# Nature Ethics

## Studies in Social, Political, and Legal Philosophy
Series Editor: James P. Sterba, University of Notre Dame

This series analyzes and evaluates critically the major political, social, and legal ideals, institutions, and practices of our time. The analysis may be historical or problem-centered; the evaluation may focus on theoretical underpinnings or practical implications. Among the recent titles in the series are:

*Child versus Childmaker: Present Duties and Future Persons in Ethics and the Law*
   by Melinda A. Roberts
*Gewirth: Critical Essays on Action, Rationality, and Community*
   edited by Michael Boylan
*The Idea of a Political Liberalism: Essays on Rawls*
   edited by Victoria Davion and Clark Wolf
*Self-Management and the Crisis of Socialism: The Rose in the Fist of the Present*
   by Michael W. Howard
*Ecofeminist Philosophy: A Western Perspective on What It Is and Why It Matters*
   by Karen J. Warren
*Controversies in Feminism*
   edited by James P. Sterba
*Faces of Environmental Racism: Confronting Issues of of Global Justice, Second Edition*
   edited by Laura Westra and Bill E. Lawson
*Theorizing Backlash: Philosophical Reflections on the Resistance to Feminism*
   by Anita M. Superson and Ann E. Cudd
*Just Ecological Integrity: The Ethics of Maintaining Planetary Life*
   edited by Peter Miller and Laura Westra
*American Heat: Ethical Problems with the United States' Response to Global Warming*
   by Donald A. Brown
*Exploitation: What It Is and Why It's Wrong*
   by Ruth J. Sample
*The Principle of Fairness and Political Obligation, New Edition*
   by George Klosko
*Moral Thinking: Reason, Aesthetics, and Pluralism*
   by Duane L. Cady
*Nature Ethics: An Ecofeminist Perspective*
   by Marti Kheel

# Nature Ethics

## An Ecofeminist Perspective

Marti Kheel

ROWMAN & LITTLEFIELD PUBLISHERS, INC.
*Lanham • Boulder • New York • Toronto • Plymouth, UK*

ROWMAN & LITTLEFIELD PUBLISHERS, INC.

Published in the United States of America
by Rowman & Littlefield Publishers, Inc.
A wholly owned subsidary of The Rowman & Littlefield Publishing Group, Inc.
4501 Forbes Boulevard, Suite 200, Lanham, Maryland 20706
www.rowmanlittlefield.com

Estover Road
Plymouth PL6 7PY
United Kingdom

Copyright © 2008 by Rowman & Littlefield Publishers, Inc.

British Library Cataloguing in Publication Information Available

**Library of Congress Cataloging-in-Publication Data:**
Kheel, Marti.
  Nature ethics : an ecofeminist perspective / Marti Kheel.
     p. cm. — (Studies in social, political, and legal philosophy)
  Includes bibliographical references.
  ISBN-13: 978-0-7425-5200-5 (cloth : alk. paper)
  ISBN-10: 0-7425-5200-4 (cloth : alk. paper)
  ISBN-13: 978-0-7425-5201-2 (pbk. : alk. paper)
  ISBN-10: 0-7425-5201-2 (pbk. : alk. paper)
  1. Ecofeminism. 2. Philosophy of nature. 3. Animal welfare—Moral and ethical
aspects. 4. Human–animal relationships—Philosophy. 5. Environmental ethics. 6.
Feminist ethics. 7. Holism. I. Title.
  HQ1233.K48  2008
  179'.1—dc22                                                                 2007023940

Printed in the United States of America

$\infty$ ™ The paper used in this publication meets the minimum requirements of American
National Standard for Information Sciences—Permanence of Paper for Printed Library
Materials, ANSI/NISO Z39.48-1992.

Dedicated to my parents,
Ted and Ann Kheel,
who continue to inspire me

# Contents

# Foreword

*Rosemary Radford Ruether*

This volume on an ecofeminist perspective on nature ethics represents a more than twenty-five year commitment by environmental philosopher Marti Kheel to bridge the seemingly disparate movements of feminism, environmental ethics, and animal liberation. Marti Kheel's work is well known in these fields as the author of major articles that have been published in numerous journals and anthologies and translated into several languages. Kheel first developed her critique of the philosophical dualisms that linked environmental ethics and animal rights in a 1984 article, "The Liberation of Nature: A Circular Affair," originally published in *Environmental Ethics*. In 1982 she cofounded Feminists for Animal Rights.

Marti Kheel's book, *Nature Ethics: An Ecofeminist Perspective*, brings together in a fuller form her work in earlier articles. In this book she studies the defects and limitations of mainline environmental practice and thought. Kheel focuses on four major founders of the environmental movement: Theodore Roosevelt, whose concern for conservation helped set up the national parks system; environmental philosopher Aldo Leopold, author of the classic work in the field, *A Sand County Almanac*; leading ecophilosopher Holmes Rolston III, author of such volumes as *Conserving Natural Value* (1994); and deep ecology thinker Warwick Fox, author of such works as *Toward a Transpersonal Ecology: Developing New Foundations for Environmentalism* (1990).

Kheel does not totally discount the contributions of these four environmental leaders. She expresses her appreciation for their significant contributions. She credits Roosevelt as "an early harbinger of the message of limits, the notion that abundance should not be taken for granted." Leopold's work contributed to a "perceptual shift, based on the ecological notion of interdependence." Rolston's work suggested "the importance of lived experience and local stories," while Fox's idea that "humans, like other 'species,' are merely individual leaves on a metaphorical tree is also a beneficial antidote to the presumption of human superiority."

But Kheel finds all these thinkers wanting primarily because of their inability to value animals as distinct individuals in their own right. Each has marked preferences for thinking of "nature" in terms of large abstractions — species, ecosystems, even the cosmos — rather than rooting their concern in real empathy for living and often suffering fellow "other-than-human animals," as Kheel calls them. There is also a strong tendency to value "nature" in the abstract primarily for its beneficial effect on the human psyche, rather than really being concerned with the quality of life of particular "nonhumans" in their own right.

For Roosevelt and Leopold in particular, "roughing it" in "nature" is also linked to sport hunting. Nonhuman animals are to be "preserved" so they can be killed by sportsmen-hunters, thereby enhancing intergenerational manliness and virility of men and boys. Although hunting and its value for "manliness" is not as central for Rolston, it is also not disavowed. Warwick does not promote hunting, but his concept of ecological consciousness as a transpersonal expansion of the ego to include the cosmos suggests a kind of transcendental inclusivism of all reality within the human (male) self.

Kheel sees these defects of abstractionism — the quest for transcendence, alienation from nature and body, the need to prove oneself through killing animals — as deeply linked with the social construction of masculinity in Western societies, and patriarchal societies in general. She calls for a deep revision of such patriarchal thinking in environmental thought by a real inclusion of concrete empathy with "other-than-human animals" as individuals in their own right. She sees ecofeminism as a movement that recognizes the interconnection of sexism and abuse of both women and animals as an important corrective to these myopias.

The extent to which the dominant theories in contemporary environmental ethics are linked to male bias has not been generally appreciated, and Kheel makes the case more clearly and convincingly than anyone else has done to date. For Kheel, these concerns are deeply linked to veganism, the eschewing of abuse or killing animals for food, clothing, or laboratory experiments. Vegan ecofeminism is, for Kheel, not so much an ethic as an ethos — a way of life that one is called to adopt if one becomes really serious about overcoming these interlinked abuses of women, animals, and the natural world. Kheel's book is a groundbreaking contribution to the literature and a must read for anyone concerned with the links among environmental ethics, animal liberation, and feminist critique of male cultural bias.

# Acknowledgments

One of the most basic lessons of ecology is that no part of nature exists apart from a web of relations. So, too, the process of writing takes place within a network of relations that provide the "soil" in which the printed words comes to fruition. The creation of this book has benefited from far too many people to adequately express my gratitude to all those involved. I can only attempt to single out some of the most significant ones.

I am especially indebted to James Sterba for the propitious suggestion that I submit my manuscript to Rowman & Littlefield as part of his series on Social, Political, and Legal Philosophy. A special thanks, too, to Rosemary Radford Ruether for her enthusiasm about my work and for graciously writing the foreword.

The earliest incarnation of this book was my dissertation at the Graduate Theological Union in Berkeley, California. I am particularly grateful to the chair of my committee, Carol Robb, whose skillful mentoring helped me to fine tune an unwieldy idea into a manageable project. I also wish to thank my other committee members, Michael Mendiola and Jim Cheney, for useful advice at that stage of my work.

I am indebted to the Women's Leadership program at Mills College for the 2000–2001 year as a visiting scholar. During that time, I was afforded the opportunity to develop and present some of the ideas for this book in a supportive environment of peers. I am similarly grateful to the Graduate Theological Union for awarding me the position of visiting scholar since 2006, thereby giving me access to important library resources.

Many people have assisted me in various aspects of the writing process. I am particularly grateful to Joan Stenau Lester for her assistance in multiple roles throughout the entire project. As mentor, editor, and coach, she has provided the best gift an author could hope for—critical feedback balanced with enthusiastic support. In addition to her expert editing, she has been a guiding light helping me to persevere when the going got rough. Morgan also provided invaluable assistance in numerous ways. Her keen attention to detail and unparalleled capacity for rigorous thought saved me from many errors and lapses in logic. I am grateful to her and to Joan for their ceaseless efforts in encouraging me to convey complex philosophical ideas in a succinct and accessible manner.

Nahrain Al Moussawi has been a wonderful support, assisting me from the inception of the project, as both an excellent editor and researcher. I am especially grateful to her and to Kyla Wagener for helping me with bibliographical references in the midst of a time crunch. Rosann Greenspan also read parts of *Nature Ethics*, always offering insightful editing and feedback, and a cheerful sounding board. Her friendship and enthusiasm for my work have been a wonderful support over the years. Ellen Radovic provided valuable assistance, both through her friendship and through her diligent reference-checking. Thanks also to Heather Madar and Kyla Wagener for invaluable assistance in reviewing aspects of the manuscript for accuracy. Heather has also been of immense help in accessing bibliographical references.

The emotional sustenance I received over the years from friends has been no less valuable than other forms of assistance. Among others, I am grateful to Angela Graboys, Rosann Greenspan, Elise Peeples, Ellen Radovic, Linda Rollins, Diana Russell, and Linda Rae Savage for modeling the caring and attentiveness that I propose in these pages as a basis for a nature ethic. My gratitude goes as well to my family for demonstrating the possibility of a diverse community based on love and respect.

My thanks go to those who graciously read chapters or excerpts pertaining to their respective areas of expertise: Alan Drengson, J. Baird Callicott, Stephen J. Ducat, Christopher Preston, Diana E. H. Russell, Steve F. Sapontzis, and Keith K. Schillo. I am especially thankful to those readers who offered advice even when they did not agree with my conclusions. An additional thanks to Diana for long conversations over dinner about the joys and sorrows of the writing process.

I presented earlier formulations of the ideas in this book at numerous academic conferences and institutional forums, where I received the benefit of useful feedback. Some of these include the National Women's Studies Association, the American Academy of Religion, the Pacific Division of the Society for Women in Philosophy, the American Psychological Association, the University of California at Berkeley, the University of California at Irvine, Whittier Law School, Mills College, Bard College, University of North Texas, University of Vermont, and San Francisco State University.

As someone who works within a variety of disciplines, I owe a debt of gratitude to multiple communities, both intellectual and activist. *Nature Ethics* was conceived in dialogue with all of these: ecofeminists, environmental philosophers, animal advocates, vegetarians and vegans, theologians, and feminist philosophers. Although I critique particular environmental philosophers in the following pages, my purpose is not to dismiss their importance, but rather to engage in respectful dialogue. My colleagues in the feminist animal advocacy movement have sustained me in multiple ways. Batya Bauman, a longtime friend and former colleague in the operation of Feminists for Animal Rights, has always offered an enthusiastic audience for my ideas, encouraging me to continue underscoring the vital distinction between caring about "species" and caring for individual beings. Carol Adams has also been an ongoing inspiration and catalyst for my work. As author of the earliest book elucidating the connections between feminism and animal advocacy, she helped prepare the conceptual soil for the work of authors such as myself. The articles and books of Greta Gaard, along with her friendship, have also sustained me over the years, reassuring me that a viable niche for other-than-human animals can be found within the field of ecofeminism.

I am indebted to a number of people for relaying useful bits of information that I was able to incorporate into *Nature Ethics*. Thanks to Pattrice Jones for drawing my attention to the moving passage by Simone de Beauvoir about her first-hand experience of a U.S. slaughterhouse. And to Curt Meine for informing me about the University of Wisconsin departmental lore concerning the last act of defiance of the wolf that Aldo Leopold killed. I am also grateful to Adam Weissman for suggesting the term "rape culture" to characterize the treatment of other-than-human animals on factory farms.

I feel fortunate to have had the benefit of a wonderful team at Rowman & Littlefield: Ross Miller, Ruth Gilbert, Elaine McGarraugh, Amanda Gibson, and Lynn Gemmell. A special thanks to Amanda for her excellent copy editing. Thanks also to Jen Burton for her detailed and thorough indexing.

On the visual front, I am grateful to my nephew, Rick Stanley, for the cover photograph. A gifted photographer and naturalist, he gives me hope that the next generation will genuinely care about the other-than-human world, not only as a beautiful backdrop but as a living, breathing community of individual beings.

Last but not least, I am grateful to my family and friends for their patience about my lack of availability during the time I have been working on *Nature Ethics*. Their understanding made all the difference.

# Finding a Niche for All Animals in Nature Ethics

While out on a walk one bright summer afternoon, a woman discovered several fox kits huddled together outside a dilapidated house. A "condemned" sign hung on the broken door. Spotting a bulldozer down the street, she ran to the nearest phone to call the Division of Wildlife for Colorado. After finally reaching the appropriate agency official, she was offered this reassurance: "There is no need for concern, since there are plenty of foxes in Colorado."

A philosophy professor with an interest in environmental ethics found himself seated next to a United States Department of Agriculture official on a cross-country flight. Before long, the professor was expressing his concerns about the rapid decline in species, eager to know what the USDA could do to help out. The government official listened intently and then relayed the good news: "In the future, we will not have to worry about protecting animals, because the USDA will eventually have a gene library for the propagation of endangered species."[1]

## INTRODUCTION

It has become commonplace to observe that the destruction of the natural world has reached unprecedented heights. The protective response to this crisis takes many forms. While environmental activists seek to change existing laws and practices, ethical theorists have been engaged on a more abstract plane, developing theories designed to compel moral conduct through their conceptual force. Although numerous ideas compete for the distinction of having the greatest theoretical cogency, the dominant philosophy in the field of nature ethics,[2] as well as the environmental movement more generally, is holism. Holist nature philosophy,[3] commonly referred to as ecocentric philosophy, postulates that larger entities such as "species," "the land," or the "the ecosystem" should be accorded the highest value in ethical conduct toward nature. Holists contrast their philosophy with the atomistic and egocentric orientation of modern Western culture, arguing that humans should see themselves as part of the larger matrix of nature. Holists maintain that their emphasis on larger constructs does not preclude a respect for other-than-human animals,[4] since they too are included within an all-inclusive "whole."[5] But is this the case?

My analysis suggests that holists typically care about "species," "the ecosystem" or "the biotic community" over and above individual beings. Many see no contradiction in killing wolves in order to save "the wolf," or experimenting on animals in order to make the environment "safe."[6] The major environmental organizations condone or endorse hunting,[7] and none promote vegetarianism as a means of reducing animal suffering.[8]

I will argue that in expanding their moral allegiance to the larger "whole," holist nature philosophers reflect a masculinist orientation that fails to incorporate care and empathy for individual other-than-human animals. I contrast the notion of *care-taking* for the whole of the ecosystem with direct, unmediated care for and about individual beings. Rather than dismissing this absence of concern for individuals as an oversight, I explore whether it might have deeper, psychological roots based on the construct *masculine identity*.

Before proceeding, it is useful to explain my use of the terms "masculinism," "masculinity," and "manliness," and to provide a brief history of their evolution. Throughout the nineteenth century, in Western Europe and the United States, "manliness" was commonly used as a term of praise, designating high mindedness and civility. Middle-class men were seen as the embodiment of the manly ideal, due to their ability to control their (animal) passions. As rapid industrialization and economic hardships increased in the late nineteenth century, the manly ideal of self-denial became less tenable, and the new term "masculinity" came into vogue. Masculinity, unlike manliness, referred to a constellation of characteristics, both good and bad, that all men shared. Masculinity thus slowly made its way into the language to describe a state or quality associated with particular collective traits. By the 1930s, "masculinity" had begun to be associated with more familiar male ideals of aggressiveness, physical force, and male sexuality. Despite their respective change in meanings over the years, the terms "manliness," "masculine," and "masculinity" were all conceived in direct opposition to the female world. Moreover, they were typically viewed as universal traits superior to those of females and other-than-human nature.

I use the term "masculinism" in this study to refer to an *ideology* that endorses the explicit or implicit belief in the superiority of a constellation of traits attributed to men.[9] Many theorists have pointed out that no single expression of masculine identity exists. Distinctions exist across the lines of class, race, ethnicity, sexual orientation, and historical period, making it more accurate to refer to "masculinities" than to a sole masculine identity to which all men conform. Nonetheless, the disparate expressions of masculinity all exist in relation to a culturally exalted *hegemonic ideal*, which has exerted a powerful influence on Western culture.[10]

Despite temporal and geographical variations, masculinist traits are characteristically opposed to traits commonly perceived as female.[11] In addition, they are assessed through their (superior) relation to the larger natural world, which they symbolically transcend. In the modern era, the traits most commonly associated with masculinity are: (1) rationality, (2) universality, and (3) autonomy. These traits are counterposed to (1) nonrationality (or emotionalism), (2) particularity, and (3) relation and dependence.[12] From these contrasting traits a series of dualisms emerge: culture/nature, male/female, good/evil, domestic/wild, conscious/unconscious, subject/object, human/animal. A common thread uniting these dualities is the theme of transcending the female-imaged biological world. It is this motif of transcendence that I investigate in this study.

I examine four representatives of holist philosophy—Theodore Roosevelt, Aldo Leopold, Holmes Rolston III, and Warwick Fox—focusing on the scope of their moral concern for nature, as well as the criteria they use for delineating the parameters of moral considerability. My intention is to understand the underlying worldview that shapes their attitudes toward other-than-human animals, as well as the place they accord to empathy and care for individual other-than-humans. My central thesis is that the failure of holist theorists to incorporate a respect for individual other-than-humans stems from an orientation that idealizes transcending the biological realm, as represented by other-than-human animals and affiliative ties. I furthermore argue that the holists in this study use other-than-humans as symbols or psychological props to support their constructs. I make the case that these attitudes are masculinist in that they subordinate empathy and care for individual beings to a larger cognitive perspective or "whole."

I focus on eight masculinist characteristics, or themes, which are embedded in the broader concepts of rationality, universality, and autonomy:

- A belief that humans, particularly men, are driven by aggressive, self-centered biological drives that must be given controlled, rational expression.

- A belief in the superiority of sport over spontaneous play, which is typically conceived as a purposeless activity and has long confounded philosophers who have struggled to explain why it exists. In contrast, sport, with its publicly recognized rules of competition, has long been associated with the masculine traits of valor, power, and prestige.[13]
- The idea of preserving the "primitive" environment (or frontier experience) as a legacy for future generations and, in particular, young boys.
- The notion of adventure as a counter to the repetitive realm of biological nature.
- An emphasis on the science of ecology and natural evolutionary history as a rationally conceived base for connecting with past and future generations.
- A belief in the moral importance of stewardship or care-taking of the "whole" of nature.
- An anthropocentric (or I would argue, an androcentric)[14] philosophy, based on the unique capacity of humans for self-conscious deliberation and the attainment of a transcendent perspective.
- A belief in the necessity of subordinating concern for individual other-than-humans to larger constructs.

Common to all these themes is the idea that human maturity consists in transcending the biological realm through the construction of a transcendent identity.

It might seem that the four holists examined in my research do not exemplify these masculinist themes. Some preliminary comments may, therefore, be helpful to dispel this misconception. Although the individual philosophies of the authors in this study do not exhibit all of these themes, each contains many of them. The conservation movement — the foundation upon which they built — replaced an earlier ethos of unrestrained aggression toward nature with a more gentlemanly ethic of protection and "self-restraint." Some of these individuals further developed the idea of protecting nature, proposing the ideas of human interdependence with nature as well as love and respect for it.

At first glance, interdependence appears to diverge from the masculine quality of autonomy, and love and respect appear at odds with the masculine emphasis on rationality. The question that I pursue here is whether these changes in attitude toward nature fully escape the masculinist paradigm. I will argue that the authors' emphasis on feelings and interdependence is directed toward "species," "the ecosystem," or "the land," rather than individual beings, and question how different this is from masculinist ideas of universality and autonomy. Under the aegis of management or science, Roosevelt, Leopold, and Rolston argue for a care-taking orientation toward these larger entities, over and above concern for individual beings. I will compare this stewardship idea of care-taking for the whole of nature to an orientation, more commonplace in women's subcultures of care, which foregrounds the moral importance of direct empathic ties to individual beings. I argue, in addition, that the emphasis on larger constructs leads holists to overlook or devalue domestic animals, who are seen to lie outside the ecological or biotic "whole."[15] Thus, the noted environmentalist John Muir expressed a common disdain toward domesticated animals when he described the dignity of wild goats as "bold, elegant and glowing with life," in contrast to domesticated goats who are "only half alive."[16]

Holist nature philosophers' neglect of individual and domestic other-than-humans is not only a matter of academic interest or theoretical quibbling. The conceptual "sacrifice" of other-than-human animals contributes to the death of millions every year, at the hands of hunters, agribusiness owners, and animal experimenters. The animals in these practices function as sacrificial victims who suffer and die for the purported benefit of the "whole," which is conceived as humanity or the ecosystem.[17]

A personal example helps to illustrate how holist philosophy operates in practice. One evening after dinner, I received a call from a telephone solicitor for a well-known environmental organization. She took several minutes to enumerate the organization's many accomplishments, going on to explain its future projects. One, she told me, called for a temporary halt to all genetic engineering "until further testing can be done." As an ardent opponent of genetic engineering, I was eager to hear the details of her organization's plans. I asked her what kind of testing they were calling for, and whether it would involve the use of animals. The solicitor on the phone paused, seeming somewhat confused, and then went on to reassure me that her organization does not perform animal experiments, nor does it request that they be performed. After several minutes of cross dialogue, she conceded that the tests that they are asking the genetic engineering industries to perform will in all probability involve the use of animals. For this environmental organization, animals functioned as sacrificial victims for the purported purpose of ensuring human safety. I will suggest that a similar sacrificial mentality can be found in hunters who sanction the killing of "wild" animals for the well-being of the larger "species" or "the ecosystem."

## TERMINOLOGY

A word about my use of terminology is in order. The authors in this study are commonly viewed as representatives of (or precursors to) the field of environmental ethics or ecophilosophy. The term *ecophilosophy* was developed in the early 1970s in reaction to the emphasis within environmental ethics on axiological theory, which relies on abstract, rational arguments about moral conduct toward nature. It was designed to refer to philosophies that emphasize personal experience and consciousness, rather than disembodied "ethics." In this study I prefer to use the terms "nature ethics" and "nature philosophies," since they encompass both environmental and animal advocacy philosophies. I do not share the aversion of ecophilosophers to the term "ethics," and in the last chapter I outline an ecofeminist understanding of nature ethics. My use of the term "ethics" relies on the notion of "ethos," or way of life, rather than on axiological theory. Additionally, "nature ethics," as I conceive it, is broad enough to encompass the diverse perspectives of the key figures examined in this study: "conservationist," "environmental philosopher," and "ecophilosopher."[18]

Language conveys (and reproduces) the attitudes and practices of the societies in which it evolves. It is therefore not surprising that the devaluation of other-than-human animals is an inescapable aspect of the English language. The term "animal," for example, is usually employed with little awareness that humans also are animals. My use of the phrases "other-than-human animals" and "other animals" is intended as a reminder of our kinship. Although humans remain the referent in this usage, as long as we distinguish ourselves in ways that require distinct terms to describe our unique impact on the natural world, such terminology may be necessary.

I also use the word "individual" throughout this project in reference to other-than-human animals, for lack of a better alternative. Etymologically, the term "individual" means "undivided." It has been an important term within the Western Enlightenment tradition, bringing into prominence the idea of human beings as uniquely rational and autonomous. Feminists have pointed out that the Enlightenment notion of an abstract, isolated individual, unencumbered with ties to others, reflects a masculinist ideal of independence.[19] It is not my intention to reinforce or extend this problematic conception of the "individual" to other-than-humans. I am aware that in this sense the term "individual" may be viewed as an abstract construct itself.[20] However, since what has been lacking in the Western tradition, and especially within holist theories, is the ability to establish respectful boundaries that acknowledge the integrity or discrete identity of other-than-humans, I still find the term "individual" helpful and use it to suggest this sense of "integrity."[21]

The assumption that rationality and autonomy are unique to humans has been reinforced in the Jewish and Christian notion that only "man" is made in the image of God. As a consequence, only men (and, by extension, women) have been viewed as "persons" who are unique and irreplaceable creations worthy of dignity.[22] President Bill Clinton emphasized the relevance of the belief that human beings are unique creations when he referred to the scientific research on cloning humans as "troubling," arguing that

any discovery that touches upon human creation is not simply a matter of scientific inquiry. . . . It is a matter of morality and spirituality, as well. . . . Each
human life is unique, born of a miracle that reaches beyond laboratory science.
I believe we must respect this profound gift and resist the temptation to replicate
ourselves.

In the same breath, however, Clinton praised the continued research on
cloning of other-than-humans, asserting that cloning could "yield enormous
benefits" for human beings in reproducing the most productive livestock
strains and "revolutionary new medical treatments and cures."[23] The message, of course, is that other-than-human animals are interchangeable or replaceable, whereas human beings are unique and inviolable.[24] As long as the
aggregate number of animals is maintained at an optimum level, no moral
wrong has been committed in using them for human benefit. A similar attitude can be found in gubernatorial candidate Ronald Reagan's statement, "A
tree is a tree, how many more do you need to look at?"[25]

The tendency to view other-than-human animals as aggregate categories,
rather than individuals, is built into our language. Thus, those that are undo-
mesticated are collectively known as "wildlife." Similarly, large numbers of
individual animals are routinely referred to with the use of singular words,
such as "deer" or "buffalo," blurring the distinction between individuals and
species. The psychologist Kenneth Shapiro, noting the irony contained in the
semantic absorption of the individual into the species, observes "there is an
extensive literature in the philosophy of biology on the controversial question
of whether a species is 'objectively real.'"[26] The Endangered Species Act
epitomizes the obfuscation that is built into our language as a result of the interchangeable use of a single word to refer to both individuals and abstract
categories of thought. Under its auspices, government agencies enact laws to
preserve *the wolf*, while promoting the continued hunting and killing of individual *wolves*.

In this study I have sought to avoid the use of a singular term to refer to animals in the aggregate. Thus, I sometimes refer to "deers," rather than to
"deer," even though such usage may appear grammatically incorrect.[27] Because all of the authors examined in this study employ the conventional usage, however, I sometimes use their terminology when conveying their ideas
(for example, "wildlife"). Unless quoting directly, I also avoid terms such as
"it" or "that" when referring to other-than-human animals, as they fail to respect subjective identity.

The reader will note that I abstain from the widespread usage among nature philosophers of the terms "intrinsic value" or "inherent value," choosing
instead to refer to the "integrity" or "importance" of nature and individual beings. I believe that terms like "value" connote an economic framework by

which humans rate the rest of the natural world in order to determine who is "owed" rights or responsibilities. I do not argue that my friends and family have intrinsic value; nor do I wish to make this argument for other-than-humans.

As a concession to common usage, I sometimes refer to "domestic" and "wild animals." This distinction is not intended to endorse the customary division, which conceives of other-than-human animals who are not serviceable to humans as unruly or "wild,"[28] an attitude typified in a children's story book that explains the distinction between domestic and wild animals. Juxtaposed to an image of a nursing cow and calf, the caption states, "there are different kinds of mammals . . . there are tamed animals that work for people or human beings. And there are wild animal that will do nothing for anyone."[29]

Finally, I use the term *ecofeminism* in this book with deliberation. While ecofeminism is not a single movement or philosophy, it can be described at the broadest level as a loosely knit philosophical and practical orientation linking the concerns of women to the larger natural world.[30] More specifically, ecofeminism examines and critiques the historical and mutually reinforcing devaluation of women and nature with a view to transforming existing forms of exploitation. Conceived in the early 1970s,[31] the term ecofeminism was immediately embraced by a number of feminists who welcomed the widening of feminist concerns to the larger natural world. From its inception, however, the term and the movement it represents have also been plagued by criticism, most commonly the charge of "essentialism."

The term *essentialism* has a number of different meanings, but in common current usage, it refers to the notion of a biologically based, unchanging "nature" or "essence." Since essentialist characterizations of women's "nature" have been used throughout history to justify women's consignment to a secondary status, challenging these stereotypical views has been a central goal of the feminist movement. As deconstructive postmodernist philosophy began to permeate the academic world, essentialism was further critiqued, and references to general categories of analysis, such as "women," "men," and "nature," came to be viewed as at best mistaken fictions and at worse as "grand totalizing" discourses. Since masculine identity was viewed as multifarious, feminists who spoke or wrote of male domination were regarded as guilty of participating in this totalizing discourse. Women of color, third world women, and lesbian feminists also argued that the use of an all-inclusive category such as "women" erases differences along the lines of race, class, nationality, ethnicity, and sexual orientation. In this milieu, the term essentialism, used to describe any general attribution or causation, came to be viewed by many feminists as a term of opprobrium, immediately dismissing an author's work.

Perhaps no group of feminists has been more riddled by this criticism than ecofeminists. Social ecologist Janet Biehl led the early attack, accusing ecofeminism of a "psychobiologistic" orientation.[32] Over the years, the accusations against ecofeminism have prodded ecofeminists to modify and clarify their relation to essentialism. Several of those who were the object of early criticisms—Charlene Spretnak, Susan Griffin, and Ariel Salleh—subsequently wrote articles or books clearly disassociating themselves from simplistic understandings of essentialism.[33] More recently, even those allied with the movement commonly known as ecofeminism often shun use of the term, for fear of being linked with essentialism. Still others have opted for distinct terms, such as "ecological feminism," "feminism and ecology," "feminist environmentalism," "environmental feminism," or "eco/feminism."[34]

The term ecofeminism, which linguistically conjoins women and nature into a single word, is particularly susceptible to the charge of essentialism. Not only does the single word appear to conjure up images of a merging of the categories of "woman" and "nature," but it seems to imply an "essential" or "universal" bond uniting them together. While the concerns over reinforcing a stereotypical link between women and nature are not devoid of merit, the presumption that all ecofeminism makes this claim constitutes its own form of essentialism. Often descriptive analyses of the historical treatment of women and nature under patriarchal society are mistaken for universal or ontological claims. Although the original fears that fueled the early essentialist critiques are legitimate and important, the heightened state of surveillance directed toward essentialism seems to have lost sight of the original intent underlying the critiques. As Noël Sturgeon points out, rather than simply dismissing all expressions of essentialism, it is helpful to understand where essentialist tendencies came from and what functions they served.[35] While acknowledging the risk of making universal generalizations about "women" and "nature," Sturgeon points to the advantages of momentarily adopting particular symbols and language that may be seen as essentialist to enable women activists to politically unite across the lines of race, class, and national identity.[36] Along similar lines, Ariel Salleh argues that "understanding how experiences are shared by women across special and discursive boundaries is crucial to ecofeminist mobilization."[37]

The repudiation of the term ecofeminism, however, also reflects a desire to acknowledge the evolution in thinking among feminist nature theorists. Over the past two decades, increasing numbers of theorists have extended their analysis beyond the commonalities of the objects of oppression ("women" and "nature") to the dynamic of oppression embedded in multiple forms of abuse. Some, therefore, prefer to reserve the word "ecofeminism" for the former approach, employing terms such as "ecological feminism" for those who

emphasize the *similar ideologies* underlying the interlocking forms of subordination.[38] Yet the word "ecology," which derives from the Greek "logos,"
has problems of its own. In Greek philosophy, *Logos* referred to the rational
principle ordering the world; "ecology," moreover, is "the science of the relationships between organisms and their environments."[39] By embracing the
term "ecological" to describe their approach, feminists may inadvertently reinforce the rational emphasis within philosophy that they seek to critique. Despite its troubled history, I prefer to retain the term ecofeminism, while qual-
ifying that I support the broader interpretation of its aims.

## FORMAT

Though I apply a multidisciplinary approach in this book, I use the particular
lens of gender analysis to focus upon the relation of masculine identity to nature ethics. Drawing on the literature of gender psychology and feminist
ethics in the second chapter, I examine the binary construction of masculine
identity, as well as the notion of masculine maturity as a transcendence of direct ties to others. Simone de Beauvoir was the first to coin the term "the
other" to characterize women's status under patriarchal society.[40] A growing
body of feminist literature, including object relations theory, suggests, however, that it is more accurate to state that it is men's identities that are constructed as "the other." According to this research the maturation of young
boys entails a process of constructing an identity that is not simply distinct
from women, but diametrically opposed.[41] Some of this literature also suggests that men's identities have been established not only through a negation
of the female world, but through a negation of the entire realm of nature.[42] Simone de Beauvoir elucidates the implications for other-than-human animals,
arguing that men seek to attain full human maturity by engaging in acts of violence toward the natural world, including hunting, fishing, and war.[43] According to de Beauvoir, these activities represent a transcendence of the realm
of biological necessity to which women have been confined. I argue that the
notions of drama, adventure, and transcendent perspectives found in the figures in this study imply a similar urge to transcend the repetitive, cyclical
realm of the natural world.

   In the second chapter, I also examine the feminist research that contends
that the "masculine" quest to renounce ties to the biological realm derives
from a lack of a sense of connection and continuity with nature. Some have
argued that this sense of disconnection results from men's inability to give
birth. According to this view, masculine identity has been conceived, structurally, as a kind of second birth that is independent of the biological realm. I

examine the relevance of this idea for conceptions of nature ethics in subsequent chapters. For Roosevelt and Leopold, a sense of rebirth was found in the adventure and drama of the hunting experience, which they conceived as a cross-generational legacy to be "conserved" for future generations of boys.[44] I will argue that this tradition of forging cross-generational links through acts of violence represents a masculinist attempt to transcend nature and achieve immortality.

I also draw on the feminist literature on an ethic of care, inspired by educational psychologist Carol Gilligan, which identifies a greater tendency among men to resolve disputes through the development of abstract principles and universal rules, rather than through a contextual approach that recognizes feelings of care.[45] I argue that the emphasis of the figures in this study on transcendent construct suggests a similar devaluation of empathetic ties to individuals.

My use of these feminist theories concerning men's predisposition toward transcendence is designed to be suggestive. Theorizing about the psychological basis of gender difference and gendered worldviews is inherently speculative. While I am aware of the dangers of overgeneralization, I believe that the recurrence of particular themes across a wide variety of cultures and historical periods merits further investigation. In distinct ways, the philosophies of all of the theorists discussed in this chapter suggest the common masculinist quest to transcend the female-associated biological world. Although this book is primarily concerned with the late nineteenth and twentieth century time period, I avail myself of broader theories in order to further illuminate my analysis.

Chapters 3 and 4 explore the historical background to holist philosophy, examining the origins of conservation philosophy, with particular focus on the ideas of Theodore Roosevelt and Aldo Leopold. In these chapters I direct attention to the central importance of hunting and the concept of manliness in the development of conservationist and environmental ideas. I highlight the use of other-than-human animals as psychological props for the construction of masculine identity and worldview.

The central figure in chapter 3, Theodore Roosevelt, does not readily jump to mind as an example of a holist philosopher. I contend, however, that the philosophy of sport hunting that he endorsed provided an important historical foundation for subsequent holist philosophy. The early sport-hunter conservationists most clearly exemplify the connection between a holist orientation and masculine identity. They also demonstrate with clarity the oppositional attitude toward individual other-than-human animals that, I argue, is implicit in holist theories. The sport hunters in the early conservation movement were intent on conserving species, not individual animals, in order to provide an

arena in which they could continue their displays of "manly" sport and adventure.

Roosevelt was deeply influenced by Darwinian philosophy, and his views
of human nature reflected the prevailing belief in an innate drive (within men)
toward aggression. The curbing of this aggressive drive was regarded by
many as evidence of a new, gentlemanly conception of maturity and manhood. The type of manhood achieved through the activity of hunting was valued both for its ability to transcend sentimental attachments to animals and
for its contribution to building the type of character that could advance U.S.
imperial ideals. In this chapter I also identify the theme of patrilineal heritage,
based upon the notion of protecting nature in order to pass on the frontier experience to future generations of boys.

In chapter 4, I examine the figure best known as the originator of holist philosophy, Aldo Leopold, and challenge the commonly held view that he made
a decisive break with earlier instrumental views of nature. I argue that
Leopold's notion of the "land community" did not extend to individual other-
than-human animals, but rather to "species" and ecological processes. Moreover, the experience of hunting and killing individual animals was an integral
aspect of Leopold's famous "land ethic." I argue that his well-known experience of identification with the land, symbolized by a mountain, was identification with the larger ecological arena, not individual beings.

Although Leopold continued many of the early themes found in Roosevelt's writings, he also demonstrated an increased emphasis on spirituality,
exemplified by the idea of an internalized "ecological conscience." This notion was intimately tied to his beliefs about the necessity of restraining the innate propensity (of men) for aggression through the activity of sport hunting.
Like Roosevelt, Leopold saw the exercise of restraint as an evolutionary and
psychological advance and mark of moral maturity. Leopold also elaborated
on the theme of both witnessing and participating in the drama and adventure
of evolutionary history. Although Leopold played a major role in advancing
awareness of the importance of ecological principles and nature's fragility, he
never relinquished an instrumental orientation toward nature. The overriding
theme that emerges in his philosophy is the notion of treating the earth (and
other-than-human animals) according to the scientific principles of agricultural "husbandry," which value nature for her reproductive potential and, in
particular, her ability to produce crops. Although Leopold sought to move beyond this materialist orientation, he retained the view of animals as one of the
"crops" that nature produced. I argue that this model of "harvesting" other animals reflects an instrumental attitude and a failure of empathy and care.

In the chapters on Holmes Rolston III and Warwick Fox, I investigate the
more subtle use of other-than-human animals as psychological props, despite
the fact that other animals do not figure prominently in their philosophies.

The fifth chapter examines the work of Holmes Rolston III, focusing on his arguments for the superiority of humans over the rest of the natural world. He bases this assertion upon the ability of humans to view the "whole" of nature. The theme of rebirth and immortality can be seen in his idea of identification with the never-ending "adventure" and "drama" of evolutionary history. He views the highest moral achievement as the God-like ability to bring forth conceptual order out of the seeming chaos and conflict of the natural world. I critique Rolston's use of sexual and industrial metaphors, arguing that they suggest an instrumental view of nature wherein other-than-human animals are "fertile" but not fully developed without the "fuel" provided by the superior perspective of humans. I furthermore argue that Rolston's emphasis on the pivotal role of humans in the "production of value" reflects an anthropocentric view, based upon traditional masculinist dualisms between mind and matter.

In the sixth chapter I examine the transpersonal ecology of Warwick Fox, in particular his development of Arne Naess's ecosophy T and notion of Self-realization. Fox believes that transpersonal ecology represents the most mature form of identity in that it transcends the realm of direct, affiliative ties and feelings of care and personal connection. Yet this philosophy uses other-than-human animals as symbols that represent the biological realm that must be transcended in order to attain full maturity. I also critique Fox's notion of identity for its failure to establish respectful boundaries between the self and others, as well as for its failure to acknowledge the moral importance of feelings of care.

Although Fox rarely mentions other-than-humans directly, I argue that they still play a central role in his (and Rolston's) ideas as a foil against which human maturity and identity are established. In place of Roosevelt and Leopold's explicit emphasis on hunting as a means for establishing masculine identity, I point to the "sacrifice" of other-than-human animals for larger and, purportedly, more evolved constructs, that is, the ecosystem or the larger philosophical "Self."

In the final chapter I examine the potential within ecofeminism to offer an alternative conceptualization of holist philosophy that integrates a respect for both the "biotic whole" *and* individual beings. I propose that rather than focusing on challenging aggressive practices toward nature, ecofeminist philosophy can attempt to understand why aggressive impulses toward nature have arisen and begin to explore the necessary measures for their prevention. Much as holistic healing focuses on the importance of preventing disease through an understanding of its origins, a holistic ecofeminist philosophy can help to identify the psychological and historical factors that have contributed to the degradation of nature. In light of evidence that suggests masculine identity may be a major contributor toward violence against nature, I argue that nature ethicists would do well to address the ways the current construction of masculine identity can be challenged. While I do not claim to have a blueprint for how to accomplish this daunting task, I believe that naming the factors motivating violence toward nature is an important first step in its elimination. Whereas the holists in this study situate humans within grand scientific and evolutionary dramas, an ecofeminist holist philosophy seeks to piece together the truncated narratives that exist within patriarchal society and weave them into a tapestry of stories situated within particular social and historical contexts. And just as holistic healing seeks to facilitate the body's natural ability to heal, so too I argue that ecofeminism can attempt to identify the conditions that facilitate the development and flourishing of appropriate care. This process entails freeing up our fettered imaginations. Can we imagine, for example, a Federal Department of Care along with a Department of Justice?

In this chapter I also examine the feminist literature on the moral importance of the act of "attention" in the development of appropriate care, and the role of metaphors and other unconscious influences in promoting or impeding ethical interactions with nature. I suggest that appropriate care springs from a sense of shared kinship, respectful boundaries, and recognition of needs. However, an ecofeminist nature philosophy cannot (and should not) seek to emulate masculinist theories by futilely attempting to mandate universal care. My intention in this chapter is not to construct a new "foundation" for a nature ethic, but rather to identify the factors that both facilitate and impede moral conduct and thought toward nature. I emphasize the potential of metaphor to inspire empathy. It may therefore be accurate to say that I am contributing insights to a public discussion of what constitutes appropriate care for the natural world. However, I do not rest my ultimate position on arguments for the importance of caring for individual other-than-humans on rational argumentation. Rather, I present my commitment, shared by a growing body of nature philosophers, to express and promote empathy for other-than-human animals, and I invite others to do the same.

## CONCEPTUAL APPROACH

I investigate the work of the four theorists in this study with a focus on their treatment of other-than-human nature, and in particular individual other-than-human animals. The time frame spans the United States conservation movement from its early days to the present, and includes three U.S. writers and one Australian, Warwick Fox. I apply historical and conceptual analysis to the work of each individual, focusing on common themes as well as differences, with a lens shaped by the research in feminist social psychology and philosophy regarding the process of gender formation. My working hypothesis is that gendered ideas and themes characterize not only the ideology that has supported domination of the natural world, but also the theories of some nature philosophers who seek to counter this destruction.

I bring to my critical work a perspective informed by (1) an ethical orientation that emphasizes the centrality of feelings of attachment and care; (2) a view of human maturity that entails deepening, not transcending, these feelings; (3) a vision of a post-patriarchal world that affirms diversity, not dualism; (4) an affirmation of the individual integrity of other-than-humans; (5) a belief in the importance of forging cross-generational links in nonviolent ways; and (6) an affirmation of the repetitive cycles of nature, including life and death. With these criteria, I seek to evaluate particular constructions of masculine identity within their social and historical context. Although my analysis of the connection between masculinism and violence may be viewed as grounds for pessimism, that perspective is not what I wish to convey. On the contrary, the malleability of human nature inspires me with hope for the future.

I selected the theorists in this study both because of their prominence within the field and because they represent distinct expressions of holism. The selections are not intended, however, to represent all varieties of holist nature philosophy. Other significant figures might have been examined, such as, most prominently, J. Baird Callicott, who conceives his philosophy as a direct extension of Aldo Leopold's ideas. I chose those theorists that I believe best convey the masculinist themes under consideration. I would argue, however, that my critique is equally relevant to other expressions of holism.

The criticism of holism for failing to recognize the importance of individual beings can be (and has been) made in relation not only to other-than-human animals, but to human beings as well. Thus, the followers of deep ecology have frequently been charged with sexism and racism in their holistic-based arguments for population control. A number of feminists, for example, have criticized the platform statement of the deep ecology movement that calls for a reduction in the rate of population without examining the larger societal factors that influence women to give birth.[46] Earth First! co-founder Dave Foreman, a self-proclaimed deep ecologist, also shocked many by calling for a policy that allowed Ethiopians to starve in an effort to forestall future overpopulation.[47]

Since the masculinist orientation that I explore is not always explicit, I often draw on the authors' use of metaphors to reveal their unstated premises. I argue, for instance, that the common use of economic imagery and modes of thought reflects and reinforces the devaluation of individual other-than-humans as well as domesticated animals. Beginning with Roosevelt, holist philosophers have tended to view other-than-human animals in instrumental terms, as a "stock" or "resource" to be "conserved" for present "value" and as an "investment" for future generations. Although succeeding holists increasingly perceived these benefits in psychological or spiritual terms, the persistence of economic language suggests the continuation of instrumental thought. The utilitarian idea of "conserving" nature for human well-being is accompanied by the willingness to "sacrifice" individual animals for the well-being of the ecosystem.

I argue that holist theorists fail to examine the unconscious factors that promote (or discourage) the development of feelings of care and empathy for individual other-than-humans, both within society at large and within their own theories. Applying insights from gender psychology, feminist ethics, and ecofeminist theory, I suggest that, rather than seeking to establish objective grounds for moral considerability, holist philosophers would do well to focus on the task of exploring the social, cultural, and psychological conditions necessary for care to flourish, for individuals as well as the larger "whole."

In my critique of holist philosophy, I draw on Sarah Hoagland's metaphor, adapted from Wittgenstein, of an axis that is held in place by what surrounds it.[48] According to Hoagland, the oppressive structures within patriarchy cannot be dismantled through rational argumentation, but rather by undermining the beliefs and practices that support them. As she contends, it is not a matter of arguing why rape is wrong, but rather of creating a society where rape would be unthinkable. So, too, in my concluding chapter, I focus on the practices, beliefs, and psychological mind-sets that must be dismantled in order to promote empathetic ties with other-than-human animals.

From Hoagland, I have also adapted the idea of the underlying structural similarities in the concepts of "predation" and "protection." Although holist nature philosophers purport to dismantle predatory attitudes toward nature, in many ways their protective approach perpetuates the same aggressive stance. I argue that the stewardship idea of care-taking for the whole of nature perpetuates a similar hierarchical worldview in which humans are above the rest of nature, albeit in a kindly, care-taking capacity. Moreover, by focusing on "species," "the land," or "the ecosystem" over individual beings, holist philosophers have promoted a socially acceptable context for the expression of aggression toward individual (other-than-human) beings.

I also draw upon Catherine Keller's insights into the multiple manifestations of masculine identity. According to Keller, a commonality exists between the "heroic" separation of men from the female world, attained through outright conquest, and the purportedly more "objective" disassociation attained through the elevation of rationality vis-à-vis the natural world. This analysis parallels my discussion of the relationship between the "heroic" con-

quest of animals through hunting and the emphasis on a scientific management of animals in which individual beings are "sacrificed" for the well-being of the whole.

One of the working hypotheses of this book is that feelings of care for individual animals are best fostered when humans have the opportunity to perceive them as subjective beings. This in turn is facilitated by learning their individual stories. With this in mind, I discuss the efficacy of stories from real
life, as well as from literature and film, in heightening human awareness of
other animals as subjects of their own lives. I also provide details about the
living conditions of other-than-human animals that might not otherwise be
heard.

## PERSONAL BACKGROUND

This project was inspired by my frustration with the inadequate consideration
of animals within the larger field of nature ethics. My interest arose out of the
pain and empathy I experienced upon learning of the harrowing treatment of
other-than-human animals throughout modern society. To understand how
people could condone so much suffering and how to eliminate it, I turned to
the philosophical literature on "animal liberation" or "animal rights." In the
work I read, I discovered a plethora of arguments founded upon rational principles and abstract rules. Two of the most influential philosophers of animal
advocacy, Peter Singer and Tom Regan, present distinct theories, yet both devalue personal and affective ties.

Peter Singer develops a preference-based, utilitarian moral theory, founded
upon the idea of the shared capacity of humans and other-than-humans for
sentience.[49] According to Singer, if moral consideration derives from the ability to suffer, and if animals share this capacity with human beings, it is only
logical that animals should be included within the scope of moral concern.
Tom Regan, on the other hand, argues that moral considerability derives from
the idea that animals (or, more specifically, mammals of one year or more) are
"subjects of a life." If beings are "subjects of a life," according to Regan, they
may be said to have "inherent value," and if they have "inherent value," they
must therefore be accorded "rights."[50]

Although I am sympathetic to Singer's and Regan's quest to find a socially
acceptable basis for ending the exploitation and suffering of the majority of
other-than-human animals, the criteria that they use to advance their cause do
not accord with my personal experience. Singer claims that nowhere in his
book did he "appeal to his readers' emotions where they cannot be supported
by reason,"[51] and yet it was emotional outrage that had kindled my interest in

the animal advocacy movement. Although he does not ostensibly "ground" his argument in appeals to emotion, his detailed and poignant description of the plight of other-than-human animals in laboratories and factory farms exerted a powerful emotional influence upon me. Furthermore, the logic of Singer's and Regan's arguments leads them to disconcerting conclusions. Singer's emphasis on the singular notion of sentience leads him to conclude that killing an animal may be acceptable if it is performed without the infliction of pain. He argues that a being that cannot see itself as an entity with a future cannot have a preference about its future existence.[52] Nonconscious beings, who are unaware of themselves as "distinct entities," are, therefore, "replaceable" within a preference-based utilitarian framework.[53] Thus, the enjoyment that a human derives from eating meat justifies the killing of a chicken, as long as that chicken led a good life, is killed without the infliction of pain, and is replaced with another chicken who enjoys life equally. By contrast, the human ability for self-conscious thought (shared only by such creatures as chimpanzees, gorillas, dolphins, and whales) "makes their suffering worse."[54] Thus, persons, unlike animals, should never be killed since the thwarting of their future plans would subject them to undue suffering.

Like Singer, Regan's ethic allows for the killing of some other-than-human animals as opposed to humans. He, too, argues for the human capacity for self-consciousness and, in particular, the ability to project one's plans into the future. Regan argues that in a lifeboat scenario, it would be acceptable to throw over "one million dogs" to save four human beings.[55] Each of the one million dogs may be sacrificed for failing to meet Regan's criteria for human subjectivity.

Regan, like Singer, discounts feelings of empathy and care as morally significant factors in ethical thought.[56] In *The Thee Generation*, he critiques the feminist idea of an ethic of care for its inability to extend beyond one's immediate circle of friends.[57] According to Regan, only the universalizing power of rights logic can lead to the realization that one should extend care. "Whether I care or not [emotionally for the neighbors' children], I ought to and it is logic that leads me to the realization of this 'ought.'"[58]

The moral criteria used by Singer and Regan run counter not only to my own experience and intuition, but also to my feminist views. Both emphasize in distinct ways the moral importance of the capacity for autonomy, deliberation, and the ability to engage in future projects.[59] Yet these are the very qualities that many feminists have identified as common masculinist ideals within the Western tradition. The competitive paradigm, exemplified by the lifeboat scenario, also demonstrates the dualistic and atomistic worldview that feminists have associated with masculinism, in which the well-being of one group occurs at the expense of others. The lifeboat dilemma depicts a tragic drama, leading ineluctably toward the "sacrifice" of some for the well-being of others.[60] Life, however, rarely presents itself as a simple dualism. I have come to believe that it is lifeboat scenarios that should be thrown overboard!

Equally disturbing for me was Singer and Regan's reduction of nature to a backdrop for humans and other-than-human animals. Regan's "rights" and Singer's "equal consideration" for preferences exclude such entities as mountains, rivers, and forests. Although the moral borderline is reconfigured so as to allow some other-than-humans entry into the realm of moral considerability, the rest of the natural world is left behind.[61]

Dissatisfied with the moral philosophies of the animal advocacy movement, I turned to the holist theories in the field of nature ethics in the hope of encountering more inclusive ideas. Once again, I encountered a tendency to neglect the role of empathy and care for individual beings. Individual animals appear to be swallowed up or "sacrificed" for the larger "whole." Holist theories particularly neglect domestic animals, who are typically considered irrelevant or detrimental to the ecological arena and hence of no direct moral concern for nature philosophers. Expressing a common view, the philosopher J. Baird Callicott argued in a controversial article that "environmental ethics sets a very low priority on domestic animals as they very frequently contribute to the erosion of the integrity, stability, and beauty of the biotic communities into which they have been insinuated."[62]

Still hoping to find a more inclusive nature philosophy, I turned to the literature in ecophilosophy. Ecophilosophers held forth a promise of incorporating feelings of care through their emphasis on the importance of experience and personal consciousness. Once again, however, I was disappointed to learn that reverence and respect among ecophilosophers often did not extend to individual other-than-human animals, but rather to "species" or the "land." Both environmental ethicists and ecophilosophers invoked Leopold's dictum to "think like a mountain," but virtually none spoke of thinking like an animal in a laboratory or factory farm.

I first encountered Aldo Leopold's *A Sand County Almanac* in a class at the University of Wisconsin, Madison, the school where he had taught. The teacher was eager to impress upon his students Leopold's love of nature and the significance of his attempt to bring the larger community or the "land" into the orbit of moral concern. Despite the teacher's best efforts, what impressed me most deeply was my shock and horror at Leopold's vivid accounts of the delight that he experienced while hunting. Where, I pondered, was Leopold's love and respect for birds, deers, and other animals when he was shooting them? Was there, in fact, a place for individual animals within Leopold's notion of the "land community"? And for what reasons did he wish to preserve the "land"?

Feeling discouraged with the nature philosophies I had encountered, I turned to ecofeminism in hopes of finding a more hospitable niche for other-than-human animals. I was disappointed, however, to discover that ecofeminists too often displayed a similar absence of concern for other-than-humans. With noticeable exceptions, such as Carol Adams, Greta Gaard, and Lori Gruen, ecofeminists rarely discussed other animals; nor did they write about vegetarianism.[63] Although ecofeminists embraced a holist philosophy, often little was said about what this meant in everyday practice.

I was beginning to suspect that the neglect of other-than-humans was not an incidental aspect of the Western nature philosophies, but rather central to it. Instead of continuing to seek an ethic or philosophy that expressed a concern for individual beings, I therefore began to investigate why this concern was lacking. I became interested in understanding the worldviews that underlay nature philosophies and, in particular, their focus on larger transcendent constructs. This, in turn, led me down an unexpected path: the study of religion.

It was at this point that I decided to return to school and get a doctorate in religious studies. I had been warned that it would be difficult to be a feminist in a religious institution, but I discovered that the challenge posed by my interest in other-than-human animals was even more daunting. Both Judaism and Christianity are founded upon the notion of a profound distinction between humans and the rest of nature. Questioning the unique status of humans therefore threatens the very foundation of the religions themselves. Critics of the Western religious traditions have indicted the passage in Genesis where God "gave Man dominion over the earth and all of the creatures of the Earth," entrusting "him" with the mandate to subdue it. The best-known critic of the "Judeo-Christian tradition," Lynn White, argues that, historically, the Genesis passage has lent itself to the interpretation that all of nature was created by God expressly to serve "man's" needs.[64] God's mandate to Adam to "till the earth" in the Garden of Eden has also been interpreted as conferring upon humans the role of God's deputy on Earth. As God's representatives, humans are granted the authority to manage God's creation.[65]

Recently, a number of theologians and philosophers have reinterpreted the Genesis passage, positing that dominion does not imply human domination of nature but rather stewardship. Thomas Sieger Derr expresses this attitude, arguing that "the real, orthodox Christian attitude toward nature . . . is, in a word, stewardship. We are trustees for that which does not belong to us."[66] However, although humans are made "in the image of God" and are "definitely above nature and in charge," Derr cautions that "we cannot do whatever pleases us. Our dominion is one of responsibility and is exercised for the benefit of the true owner, as God's steward. It is an act of *service* to the creation."[67] Derr's concept of stewardship allows humans to "treat the non-human creation with respect and to use it properly for human need." It entreats humans "to love the world both for our own sakes, and for the love of its Maker."[68] In the same volume James A. Nash expresses an increasingly common view among theologians of nature. For Nash, stewardship means "loving care and service for the sake of both humans and other life forms."[69]

The new conception of human stewardship is thought to imply an attitude of kindness toward all of God's creatures. A number of adherents cite biblical passages as evidence of God's concern for other-than-human animals, such as the mandates not to boil a kid in the milk of its mother, or not to "plow with an ox and ass together."[70] But these passages fail to challenge the human prerogative to use other-than-humans for forced labor and food. Furthermore, a triadic relationship is established whereby individuals and all of nature are valued indirectly, because they are the property of a larger "whole," conceived as God.[71] Whether as dominators or as caretakers, humans still occupy the hierarchical position of managers of the rest of the natural world.[72] I found the idea of a God who, through a divine act of nepotism, selects a "chosen species" to manage the rest of the natural world deeply disturbing, and at odds with my feelings of kinship with the rest of the nature.

I was never drawn to any of the mainstream Western religious traditions. Buddhism, although strictly speaking not a religion, held some appeal for me, due to its emphasis on concern for the suffering of all sentient beings. But even Buddhism reinforces a hierarchy that places humans at the top. If humans accrue bad karma they risk returning in the next life as other-than-human animals, a turn of events clearly seen as undesirable. Furthermore, although the early Buddhist writings in the Lankavatara Sutra made strong statements in favor of vegetarianism,[73] subsequent Buddhists have often condoned meat eating by focusing on the circumstances in which the meat was obtained. If a Buddhist monk is offered meat, for example, it is considered a worse offense to refuse it than to eat it. I was disillusioned with a religion or philosophy that could engage in these kinds of rationalizations.[74]

The focus on the purity of one's mental or spiritual state has been an integral part of both Eastern and Western religious traditions. It has also become increasingly popular in New Age spirituality, and is often applied to our treatment of other-than-humans. People frequently condone their consumption of meat with the argument that they give "thanks" to the animals that they consume, or they "ask for their forgiveness." One woman even claimed she had a spiritual experience where she heard the words of animals as they entered a slaughter house. They told her it was "okay" that they were going to be killed.[75] But do animals really acquiesce so willingly in their deaths? And do the kind thoughts of those who consume them give them consolation?

My own spirituality developed in partial reaction to this focus on intention over embodied acts. Mental and spiritual states were meaningless, I felt, unless they were accompanied by appropriate actions. Veganism, therefore, became an important part of my spiritual practice. Veganism has never been a religion for me, however, nor is it a set of dogmatic beliefs. When I dine with nonvegetarians I am often told that I cannot eat a certain item on the menu. I always correct this misunderstanding. "I can eat anything I want," I explain. "I *choose* not to eat other animals." Not eating other-than-human animals is an outward expression of my feelings of care and connection, not a rigid belief to which I owe obedience.

## ECOFEMINIST IDEAS OF HOLISM

Despite my disillusionment with ecofeminism, I have remained optimistic that it has the potential to develop a genuinely inclusive and embodied philosophy. Ecofeminists have endorsed the idea of holistic thought and critiqued dualisms, including reason and emotion, the domestic and the wild, the universal and the particular. I stress the word "potential" since ecofeminists, like many other nature theorists, often fail to directly address the plight of other-than-human animals. My ideas about ecofeminism, therefore, are not intended as a generalization about this diverse school of thought, but rather as my personal hopes for its future direction. Feminist and ecofeminist philosophy is both the lens through which I have developed my critique of holist philosophy, and the field within which I seek to set forth an alternative view of nature ethics.

One of my purposes in focusing on holism has been to highlight the significant differences between the ecofeminist understanding of holism and that of mainstream holists. I will suggest that ecofeminist philosophy can critique the current understanding of holist nature philosophy, and also point to ways in which the understanding of "holism" itself might be transformed. Ecofeminist holist philosophy, as I conceive it, transcends neither individual beings nor feelings of care and empathy. On the contrary, it embraces these, while simultaneously seeking to understand the larger historical and current context (or larger story) within which moral problems arise. It also bridges the dichotomy between an inward spirituality and outward actions. Ecofeminism cannot mandate feelings of care, but it can help to sow the seeds of change by examining the conditions that facilitate it.

My critique is not intended to reinforce new dualisms, such as that between "ecofeminists" and "other" nature philosophers. I also do not wish to deny the achievements of the theorists under study, or their genuine love of the natural world. My insights are offered, however, in the belief that as long as nature ethicists continue to analyze the environmental crisis in gender-neutral terms, we will overlook important information that can help to alleviate suffering and achieve fundamental change. Finally, although I focus on some of the historical and philosophical roots of the conceptual divide between animal advocates and other nature philosophers, my hope is that we can ultimately find the common ground that will bring us together in our efforts.

## NOTES

1. The above examples are based on anecdotes provided by Bernard Rollin. Personal communication with author, March 20, 2000.

2. I use the term "nature ethics" in my work rather than the more usual "environmental ethics" to avoid the implicit assumption that humans are distinct from "the environment," and because it helps to bridge the divisions between the animal advocacy and environmental movements.

3. Holist nature philosophy has roots in the broader philosophy of holism, which spans diverse fields, such as spirituality, science, and philosophy. The term *holism* was coined in 1926 by the South African statesman Jan Christiaan Smuts (1870–1950) to indicate the unifying whole underlying matter, life, mind, and personality. Critiquing the mechanistic views of science and the determinism of moral philosophy, Smuts argued that the creation of wholes is a "fundamental factor" operating in the universe. Smuts, *Holism and Evolution: The Original Source of the Holistic Approach to Life*, ed. Sanford Holst (Sherman Oaks, Calif.: Sierra Sunrise Books, 1999), 94. Carolyn Merchant summarizes the major ideas of holism as (1) everything is connected; (2) the whole is greater than the sum of its parts; (3) knowledge is context dependent; (4) the primacy of process over parts; and (5) the unity of humans and nonhuman nature. Carolyn Merchant, *Radical Ecology: The Search for a Livable World* (New York: Routledge, 1992), 76–78. For a historical overview of the holist origins of ecology, see Anna Bramwell, *Ecology in the 20ᵗʰ Century: A History* (New Haven, Conn.: Yale University Press, 1989). See also Donald Worster, who argues that although holism has assumed various guises throughout history (arcadianism, vitalism, and organicism) the common underlying theme has been "an intense distaste for the fragmentation of the industrial culture and its isolation from the natural world," in *Nature's Economy: The Roots of Ecology* (San Francisco: New York: Cambridge University Press, 1990), 21. For an overview of holism's relation to the social sciences, see D. C. Phillips, *Holistic Thought in Social Science* (Palo Alto, Calif.: Stanford University Press, 1976).

4. I use the phrase *other-than-human animals* to avoid reinforcing the conventional dualism that separates humans from the other animals.

5. For contemporary discussions of holism in nature philosophy, see Kristin Shrader-Frechette, "Individualism, Holism, and Environmental Ethics," *Ethics and the Environment* 1, no. 1 (1996): 55–69; Frederick Ferré, "Persons in Nature: Toward

an Applicable and Unified Environmental Ethics," *Ethics and the Environment* 1, no. 1 (1996): 15–25; William Aiken, "Ethical Issues in Agriculture," in *Earthbound: New Introductory Essays in Environmental Ethics*, ed. Tom Regan (New York: Random House, 1984), 274–288; Don Marietta, *For People and the Planet: Holism and Humanism in Environmental Ethics* (Philadelphia: Temple University Press, 1994); Joseph DesJardins, ed., *Environmental Ethics: Concepts, Policy and Theory* (New York: McGraw Hill, 1999) — see especially chapter 7, "Holism: Ecology and Ethics"; Michael P. Nelson, "Holists and Fascists and Paper Tigers . . . Oh My!" *Ethics and the Environment* 1, no. 2 (1996): 103–118; Arthur Zucker, "Ferré, Organicistic Connectedness — But Still Speciesistic," *Ethics and the Environment* 1, no. 2 (1996): 185–190; Lawrence E. Johnson, "Humanity, Holism, and Environmental Ethics," *Environmental Ethics* 5 (Winter 1983): 345–354; J. Baird Callicott, "Holistic Environmental Ethics and the Problem of Ecofascism," in *Environmental Philosophy: From Animal Rights to Radical Ecology*, ed. Michael E. Zimmerman et al., 4th ed. (Upper Saddle River, N.J.: Prentice Hall, 2005), 116-129; Y. S. Lo, "Non-Humean Holism, Un-Humean Holism," *Environmental Values* 10, no. 1 (2001): 113–123; G. E. Varner, "The Schopenhauerian Challenge in Environmental Ethics," *Environmental Ethics* 7 (Fall 1985): 209–230; and *In Nature's Interests?: Interests, Animal Rights and Environmental Ethics* (Oxford: Oxford University Press, 1998).

6. Citing animal experiments to prevent the release of dangerous chemicals into the environment is a common strategy used by environmental advocates. In addition to the ethical problems entailed in experimenting on sentient beings, interspecies variability makes the results unreliable. For a critique of the spurious scientific validity of animal experimentation, see Jean Swingle Greek and C. Ray Greek, *What Will We Do If We Don't Experiment on Animals? Medical Research for the Twenty-first Century* (Victoria, BC: Trafford Publishing, 2004).

7. Environmental organizations that condone or endorse hunting include the Sierra Club, World Wildlife Fund, the Nature Conservancy, the National Wildlife Federation, and the National Audubon Society. *The Watchdog Report on Animal Protection Charities* (Clinton, Wash.: Animal People, 2006). For summaries of environmental organizations' positions on hunting, see National Shooting Federation, "What They Say About Hunting," http://www.nssf.org/lit/WTSAH2.pdf?AoI=hunting (accessed August 11, 2007). Additional information about support for hunting and alliances with hunter organizations may also be found on the websites of these organizations.

8. At first glance, the failure to promote vegetarianism among environmentalists appears puzzling. My analysis suggests, however, that the adherence to an animal-based diet may have psychological roots that extend beyond the reach of rational discourse. See chapter 7.

9. I will restrict my understanding of masculinism to nineteenth and twentieth century Western conceptions of masculine identity. For further discussion of masculinism and masculine identity, see chapter 2.

10. On the subject of masculine hegemony, see Tim Carrigan, R. W. Connell, and John Lee, "Towards a New Sociology of Masculinity," *Theory and Society* 14, no. 5 (1985): 551–604. See also R. W. Connell, *Masculinities* (Berkeley: University of Cal-

ifornia Press, 1995), 76–77, and Andrea Cornwall and Nancy Lindisfarne, eds., *Dislocating Masculinity: Comparative Ethnographies* (New York: Routledge, 1994), 20.

11. The conceptual opposition between male and female has assumed different forms throughout history. Up until the modern bourgeois era, women were viewed as inferior according to a singular standard of male excellence. With industrialization and the rise of the cult of domesticity, the notion of the complementary nature of the sexes came to the fore. Throughout these permutations, however, manhood or masculine identity typically has been conceived as the renunciation of ties to the (devalued) female world. For further discussion of the concept of gender identity see chapter 2.

12. I do not argue that the philosophies of the prominent holist authors examined in this study must always include all three traits in order to qualify as masculinist. Typically, the traits are found together, however, and function to modify one another. For example, while the holists under review attempt to develop a caring ethic for nature, their focus is on larger, universal constructs, rather than the realm of particular individual beings. Thus, with respect to individual other-than-humans, this form of relation functions to reinforce the masculine ideal of autonomy or detachment.

13. Donald Sabo and Ross Runfola, eds., *Jock: Sports and Male Identity* (Englewood Cliffs, N.J.: Prentice Hall, 1980); Michael A. Messner and Donald F. Sabo, eds., *Sport, Men and the Gender Order: Critical Feminist Perspectives* (Champaign, Ill.: Human Kinetics, 1990).

14. I use the term *anthropocentric* in deference to convention, although I believe that it is more accurate to use the term *androcentric*, since the qualities cited as a basis for human superiority are also stereotypical "masculine traits" (i.e., rationality, autonomy, and universal awareness).

15. The generalization that low regard for domestic animals exists among holist nature philosophers does not always apply to pets, who at times have been accorded honorary entry into the human family. This was particularly true in the latter part of the nineteenth century. However, this honorary status does not preclude an instrumental orientation. Attitudes toward pets typically reflect a psychological, rather than a material, form of instrumentalism. Thus, Victorians valued pets for their ability to teach young boys a new conception of manliness, based upon the ideas of self-control and care-taking of others. See Katherine C. Grier, "Childhood Socialization and Companion Animals: United States, 1820–1870," *Society and Animals* 7, no. 2 (1999): 95–120.

16. John Muir, "The Wild Sheep of California," *Overland Monthly* 12 (1874): 359.

17. The word "sacrifice" is the actual word used by laboratory experimenters when they kill animals. The choice of terms exposes the underlying mentality, which presumes that if other-than-human animals suffer and die, human beings will be allowed to live. On the connections between the philosophy of sacrifice and animal experimentation, see Brian Luke, "Animal Sacrifice: A Model of Paternal Exploitation," *International Journal of Sociology and Social Policy* 24, no. 9 (2004): 18–44, and *Brutal: Manhood and the Exploitation of Animals* (Chicago: University of Illinois Press, 2007).

18. Aside from Roosevelt, readily known as a conservationist, the holists under study defy rigid categorizations. Both Leopold and Rolston are referred to as "environmental philosophers," "ecophilosophers," "ecocentric philosophers," and "environmental ethicists." Although Leopold never used the term, Warren argues that he

was "arguably the first bona fide Western environmental ethicist." Karen J. Warren, "The Philosophical Foundations of a New Land Ethic," in *The Land Ethic Toolbox: Using Ethics, Emotion and Spiritual Values to Advance American Land Conservation*, ed. Robert T. Perschel (Washington, DC: Wilderness Society, 2004). Warwick Fox, in addition, self-identifies as a "transpersonal" ecologist, rather than a "deep" ecologist. For the distinction between environmental ethics and ecophilosophy, see chapter 6.

19. As political theorist Carole Pateman points out, in the modern era the "individual" came to be viewed as "a collection of pieces of property that can, through rational calculation of the mind, be made the subject of contract." According to this male ideal of autonomy, bonds with other citizens were based on the pursuit of self-interest, which women were unable to achieve, given their deficient capacity for objectivity and rationality. Pateman, *The Disorder of Women: Democracy, Feminism and Political Theory* (Stanford, Calif.: Stanford University Press, 1989), 48. For feminist critiques of Western individualism for its devaluation of dependency, see Eva Feder Kittay, *Love's Labor: Essays on Women, Equality, and Dependency* (New York: Routledge, 1998). For further discussion of the modern Western notion of the individual, see chapter 6.

20. Biological "hierarchy theory" asserts this point as a scientific theory. According to hierarchy theory, different objects come into perspective, depending upon one's spatiotemporal scales, methods, or instruments of perception. Thus, depending upon one's epistemological standpoint, "chromosomes" may be viewed as individual beings. Although I am not averse to entertaining the idea that chromosomes and other microscopic and macroscopic entities are "individuals," my particular focus is on more tangible beings, namely, other-than-human animals. For a consideration of the place of plants within an ecofeminist philosophy, see chapter 7.

21. Andrée Collard argues that "individualism in the sense of integrity (wholeness)—the integrity of human groups *and* animals, animals *and* plants, plants *and* the earth, the earth *and* the heavens held together by indivisible bonds of kinship—this type of individualism is incompatible with the patriarchal notion of individualism as an isolated member of the group whose integrity is broken." Collard with Joyce Contrucci, *Rape of the Wild: Man's Violence Against Animals and the Earth* (Bloomington: Indiana University Press, 1989), 31–32.

22. A number of animal advocates have sought to bring some other-than-human animals (e.g., great apes) into the orbit of moral considerability by conferring upon them the status of "persons." Although well-intentioned, I believe this strategy is misguided, since it leaves unchallenged the dualism between "persons" (or "individuals") and all other animals, merely changing the boundary line. For essays that advocate this strategy, see Paola Cavalieri and Peter Singer, eds., *The Great Ape Project: Equality Beyond Humanity* (London: Fourth Estate Limited, 1993).

23. David Perlman, "Clinton Bans Human Clone Funding," *San Francisco Chronicle*, March 5, 1997.

24. It is interesting to note that since humans are a relatively young species, they are much less individually differentiated than other species. An individual human, for example, may have one unique gene in a thousand (i.e., one gene that is not the same as in every other human), a chimpanzee has twice as many (two), and a fruit fly has

ten. Thus, individual fruit flies and chimpanzees are more genetically distinct than individual humans. It appears, therefore, that the presumption of the uniqueness of individual humans rests on shaky grounds. "The Difference Between Us," produced and directed by Christine Herbes-Sommers. Episode 1 of the three-part PBS documentary series *The Power of An Illusion*, created and produced by Larry Adelman (San Francisco, Calif.: California Newsreel, 2003).

25. Ronald Reagan, campaign speech to Western Wood Products Association (San Francisco, Calif., March 12, 1966).

26. Kenneth Shapiro, "Animal Rights versus Humanism: The Charge of Speciesism," *Journal of Humanistic Psychology* 30, no. 2 (1990): 9–37. For the argument that species are "abstract, or spatio-temporal" rather than "concrete entities," see John R. Gregg, "Taxonomy, Language, and Reality," in *American Naturalist* 84 (1950): 419–435, quoted in Shapiro, "Animal Rights versus Humanism," 17. Even when biologists do agree on the existence of "species" there is no consensus on the criteria used for its definition. As Carl Chung points out, "there are anywhere from three to twenty-two definitions, and there is ongoing debate about which definition is the right one." Chung, "The Species Problem and the Value of Teaching the Complexities of Species," *American Biology Teacher* 66, no. 6 (August 2004): 413. See also M. F. Claridge, H. A. Dawah, and M. R. Wilson, "Practical Approaches to Species Concepts for Living Organisms," in *Species: The Units of Biodiversity*, ed. M. F. Claridge, H. A. Dawah, and M. R. Wilson (New York: Chapman and Hall, 1997), 1–15; and Robert A. Wilson, ed. *Species: New Interdisciplinary Essays* (Cambridge, Mass.: MIT Press, 1999). For an ecofeminist analysis that calls for recognizing the commonalities between humans and other animals, while also acknowledging relevant differences that affect the well-being of other animals, see Ronnie Zoe Hawkins, "Ecofeminism and Nonhumans: Continuity, Difference, Dualism, and Domination," *Hypatia* 13, no. 1 (Winter 1998): 158–197.

27. For further discussion of the idea of the "mass term" and other speciesist language practices, see the discussion in chapter 7. For an in-depth analysis of speciesist language, see the work of Joan Dunayer, *Animal Equality: Language and Liberation* (Derwood, Md.: Recycle Publishing, 2001).

28. According to Roderick Nash, the root of the word *wild* "seems to have been 'will' with a descriptive meaning of self-willed, willful, of uncontrollable. From 'willed' came the adjective 'wild' used to convey the idea of being lost, unruly, disordered or confused." "Wild" animals, thus, are literally conceived as animals with "wills." Roderick Nash, *Wilderness and the American Mind* (New Haven, Conn.: Yale University Press, 1967).

29. José Luis García Sánchez and Miguel Angel Pacheco, illustrated by José Antonio Alcázar, *I Am a Wild Animal* (New York: Santillana Publishing, 1975), 7. A parallel view of human females' tameness and serviceability to others is visually underscored by an adjacent image of a human mother nursing her infant.

30. The link between women and nature is often discussed in abstract terms, providing little or no indication of what it might entail. Karen J. Warren identifies a number of connections linking the domination of women, other subordinated humans, and "nonhuman nature," including "historical, conceptual, empirical, socio-economic,

linguistic, symbolic and literary, spiritual and religious, epistemological, political, and ethical interconnections." Warren, *Ecofeminist Philosophy: A Western Perspective on What It Is and Why It Matters* (Lanham, Md.: Rowman & Littlefield, 2000), 21–38. For further discussion of ecofeminism see chapter 6.

31. Françoise D'Eaubonne is often credited with the first use of the term ecofeminism in *Le Feminisme ou la Mort* (Paris: Pierre Horay, 1974). Although D'Eaubonne's work was never translated into English, the term spread rapidly across several continents during the 1970s, leading some analysts to speculate that it emerged synchronistically. Ariel Salleh, *"Staying Alive: Women, Ecology and Development,* by Vandana Shiva." *Hypatia* 6 (Spring 1991), 206–14.

32. Janet Biehl, *Rethinking Ecofeminist Politics* (Boston: South End Press, 1991), 11.

33. Numerous charges and countercharges can be found in ecofeminists' texts. For example, Victoria Davion charges that in "Deeper than Deep Ecology: The Ecofeminist Connection," Salleh implies the existence of a female-based consciousness and knowledge deriving from women's embodiment in nature. Davion claims that while Salleh recognizes the socially constructed dualisms that characterize patriarchal society, she perceives women's cycle of fertility, pregnancy, and childbirth as a "fact of life." Davion, "Is Ecofeminism Feminist?" in *Ecological Feminism,* ed. Karen J. Warren (New York: Routledge, 1994), 8–28. In her subsequent work, to dispel all doubt about her affiliation with essentialism, Salleh states that "it is nonsense to assume that women are closer to nature than men." Salleh, "The Ecofeminism/Deep Ecology Debate: A Reply to Patriarchal Reason," *Environmental Ethics* 14, no. 3 (Fall 1992): 208. Both Charlene Spretnak and Susan Griffin also wrote nuanced responses to the charge of essentialism, critiquing the nihilistic implications of an extreme postmodern view. Spretnak points out that while humans socially construct the world through discourse, these collective narratives are "grounded in our bodily experiences in nature and society." Charlene Spretnak, *The Resurgence of the Real: Body, Nature and Place in a Hypermodern World* (New York: Routledge, 1999), 4. In addition, Susan Griffin argues that although we need to give up the illusion that language can master reality, the terms "woman" and "nature" do have contextual meanings "as they are perceived to be connected to a web of other meanings." Griffin, "Ecofeminism and Meaning," in *Ecofeminism: Women, Culture, Nature,* ed. Karen J. Warren (Bloomington: Indiana University Press, 1997), 224. Seeking to avoid both essentialism and postmodernism, other feminists have located women's link with nature in their shared material exploitation under patriarchal culture. As Mary Mellor explains, these analyses concentrate not on what women *are,* but on "what most women *do,*" namely, "women's unpaid and underpaid work." Mellor, *Breaking the Boundaries* (London: Virago Press, 1992), 196. See also Ariel Salleh, *Ecofeminism as Politics: Nature, Marx and the Postmodern* (New York: Zed Books, 1997).

34. Reflecting the strength of the backlash against ecofeminism, Noël Sturgeon relates that when presenting her work on ecofeminism in academic contexts, it has often been presumed (incorrectly) that she was making essentialist claims. Some of her colleagues went so far as to pressure her to change the name of a paper that used the term "ecofeminism," arguing that "such essentialisms permanently and thoroughly tarnish ecofeminism as a political position." Sturgeon admits that this external pres-

sure, in combination with her own qualms about the essentialism of some ecofeminist arguments, led her to struggle with the question of whether she wanted to identify herself and her work as ecofeminist. Sturgeon, *Ecofeminist Natures: Race, Gender, Feminist Theory and Political Action* (New York: Routledge, 1997), 168.

35. Sturgeon, *Ecofeminist Natures*, 59. In a similar vein, Elizabeth Carlassare critiques the characterization of "spiritual and intuitive ways of knowing" as inherently "essentialist," arguing that "the uses of essentialism by ecofeminists can be explored for their political intentions and their points of effectiveness and ineffectiveness in liberatory politics, instead of dismissed unconditionally as 'regressive.'" She advocates an "umbrella" approach that sees differences within ecofeminism as "a sign of the movement's vitality." Carlassare, "Essentialism in Ecofeminist Discourse," in *Ecology*, ed. Carolyn Merchant (Atlantic Highlands, N.J.: Humanities Press, 1994), 231. Erika Cudworth further maintains that "there is merit . . . in the range of ecofeminist approaches and the allegations of essentialism, are, more often than not, based on cursory readings, de-contextualization and attribution." Cudworth, *Developing Ecofeminist Theory: The Complexity of Difference* (New York: Palgrave Macmillan, 2005), 102.

36. Sturgeon, *Ecofeminist Natures*, 60. Sturgeon contends that this form of strategic essentialism is a momentary event, which becomes destabilized as women advance in their organizational activism and require recognition of differences.

37. Salleh, *Ecofeminism as Politics*, 171.

38. See for example, Chris J. Cuomo, *Feminism and Ecological Communities: An Ethic of Flourishing* (New York: Routledge, 1998), 36.

39. *The American Heritage Dictionary*, 4th ed., s.v. "logos."

40. Simone de Beauvoir, *The Second Sex*, trans. H. M. Parshley (New York: Vintage Books, 1974).

41. For psychological analyses, see Nancy J. Chodorow, *The Reproduction of Mothering: Psychoanalysis and the Sociology of Gender* (Berkeley: University of California Press, 1978) and Jessica Benjamin, *The Bonds of Love: Psychoanalysis, Feminism, and the Problem of Domination* (New York: Pantheon Books, 1988). For philosophical and political perspectives, see Catherine Keller, *From a Broken Web: Separation, Sexism, and Self* (Boston: Beacon Press, 1986); Wendy Brown, *Manhood and Politics: A Feminist Reading in Political Theory* (Totowa, N.J.: Rowman & Littlefield, 1988); and Marilyn French, *Beyond Power: On Women, Men, and Morals* (New York: Summit Books, 1985).

42. See Dorothy Dinnerstein, *The Mermaid and the Minotaur: Sexual Arrangements and Human Malaise* (New York: Harper and Row, 1976) and Sherry Ortner, "Is Female to Male as Nature Is to Culture?" in *Woman, Culture and Society,* ed. Michelle Z. Rosaldo and Louise Lamphere (Stanford, Calif.: Stanford University Press, 1974).

43. Beauvoir, *Second Sex,* 71–72.

44. The importance for men of passing on the hunting experience was underscored in the 2004 murder trial of Californian Scott Peterson. Peterson displayed no emotional response throughout the entire trial, even during testimony about the discovery of the body of his pregnant wife. Yet, when a friend described a conversation in which the two men imagined future hunting expeditions with their yet-to-be-born boys, he

reported that Peterson wept. Diana Walsh, "The Peterson Trial: Defendant Moved to Tears," *San Francisco Chronicle*, August 5, 2004.

45. Carol Gilligan, *In a Different Voice: Psychological Theory and Women's Development* (Cambridge, Mass.: Harvard University Press, 1993). My use of the literature on women and care is not intended to reinforce yet another binary opposition that relegates women to the role of caring for men as well as the natural world. As Alison Jaggar points out, radical feminists seek to create an alternative culture to patriarchy, not a mirror image, rejecting those aspects of the culture that keep women subservient, while also incorporating and reinterpreting traditionally conceived values, such as power and strength. Jaggar, *Feminist Politics and Human Nature* (Lanham, Md.: Rowman & Littlefield, 1988), 252.

46. The ecofeminist Greta Gaard argues that critique of population must include the following components: (1) an examination of the overconsumption of the first world nations in relation to the third and fourth world; (2) a consideration of the problems of poverty, which lead families to have many children; (3) the role of sexism in confining women's social worth to childbearing; (4) the quality of infant and maternal health care; (5) the definition of masculinity as entailing the ability to "father"; (6) the resolution of colonial relations between nations as well as the problem of militarism; and (7) a challenge to sexual mores, including free and safe contraception, and a challenge to the assumptions that heterosexuality and childbearing are women's "only and proper fulfillment." Gaard, *Ecological Politics: Ecofeminists and the Greens* (Philadelphia: Temple University Press, 1998), 185. See also Christine J. Cuomo, "Ecofeminism, Deep Ecology, and Human Population," in *Ecological Feminism*, ed. Karen J. Warren (New York: Routledge, 1994), 88–105.

47. Quoted in Rik Scarce, *Eco-warriors: Understanding the Radical Environmental Movement* (Chicago: Noble Press, 1990), 92–93. The racism in Foreman's call to allow Third World people to starve was not lost on many environmental critics. Foreman subsequently softened his position, acknowledging that it "was insensitive and simplistic." His point was that humanitarian responses "may not have the result that we hope, and may even have the opposite result."

48. Sarah Lucia Hoagland, *Lesbian Ethics: Toward New Value* (Palo Alto, Calif.: Institute of Lesbian Studies, 1989).

49. Peter Singer, *Animal Liberation: A New Ethics for Our Treatment of Animals* (New York: Avon Books, 1975).

50. Tom Regan, *The Case for Animal Rights* (Berkeley: University of California Press, 1983).

51. Singer, *Animal Liberation*, x.

52. Peter Singer, *Practical Ethics* (New York: Cambridge University Press, 1979), 80.

53. Singer, *Practical Ethics*, 104, 102. This argument appears in Singer's *Practical Ethics* and is overlooked by those who are only familiar with Singer's more popular *Animal Liberation*. Singer attempts to soften the pernicious implications of his thesis by pointing to its limited applications: "It cannot justify factory farming, where animals do not have pleasant lives. Nor does it normally justify the killing of wild animals . . . the shooting of a duck does not lead to its replacement by another . . . al-

though there are situations in which it is not wrong to kill animals, these situations are special ones, and do not cover very many of the billions of premature deaths humans inflict, year after year, on nonhumans." *Practical Ethics*, 105.

54. Singer, *Practical Ethics*, 51.

55. Regan, *Animal Rights*, 325.

56. Regan, *Animal Rights*, 199.

57. Tom Regan, *The Thee Generation: Reflections on the Coming Revolution* (Philadelphia: Temple University Press, 1991).

58. Regan, *Thee Generation*, 140. For a critique of Regan's emphasis on logic over feelings of care in moral theory, see Josephine Donovan, "Attention to Suffering: Sympathy as a Basis for Ethical Treatment of Animals," in *Beyond Animal Rights: A Feminist Caring Ethic for the Treatment of Animals*, ed. Josephine Donovan and Carol J. Adams (New York: Continuum Publishing, 2000). Donovan asks, "Isn't it unlikely that one would stop to figure out principles of logic and consistency to determine an appropriate moral action, if say [the neighbor's children] were crying in pain?" (157). For additional feminist critiques of mainstream animal rights theories, see Cuomo, *Feminism and Ecological Communities*, 91–98; Marti Kheel, "The Liberation of Nature: A Circular Affair," *Environmental Ethics* 7, no. 2 (Summer 1985): 135–149; and Brian Luke, "Taming Ourselves or Going Feral? Toward a Nonpatriarchal Metaethic of Animal Liberation," in *Animals and Women: Feminist Theoretical Explorations*, ed. Carol J. Adams and Josephine Donovan (Durham, N.C.: Duke University Press, 1995), 290–319.

59. Although both Singer and Regan emphasize the moral importance of the ability to project oneself into the future, the theoretical bases to their arguments are distinct. Regan draws on the Kantian tradition's emphasis on the moral importance of self-conscious reflection. For Singer, by contrast, self-consciousness is morally significant because of its implication for the increased capacity to suffer. Despite their distinct grounds of argumentation, both philosophies share a focus on the masculinist ideal of autonomy.

60. Joseph Mellon critiques mainstream philosophy's emphasis on crisis situations, and in particular the spurious logic of developing a hierarchy of value based upon decision-making in dramatic, lifeboat scenarios, where rational decision-making is hardly the norm. Joseph Mellon, "Nature Ethics without Theory" (PhD diss., University of Oregon, 1989).

61. Regan seems to show some concern over the limitation of his own ethic. In his words, "But limiting the class of beings that have inherent value to the class of living beings seems to be an arbitrary decision and one that does not serve well as the basis for an environmental ethic. . . . If I am right, the development of what can properly be called an environmental ethic requires that we postulate inherent value in nature." Tom Regan, *All That Dwell Therein* (Berkeley: University of California Press, 1982), 202–203.

62. J. Baird Callicott, "Animal Liberation: A Triangular Affair," in *In Defense of the Land Ethic: Essays in Environmental Philosophy,* ed. J. Baird Callicott (Albany: State University of New York Press, 1989), 37. In a subsequent article, Callicott attempted to make amends for his former stridency, arguing for moral obligations to

animals based upon the "social instincts." However, the "social instincts" still sanction the use of domestic animals for work and allow their slaughter for food, due to
an "evolved and unspoken social contract between man and beast [*sic*]." J. Baird Callicott, "Animal Liberation and Environmental Ethics: Back Together Again," in Callicott, *In Defense of the Land Ethic*, 56.

63. For ecofeminists who focus on concern for other-than-human animals, see the
anthologies of Greta Gaard, ed., *Ecofeminism: Women, Animals, Nature* (Philadelphia: Temple University Press, 1993); Adams and Donovan, *Animals and Women*; and
Donovan and Adams, *Beyond Animal Rights*. Also see Carol J. Adams, *The Sexual
Politics of Meat: A Feminist-Vegetarian Critical Theory* (New York: Continuum Publishing, 1990).

64. Lynn White, Jr., "The Historical Roots of Our Ecological Crisis," *Science* 155,
no. 3767 (1967): 1203–1207. White also argued that Christianity laid the groundwork
for the exploitation of the natural world by destroying the earlier pagan image of nature as sacred and animate. For a critique of White's thesis, see Elspeth Whitney, who
argues that White ignored the material factors that led to the groundwork for the attitudes he indicts. Whitney, "Lynn White, Ecotheology, and History," *Environmental
Ethics* 15, no. 2 (1993): 151–169.

65. Keith Thomas has argued that the Judeo-Christian tradition has been an ambiguous legacy that has at times functioned to promote the domination of nature and
at other times functioned to encourage protection. Thomas, *Man and the Natural
World: A History of the Modern Sensibility* (New York: Pantheon, 1983), 24. My thesis is that both orientations (protector and dominator) are characterized by a masculinism that generally has failed to accord importance to individual beings. Thomas
argues that the humane movement that arose in England in the seventeenth century
had roots in the stewardship tradition. Advocates for kindness to other-than-human
animals did in fact draw on both the stewardship tradition and transcendental ideas
about the divinity of all of creation. However, by and large, even the benevolent view
of other animals within the Jewish and Christian religions has entailed treating them
as symbols or instruments for a transcendent good. Thus, according to St. Thomas
Aquinas, the only reason for condemning human cruelty to animals-other-than-hu-
mans is that such behavior degrades the human soul and leads to cruelty toward other
humans. Some recent theologians have sought to correct this emphasis on the instrumental value of animals, arguing that other-than-humans have value independently of
humans. Process theologians such as Jay B. McDaniel, Charles Birch, and John B.
Cobb have been in the forefront of this attempt. In *Of God and Pelicans: A Theology
of Reverence for Life*, McDaniel employs a panentheistic notion of God to develop the
idea of a life-centered God and a life-centered ethic (Louisville, Ky.: Westminster/
John Knox, 1989). McDaniel stands out as one of the few theologians to emphasize
respect for the whole of creation as well as the individual parts of the natural world,
including domestic animals. He also argues for the importance of vegetarianism.
Birch and Cobb suggest the idea of a continuous process in which no great gulf exists between humans and other living beings. Charles Birch and John B. Cobb, Jr., *The
Liberation of Life: From the Cell to Community* (Denton, Tex.: Environmental Ethics
Books, 1990). Nevertheless McDaniel, Birch, and Cobb concede their willingness to

use other-than-human animals for experimentation out of "absolute necessity." Birch and Cobb, in addition, endorse a total utilitarian philosophy in which a chicken may be killed if "replaced" by another one. Birch and Cobb, *Liberation of Life*, 155, 159; McDaniel, *Of God and Pelicans*, 70. In this respect, their philosophies have not fully relinquished an instrumental orientation toward nature.

66. Thomas Sieger Derr, "Environmental Ethics and Christian Humanism," in *Environmental Ethics and Christian Humanism*, ed. Thomas Sieger Derr with James A. Nash and Richard John Neuhaus (Nashville, Tenn.: Abingdon Press, 1996), 22. For additional arguments for the idea of stewardship, see Loren Wilkinson, ed., *Earthkeeping in the '90s: Stewardship of Creation*, rev. ed. (Grand Rapids, Mich.: Wm. B. Eerdmans Publishing, 1991); Douglas Hall, *The Steward: A Biblical Symbol Come of Age* (Grand Rapids, Mich.: Wm. B. Eerdmans Publishing, 1990); Andrew Linzey, *Animal Theology* (Chicago: University of Illinois Press, 1995); and Matthew Scully, *Dominion: The Power of Man, the Suffering of Animals and the Call to Mercy* (New York: St. Martin's Griffin, 2002).

67. Derr, "Environmental Ethics," 22. The notion of nature as God's property is also represented in a statement by the ecotheologian Richard A. Baer, Jr., "The earth is property that does not belong to us," in "Higher Education, the Church, and Environmental Values," *Natural Resources Journal* 17 (July 1977): 48. As Roderick Nash comments, "From Baer's perspective *Homo sapiens* rents an apartment called nature. God is, quite literally, the landlord. He expects compliance with basic 'principles of etiquette' in the use of his creation." *The Rights of Nature: A History of Environmental Ethics* (Madison: University of Wisconsin Press, 1989), 101.

68. Derr, "Environmental Ethics," 23.

69. James A. Nash, "In Flagrant Dissent: An Environmentalist's Contentions" in Derr, *Environmental Ethics and Christian Humanism*, 107.

70. Exodus 23:19, 34:26; Deuteronomy 14:21 and 22:10. See, for example, Roberta Kalechofsky, ed., *Judaism and Animal Rights: Classical and Contemporary Responses* (Marblehead, Mass.: Micah Publications, 1992).

71. For a contrasting view arguing that the Christian God is concerned for individual other-than-humans, see McDaniel, *Of God and Pelicans*.

72. Even Christian saints, like St. Francis of Assisi, conform to this hierarchical aspect of the stewardship tradition. In the typical hagiographical tradition, other-than-human animals are depicted as subservient to their kindly caretaker, and as a mirror image of the saints' subservience to God. The taming of the animals reflects the internal taming of the saints' souls in their service to God. I contrast the idea of caring for (or taking care of) the whole of creation or the biotic community and a direct, unmediated caring for and about individual other-than-humans. On the subject of the symbolic role of animals in medieval hagiography, see William J. Short, "Saints in the World of Nature: The Animal Story as Spiritual Parable in Medieval Hagiography, 900–1200" (PhD diss., Pontificia Universitas Gregoriana, 1983).

73. "For the sake of love of purity, the Bodhisattva should refrain from eating flesh, which is born of semen, blood, etc. For fear of causing terror to living beings, let the Bodhisattva, who is disciplining himself to attain compassion, refrain from eating flesh. . . . Meat eating, I have unconditionally not permitted to anyone." *The*

*Lankavatara Sutra*, trans. Daisetz Suzuki (London: Routledge, 1932), quoted in Philip Kapleau, *To Cherish All Life: A Buddhist Case for Becoming Vegetarian* (New York: Harper and Row, 1982), 34–38.

74. On attitudes toward other-than-human animals in Asian traditions, see Christopher Key Chapple, *Nonviolence to Animals, Earth, and Self in Asian Traditions* (Albany: State University of New York Press, 1993). For a critical analysis of the speciesism underlying both Christianity and Buddhism, see Paul Waldau, *The Specter of Speciesism: Buddhist and Christian Views of Animals* (New York: Oxford University Press, 2002).

75. Personal communication to author, 2001.

# 2

## Masculine Identity
### *Born Again "Man"*

Zeus takes a break from flinging thunderbolts to incubate Dionysus in his thigh, later giving birth to Athena from his head.

Abraham sets out to sacrifice his son, in compliance with God's command.

Millennia later, Claude Bernard, nineteenth-century physiologist and founder of experimental medicine, dissects living animals and "does not hear the cries. . . . He does not see their flowing blood, he sees nothing but his idea, and is aware of nothing but an organism that conceals from him the problem he is seeking to resolve."[1]

### INTRODUCTION

What links a Greek god, a biblical figure, and a nineteenth century vivisectionist? Each example above illustrates a single theme: an attempt to construct masculine identity through an act of transcendence over nature, conceived as bodily functions or affective ties. Zeus usurps women's capacity to give birth by appropriating the act of reproduction; Abraham transcends kinship ties by demonstrating his greater allegiance to divine law; and Claude Bernard overrides feelings of empathy for the other-than-human world in his pursuit of a detached scientific ideal.

Men's greater propensity for aggression is widely recognized;[2] less well understood are its ties to masculine identity and the ideal of transcendence.[3] In this chapter I review some of the major theories of gender identity. I explore a range of sources, including feminist social and historical analysis, men's studies, object relations theory, and feminist ethics. All of the theories examined elucidate the confluence of masculine identity, aggression, and transcendent ideals.

## MASCULINE IDENTITY:
## THE CONSTRUCTION OF THE "OTHER"

It has become commonplace among theorists of postmodernism, postcolonial studies, and contemporary psychology to distinguish gender from biological differences between men and women. Sex differences exist in the realm of anatomy, whereas gender differences reside in culture.[4] As the men's studies theorist R. W. Connell states, gender is a linking concept that organizes social life in particular ways; it is a *practical engagement* with biological differences.[5] Gender, however, is more than a means of organizing sexes according to their differences; it is a binary system that posits an opposition. As many gender theorists have noted, masculinity is part of a symbolic binary order in which identity is defined by what it is not, namely, female. In other words, masculinity is a relational construct defined by what it excludes or negates. This binary organizational system is imbued with values which give higher status to men.

Women are not only viewed as the "opposite" sex in relation to men, however. At times, they are also seen as men's complement. In the Western world, the idea of the complementary nature of the sexes first emerged in the modern bourgeois era, along with the idea of the family as a safe haven from the competitive public sphere. Previously, women were viewed as inferior to a single standard of rational (male) excellence.[6] Although the modern complementary notion of the sexes might suggest the idea of separate but equal spheres, a hierarchy of value still exists in which the male-dominated public sphere is conceived as a superior arena to that of the more insular family unit, reserved for women.

Despite the changing conceptions of "manhood" and "masculinity" throughout the ages, the idea of a dynamic, hierarchical, binary relation between the genders remains a constant in Western society. This assumes a number of forms: "norms" and "difference," the "essential" and the "complementary," and "positive" and "negative."[7]

Generalizations about gender differences, however, must be made with great caution. As postmodernist, psychoanalytic, and postcolonial theorists argue, gender is not a fixed construct that transcends time, culture, and geographical location. Nor is it a unitary identity that can be affixed to members of diverse classes, ethnic groups, and sexual orientations. Instead, they claim that a plurality of *masculinities* exists.[8] These cautionary notes are well taken. Masculinity for an upper-class man from Japan will not be the same as it is for a middle-class Latino from the United States. Nor will it be the same for a gay, middle-class black man and a heterosexual, white working-class Jew. Nevertheless, the binary nature of gender identity continues to operate within and across these identities. And particular conceptions of femininity still operate as a construct against which masculine identity is formed.

The establishment of masculine identity is not only based on relations between men and women, however, but also on male-to-male relationships. More specifically, as gender theorists have argued, it operates in relation to a hegemonic masculinist ideal.[9] One particular definition is held up as a model against which all men in a given society measure themselves. As Erving Goffman states,

> in an important sense there is only one complete unblushing male in America: a young, married, white, urban, northern, heterosexual Protestant father of college education, fully employed, of good complexion, weight, and height, and a recent record in sports. . . . Any male who fails to qualify in any one of these ways is likely to view himself—during moments at least—as unworthy, incomplete, and inferior.[10]

Thus, although hegemonic masculinity is conceived as dominant to women, it is also dominant over "subordinate masculinities."[11] Most importantly, the modern construction of masculinity is based on a hetero-normative ideal, which designates one category of beings (women) as potential sexual objects for another category (men). Males who reject this norm are not regarded as bonafide men. They too are relegated to a subordinate status, associated with the female world.

R. W. Connell developed the concept of hegemonic masculinity, drawing from Antonio Gramsci's theories on how class dominance is maintained.[12] According to Gramsci, hegemony operates though both external force and internalized consent. Dominance (as opposed to domination) is achieved through the influence of cultural institutions, mores, and laws. In a similar manner, hegemonic masculinity is conceived not simply as an attribute of individual men, but rather as a diffuse worldview that inheres in institutions, power relations, and ideas. The significance of this understanding is its implication that people may hold masculinist ideas independently of their conscious awareness.

The conception of masculine identity as a form of hegemony has been the subject of debate.[13] Particularly relevant to this study is the accusation that this perspective implies a unitary subject and normative masculinity, overlooking unconscious motives and desires.[14] Drawing from Moira Gatens's theory of the "imaginaries," Richard Collier argues that to the extent that hegemonic masculinity is conceptualized as operating at the level of ideas, it implies a "dubious voluntarism which underestimates the *unconscious* embedding of . . . 'patriarchal' imperatives."[15] The term hegemonic masculinity as I conceive it, however, does not simply encompass a systematic ideology (for example, the idea "men are superior to women"), but also the unconscious motives and desires of a misogynist society (for example, I must control women in order to feel safe). This suggests that far from being a rational system or set of practices, hegemonic masculinity may express a form of mass pathology.[16]

Connell concurs that there are "serious difficulties" with a theoretical approach that "gives an absolute priority to ideology."[17] Drawing upon Sartre's notion of *practice,* he develops the concept of masculinity as an ongoing project. In this construction, masculinity occurs within particular contexts and is connected to "things people do."[18] And just as practices are ongoing activities, so too the attempt to establish masculinity is an unfinished, ever-changing project, requiring repeated and myriad forms of support.

Ecofeminists have contributed to the understanding of gender identity by pointing out that masculine identity has been defined not only in relation to women, but also with respect to a series of related dualisms, including reason/emotion, good/evil, culture/nature, conscious/unconscious, active/passive. In this dualistic worldview, men and women are not simply defined as polarities, but all that is associated with women is devalued and subordinated. Although the content of the polarities varies, masculine identity is the norm against which women and the natural world have been measured.

Within the Western tradition, masculine identity has been conceived as conforming to a narrative structure. Whereas women have been perceived as allied to the cyclical and repetitive realm of nature, masculine identity has been viewed as a storied achievement that transcends biology. It is not enough for men to simply mature. Masculine identity necessitates achievement. The etymological roots of the words *nature* and *culture* illustrate the connection between masculine identity and the idea of storied development. The word *culture* derives from the Latin "colere" meaning "to till" or "to cultivate." The word *nature,* by contrast, derives from the Latin "natura," meaning "birth."[19] Historically and anthropologically, women have been associated with that which is born (nature), while men have been associated with that which transforms or develops nature (culture).[20] In short, women's identities have been defined by means of an association with the unchanging, non-storied aspect of nature, whereas men's identities have been defined by their narrative of transcendence of biology.

In her monumental book *The Second Sex*, Simone de Beauvoir provides insight into the connection between men's transcendence of the realm of nature and women's constructed identities. According to de Beauvoir, under patriarchal society men have constructed women as the "other" in their attempt to escape from their biological "destiny." De Beauvoir argues that women's biological processes, such as menstruation, pregnancy, and birth, condemn them to the realm of immanence. All human beings, according to de Beauvoir, reach for transcendence and autonomy and an escape from the realm of objects. But whereas men are free to pursue their destinies by relinquishing nature, women remain tied to the animal realm. De Beauvoir argues that men's transcendence has historically been achieved by means of the subordination of both women and the natural world. As she states:

> Now, what peculiarly signalizes the situation of woman is that she—a free and autonomous being like all human creatures—nevertheless finds herself living in a world where men compel her to assume the status of the Other. They propose to stabilize her as object and to doom her to immanence since her transcendence is to be overshadowed and forever transcended by another ego (*conscience*) which is essential and sovereign.[21]

De Beauvoir developed her idea of the "other" from both structuralism and phenomenology.[22] From Claude Levi-Strauss she drew the idea that the passage from nature to culture is marked by a series of inherent dualisms. According to this structuralist view, duality is a given fact of social reality. De Beauvoir, however, also sought to understand the dualistic structures of society in terms of a phenomenological understanding of consciousness. In her analysis, she drew on G. W. F. Hegel and Jean-Paul Sartre's ideas that selfhood could only be achieved by means of antagonistic consciousness. As she argued, "If, following Hegel, we find in consciousness itself a fundamental hostility towards every other consciousness; the subject can be posed only in being opposed—he sets himself up as the essential, as opposed to the other, the inessential, the object."[23] According to de Beauvoir, human subjectivity requires the negation of the determinate, unchanging realm of objects. The highest form of human subjectivity is attained through the freedom of self-enactment, releasing one from the object realm. But, as philosopher Allison Weir points out, whereas Hegel argued for the notion of a dialectical resolution of antagonistic consciousness, de Beauvoir followed the philosopher Alexandre Kojève in accepting the eternal nature of conflict.[24]

De Beauvoir was also influenced by Sartre's philosophy of the antagonistic "look." According to Sartre, intersubjective recognition is essential in the quest for selfhood. By creating our own "projects," we humans realize our autonomous existence. But since humans need the recognition of others who, in turn, have their own projects which are often opposed to our own, human beings face a precarious situation. Sartre coined the term the *look* to refer to the danger that humans face in their quest for subjectivity. When one is looked at, one becomes the object of the other person's gaze. Since others are needed, however, in order to know oneself, the outcome is an ongoing struggle between competing "looks." Each self struggles to attain transcendence by transforming the other into an object. De Beauvoir extends Sartre's thought by arguing that it is "woman" who has been assigned the role of the looked-upon "other" in men's quest for transcendence.

De Beauvoir argues that men have denied woman her transcendence, making her into a thing, while seeking to raise themselves above the realm of nature and necessity through exploits and projects. By virtue of their bodily processes—pregnancy, menstruation, reproduction—women are confined to the realm of biology and dependence upon men for protection. Men, by contrast, seek to renounce their ties to women and the natural world. As de Beauvoir elaborates,

> What man cherishes and detests first of all in woman—loved one or mother—is the fixed image of his animal destiny; it is the life that is necessary to his existence but that condemns him to the finite and to death. From the day of his "birth" man begins to die; this is the truth incarnated in the Mother.[25]

The projects that have engaged men in their quest for transcendence are those which seek to transform the natural world: "Man's design is not to repeat himself in time: it is to take control of the instant and mold the future."[26] The prototypical activities of transcendence, according to de Beauvoir, involve risk, struggle, and violence, such as hunting, fishing and war.[27] She explains, "For it is not in giving life but in risking life that man is raised above the animal; that is why superiority has been accorded in humanity not to the sex that brings forth but to that which kills."[28] Thus for de Beauvoir the highest stage of human development entails an antagonistic confrontation with individual other animals. And only men have historically attained the status of full human maturity, realized in this manner; it is woman's "worst curse . . . that she should be excluded from these warlike forays."[29]

De Beauvoir uses the term "woman" to refer to all women. Her aggregate use of the term suggests the lack of individuality that is attributed to women in patriarchal society. Women represent species existence, whereas men are the individuals born from the species, who go on to transcend the biological realm, through an existential "second birth." For women to attain full human subjectivity, according to de Beauvoir, they must join with men in projects that transcend biology. As Andrea Nye points out, for de Beauvoir it is in the realm of self-assertion and self-creation that the highest values are attained, namely "heroism, revolt, detachment, invention, creation."[30]

Whereas de Beauvoir argues that women are used as objects in men's quest for transcendence, the anthropologist Sherry Ortner takes de Beauvoir's analysis one step further, arguing that women have been used as *symbols* by men in their attempt to achieve transcendence; women are not simply seen as identical to nature but as symbols that mediate between nature and culture. Men, by contrast, operate in the realm of cultural reproduction because of their inability to create "naturally." As Ortner argues, "Woman creates naturally from within her own being, whereas man is free to, or forced to create artificially . . . through cultural means."[31]

Ortner cites hunting as an example of an activity in which men seek to transcend the natural world symbolically. She writes:

> In other words, woman's body seems to doom her to mere reproduction of life; the male, in contrast, lacking natural creative functions, must (or has the opportunity to) assert his creativity externally, "artificially," through the medium of technology and symbols. In so doing, he creates relatively lasting, eternal, and transcendent objects, while the woman creates only perishables—human beings. [This] speaks, for example, to the great puzzle of why male activities involving the destruction of life (hunting and warfare) are often given more prestige than the female's ability to give birth. . . . [W]e realize it is not the killing that is the relevant and valued aspect of hunting and warfare; rather, it is the transcendental (social, cultural) nature of these activities, as opposed to the naturalness of the process of birth.[32]

Few feminists embrace de Beauvoir's conclusion that women must join with men in acts of violence to attain full human subjectivity, and many have criticized de Beauvoir and Ortner's analysis of women's status.[33] Nonetheless, their combined analyses provide insights into the hegemonic conception of masculine identity permeating Western culture:

- Historically, it has entailed a belief in the desirability or inevitability of struggle and conquest.[34]
- It has been defined as a maturational achievement that requires transcending the natural world.
- It has occurred through opposition to women and nature.

## THE "HEROIC WARRIOR" AND THE "TRANSCENDENT PERCEIVER"

Masculine identity in the Western patriarchal tradition has often been expressed through the use of two narratives and their accompanying imagery.[35]

In the first, selfhood is achieved through a heroic battle with an unruly Beast often depicted as female.[36] In mythology and religion, the slain Beast is typically a former divinity from the earlier matrifocal world. As feminist historians have argued, patriarchal mythology transformed the serpents, dragons, and horned gods who were once worshipped as divine into devils and monsters that must be slain. Examples of the idea of combat with a wild, female-imaged Beast can be found in numerous mythologies: "The sun-worshipping pharaohs of later Egypt slay the dragon Apophys, Apollo slays Gaia's python. The Greek hero Perseus slays the Amazonian Medusa—who is described as three-headed (the triple goddess) with snakes writhing from her three heads. St. George slays the dragon in England; even St. Patrick must drive the snake from snakeless Ireland."[37]

Frequently the death of the Beast heralds the birth of light and order, either at the beginning or end of time. Thus, in the Sumero-Babylonian Enuma Elish, Marduk kills his mother, the goddess Tiamat, the great whale-dragon or cosmic serpent, and from her body the universe is made. The dragon-slaying tradition continued in both Judaism and Christianity.[38] According to St. John the Divine, at the world's end an angel with a key will subdue the dragon that is Satan. In the Hebrew legend, the death of the serpent-like Leviathan is prophesied for the Day of Judgment. Thus the perception of birth as a creative act gives way to a conception of the birth-giving properties of violence.[39]

These myths of generative violence and conquest are a pronounced departure from the mythologies of pre-patriarchal cultures.[40] The cosmological stories of these earlier societies typically depict life emanating from a female-imaged goddess who embodied the earth. In the earliest Greek myths Gaia gave birth to the universe by herself. The snake, so much feared in our current culture, was worshipped in such societies as divine. A new worldview emerges in the biblical story of the Garden of Eden in which both a woman and an animal are the source of evil in the world, and "Man," above all other forms of life, has a special relation to the divine.

The Christian tradition added a moral dimension to the struggle against the forces of nature, transforming it into a battle with evil. The former Beasts became the "animal passions" that existed within human nature. God, saints, and archangels joined forces in heroic combat with the Devil, who was frequently depicted in animal form. The horned gods common to Mesopotamia, in both Babylon and Assyria, became transfigured in the Christian tradition into the familiar image of the horned Devil. This animal-like Devil was then depicted as the source of disorder or unruly nature that faith, prayer, and divine intervention must overcome. Providing a biblical example, Monica Sjöö and Barbara Mor state, "In Christian prophecy, in Revelation 12–21:1, the final extinction of the dragon is promised when a king-messiah kills the watery cosmic snake and takes over the world unchallenged: 'and there was no more sea.' This event was prefigured in Psalms 74:13: 'Thou breakest the heads of dragons in the waters.'"[41]

Men, too, have sometimes been portrayed as the Beast. Men who rape women are called "wolves," "beasts," or "predators."[42] The image of men as beasts has been accompanied by the idea of women as a domesticating force. The notion of women as civilizing agents and men as beasts came to the fore in the Victorian era with the cult of domesticity, when mothers were charged with the task of domesticating "savage" boys, encouraging them to channel their animal passions into such gentlemanly endeavors as exercise and sport. Yet the image of women as the "Beast" still lurked in the background, for women's sexuality was thought to bring out the "beast" in men.

The concept of the Beast has also been applied to a wide variety of humans who deviate from the white, middle-class norm. This has included people of color, third world people, gays, prisoners, the mentally and physically handicapped, the young and the old. These groups of people are stereotyped as lacking the purported mark of humanity—control over their emotions. The movements of emancipation of these and other groups have reinforced the notion of the Beast through their demands to be treated as "human beings." By leaving unchallenged the assumption of a dividing line that distinguishes humans from other animals, oppressed people have often inadvertently legitimized the idea of "brutal"[43] treatment for other-than-human animals.

In the second narrative associated with masculine identity within the Western tradition, selfhood is achieved not through heroic battle with a Beast, but rather through an act of conceptual disassociation designed to confer transcendence over women and nature, and hence masculine autonomy. Women and nature are relegated to the realm of mindless matter, in contrast to the superior realm of "rational man." As Catherine Keller argues, the serene, rational, single God depicted by Aristotle as the Unmoved Mover achieves the same ideal of autonomy as the heroic warrior:

> No wonder both the Greek and the Hebrew deities achieve an image of absolute independence from their worlds. They fulfill the heroic ego's impossible wish for an impenetrable dominion and for the final conquest of the too penetrable, permeating force-field of femaleness.[44]

A similar masculine ideal of separation and autonomy may be found in the Christian concept of a singular, omnipotent, transcendent, and eternal God, as well as in the idea of scientific detachment. In this image, nature is viewed not as wild and irrational, but rather as non-rational and inert, passively existing to serve the needs of rational "man." Although the second image of nature appears less heroic, it is equally violent. The scientist who experiments upon animals inside a laboratory violently establishes his transcendence and masculine identity, no less than the man who engages in war.

The two images of nature—wild and inert—represent different points along a single scale. In one image, nature is a demonic being that must be conquered and subdued. In the other, nature has been subdued to the point of lifelessness or death. Behind both images, however, lies a single theme—the idea of nature as the "other," a mental construct in opposition to which an autonomous masculine self is attained, through a violent severing of connection with women and the natural world.

## MASCULINE IDENTITY: PSYCHOLOGICAL CONSTRUCTIONS

The field of psychology has perpetuated the theme of heroic struggle against unwieldy animal passions. Sigmund Freud, the founder of psychoanalytic theory, argued that "man" is in reality a "savage beast" himself.[45] For Freud, however, humans are animals with a difference. Unlike other animals, humans have the capacity to struggle against the forces of nature, including their own instinctual drives. It is the human ability to combat aspects of their own instinctual nature, according to Freud, that lays the groundwork for civilization itself. Freud viewed both human maturation and civilization as ongoing battles against the baser instincts that threatened social order.[46] The conflict derives from the "economics of the libido," that is, the realistic limitations in the satisfaction of libidinal drives.[47]

Freud considers libidinal energy the force that binds humans together in all aspects of life, both personal and communal. Given that people have a limited amount of this sexual energy to expend, the family poses an ongoing source of conflict. Only a finite amount can be harnessed for the purpose of civilization, and since women's primary commitment is to conserve the nuclear family, women adopt a hostile attitude toward civilization. Freud concludes that "the work of civilization has become increasingly the business of men, it confronts them with ever more difficult tasks and compels them to carry out instinctual sublimations of which women are little capable."[48]

At the level of childhood development, the "economics of the libido" finds expression in the Oedipus complex. According to Freud, both boy and girl children are faced with the need to renounce their libidinal attachment to the mother figure. But boys, unlike girls, are driven by anger toward the rival father figure and fear of retribution in the form of castration. In order to avoid this terrifying fate, they renounce their desire for the mother and learn to identify with the father figure. It is out of an introjection of the fantasized punishing father figure that the superego is born, the locus of all future moral conduct. According to Freud, however, girls have a more difficult time in relinquishing their attachment to the mother figure since they lack the fear of castration. Lacking the intra-psychic surrogate father figure, girls grow into adulthood with a less developed superego. Freud concludes that since civilization is a matter of sublimating the instincts, and since women are less capable of this than men, women may be said to retard this process.[49] Once again, masculine identity is portrayed as conforming to a narrative structure of heroic conquest over "animal" drives. And once again, women's failure to enter into this heroic struggle renders them morally immature.

Where Freud's theory was premised on the idea that the struggle against libidinal drives is the primary impetus toward the achievement of mature selfhood and moral development, more recent psychoanalytic theorists have argued that the primary developmental impetus resides in the young child's need to establish relationships. Object relations theorists focus on "object choices" and interpersonal relations, in contrast to sexuality and drives. Where Freud saw conflict as the source of moral development, object relations theorists argue that the pre-Oedipal, reciprocal attachment to the mother is the primary motivating force of development for both boys and girls.

A number of feminists have embraced the object relations model.[50] Nancy Chodorow describes the significance of this model for the maturational development of boys. Like Freud, Chodorow argues that both boys and girls begin life experiencing an oceanic sense of oneness with the mother figure. The child then develops a self through a process of disengaging from this unified worldview. Unlike girls, however, boys go through a two-stage process. They must not only disengage from the mother figure, but to identify as male, they must deny all that is female within themselves, as well as their involvement with the female world. Since father figures and men are typically absent, the young boy must develop a sense of his masculine identity through an abstract process of identification with a role, rather than a personality. The mother thus becomes an object in the boy's transition into the role of "not-mother" and "not-female." Since the mother experiences the boy as sexually other, she reinforces the boy child's sense of otherness, thereby contributing to the oppositional nature of his identity.

Object relations theory reverses the traditional view of women as morally deficient, suggesting that it is young boys who grow up with vulnerable ego identities. According to Chodorow, the emphasis on separation and abstract role identification produces men with a fear of intimacy and attachment to others, and an inclination toward ideals of abstract reasoning and individual autonomy. Chodorow argues that, as a result, men grow up with a tendency to objectify and dominate women.[51] Since the girl child is not faced with the same need to differentiate her identity from that of the mother figure, she has a greater capacity for empathy with others. Chodorow states,

> Girls do not define themselves in terms of the denial of pre-oedipal relational modes to the same extent as do boys. Therefore regression to these same modes tends not to feel as much a basic threat to their ego. . . . *Girls come to experience themselves as less differentiated than boys, as more continuous with and related to the external object world and as differently oriented to their inner object world as well* [emphasis in original].[52]

Girls, therefore, emerge from this period with a basis for "empathy" built into their primary definition of self in a way that boys do not. The disadvantage for girls is that they may emerge into adulthood without a clear sense of their separate identities. The disadvantage for boys is that their identities can reflect a defensive rigidity.

Chodorow challenges the typical model of masculine identity in the Western tradition as the natural norm, implying instead, as Allison Weir notes, that this norm may be pathological.[53] Boys, in her thinking, must strive to repress a natural impulse of connection in favor of an atomistic model that objectifies women. Thus, where Freud postulates conflict and separation as the healthy (albeit tragic) crucible for the development of a self, Chodorow argues that the boy's ongoing struggle to deny his feelings of connection to women creates an unhealthy sense of vulnerability. While religious, philosophical, and psychological theories have emphasized woman as the "other," feminist object relations theory suggests that it is, in reality, *men's* identities that have been constructed as the "other." Chodorow finds the root cause of this situation in women's primary role in parenting. Her solution, therefore, is to bring men into the parenting process as equal partners with women.

The relational model of psychological development may help to explain why many men feel impelled toward demonstrations of masculinity throughout their lives. In patriarchal society, masculine identity entails an attempt to establish autonomy and yet men need women in order to realize their identities as "not-female." Dependence, therefore, is built into the very structure of male identity. A number of gender theorists hypothesize that men's fears and hatred of women are a projection of their anger and shame over their dependency. As psychologist Stephen Ducat describes this emotional complex, "femiphobia" is an "inner directed expression of misogyny, an unconscious dread of a part of the self experienced as feminine. . . . Like all forms of paranoia, [it] is a response to an unwanted part of the self that is projected out into the world and then experienced as a persecutory threat."[54]

Dorothy Dinnerstein extends the analysis of "otherness" beyond women, arguing that the current family structure encourages men to project "otherness" onto a conjoined image of woman and nature. The young infant, who lacks an understanding of the mother's subjective identity, experiences a sense of oneness with the mother figure. And since children experience their first caretakers as indistinguishable from the impersonal forces of nature, women take on the aspect of semi-human creatures who can confer or deny their most basic desires. Thus, nature becomes quasi-human, and the mother figure becomes semi-human. As Dinnerstein explains:

> Our over-personification of nature, then, is inseparable from our under-personi-fication of woman. We cannot listen to reason when it tells us that the mother—who was once continuous with nature—is a fully sentient fellow person; nor can we listen when it tells us that nature—which was once continuous with the mother—is wholly impersonal, non-sentient. If we could outgrow our feeling that the first parent was semi-human, a force of nature, we might also be able to outgrow the idea that nature is semi-human, and our parent.[55]

Dinnerstein argues that since the young child's first faltering steps toward separation occur in relation to the mother, women's bodies become the source of an ambivalent rage against the "knowledge of fleshly transience," and an urge to return to the original coextensive self.[56] The young child and, in particular, the young boy, seeks to deny the "primitive joy" of the body, associated with the mother, focusing instead on fantasies of mastery and control.[57]

Chodorow's and Dinnerstein's theories have been widely criticized for making universal, monocausal, and simplistic claims about men's and women's identities.[58] Both identified women's predominant role in childhood nurturing as the cause of men's problematic identity formation. The solution, for them, is for men to become equal partners in parenting. Some critics point out that Chodorow's and Dinnerstein's theories are heterosexist in presuming the need for both male and female care-takers. Still others have argued that their analyses fail to identify the material and structural roots of male domination.

Jane Flax also challenges object relations theorists' focus on infancy, given the lack of direct access to the child's inner word. She questions, for example, the inference that dependence necessarily results in feelings of helplessness, anger, and a wish for omnipotence, as well as whether infants can experience their caretaker as "female." Moreover, Flax argues, "feelings of rage and hate, resentment of authority, and the degree to which they are directly enacted or socially sanctioned also vary importantly with race, class, age, sexuality, ethnicity, and other variables."[59] Flax prefers to investigate why particular conceptions of gender emerge at particular historical times. She suggests that object relations theory may be a compensatory phenomenon, bringing mothers to the fore at time when they were particularly devalued and the destructive forces of society were generating increased anxiety. Despite her misgivings about Dinnerstein's search for the "bedrock of human behavior," Flax praises Dinnerstein for her focus on the importance of fantasy and the irrational.[60]

The philosopher Allison Weir also questions why the boy's process of individuation must entail repressing a sense of connection with women and the urge to dominate them. She suggests that *failure* to separate from another can itself be a basis for domination;[61] the process of separating from the mother can have beneficial consequences, leading to the ability to overcome egoism and achieve an equitable relation with another. Weir's analysis suggests that object relations theorists may have neglected other influences on the oppositional construction of the young boy's identity. While it is true that separation in and of itself need not produce domination, masculine identity—for whatever reason—has been achieved, in patriarchal society, through the construction of women not merely as *an* other, but as *the* other.

Chodorow's early work sought to counter essentialist views of the origin of gender differences through its focus on the ways gender differences are produced through social practices.[62] However, her generalizations about the influence of current parenting arrangements on gender development often conveyed their own sense of cultural "essentialism." In a subsequent work, Chodorow tempers her earlier ideas, arguing that clinicians and theorists have been "more likely to notice those tendencies toward which they have been sensitized," overlooking "psychological variation and complexity." Feminist psychoanalytic accounts of "normative or typical gender and sexuality," in turn, have run the risk of "selecting elements that fit a preconceived template."[63] She also drew attention to social influences beyond the immediate family.

In her most recent work, Chodorow further distances herself from potential determinist misunderstandings, arguing that "gender cannot be seen as entirely culturally, linguistically or politically constructed."[64] As she states, "Each person's sense of gender is an individual creation, and there are thus many masculinities and femininities. Each person's gender identity is also an inextricable intertwining, virtually a fusion, of personal and cultural meaning."[65] Chodorow does not entirely relinquish her earlier views, asserting her desire to "hold on to the clinical and theoretical truth that gender is a useful category for psychological thinking." However, she concludes that "there is not *a* psychology of gender but many psychologies of gender."[66]

While Chodorow's acknowledgement of the varying expressions of gender identity is valuable, her new work lacks the important insights contained in her earlier analysis concerning the significant gender differences between women and men. In particular, her new work obscures the link between masculine identity and the tendency to deny a sense of connection to the mother figure and to all women. Although people may express gender identity in unique ways, this does not change or explain the preponderance of male-perpetrated acts of violence. While the critics of object relations theory make cogent arguments, these do not detract from the core insights contained in Chodorow's and Dinnerstein's early analyses. Their inference that it is men, by and large, rather than women, who are psychologically constructed as the "other" contributes to an understanding of the abstract process by which "masculine" identities have been formed. The tenuous nature of this construction, which requires a denial of natural feelings of connection, also provides an insight into the compulsion to repeatedly "prove" masculine identity through acts of dominance and control. As Stephen Ducat concludes, "male identity will always be an unstable psychological achievement, as long as it is based on repression— on the disavowal of whatever is constructed as feminine."[67]

## MASCULINE IDENTITY AS A SECOND BIRTH

A number of feminist social theorists have argued that, in patriarchal society, men's psychological need to separate from women has taken the form of a simulated "second birth."[68] The narrative structure of masculine identity begins with a physical birth from a woman but requires a second, transcendent birth in order for a male to attain the status of "man." As Nancy Jay points out, anthropologists agree that one function of male initiation rites is to separate boys from women-and-children, to make them not-women.[69] In this second genesis, it is other men, not women, who act as the primary parents. Rites of initiation into manhood illustrate this. Anthropologist Elizabeth Fisher argues, "Most initiations of boys symbolize rebirth as a man by men: they may involve the boy being swallowed by a symbolic crocodile and emerging newborn, or being housed in a symbolic (male) womb and tended by male 'mothers.'"[70] Frequently, rites of initiation into manhood also include violence toward nature and separation from the sphere of women, celebrating the mother's death and the seizure of her power. According to some scholars, the drama of matricide is the foundation of culture itself.[71]

One of the most commonly found cross-cultural rites of initiation into manhood involves the young boy's killing of an animal.[72] The goal of the initiation is "to detach the boy from natural affection and natural role, to teach him that a man does not act on feelings but rather on meeting an external societal standard of manliness that is focused on exhibiting self-control and control over others." In contrast, a girl's initiation typically occurs at the first menstruation, in recognition of a "natural, non-volitional event."[73]

A central tenet of the men's movement is that manhood demands renunciation of the sphere of women and an initiation by men. Robert Bly, a leading proponent, laments the lack of appropriate male mentors in modern society who are capable of initiating men into masculine self-identity.[74] Bly believes that men can regain a sense of masculine power only by renouncing ties to their mothers. Although he contends that his notion of mentoring does not entail a devaluation of women, feminists have argued otherwise. Jill Johnston points out that the men's movement posits that what is crucial for the boy child is "the boy's separation from his mother, who has to stay at home and take care of the boy for the appearance of a male mentor to be significant or necessary. If the mother doesn't stay at home, the boy will have no good emotional reason for being pried away. There would be no initiation story." Johnston concludes, in contrast to Bly, that "male initiation *always* has to do with gender distinctions and the devaluation of women. If women were important, boys wouldn't need to get away from them and mothers wouldn't need to cling to their boys."[75]

Other theorists have similarly critiqued men's need to repeatedly demonstrate their independence from women. Men's problem is not that they have "not yet cut the psychic umbilical cord," but rather that they have a relentless compulsion to "consciously and unconsciously demonstrate that the cord is cut." According to this view, what we need is "more Ironing Johns, not Iron Johns."[76]

Whereas feminist object relations theorists locate the source of men's attempt to assert dominance over women in their childhood experience of alienation from a mother figure, other social theorists have focused on the formative influence of men's alienation from the natural cycles of procreation and birth.[77] Developing the Marxist notion of alienation from production, the political theorist Mary O'Brien argues that men's momentary (and minimal) participation in the act of procreation creates a lifelong sense of alienation from the process of reproduction. According to O'Brien, men's sense of alienation is found in the literal "alienation of the male seed in the copulative act."[78] As a consequence, men seek to devalue women's procreative powers, as well as familial bonds, and replace them with "superior" forms of their own creation that transcend the natural world. Instead of reproductive consciousness, men assert the "potency principle" as the new creative force, thereby assuring themselves a central place in political life. O'Brien traces the historical rise of the "potency principle" to the discovery of paternity. As she points out, paternity is an idea that is grasped conceptually, rather than in a bodily sense: "It rests very specifically on theory, not unified immediately with practice."[79]

The anthropologist Nancy Jay also develops the theme of men's alienation from reproductive processes in her analysis of the psychological motives that drive men to perform sacrifice. Pointing out that sacrifice is almost universally performed by men, she reasons that men perform it in an effort to achieve the sense of generational continuity that women are endowed with by nature. The logic of the sacrificers is governed by the urge to replicate the birthing process on a purportedly more spiritual plane. In so doing, they seek to establish a patrilineal descent that transcends both mortality and death.[80]

According to Jay, the only activity that is as serious as giving birth, and that can counter-balance it, is the act of taking life.[81] But unlike birth, which is an involuntary act of nature, sacrifice is performed with conscious intention, purportedly making it superior. The priests who perform sacrifice thereby act as spiritual "mothers," ushering the beneficiaries into a new transcendent realm in which *men*, not women, are the primary link to life.

Jay's theory shows how the two major forms of sacrifice (communion and expiatory), usually thought of as distinct, reflect and reinforce the traditional model of masculine identity. Although one form may be emphasized over another, each follows the pattern of separation and integration of men into a (superior) transcendent realm. In communion sacrifice, the male worshippers are united in relation to a realm of good (fertility, abundance, eternal life), and separated from evil; they also typically consume the sacrificed animal in a communal meal.[82] In expiatory sacrifice, by contrast, the participants are integrated through their opposition to an "evil" (disease, famine, social discord, pollution, childbirth), and the sacrificial animal is typically eaten by a select group of priests or not consumed at all. In both forms of sacrifice, however, the death of the animal functions as the generating matrix for men's rebirth into a transcendent realm.

Jay points out that sacrifice entails a complete reconfiguration of social bonds: men supplant women's primary role as progenitors of offspring; it is men, not women, who serve as a link with past and future generations through their participation in sacrifice. Women give birth to infants who mature and die, but men give birth to an eternal social order that persists throughout time.

O'Brien and Jay view men's quest for transcendence or immortality, achieved through sacrifice or the paternity principle, as a substitute for a natural sense of kinship with nature. Their theories imply that if one has a connection to the cycles of life, one will not approach one's own death with fear and denial. Similarly, the political scientist Wendy Brown suggests a relation between men's quest for transcendence and the fear of death. As she writes,

> The realization of manhood lies in transcendence of life, mere life, mortality, routines, rhythms, involvement with nature and necessity. Manhood is acquired through a relentless quest for immortality, through constructing ideals and institutions specifically contrasted to or with life.[83]

Other theorists have focused on the ways that particular myths have reinforced the superiority of a transcendent realm over kinship ties. The religious
studies scholar Mary Condren illustrates the conceptual change that accompanied the devaluation of family ties in Celtic Ireland. She states:

> In the new power structures being established, such maternal ties were to be re-
> linquished. Not the ties of particularity, but those of universality or the Common
> Good were those that mattered. Only those who acted on behalf of the Common
> Good, and not just on behalf of their own families, could be trusted to exert
> forms of power that transcended family interests.[84]

The philosopher Carol Ochs echoes this theme, contending that the shift
from matriarchy to patriarchy was accompanied by a shift from allegiance to
children and kin to a primary obligation to an abstract moral principle, the
voice of God. The allegiance to the new ethical code is illustrated in the biblical story of Abraham's willingness to "renounce the most fundamental tenet
of the matriarchal religion and kill his own child."[85] Ochs describes this transition to the new world order in her statement:

> As we enter the world historical stage, where the claims of kinship would be su-
> perseded by the ambitions of successive popes and emperors, restraints on sac-
> rifice would be lifted. Indeed sacrifice would become the means by which pa-
> triarchal forms of religion and social organization would become established.[86]

The attenuation of the story through Yahweh's decision to substitute an animal for Abraham's child does not detract from its moral lesson. Other-than-
human animals merely become the new sacrificial victims in the quest to transcend kinship and empathic ties.[87]

As Condren and Jay point out, the Christian doctrine of the atonement also
functions to reinforce allegiance to a higher social order. Atonement is based
upon the covenant between God the Father and his only Son. According to
this covenant, the sacrifice of the "Lamb of God" will redeem the community
of believers from original sin. Historically, the church based its religious and
political authority on its claim to be the exclusive administrators of this
covenant. Through the consumption of Christ's body, administered by priests
in the communal eucharist meal, men relinquish their "mother earth," becoming "brothers of Jesus and sons of the same heavenly Father."[88]

Yet another view of the life-giving properties of sacrifice can be found in
the notion of heroism. As Nancy Hartsock points out, the hero's quest entails
both risk and struggle, and confrontation with death. Scorning the realm of
daily subsistence with "its reminder that we are mortal, bodily beings," the
hero chooses to live on through the legend of his daring feats. Thus, "The he-

roes give birth to themselves in an all-male community and do so in such a way that they will not die."[89] Hartsock concludes, "whereas the first birth, from the body of a woman, is a death sentence, the second, through the bodily might of man himself, leads to immortality."[90]

In a similar vein, the philosopher Michael Nerlich contends that adventure has typically been seen as a male domain and as a contrast to the repetitive cycles of nature, as well as work.[91] Adventure, in his view, has also been an important aspect of modernity. The motive force appears to be the same fear of repetition that feminists have identified as a source of men's devaluation of the natural world. Nerlich posits that adventure can have two "sponsors": it can be performed under the auspices of violence, or it can be performed under the name of play. In the latter part of the nineteenth century, leisure (playful) activities became an important avenue for adventure.[92] The focus of the early conservationists was on establishing an arena in which men could continue to experience the sense of adventure that was rapidly disappearing along with the frontier. Sport hunting represented the fortuitous marriage of violence to "play," now rendered socially acceptable through its new incarnation as "sport."

The superimposition of structure upon play in the form of "sport" represents another expression of the age-old quest to transcend nature in order to prove virility. While play follows a spontaneous, non-linear path, the narrative structure of sport is such that it must have an object or "project"; sport typically entails competition, defeat of an "other," and obedience to rules.[93]

## MASCULINE IDENTITY IN MORAL THEORIES

The foregoing analysis suggests that a sense of alienation has been an integral aspect of masculine identity. In light of this alienated self, the question that has perplexed philosophers for centuries is how to forge bonds, or a sense of community. In the Western tradition, the establishment of moral conduct and social integration typically has been conceived as a matter of transcending the (animal) realm of necessity, including instincts and feelings, through the exercise of reason.

In ancient Greece, Plato invoked a metaphor of animal conquest to depict the soul's ascent toward true knowledge. In *The Phaedrus*, he likens the soul's journey to the struggle of a charioteer to establish control over the non-rational (animal) aspects of the soul. In Plato's allegory, the charioteer represents reason, and two winged steeds symbolize the non-rational parts of the soul. The journey of the soul toward the heavens begins when the onlooker attempts to transform the sight of the "beloved" into a voyage of return to an original unified state. The desired union is ultimately not with an individual but with the forms of Truth and Beauty, situated within a transcendent realm. While one horse obeys the driver's commands, the other, "for want of courage and manhood," plunges impulsively "toward the love object, heedless of the blows of the whip." As Plato describes the charioteer's task:

> But the driver, with resentment even stronger, . . . like a racer recoiling from the starting-rope, jerks back the bit in the mouth of the wanton horse with an even stronger pull, bespatters his railing tongue and his jaw with blood and forcing him down on legs and haunches delivers him over to anguish. . . . And so it happens, time and again, until the evil steed casts off his wantonness; humbled in the end, he obeys the counsel of his driver.[94]

Plato's philosophy does not dismiss the value of all feeling. On the contrary, in both *The Phaedrus* and *The Symposium*, passionate, erotic feelings are centrally important. But it is the love of truth, knowledge, and beauty that Plato valorizes over and above individual beings. In addition, although his philosophy grants women certain privileges, including the ability to serve as guardians in the republic, most of his dialogues link women with the nonrational private realm that must be transcended for the life of virtue.[95]

Centuries later, Immanuel Kant sought to further strip morality of its association with the natural realm of emotion. Kant's *categorical imperative* argues that one should "act only according to that maxim by which you can at the same time will that it would become a universal law."[96] Thus, a moral person must evaluate the maxim "it is okay to steal in order to obtain what I want" by willing that it become a categorical law for all rational persons under all circumstances. A moral will, according to Kant, reveals virtue "stripped of all admixture with the sensuous and of all the spurious adornments of reward or self love."[97] As he explains, "It is just this freedom from dependence on interested motives which constitutes the sublimity of a maxim and the worthiness of every rational subject to be a law making member in the kingdom of ends." In contrast, those who pursue interested motives are subject to the mere "law of nature—the law of [one's] own need."[98] For Kant, "interested motives" include all forms of inclination, even feelings of love. As he states, "It is precisely in this that the worth of character begins to show—a moral worth and beyond all comparisons the highest—namely, that he does good not from inclination, but from duty."[99] Thus, an act done out of an "inner pleasure in spreading happiness . . . however amiable . . . has still not genuine moral worth."[100]

Kant grants women certain positive qualities, including "a strong inborn feeling for all that is beautiful, elegant, and decorated."[101] Women therefore have a natural capacity for compassion and sympathy which inclines them toward acts of *benevolence*. In contrast, men are more drawn toward the *noble* and *sublime*, allowing them to act out of duty rather than mere inclination. Although, as Mason Cash notes, Kant does not deny that women have the capacity for reason, he does argue that they lack the ability to conquer their animal emotions and follow the dictates of duty.[102]

In the 1970s, Lawrence Kohlberg articulated a moral theory of development that was indebted to the impartialist theories of Kant and John Rawls. In Kohlberg's conception, human moral development has a fixed endpoint toward which all children ideally progress, with each stage representing an advance in the capacity for autonomous thinking. The six moral stages fall within three overarching classifications—namely, pre-conventional, conventional, and post-conventional morality. At the pre-conventional level, the child's moral actions are governed by egoistic concerns and the desire to avoid offending parental authority figures. In the second stage of morality, moral behavior is governed by a desire to conform to the rules and standards of groups, such as a school or surrounding community. In the final stage, the child progresses to the most abstract level of moral reasoning, arguing for the rightness of a given action based upon self-chosen, universal, ethical principles and laws, first of a utilitarian and finally of a Kantian nature.

Since Kohlberg's typology, developed from research on boys, suggested that girls typically did not progress beyond the conventional stage of morality, the educational psychologist Carol Gilligan decided to conduct her own studies, which she published in her 1982 landmark book, *In a Different Voice*. Her premise was that something had been left out of moral theory, both by omitting women from investigative study and by failing to attend to the priorities and sensibilities that women bring to moral problems. Gilligan sought to listen to the "different voice" of women not simply to contrast how women and men solve moral problems, but to explore whether women pose different moral questions. She hypothesized that the differences between women and men may reflect the distinct questions that they bring, rather than women's deficiency in solving moral dilemmas.[103]

Gilligan developed Chodorow's thesis that the process by which boys separate from the mother figure has served to produce men who have a fear of intimacy and attachment to others, as well as an inclination toward the ideals of abstract reasoning and individual autonomy. By contrast, since girl children do not have to dissociate themselves from their mothers, they are able to develop empathy and compassion, based on a sense of self that is defined through its embeddedness in relationships.

Gilligan concludes that women's moral development follows its own trajectory, based upon a distinct conception of self. Women, therefore, speak in a "different," not inferior, moral voice. They respond to moral dilemmas not on the basis of abstract principles and universal rules, but rather out of a concern for maintaining relationships and causing the least amount of harm, given the situational constraints. Women tend to perceive moral problems as arising from conflicting responsibilities, rather than conflicting rights. Their resolution is "contextual and narrative rather than formal and abstract."[104] Gilligan observes,

> The moral imperative that emerges repeatedly in interviews with women is an injunction to care, a responsibility to discern and alleviate the "real and recognizable trouble" of this world. For men, the moral imperative appears rather as an injunction to respect the rights of others and thus to protect from interference the rights to life and self-fulfillment.[105]

Gilligan also notes that the "truth" of women's experience, hitherto ignored by psychologists, is "a territory where violence is rare and relationships appear safe."[106] She notes that male fantasy, in contrast, "is consonant with a view of aggression as endemic in human relationships."[107] Gilligan concludes that, far from being morally deficient, "women's development delineates the path both to a less violent life and to a maturity realized through interdependence and taking care."[108] She elaborates in one of her essays,

> Since morality is closely tied to the problem of aggression—an area where sex differences are uncontested—it may be of particular interest at this time for both sexes to explore whether women's experience illuminates the psychology of nonviolent strategies for resolving conflicts.[109]

She concludes that maturity for women involves appreciating what justice requires for themselves, while maturity for men involves learning that affiliation is not dangerous.

Gilligan's early research has been widely criticized for making "essentialist" claims about boys' and girls' moral development. A number of critics have challenged her methodology, pointing out that just as Kohlberg had excluded girls, Gilligan's research, based on white middle-class girls, excluded individuals of other races, classes, and ethnic orientations. Some have argued that gender differences disappear when these groups are included, while others note that it is not only women and girls who demonstrate the care perspective.[110]

Yet Gilligan never made the claim that all girls conformed to the care perspective, nor that boys adhered exclusively to the rights approach. In addition to pointing out that considerable overlap existed between girls and boys, she maintained that healthy individuals would eventually integrate both orientations into their identity. As Kathy Davis points out, many of Gilligan's critics appear to have lost sight of the main purpose of Gilligan's research, which was to correct a bias toward men and boys in the traditional moral research, not to make universal claims for either gender. As Davis explains, "By taking Gilligan's theory out of the context in which it was formulated, including what she was arguing against; namely, the gender bias in Kohlberg's theory, the debate becomes caught up in a search for secure and unambiguous foundations rather than a self-reflective and admittedly tentative discussion of the adequacy of a specific theoretical account in a specific argumentative context."[111] Despite some of its limitations, Gilligan's work helped bring the issue of care to the forefront of both psychological and moral theory, showing the critical importance of the link between moral reasoning and self-identity.

The discounting of care, and the concomitant elevation of a universalistic ethic in modern thought, is best understood in its historical context. The view of the family or household as a personal enclave, distinct from the public sphere, arose with the modern state. During this time, an emphasis on non-personal law, associated with the traits of masculinity, developed in contrast to the private realm of family life, which was allied with the feminine domain of affectivity and personal bonds.[112] The public arena of law was conceived as abstract, rational, and universal, free from the fluctuating contingencies of the private realm of personal desires.

In Enlightenment thought, the attainment of impartial knowledge came to be seen as part of a linear moral progression. The "progress" made possible in the quest for universal reason entailed leaving behind not only the household, but also "childish emotions." Thus, "modernity can be considered as an attack on 'childishness' and so on the child within." As British sociologist Victor Seidler states, modernity held that "the child has an 'animal' nature that had to be trained out if children were ever to make a move towards existing as 'rational selves.'. . . Men in particular had to learn to curb their 'animal natures.'"[113]

Meanwhile, under the influence of Darwinism, Americans had developed new ideas of how to cope with the animal passions believed to be lurking within men. Denying or suppressing these "primitive" emotions was no longer considered a viable option. Yet when men expressed their animal impulses without *controlled* expression, they risked descending to the level of other-than-human animals. The men in the early conservation movement thus inherited a dual intellectual legacy. From Darwinian scientific theory they learned the idea that humans are animals; yet their religious and intellectual traditions continued to emphasize human superiority over the rest of the natural world. Young boys were advised simultaneously to express their animal instincts and to control their passions. How the sportsmen in the early conservation movement resolved these contradictory imperatives is the subject of the next chapter.

## CONCLUSION

In this chapter I presented several of the major feminist ideas on masculine identity. The literature shows that although it is established in various ways, separation (or autonomy) from women and nature is a recurring theme. It suggests that moral maturity for men requires the transformation of female, animal nature into a superior, rational, cultural construct. The heroic warrior, the transcendent perceiver, and the sacrificer all seek to establish their identity as superior, and opposed, to the natural world. Furthermore, the devaluation of nature has gone hand in hand with a devaluation of kinship ties and emotional bonds. Moral philosophers reflect this devaluation through the elevation of rational rules and universal principles and ideals over ties of affection. In the following chapters I will attempt to show that the philosophies of the authors in this study reflect these masculinist ideas and themes, albeit in distinct ways.

## NOTES

1. John Vyvyan, *In Pity and in Anger: A Study of the Use of Animals in Science* (Marblehead, Mass.: Micah Publications, 1969), 44. As Reino Virtanen points out, "MMe. Bernard was not only unsympathetic toward her husband's work but succeeded in having their two daughters share this hostility. In her opinion Bernard would have done better to apply his energies toward a prosperous medical practice instead of tormenting helpless animals in his laboratory. To make amends for his activities, she contributed money to anti-vivisectionist societies." Virtanen, *Claude Bernard and His Place in the History of Ideas* (Lincoln: University of Nebraska Press, 1960), 2.

2. According to evolutionary psychologists Martin Daly and Margo Wilson, "There is cross-culturally universal sex difference in human use of physical violence, whether it be fist fights or homicides, warfare or the slaughter of nonhuman animals. There is no evidence even suggesting that this sex difference is contravened anywhere." Daly and Wilson, "Evolutionary Psychology of Male Violence," in *Male Violence*, ed. John Archer (New York: Routledge, 1994), 275. Psychologist John Archer asserts "it is still the case that there are vast differences in overt acts of violence when we look at homicide statistics, violent crime statistics, accounts of violent acts in public, major acts of violence in a domestic context, and the use of violence by organized groups, whether the police, army or politically motivated groups outside the law." Archer, "Male Violence in Perspective," in Archer, *Male Violence,* 3. Criminologist James W. Messerschmidt, though unsympathetic to radical feminist gender analysis, acknowledges that "gender has consistently been advanced by criminologists as the strongest predictor of criminal involvement. Gender explains more variance in crime cross-culturally than any other variable." Messerschmidt, *Masculinities and Crime: Critique and Reconceptualization of Theory* (Lanham, Md.: Rowman & Littlefield,

1993), 1. Nancy J. Chodorow also notes that "[M]en . . . are directly responsible for and engage in the vast majority of both individual violence and rape as well as collective violence." Chodorow, "The Enemy Outside: Thoughts on the Psychodynamics of Extreme Violence with Special Attention to Men and Masculinity," *Masculinity Studies and Feminist Theory: New Directions*, ed. Judith Kegan Gardiner (New York: Columbia University Press, 2002), 251. See also Eleanor E. Maccoby and Carol Nagy Jacklin, *The Psychology of Sex Differences* (Stanford, Calif.: Stanford University Press, 1974) and Ronald P. Rohner, "Sex Differences in Aggression," *Ethos* 4 (1976): 57–72.

3. Nancy Chodorow notes that curiously "books about masculinity barely mention aggression except to suggest that it can be positive and normal, and they never discuss masculine violence." Chodorow, "Enemy Outside," 251.

4. Under the influence of Foucault's theories on "regulatory regimes" and the production of sexuality, a number of feminist scholars, most prominently Judith Butler, have argued that sex differences, as well as gender, are "produced" through discursive practices. Disputing the expressive understanding of sex and gender identity, Butler advances a *performative* model in which gender identity is constituted by repeated linguistic performances. According to this model, the subject's utterances are a *doing* or an action of some kind. See Butler, *Gender Trouble: Feminism and the Subversion of Identity* (New York: Routledge, 1990) and *Bodies that Matter: On the Discursive Limits of Sex* (New York: Routledge, 1993). Research on intersex children in the 1970s by John Money and Anke Ehrhardt also challenged the seemingly "natural" existence of only two sexes. Money and Ehrhardt, *Man and Woman, Boy and Girl: The Differentiation and Dimorphism of Gender Identity from Conception to Maturity* (Baltimore: Johns Hopkins University Press, 1972). More recently, biologist Anne Fausto-Sterling has argued that at least five biological types of sexed humans exist and that the focus on only two reflects ideology, not biology. As she expands, "Sex is a vast, infinitely malleable continuum that defies the constraints of even five categories." Fausto-Sterling, "The Five Sexes: Why Male and Female are Not Enough," *Sciences* 2, no. 2 (March–April 1993): 20–24. Nevertheless, the notion of both sex and gender as binary categories persists in most cultures of the world. It is this perception of gender differences that I examine in this chapter, not their questionable basis in biology.

5. R. W. Connell, *Gender and Power: Society, the Person and Sexual Politics* (Stanford: Stanford University Press, 1987), 140.

6. Genevieve Lloyd, *The Man of Reason: "Male" and "Female" in Western Philosophy* (Minneapolis: University of Minnesota Press, 1984), 75.

7. Lloyd, *Man of Reason*, 103–104.

8. Michael S. Kimmel, *Manhood in America: A Cultural History* (New York: Free Press, 1996), 5.

9. The phrase *hegemonic masculinity* first appeared in field reports from a study of social inequality in high schools. S. J. D. Kessler, Dean Ashenden, R. W. Connell, and G. W. Dowsett, *Ockers and Disco-Maniacs* (Sydney, Australia: Inner City Education Centre, 1982). See also R. W. Connell, *Masculinities* (Berkeley: University of California Press, 1995) and Connell, *Gender and Power*.

10. Erving Goffman, *Stigma: Notes on the Management of Spoiled Identity* (New York: Simon and Schuster, 1963), 128, quoted in Kimmel, *Manhood in America*.

11. See Connell, *Gender and Power*, 183 and *Masculinities*, 78–79.

12. Antonio Gramsci, *Selections from the Prison Notebooks*, ed. and trans. Quintin Hoare and Geoffrey Nowell Smith (New York: International Publishers, 1971). For further analysis of the relevance of Gramsci's theory of hegemony to the understanding of masculinity, see Connell, who points out "there is no femininity that is hegemonic in the sense that the dominant form of masculinity is hegemonic among men." *Gender and Power*, 183.

13. Critics have argued that hegemonic masculinity implies a static construct, impervious to the fluctuating realities of men's lives. However, as Connell argues, Gramsci understood hegemony as "dynamic" and always "had in mind social struggle for leadership in historical change." *Masculinities*, 249. For responses to the criticisms of hegemonic masculinity, see R. W. Connell, "Hegemonic Masculinity: Rethinking the Concept," *Gender and Society* 19, no. 6 (2005): 829–858. According to Connell, some of the criticisms are based upon misunderstandings or mistaken usages by theorists.

14. Richard Collier, *Masculinities, Crime and Criminology* (Thousand Oaks, Calif.: Sage Publications, 1998).

15. Collier contends that the conception of masculine identity as hegemony is "premised on a false distinction between 'mind/consciousness' and the 'body.'" Disputing the belief that consciousness is primary, he points to the limitations of an approach that simply encourages men to renounce their masculinism, particularly given the "disparagement of femininity in the wider culture." *Masculinities, Crime and Criminology*, 173, 178. For further discussion of the neglect of the unconscious in social and political philosophy, see Moira Gatens, *Imaginary Bodies: Ethics, Power and Corporeality* (New York: Routledge, 1996).

16. For the view that misogyny is "a neurosis of the male collective psyche," see J. C. Smith and Carla J. Ferstman, *The Castration of Oedipus: Feminism, Psychoanalysis, and the Will to Power* (New York: New York University Press, 1996), 12.

17. Connell, *Gender and Power*, 242.

18. Connell, *Gender and Power*, 244.

19. Eric Partridge, *Origins: A Short Etymological Dictionary of Modern English* (New York: Macmillan, 1958), 134, 428.

20. On the theme of masculine identity as a storied achievement that transcends and opposes women and nature, see the works of Simone de Beauvoir, *The Second Sex*, trans. H. M. Parshley (New York: Vintage Books, 1974) and Sherry Ortner, "Is Female to Male as Nature Is to Culture?" in *Woman and Culture and Society*, ed. Michelle Z. Rosaldo and Louise Lamphere (Stanford, Calif.: Stanford University Press, 1974).

21. De Beauvoir, *Second Sex*, xxxiii.

22. Allison Weir, *Sacrificial Logics: Feminist Theory and the Critique of Identity* (New York: Routledge, 1996), 17–18.

23. De Beauvoir, *Second Sex*, xx.

24. Weir points out that Hegel's notion of the struggle between master and slave was only one stage in the historical development of human "self-consciousness." As she states, "For Hegel, the ultimate aim of the dialectic of self-consciousness is the recognition of the object/other as, in Charles Taylor's words, an 'expression' of universal *Geist*, or Spirit." *Sacrificial Logics*, 19, 20.

25. De Beauvoir, *Second Sex*, 70, 187.

26. De Beauvoir, *Second Sex*, 74.

27. De Beauvoir, *Second Sex*, 70–72.

28. De Beauvoir, *Second Sex*, 72.

29. De Beauvoir, *Second Sex*, 72.

30. Andrea Nye, *Feminist Theory and the Philosophies of Man* (New York: Routledge, 1988), 84.

31. Ortner, "Is Female to Male," 77.

32. Ortner, "Is Female to Male," 75.

33. See, for example, Iris Young, *Throwing Like a Girl and Other Essays* (Bloomington: Indiana University Press, 1990), and Mary O'Brien, *The Politics of Reproduction* (Boston: Routledge and Kegan Paul, 1981), 65–92.

34. In chapter 3, I discuss the connection between masculine identity and the concept of self-restraint.

35. The following analysis has been inspired by Catherine Keller's understanding of the dual modes of attaining masculine autonomy, or what Keller refers to as the masculine "separative self." See Keller, *From a Broken Web: Separation, Sexism, and Self* (Boston: Beacon Press, 1986). On a related theme, see Evelyn Fox Keller, *Reflections on Gender and Science* (New Haven, Conn.: Yale University Press, 1985). Portions of this analysis are drawn from Marti Kheel, "From Heroic to Holistic Ethics: The Ecofeminist Challenge," in *Ecofeminism: Women, Animals, Nature*, ed. Greta Gaard (Philadelphia: Temple University Press, 1993).

36. I am indebted to Mary Midgley for my use of the term "Beast." Midgley argues that the term functions as a symbol for the unwanted aspects of human nature. She argues that in ancient Greek society, people blamed the gods for wicked human conduct. Beginning with Plato, however, the gods were exonerated, and the Beast was placed in the scapegoat role. Midgley concludes that "the use of animals as symbols of wickedness has done ethics no good, and the arguments based on it are irrelevant." Mary Midgley, *Beast and Man: The Roots of Human Nature*, rev. ed. (New York: Routledge, 1995), 36–46.

37. Monica Sjöö and Barbara Mor, *The Great Cosmic Mother: Rediscovering the Religion of the Earth* (San Francisco: Harper and Row, 1987), 250–251.

38. Sjöö and Mor, *Great Cosmic Mother*, 249.

39. Sjöö and Mor, *Great Cosmic Mother*, 251.

40. Marija Gimbutas, *The Civilization of the Goddess: The World of Old Europe* (San Francisco: HarperCollins, 1991).

41. Sjöö and Mor, *Great Cosmic Mother*, 251.

42. It is interesting to note that the word "predator" has become so tarnished from its application to "rapists and child molesters," that a well-known animal rights

organization has relinquished its use, preferring to employ the more neutral term "carnivores." Monica Engebretson, senior program coordinator, Animal Protection Institute, personal communication to the author, January 11, 2005.

43. The words "brutal" and "brute" are value-laden terms that project onto other animals the character trait of cruelty and then are applied to some humans. Although the word "brute" originally referred to "heavy" and later "stupid," it subsequently came to be associated with "lower animals" and in the seventeenth century with "cruelty." John Ayto, *Arcade: A Dictionary of Word Origins* (New York: Arcade Publishing, 1990), 82. Ironically, it is humans who are the perpetrators of the vast majority of "brutality" toward other living beings.

44. Keller, *From a Broken Web*, xxi.

45. Sigmund Freud, *Civilization and Its Discontents*, trans. and ed. James Strachey (New York: W. W. Norton and Company, 1961), 69.

46. Freud, *Civilization and Its Discontents*, 51–52. Elsewhere, Freud states, "Human civilization, by which I mean all those respects in which human life has raised itself above its animal status and differs from the life of beasts." Sigmund Freud, *The Future of an Illusion*, trans. and ed. James Strachey (New York: W. W. Norton and Company, 1961), 6.

47. Freud, *Civilization and Its Discontents*, 106.

48. Freud, *Civilization and Its Discontents*, 59.

49. Freud, *Civilization and Its Discontents*, 59.

50. See for example, Nancy J. Chodorow, *The Reproduction of Mothering: Psychoanalysis and the Sociology of Gender* (Berkeley: University of California Press, 1978); Dorothy Dinnerstein, *The Mermaid and the Minotaur: Sexual Arrangements and Human Malaise* (New York: Harper and Row, 1976); and Jessica Benjamin, *The Bonds of Love: Psychoanalysis, Feminism, and the Problem of Domination* (New York: Pantheon Books, 1988). For an earlier analysis that argues for the pivotal importance of the mother figure for both boys and girls, see Melanie Klein, "Love, Guilt and Reparation," in *Love, Guilt and Reparation and Other Works, 1921–1945* (New York: Free Press, 1975), 306–343.

51. In a subsequent article, Chodorow expands on her analysis by heuristically dividing expressions of masculinity and manhood into two components. In some cultures, manhood is conceived as not being a woman whereas in others it is seen as not being a little boy, subject to humiliation by other men. In both instances, masculinity is conceived as a binary construct that seeks to avoid the stigma of association with the excluded category. Chodorow, "Enemy Outside," 255.

52. Chodorow, *Reproduction of Mothering*, 167.

53. Weir, *Sacrificial Logics*, 49.

54. Stephen J. Ducat, *The Wimp Factor: Gender Gaps, Holy Wars, and the Politics of Anxious Masculinity* (Boston: Beacon Press, 2004), 47. For a discussion of the cross-cultural phenomenon of misogyny, see David D. Gilmore, *Misogyny: The Male Malady* (Philadelphia: University of Pennsylvania Press, 2001).

55. Dinnerstein, *Mermaid and the Minotaur*, 108. Dinnerstein's work builds on Melanie Klein's earlier analysis of the infant's ambivalent feelings for the mother, as both provider and denier of nurturance. Like Dinnerstein, Klein argues that parallel

feelings of love and hate are revived in the infant experiences of nature withholding her gifts. Klein, "Love, Guilt and Reparation." Catherine Roach draws on both Klein and Dinnerstein to critique modern society's unconscious projections onto "mother nature." Roach is one of the few ecofeminists to emphasize the limitations of a voluntarist approach which presumes that we can simply choose to replace destructive environmental practices with environmentally friendly ones. See Roach, *Mother/Nature: Popular Culture and Environmental Ethics* (Bloomington: Indiana University Press, 2003).

56. Dinnerstein, *Mermaid and the Minotaur*, 246.

57. Dinnerstein, *Mermaid and the Minotaur*, 122.

58. See, for example, Pauline Bart, review of *The Reproduction of Mothering* by Nancy Chodorow, in *Mothering: Essays in Feminist Theory,* ed. Joyce Trebilcot (Totowa, N.J.: Rowman & Littlefield, 1993), 147–152; Janice Raymond, "Female Friendship: Contra Chodorow and Dinnerstein," *Hypatia* 1, no. 2 (Fall 1986): 37–48; Jean Bethke Elshtain, *Public Man, Private Woman: Women in Social and Political Thought* ( Princeton, N.J.: Princeton University Press, 1981); Alice Rossi, "On *The Reproduction of Mothering*: A Methodological Debate," *Signs* 6, no. 3 (Spring 1981): 497–500; Rosemary Putman Tong, *Feminist Thought* (Boulder, Colo.: Westview Press, 1998); and Jane Flax, "Reentering the Labyrinth: Revisiting Dorothy Dinnerstein's *The Mermaid and the Minotaur*," *Signs* 27, no. 4 (Summer 2002), 1037–1057.

59. Flax, "Reentering the Labyrinth," 1055.

60. Flax, "Reentering the Labyrinth," 1050.

61. Weir, *Sacrificial Logics*, 63. Similar points are made in the works of Jean Grimshaw, *Philosophy and Feminist Thinking* (Minneapolis: University of Minnesota Press, 1986) and Marilyn Frye, *The Politics of Reality: Essays in Feminist Theory* (Trumansburg, N.Y.: Crossing Press, 1983).

62. Chodorow, *Reproduction of Mothering*.

63. Nancy J. Chodorow, *Femininities, Masculinities, Sexualities: Freud and Beyond* (Lexington: University of Kentucky Press, 1994), 72–73.

64. Nancy J. Chodorow, *The Power of Feelings: Personal Meaning in Psychoanalysis, Gender, and Culture* (New Haven, Conn.: Yale University Press, 1999), 71.

65. Chodorow, *Power of Feelings*, 69–70.

66. Chodorow, *Power of Feelings*, 125.

67. Ducat, *Wimp Factor*, 23.

68. See, for example, O'Brien, *Politics of Reproduction*; Nancy Jay, *Throughout Your Generations Forever: Sacrifice, Religion and Paternity* (Chicago: University of Chicago Press, 1992); Wendy Brown, *Manhood and Politics: A Feminist Reading in Political Theory* (Totowa, N.J.: Rowman & Littlefield, 1988); and Susan R. Bordo, *The Flight to Objectivity: Essays on Cartesianism and Culture* (Albany: State University of New York Press, 1987).

69. Nancy Jay, "Gender and Dichotomy," *Feminist Studies* 7, no. 1 (Spring 1981): 45.

70. Elizabeth Fisher, *Woman's Creation: Sexual Evolution and the Shaping of Society* (Garden City, N.Y.: Anchor Press, 1979), 78.

71. Erich Neumann, *The Origins and History of Consciousness*, trans. R. F. C. Hull (New York: Pantheon Books, 1949).

72. On the cross-cultural connection between hunting and rites of initiation into manhood, see David D. Gilmore, *Manhood in the Making: Cultural Concepts of Masculinity* (New Haven, Conn.: Yale University Press, 1990).

73. Marilyn French, *Beyond Power: On Women, Men and Morals* (New York: Summit Books, 1985), 78.

74. Robert Bly, *Iron John: A Book About Men* (Reading, Mass.: Addison Wesley, 1990). See also Sam Keen, *Fire in the Belly: On Being a Man* (New York: Vintage Books, 1991).

75. Jill Johnston, "Why Iron John Is No Gift to Women," *New York Times Book Review*, February 23, 1992.

76. Michael S. Kimmel and Michael Kaufman, "Weekend Warriors: The New Men's Movement," in *Theorizing Masculinities: Research on Men and Masculinities*, ed. Harry Brod and Michael Kaufman (Thousand Oaks, Calif.: Sage Publications, 1994), 271–272.

77. There is a large body of literature on the subject of "womb envy." The concept was introduced by Karen Horney as a contrast to Freud's view of penis envy as a definitive factor in girls' development. See Horney's "The Flight from Womanhood: The Masculinity-Complex in Women as Viewed by Men and by Women," and "The Denial of the Vagina: A Contribution to the Problem of the Genital Anxieties Specific to Women," in *Feminine Psychology*, ed. Harold Kelman (New York: W. W. Norton, 1967). Both articles originally appeared in German psychoanalytic journals in 1926. Later, Melanie Klein further theorized that both sexes experienced envy of women's sexual organs and ability to give birth, but the boy's discovery of his reproductive incapacity resulted in anger and humiliation, followed by compensatory practices to assuage the psychic trauma. Melanie Klein, "The Oedipus Complex in the Light of Early Anxieties," in *Love, Guilt and Reparation and Other Works*, 370–414. Jacqueline Stevens speculates that the creation of kinship rules establishing men's legal claim to progeny exemplifies this compensatory phenomenon. Stevens further suggests that men's efforts to naturalize affiliations such as family, nationality, ethnicity, and race reflect their attempt to recreate a sense of intergenerational continuity comparable to giving birth. Stevens, "Pregnancy Envy and the Politics of Compensatory Masculinities," *Politics and Gender* 1, no. 2 (2005): 265–296. For other theories on womb envy, see Josef Michael Eisler, "A Man's Unconscious Fantasy of Pregnancy in the Guise of Traumatic Hysteria," *International Journal of Psychoanalysis* 2 (1921): 255–286; Felix Boehm, "The Femininity Complex in Men," *International Journal of Psychoanalysis* 11 (1930): 444–469; Ernest Jones, "Psychology and Childbirth," in *Papers on Psychoanalysis* (London: Baillier, Tindall and Cox, 1942); Margaret Mead, *Male and Female* (New York: William Morrow, 1949); Bruno Bettelheim, *Symbolic Wounds: Puberty Rites and the Envious Male* (New York: Collier, 1962); and Erich Fromm, *The Forgotten Language* (New York: Rinehart and Winston, 1951). For recent feminist analyses of womb envy, see Eva Feder Kittay, "Mastering Envy: From Freud's Narcissistic Wounds to Bettelheim's Symbolic Wounds to a Vision of Healing," *Psychoanalytic Review* 82 (February 1994): 124–158, and "Rereading Freud on 'Femininity' or Why Not Womb Envy?" *Women's Studies International Forum* 7, no. 5 (1984): 385–391. See also Smith and Ferstman, *Castration of Oedipus*, and Ducat, *Wimp Factor*.

78. O'Brien, *Politics of Reproduction*, 29.

79. O'Brien, *Politics of Reproduction*, 29–30. Wendy Brown criticizes the "biologism" underlying O'Brien's analysis. Nonetheless, she contends that "there may be something to her conviction that the work of childrearing has historically offered women partial satisfaction of a desire for continuity." According to Brown, "the continuity a woman experiences in childrearing is literally embodied in another live being." *Manhood and Politics,* 205.

80. Nancy Jay, "Sacrifice as a Remedy for Having Been Born of Woman," in *Immaculate and Powerful: The Female in Sacred Imagery and Social Reality*, ed. Clarissa Atkinson et al. (Boston: Beacon Press, 1985); see also Jay, *Throughout Your Generations Forever*.

81. Jay, "Sacrifice as a Remedy," 294.

82. According to historian Richard W. Bulliet, the desire for a steady supply of animals for ritual sacrifice was a primary motivation behind the domestication of other animals. The spiritual benefits thought to derive from sharing meat with divinities was thus the primary motivator in keeping animals in captivity, not meat consumption per se. Bulliet, *Hunters, Herders, and Hamburgers: The Past and Future of Human-Animal Relationships* (New York: Columbia University Press, 2005), 122–128.

83. Brown, *Manhood and Politics*, 180.

84. Mary Condren, *The Serpent and the Goddess: Women, Religion, and Power in Celtic Ireland* (San Francisco: Harper and Row, 1989), 121.

85. Carol Ochs, *Behind the Sex of God: Toward a New Consciousness-Transcending Matriarchy and Patriarchy* (Boston: Beacon Press, 1977), 45.

86. Ochs, *Behind the Sex of God*, 122.

87. French philosopher Jacques Derrida also points to the symbolic role of animal sacrifice in affirming human beings' privileged status over the rest of the natural world. The divine sanction for sacrifice is found in the biblical story of God's preference for Abel over Cain, due to his willingness to engage in animal sacrifice. Jacques Derrida, "The Animal That Therefore I Am," in *Animal Philosophy: Essential Readings in Continental Thought*, ed. Matthew Calarco and Peter Atterton (New York: Continuum, 2004): 113–128.

88. Condren, *Serpent and the Goddess*, 125. As Nancy Jay points out, "During the entire period from Augustine to Thomas . . . the priesthood was specifically identified by its exclusive right to sacrifice and its other functions receded into the background." Jay, "Sacrifice as a Remedy," 302.

89. Nancy C. M. Hartsock, "Masculinity, Heroism and War," in *Rocking the Ship of the State: Toward a Feminist Peace Politics*, ed. Adrienne Harris and Ynestra King (Boulder, Colo.: Westview Press, 1989), 144–145.

90. Hartsock, "Masculinity, Heroism and War," 141.

91. Michael Nerlich, "The Unknown History of Our Modernity," *Center for Humanistic Studies Occasional Papers 3* (Minneapolis: University of Minnesota, 1986). Cited in Martin Green, *The Adventurous Male: Chapters in the History of the White Male Mind* (University Park: Pennsylvania State University Press, 1993), 75–76.

92. I will return to the theme of adventure and play in the early conservation movement in chapters 3 and 4.

93. An association between men and sport, and women and play, has been empirically demonstrated. Building on Piaget's studies on rules of the game, Janet Lever found that boys tend to play far more competitively than girls and are more likely to play at structured games, which accord importance to being the winner. By contrast, girls tended to "keep their play loosely structured and played until they were bored." Lever's study also demonstrates that girls' games were "mostly spontaneous, imaginative, and free of structure or rules. Turn-taking activities like jump rope may be played without setting explicit goals." In addition "disputes are not likely to occur," and when they do, the game tends to be stopped. Girls' play in smaller, more intimate groups fosters the development of empathy and sensitivity necessary for taking the role of "the particular other," and points toward "knowing the other as different from the self." Lever, "Sex Differences in the Complexity of Children's Play and Games," *American Sociological Review* 43 (1978): 479. For further discussion of gender differences in play and sport, see Willard Gaylin, "Playing the Game," in *The Male Ego* (New York: Penguin Books, 1992).

94. Plato, *The Phaedrus,* in *Greek Philosophy: Thales to Aristotle,* ed. Reginald E. Allen, rev. ed. (New York: Macmillan Free Press, 1985), 254. In *The Republic,* Plato further delineates the components of the tripartite soul as *logos* (reason), *thumos* (spirit or the will) and *epithumia* (the appetites). *The Republic* portrays a more harmonious integration of the parts of the soul, with justice requiring a balanced relationship among the distinct elements. Nonetheless, reason is still accorded the position of dominance. See Plato, *The Republic of Plato,* trans. with introduction and notes by Francis Macdonald Cornford (Oxford University Press, 1941).

95. For an in-depth discussion of Plato's devaluation of nature and its links to the debasement of women and the "feminine," see Val Plumwood, who points out that Plato explicitly associates the feminine with "disorder and ungoverned emotion, with idle gossip and opinion (*doxa*), and with moral evil, incompetence, animal nature and distance from *logos*, with lower slavelike nature unsuited to the public sphere, and with the baser self and bodily appetite." Plumwood, *Feminism and the Mastery of Nature* (New York: Routledge, 1993), 77.

96. Immanuel Kant, *Groundwork of the Metaphysic of Morals,* trans. H. J. Paton (New York: Harper and Row, 1964), 70.

97. Kant, *Groundwork of the Metaphysic of Morals,* 94.

98. Kant, *Groundwork of the Metaphysic of Morals,* 106.

99. Robin Schott argues that Kant's devaluation of feelings reflects the ascetic influence of his Protestant upbringing, as well as Pietism. He shared the Protestant emphasis on the moral significance of one's inner state, as opposed to external "works" or moral acts. Thus, the consequences of an action do not "justify" it as morally worthy, only the intentions of the individual moral actor. In addition, although he denounced the Pietist emphasis on emotion, he concurred with its challenge to external forms of authority. Schott, *Cognition and Eros: A Critique of the Kantian Paradigm* (Boston: Beacon Press, 1988).

100. Kant, *Groundwork of the Metaphysic of Morals,* 66. In spite of Kant's valiant attempt to expunge emotions from moral theory, they insinuate themselves back into his philosophy as more "elevated" responses. Thus, an act of duty "uplifts the soul,"

while the categorical imperative inspires "feelings" of "reverence." He is quick to point out that they are different from other feelings in that they are inspired by a thought. Reverence for the law is not spontaneously produced by a subject; rather, it is the *effect* of the law on the subject. *Groundwork of the Metaphysic of Morals*, 68–69.

101. Immanuel Kant, *Observations on the Feeling of the Beautiful and the Sublime*, trans. J. T. Goldthwait (Berkeley: University of California Press, 1960), 77.

102. Mason Cash, "Distancing Kantian Ethics and Politics from Kant's View on Women," *Minerva: An Internet Journal of Philosophy* 6 (November 2002): 133, at www.mic.ul.ie/stephen/kantian.pdf. Kant argued that women's inability to control their emotions required their subjection to the legal tutelage of a husband and their exclusion from active citizenship. Kant, *Anthropology from a Pragmatic Point of View*, trans. Victor Lyle Dowdell (Carbondale: Southern Illinois University Press, 1978), 105. Mason Cash argues that Kant's devaluation of women is not inherent to his philosophy but rather an inconsistency characteristic of his era. "Distancing Kantian Ethics," 143–147. For contrary views that argue that Kant's philosophy is inherently misogynist, see Hannelore Schröder, "Kant's Patriarchal Order," trans. Rita Gircour, in *Feminist Interpretations of Immanuel Kant,* ed. Robin May Schott (University Park: Pennsylvania State Press, 1997), 275–296; Cornelia Klinger, "The Concepts of the Sublime and the Beautiful in Kant and Lyotard," in *Feminist Interpretations,* 191–212; and Sally Sedgwick, "Can Kant's Ethics Survive the Feminist Critique?" in *Feminist Interpretations,* 77–100.

103. Carol Gilligan, *In a Different Voice: Psychological Theory and Women's Development* (Cambridge, Mass.: Harvard University Press, 1993), 3–4.

104. Gilligan, *In a Different Voice,* 19.

105. Gilligan, *In a Different Voice,* 100.

106. Gilligan, *In a Different Voice,* 62.

107. Gilligan, *In a Different Voice,* 45.

108. Gilligan, *In a Different Voice,* 172.

109. Carol Gilligan, "A Reply to Critics," in *An Ethic of Care: Feminist and Interdisciplinary Perspectives*, ed. Mary Jeanne Larrabee (New York: Routledge, 1993), 214.

110. See chapter 7 for a more detailed account of the most salient substantive and methodological critiques of Gilligan's work.

111. Kathy Davis, "Toward a Feminist Rhetoric: The Gilligan Debate Revisited," *Women's International Forum* 15, no. 2 (1992): 224.

112. Linda J. Nicholson, "Women, Morality and History" in Larrabee, *An Ethic of Care*, 92.

113. Victor Seidler, *Man Enough: Embodying Masculinities* (Thousand Oaks, Calif.: Sage Publications, 1997), 35.

# 3

# Origins of the Conservation Movement

## *Preserving Manhood*

"On January first, not far from the Mexican border, a father and son chased bird dogs through the south Texas brush, flushing coveys of quail in the early morning mist. Although many families rise before dawn to hunt on New Year's Day, this scene was different; this father and son were both Presidents of the United States."[1] As the younger president [George W. Bush] commented, "I'm not that good a shot, but it was a lot of fun."[2]

"Why do I hunt and fish?" another president [Jimmy Carter] reflects. "The easiest answer is: My father and all my ancestors did it before me. It's been part of my life since childhood, and part of my identity, like being a southerner or a Baptist."[3]

In the final days leading up to the presidential election, Senator John Kerry made a campaign pitch that required no words. He invited the press to follow him and three companions into the Ohio woods on a hunting trip. Clad in hunting attire, with blood dripping from his hands, a double-barreled shotgun in tow, he was photographed, along with his companions, emerging from an Ohio cornfield brandishing three dead geese.[4]

More than a century earlier, on November 14, 1902, Theodore Roosevelt took time off from settling a border dispute between Mississippi and Louisiana to engage in one of his favorite pastimes, big game hunting. Worried that the president would return empty-handed, his guides tied a bear to a tree and waited for him to deliver the fatal blow. Roosevelt gained national acclaim when he refused to kill the unfortunate bear, claiming that the animal did not have a sporting chance.[5]

## INTRODUCTION

Since the turn of the century, sport hunting has become a veritable rite of passage for presidents and presidential hopefuls. While news commentators speculated that Kerry's foray into the woods was designed to win the rural vote, a larger motive may underlie these demonstrations of violence—proof of virility. By showcasing their ability to hunt and kill, these candidates sought to dramatize that they were man enough to serve in the role of "protector" of the American public.

Roosevelt's hunting expedition, however, demonstrated another way in which virility could be expressed, while also winning public appeal. By sparing the cub's life, Roosevelt illustrated a new concept of manliness based on self-restraint. It was this model of manhood and good sportsmanship that was integral to the development of the early conservation movement.

In the latter half of the nineteenth century, many middle-class Americans viewed manhood and the environment as endangered phenomena. The environment was imperiled by the excesses of commercial hunters, and manhood was threatened by an increasing "effeminacy" among men.[6] Sport hunting came to be seen as the felicitous solution to these twin threats. It gave men an outlet for their virile impulses while simultaneously moderating these impulses through the development of rules of good sportsmanship, and it conserved the diminishing populations of animals in the wild. In addition, sport hunting helped to develop character traits viewed as vital to the security of the nation, and hence the world.

Theodore Roosevelt, the twenty-sixth president of the United States and a respected naturalist, had enormous influence on this new movement for conservation. His numerous publications provide unusual insight into the role of manliness in early conservationist thought. These writings also illustrate the growing emphasis on scientific detachment and the devaluation of feelings or "sentiment." Along with other naturalists of his time, Roosevelt believed that: (1) nature was an arena of Darwinian conflict and struggle; (2) sport hunting was an evolutionary advance over subsistence hunting, practiced by the "lower classes"; (3) hunting was a means of developing "manly" character; (4) rational rules and regulations were important tools for managing the natural world; (5) the detached approach of science was superior to one based on that of "sentiment" for interacting with nature; (6) "species" had greater value than individual other-than-human animals; (7) self-restraint was the foundation for ethical interactions with nature, as well as the world at large; and (8) hunting was a patrilineal, cross-generational inheritance, to be passed on from fathers to sons.

I argue that the sport hunters of the nineteenth century organized these ideas into a series of hierarchical oppositions which provided the basis for a common identity: nature/culture, animal/human, female/male,[7] savage/civilized, play/sport, unregulated predation/rational management (or protection).

Deeply influenced by Darwinian philosophy, Roosevelt and his contemporaries held views of human nature that reflected a belief in an innate drive toward aggression among men.[8] The curbing of this drive through the activity of sport hunting was seen as an evolutionary advance, and as a modern, "mature" conception of manhood. The new, gentlemanly approach to sport hunting offered a rational system of principles and rules, which transcended "sentimental" ties to animals, as well as unregulated "animal" drives.

The hunter-conservationists of the late nineteenth and early twentieth centuries distinguished themselves from previous generations of hunters by developing the first explicit moral discourse on hunting in the nation. The significance of the change was not merely that moral rules were now attached to the conduct of hunting, but rather that hunting was, for the first time, conceived as an essential activity for the conservation of the country's natural resources, and simultaneously as a morally beneficial activity, especially for men.[9]

Sport hunters, however, directed their moral concern not toward individual beings, but rather toward larger transcendent constructs, such as the "species," the "frontier," "manhood," "natural science," or the "land." Not only did the early conservationists exclude other-than-human animals as individuals in their sportsman's code, but they specifically sought to ensure a permanent arena for their ritualized slaughter.

## HISTORICAL BACKGROUND TO SPORT HUNTING

Hunting has a dual historical heritage. Many historians and anthropologists have interpreted hunting as the principal catalyst of human culture through its contribution to the development of technology, language, singing, art, social organization, and dance—in short, everything that is thought to define us as human beings.[10] Yet hunting has also been viewed as both the source and proof of "man's" depravity, sinfulness, and violent nature. In ancient Rome, the philosopher Plutarch condemned hunting for promoting insensitivity and fortifying "the natural lust to kill in man."[11] And with the dawn of humanism in the sixteenth century, Thomas More bemoaned, "O stony-hearted race, more savage than any wild beast, to find cruel amusement in bitter murder!"[12]

Images of hunting as blessing and curse have not only alternated throughout history; at times they have coalesced into a single worldview. Such is the case with "the hunting hypothesis," a theory that arose in the aftermath of

World War II. Analyzing damaged bones found in South African caves, professor of anatomy Raymond A. Dart concluded that early hominid australopithecines were "confirmed killers: carnivorous creatures that seized living quarries by violence, battered them to death, tore apart their broken bodies, dismembered them limb from limb, slaking their ravenous thirst with the hot blood of victims and greedily devouring livid writhing flesh."[13]

Moving beyond the scene of the crime, Dart imaginatively reconstructed the trajectory that led to the kill. According to Dart, these "killer-apes" relinquished the safety of their arboreal existence "through a spirit of adventure" and the lure of "fleshy food."[14] Setting forth into the savannas and southern plains with tooth and claws—weapons fashioned from the horns, teeth, jaw, and thigh bones of their prey—a group of bloodthirsty proto-humans embarked upon organized hunting.[15] As Dart elaborates, "The blood-bespattered, slaughter-gutted archives of human history . . . [proclaim] this common bloodlust differentiator—this predacious habit . . . that separates man dietetically from his anthropoidal relatives and allies him rather with the deadliest of Carnivora."[16] In a secularized version of original sin, Dart concluded that the violent traits found in our bloodthirsty ancestors are embedded in our genes.[17]

The conception of humans as "confirmed killers" gained popularity in the 1960s and 1970s with the publication of several books by dramatist Robert Ardrey.[18] Building on Dart's theory, Ardrey coined the term "the hunting hypothesis" to characterize the view that hunting was the major catalyst in human evolutionary development.[19] Ardrey's views about hunting crystallized when he visited Africa to report on Kenya's Mau Mau uprising, where he also met and interviewed Raymond Dart. Reflecting on his experience, Ardrey confessed that he "learned to fear for my life in a thousand ways. . . . Africa scared me."[20] Surrounded by political turmoil, he concluded that "man is a predator whose natural instinct is to kill with a weapon."[21]

A more optimistic understanding of the hunting hypothesis was brought forward by another group of scientists in the 1960s. While Dart and Ardrey regarded the hunting hypothesis as a testament to our "savage nature," these researchers viewed it as the path to human salvation and world peace. Spurred by the violence unleashed during World War II, and inspired by the United Nations model of rational man, they sought to locate a "ground for human unity" in our shared ancestral past.[22] They proposed that all humans were the by-products of a single cultural legacy—organized hunting. Group hunting with weapons demonstrated the human (or more specifically, male) ability to overcome biological limitations, such as lack of fangs and claws, and create culture for the first time. As anthropologists Sherwood Washburn and C. S. Lancaster proclaimed, "in a very real sense, our intellect, interests, emotions, and basic social life—all are evolutionary products of the success of the hunting adaptation."[23] And as William S. Laughlin concludes, "Hunting is the master behavior pattern of the human species."[24] With this new awareness of our unique species identity, scientists believed that humans could function as a single family, ending racial and national conflicts.

The hunting hypothesis received a major blow in the 1970s when scientists reevaluated the fossil evidence for proto-human violence.[25] Reexamining the markings on Dart's *Australopithecene* bones, paleontologist C. K. Brain concluded that the puncture wounds were inflicted not by bone-wielding killer-apes, but by leopards, lions, and hyenas.[26] According to Brain, early *Australopithecines* were more likely the *victims* of "professional carnivores"; when early hominids dined on flesh, they were most probably scavengers, eating the leftovers of bonafide predators.[27] The preponderance of the evidence now suggests that it was human beings' experience as prey, rather than predator, that has exerted a more definitive influence on human development.[28]

The narrative of hunting as the generating matrix of human identity echoes the idea of masculinity as a second birth. Donna Haraway points out that the hunting hypothesis reflects the effort to "father" a common species identity in opposition to the rest of the natural world. The evolutionary benefits of hunting were akin to a cross-generational patrilineal heritage, from which all men (and, by extension, women) derived benefit. As Haraway argues, the effort to identify a transcendent, universal activity common to all humanity (or more specifically, men) functioned as a "potent sacrifice, where the animal is consumed to make the man." She concludes, "hunting was not about getting enough vitamin B-12."[29]

Although some twentieth-century scientists believed that an understanding of the pivotal role of hunting in human development might abolish racial and ethnic divisions, a glance at the history of hunting illustrates its recurring role in establishing, reinforcing, and reproducing gender, class, and race distinctions. Gender dualisms, in particular, have frequently been linked to hunting. As previously discussed, the killing of the hunted animal marks the death of a boy's identity and his rebirth into an adult male community that transcends nature. The historian Matt Cartmill sums up, "the connection of hunting with masculinity runs deep and hunters and their critics often comment on it. Hunting has been a stereotypically male activity throughout most of Western history."[30]

Just as one form of masculinity has been dominant over subordinate masculinities, as discussed in chapter 2, a hegemonic hunt has been dominant over subordinate forms of hunting. Throughout a wide variety of cultures and historical periods, recreational hunting[31] has been considered the privilege of elites and superior to subsistence hunting, which satisfies "mere" biological needs. According to this view, hunting has a dual function. On the one hand, it is a symbolic display of class superiority, proclaimed through enacting the roles of conqueror and provider. On the other hand, it is an educational program for the production of the virtues, skills, and character traits appropriate to the higher classes. The meat of hunted animals has also functioned as a symbolic currency, reinforcing the power of royalty and elites. As Donald Kyle states, "Some emperors are said to have given banquets at which guests received not only regular meat but raw meat and live animals as meat-gifts."[32]

The elite hunt first emerged in the Near East as the prerogative of royalty, subsequently evolving into an aristocratic pastime in the Archaic period.[33] The narrative of The Hunt—the pursuit, conquest, and consumption of the conquered animal—has been readily adapted by rulers throughout history. Found in virtually every ancient aristocracy, including those of Persia, Rome, Assyria, Egypt, and Macedonia, hunting symbolized a contest with the "wild," "the Beast," or "the Other"— all those considered outside the human world.[34] Whether battling "beasts" or "barbarians," females or slaves, the meaning for the aristocracy of each culture remained the same: the assertion of (male) privilege and dominance.[35] The importance of maintaining a never-ending battle with the enemy as a means of asserting dominance was underscored in ancient Babylonia: when animal populations dwindled in numbers, lions were bred in zoos to provide a supply of "beasts" to perpetuate ritual slayings."[36]

In ancient Greece, Plato championed the virtues of the aristocratic "chase," the *cynegia*, which employed dogs, one's own limbs, or bows and spears for tracking large mammals, as opposed to the "ungentlemanly" pratices of the lower classes, such as fishing, use of nets and snares to catch birds, or hunting at night.[37] According to Plato, these "lazy" forms of food procurement stood in contrast to "the best kind of hunting," which renders "the souls of young men better," and elevates men to a "godlike manhood."[38]

Greek philosophers extolled recreational hunting not only for its spiritual benefits, but also for its practical military value.[39] As early as 3000 BCE hunting was viewed as ideal military training. Aristotle considered the hunting of wild animals to be the first just war.[40] And Xenophon argued that it made ideal citizens out of young boys, leading to their success in war and making them just and "self-restrained."[41] The practical value of hunting as preparation for war functioned in tandem with its role as a rite of passage into manhood. As Judith Barringer observes, in both Sparta and Crete, the hunt was conceived as a form of initiation in which young men were sent away from the city for specified periods of time to practice "tracking, ambushing, and confronting animals" as training for future battles.[42] Use of weapons and tests of courage were central to these transformational events.[43]

While the recreational hunt of the ancient world was typically conceived as a controlled, stylized group procession, myths and legends of the time also championed a "savage" hunt, undertaken by a solitary young man.[44] The legendary heroes of Greek epics are often described as driven by aggressive, predatory impulses in their pursuit of prey. As Charles Bergman observes, Odysseus, Hercules, and Orion are imaged as "lone, independent heroes, driven by will and appetite to conquer their opponents."[45] Although not precisely a sport, the heroes' battles with ferocious "beasts" resemble dramatic contests, symbolizing passage into manhood.[46] Bergman points out that on some occasions these confrontations signal the triumph of reason and culture over irrationality and nature, while on others they are linked with the unleashing of emotions. Thus, in the myth of Apollo, the hunt is considered a gift of the gods, while in the myth of Dionysus, hunting is conceived as a demonic possession inciting female maenads to rip their prey apart and consume their raw flesh in the manner of "beasts."[47] Frequently, myths and legends portray the hunting hero as victorious over evil, ushering in the birth of a masculine moral order. Throughout their changing incarnations, the heroic hunts portray the establishment of masculine identity through opposition to an "Other."

The passion-driven hunt finds still another expression when conjoined with erotic desire. Many of the best-known myths and legends define love as an erotic hunt. The notion of the erotic hunt was inherited in the West from ancient Greece and Rome. The Roman poet Ovid popularized the use of the hunting metaphor through training manuals that instructed young men in the pursuit of their coveted female "prey."[48] It came into prominence in the Middle Ages as a highly stylized aristocratic pastime, portraying sexual desire as a path to self-understanding.[49] The erotic drive was conceived as a longing that takes possession of the pursuer, transforming him into the prey of his own desire.[50] As Marcelle Thiébaux notes, it was originally conceived as an external force, a power from the gods that irresistibly impelled the smitten individual into a state of amorous pursuit: "Eros or Aphrodite govern him; later it may be Nature, Amours, Lady Venus or Frau Minne that delivers the blow to render him the impassioned quarry or drives him to his inescapable hunting."[51] Although seemingly centered on relationships, this form of hunting concerns the satisfaction of a power-hungry (erotic) drive.[52] The flesh of the hunted animal (most often a stag) was also eroticized and often "presented as a love token."[53] Significantly, the words "venison" and "venery" share the same Indo-European root as "Venus," the Roman goddess of love. "Venery" is defined as both "indulgence in or pursuit of sexual activity" and "the act or sport of hunting."[54]

As Bergman points out, since erotic desire is conceived as a lack, rather than as a relation, it is based on strategizing and quenching a bodily hunger.[55]

At times, the passionate appetite appears in a chastened form, as evidenced by the figure of the virginal goddess Diana. While the earliest records portray her as the protectress of children and animals, in later myths she is also imaged as a huntress. Bergman notes that the stories of Diana do not suggest the idea of repressing predatory instincts; rather they convey a model for redirecting them into a "pure spiritual longing."[56] Artemis is ardently virginal and guardian of the wild animals with whom she runs. Her chastity functions both as a "spur to men's desire" and as an ideal for disciplining "their more unruly predatory practices."[57] Whether expressing savage aggression, carnal lust, or tempered passion, the eroto-centric hunt is a story about the management of desire. As Bergman sums up, "In addition to offering a narrative structure for desire, a narrative of searching and longing for the elusive creature, the hunt also poses one of the central questions through which power is negotiated and structured in a relationship: Who chases whom?"[58]

The hegemonic hunt, whether in myth and legend or in real life, represents not only a story about who conquers whom, but also a narrative of who owns what. Historically, public attitudes about hunting "have been linked to shifting definitions of property and ownership," and are often associated with status, class, and race.[59] The Roman legal and social tradition classified "wild animals" as "commons," belonging to everyone and thus to no one. Animals became private property only when they were killed or captured.[60] Whoever shed the "first blood" of an animal became the proprietor of the animal's flesh, a tradition that state Fish and Game departments abide by to this day.[61]

The common-law practice was continued in England while it was still part of the Roman Empire. After the Saxon invasion, land was divided among the royalty, with vast expanses being reserved as the "royal forest" for the monarch or as "chases" for the lesser aristocracy. The common people, by contrast, were required to hunt on the "commons" or the village "waste." During this period, hunting held a dual image: for the royalty, it was a form of recreation and pleasure, whereas for the commoner it was a means of subsistence. Attitudes toward wildlife have tended to reflect these class divisions in all societies with established elites.

In the United States, early views of hunting derived from the popular conviction that all men have the prerogative to hunt. Driven by a strong repugnance to the earlier ideas of royal privilege, coupled with a belief in an unending supply of wildlife, the early colonists shunned hunting regulations. Attitudes toward "wild" animals were governed by utilitarian concerns and irrational fears. Wild animals were perceived alternately as "resources" for the provision of meat and furs and as "vermin" that should be exterminated. The early colonists regarded predators in particular as ferocious animals that incarnated the evils lurking in the wilderness. As they increasingly relied on domesticated animals on farms—and suffered an increase in attacks by wild animals—protection of "stock" became an additional rationale for hunting. Their methods reflected their desire to maximize the number of animals killed. Thomas Dunlap states:

> They shot deer at night by lantern or fire light; they killed rafts of sitting ducks with "punt guns," small cannon that fired half a pound of nails and shot; and they fished with nets or dynamite. Game laws were few and enforcement nonexistent. People took what they wanted, when they wanted, and with no thought for the future.[62]

Consequently, by 1800 the population of wild animals had diminished drastically: wolves had been nearly eliminated from New England and Canada, and only a small fraction of the large herds of buffalos remained.

The colonists were lured to the New World with inflated accounts of limitless "game" and the absence of hunting laws. But as they settled the land, it was the farmer, not the hunter, who came to be regarded as the ideal natural citizen, embodying the virtues of self-reliance, discipline, productivity, and liberty. Viewed as the backbone of republicanism, they were, in the words of Thomas Jefferson, the "chosen people of God."[63] Just as God had mandated that Adam till the Earth as God's steward, the early colonists believed they had a divine imperative to transform the wilderness into a new Garden of Eden. Imaging the land as a female waiting to be improved by men, they alternately perceived her as "virgin land" to be exploited, "fallen nature" in need of reclamation, or a "fruitful garden" to be harvested."[64]

Hunting, by contrast, was viewed as a necessary evil, brought about by the Fall, permissible only for sustenance or protection from predators or "pests." Killing domesticated animals was the more civilized way of procuring food. The colonists' "productive" use of the soil was held to be superior to the Native American form of livelihood, which relied heavily on hunting as a means of subsistence. Clearing the wilderness of "game" animals and "Indians" was seen as integral to the creation of the new Garden of Eden.

Beginning in the 1830s, attitudes toward hunting began to shift. Drawing on the British aristocratic tradition of "fair play" in field sport, a group of English immigrants began to refashion hunting by framing it within an ethical discourse. Countering the Puritan notion that sport hunting was an idle pastime comparable to gambling and other activities governed by chance, these immigrants argued for the importance of rules and regulations to govern their sport.[65] They also emphasized the utility of hunting for the development of character and, in particular, male character—a theme that gained increased importance in the course of the century.

The aristocrat Henry William Herbert, writing under the pseudonym Frank Forester, was the most influential early promulgator of this new approach. Author of several books and a contributor to sporting journals like *American Turf Register* and *Sporting Magazine* in the 1830s and 1840s, Herbert set forth a philosophy that was premised on the vital importance of gentlemanly self-restraint. The good sportsman, according to Herbert, followed an ethical code that set limits to the number and types of animals killed, as well as the time and place. He shunned selfishness, and shared shots and "bags" with fellow hunters:

> It is in the vigor, science [correct technique], and manhood displayed—in the difficulties to be overcome, in the pleasurable anxiety for success, and the uncertainty of it, and lastly in the true spirit, the style, the dash, the handsome way of doing what is to be done, and above all, in the unalterable *love of fair play*, that first thought of the genuine sportsman, that true sportsmanship consists.[66]

By the 1870s, hunting had gained a newfound respect through its association with conservation. Sport hunters were the vast majority of early conservationists, and a number of historians believe that they played a significant role in the development of the movement.[67] These avid hunters were distressed to find themselves increasingly in competition with commercial hunters and fishermen for the dwindling numbers of "game" animals. In an effort to stave off the decimation, they successfully lobbied local and state associations to pass laws to regulate sport and limit market hunting. At a time when environmental thinking was still in its early stages, few appreciated the vital role played by predators in maintaining biological integrity and balance. In many cases, hunters were intent on eliminating as many predators as possible in an effort to enlarge the number of prey that they could kill. Predators were regarded as competitors who robbed sportsmen of opportunities to hunt.

From the beginning, sport hunters sought to distinguish themselves from the "ordinary gunners, game-hogs and meat-hunters."[68] Blaming the lower classes and immigrants for the destruction of wildlife, white middle- and upper-class sport hunters sought to portray their form of hunting as uniquely civilized, in contrast to the instinctive, uncontrolled hunting of the "savage races" and lower classes. William Hornaday, a noted conservationist and director of the New York Zoological Park, devoted an entire chapter of one of his books to denouncing the "scourge on song-birds" perpetrated by immigrant Italians, arguing that the Italians were "born pot-hunters." In another chapter he decried the "devilish work of the Negroes and poor whites of the South."[69] In contrast to these "Soldiers of Destruction," sport hunters believed they were "the very bone and sinew of wildlife preservation." They were the men who were "making and stocking game preserves, public and private, great and small."[70]

In the 1870s, sport hunters established platforms for lobbying on behalf of their new creed of "conservation." They established sportsmen's clubs and new journals, including *American Sportsman* (1871), *Forest and Stream* (1873), and *Field and Stream* (1874). Together, these journals and associations helped hunters to forge a group identity whose core was a well-defined code of conduct, based upon the gentlemanly ethic of fair play and self-restraint.

Sport hunting in the nineteenth century functioned as a form of ritualized display, justifying male dominance over subordinates—women, boys, immigrants, the "lower classes," and slaves.[71] Through mock competition with animals hunters demonstrated "prowess"; and through rules and regulations they showed impulse control, necessary traits for male patriarchs. In the South, where hunters used horses, dogs, and "Negro slaves" as aids on their expeditions, sport hunting held a third symbolic function: reinforcement of mastery. By exhibiting their ability to exercise "control over other people, animals, nature, and even death," Southern slave holders sought to justify their role as masters.[72]

The sportsmen's associations attracted many of the most distinguished men in the country, including senators, artists, judges, generals, authors, and former presidents. In addition to conserving natural resources, the associations declared their intention to rescue another diminishing resource: manhood. Listed in its constitution as the first of its five objectives, the prominent Boone and Crockett Club, founded by Theodore Roosevelt, declared the club's intention: "to promote manly sport with the rifle." Membership was accordingly restricted to those who had "killed with rifle" one of each of "three of the various species of American large game."[73] According to the historian John Reiger, hunting had become more than a sport—it had become "something approaching a 'world view,' even a religion."[74] In the words of Daniel Justin Herman, it had become a "vehicle for the expression of tribal identity."[75]

As the nineteenth century progressed, hunting became a central part of imperial culture. The historian John MacKenzie argues,

> For the first time a dominant elite assumed global significance. . . . An imperial and largely masculine elite attempted to reserve for itself access to hunting, adopted and transformed the concept of the Hunt as a ritual of prestige and dominance, and set about the separation of the human and animal worlds to promote "preservation" (later "conservation") as a continuing justification of its monopoly.[76]

## CONSERVATION AND PRESERVATION: PROTECTING THE "WHOLE"

The early movement for nature protection typically is understood to have had two streams of thought: the utilitarian philosophy of the "conservationists" and the aesthetic orientation of the "preservationists."[77] For the conservationists, nature existed to serve human needs, and limitations needed to be established only for reasons of efficiency and to ensure future use. As the historian Samuel P. Hays argues, "Conservation was, above all, a scientific movement. . . . Its essence was rational planning to promote efficient development and use of all natural resources."[78] Gifford Pinchot (1865–1946), the chief forester of the Department of Agriculture, expresses this philosophy: "The object of our forest policy is not to preserve the forests because they are beautiful . . . or because they are refuges for the wild creatures of the wilderness. The forests are to be used by man. Every other consideration comes secondary."[79]

Preservationists, on the other hand, appreciated nature for its aesthetic value, independent of its use for humans. The naturalist John Muir was the most eloquent and influential representative of this philosophy. He writes:

> No dogma taught by the present civilization seems to form so insuperable an obstacle in the way of a right understanding of the relations which culture sustains to wildness, as that which declares that the world was made especially for the uses of men. Every animal, plant, and crystal controverts it in the plainest terms.[80]

These two philosophies often are thought to reflect a distinction between a secular and a religious orientation, with conservationists viewed as driven by material goals and preservationists by loftier, spiritual values. However, at times hunters of the nineteenth century claimed *both identities*. They sought to conserve wildlife as a material "resource" *and* they sought to preserve wildlife for the spiritual and moral benefits that they provided.

Sport hunting conservationists often expressed concern over the dwindling populations upon which their sport depended. Since "wild" animals and forestlands were rapidly diminishing, they were becoming more and more valuable "commodities." Just as federal regulation of the market economy had gained acceptance as a necessary corrective to the vagaries of the free market, so too federal regulations were regarded as a necessary measure to ensure the continued supply of wildlife. Furthermore, conservationists argued for the importance of protecting nature's "stock" as an "investment" for future generations. Theodore Roosevelt expresses this sentiment:

Now there is a considerable body of public opinion in favor of keeping for our children's children, as a priceless heritage, all the delicate beauty of the lesser and all the burly majesty of the mightier form of wild life. . . . We have taken forward steps in learning that wild beasts and birds are by right not the property merely of the people alive to-day, but the property of the unborn generations, whose belonging we have no right to squander.[81]

However, at times Roosevelt, usually considered a conservationist, also expressed a quasi-religious attitude toward nature:

The civilized people of today look back with horror at their medieval ancestors who wantonly destroyed great works of art, or sat slothfully by while they were destroyed. We have passed that stage. We treasure pictures and sculptures. We regard Attic Gothic cathedrals as of priceless value. But we are, as a whole, still in that low state of civilization where we do not understand that it is also vandalism wantonly to destroy or to permit the destruction of what is beautiful in nature, whether it be a cliff, a forest, or a species of mammal or bird.[82]

While preservationists sought to differentiate their orientation from conservationists, they too sometimes used language that reflected the conservationist idea of nature as a resource, especially as a "spiritual" or "moral" one for humans. As John Muir states: "Everybody needs beauty as well as bread, places to play in and pray in, where Nature may heal and cheer and give strength to body and soul."[83]

Conservationists and preservationists also shared a belief that the domestication of the wilderness was part of the march of progress.[84] Subscribing to a Darwinian vision of triumph of the fittest, they accepted as necessary the replacement of native people by European whites, and wild buffalos by cattle. Since some native tribes depended on buffalos for their livelihood, sport hunters deliberately sought to destroy them as a means of acquiring the land. The "game reserves" that preservationists sought to establish were not intended for preserving buffalos in and of themselves; rather buffalos were to be maintained in small parks and game preserves, where tourists could view them as emblems of the American frontier. They were desired as cultural icons, symbolizing the self-reliance and manliness endangered by the closing of the frontier.[85] While worshipping "wild" nature, preservationists thus "ironically contributed to the domestication of the species by confining them to managed preserves."[86] Once buffalos were safely secured on scattered preserves and the species was no longer in danger, the movement for their protection lost most of its momentum.[87]

Although the distinction between conservationists and preservationists is valid, they both shared a vision of nature as a collective spiritual and material resource for humans. While one philosophy emphasized the material value of nature, and the other its moral benefits, both advocated for nature as a collective entity, rather than as a community of individual other-than-humans.[88] Conservationists and preservationists both claimed to have replaced the earlier colonists' predatory ethos with an ethic of protection. However, the title of "wildlife protector" can only accurately be applied to hunters if animals are viewed as a collective entity. If individual other-than-humans are considered, the distinction between predation and protection collapses. The sportsman's code of early conservationists not only excluded other-than-human animals as individuals, it specifically sought to ensure the continuation of opportunities for violent confrontation with them. Thus, the new ethic of protection was designed to *perpetuate* predation. Instead of unlimited predation, the hunters of the early conservation movement substituted an ethos of controlled predation.

As Sarah Hoagland argues, predation and protection are twin aspects of the same worldview: "Protection objectifies just as much as predation."[89] Perhaps nowhere is this clearer than with the early sport hunting conservationists. The protection they sought for other-than-humans was based on a form of managed violence and restrained sport, designed to sustain their supply of "game" to hunt.

The sport hunter's claim to have replaced the early colonists' predatory ethic with one of protection is questionable in another respect. Although the hunter-conservationists were the first to develop an explicit moral code for interaction with nature, the earlier colonists also implicitly endorsed an ethical code: the felling of the primeval forests and the removal of "wild" animals and "savage" humans were all part of a collective *moral* enterprise by which they believed the raw material of nature was transformed and harnessed into an advanced civilization. The god-forsaken quality of the wilderness was to give way to a new Garden of Eden on Earth. Wild animals, like wolves who preyed on domestic animals, were regarded as impediments to the development of this garden. Their mythical narrative opened with an amoral wilderness and culminated in a tamed and godlier civilization. Although the early colonists did not explicitly invoke moral principles, they were clearly guided by an implicit moral vision in which wild animals were props in a wider drama of extermination.

Nineteenth-century conservationists and preservationists shared the conviction that interaction with nature was also *individually* morally uplifting. Just as Protestantism emphasized a personal relationship with God, members of the early conservation movement perceived interaction with nature as a means of lifting one's character to a higher, nobler realm. The ethic of sport hunting underscored the moral value derived from individual encounters with "wild" animals.

Ironically, the manly encounter with "wild" nature that was thought to confer individual identity upon men in the late nineteenth century denied the individuality of the animals they killed. Sport hunters' ethical concern applied only to animals as a collectivity, instrumental to human needs or desires. Even the parks that were established as shelters for wild animals were viewed as a "breeding" ground for future "stock." Sport hunters may have sincerely admired many other-than-humans, including the ones they killed, but their moral code required that they slaughter them.

## THE HUMANE MOVEMENT

Although occasional references to the suffering of animals can be found in the writings of both preservationists and conservationists, by and large neither group took notice. Only a third group, the humane movement for animal protection, made this a central concern. As historian Lisa Mighetto points out,

> Because humanitarians focused mostly on domestic animals, this group is not readily associated with conservation. Yet their arguments for protecting wildlife represent a significant development in attitudes toward nature, for humanitarians, unlike other conservationists, argued that animals are worthy of moral consideration.[90]

As early as 1641, a law was passed in Massachusetts forbidding cruelty to animals, but only for "the creatures which are usually kept for the use of man." A number of anti-cruelty laws were also passed in the 1820s and 1830s. The movement for animal protection, however, only gained ascendancy in the aftermath of the Civil War when the aristocrat Henry Bergh founded the first Society for the Prevention of Cruelty to Animals (SPCA) in 1866. By 1874, there were SPCAs in more than thirty cities across the Northeast.

Throughout its history, the movement for animal protection drew inspiration from Christian ideals of benevolence toward God's creatures. In the nineteenth century, however, an additional foundation for opposition to animal cruelty emerged: concern for animals' pain.[91] Darwinian science had narrowed the gap between human and other-than-human animals, facilitating an increased appreciation for their similar capacity for suffering. In addition, as belief in a heavenly reward for suffering declined, tolerance for cruel treatment also declined. Increased urbanization inspired a nostalgic longing for contact with animals, fostering the practice of pet-keeping. Living with animals in turn contributed to sympathy for their plight. For most of their early history, humane moralists focused primarily on the suffering of domesticated animals, including pets, songbirds, farmed animals, carriage horses, and other animals used for work.

Championed predominantly by women (despite the prohibition against their holding positions of leadership),[92] animal protection was seen as a "feminizing" movement, countering the aggressive traits fostered by the new industrial society with an "ideology of feminine compassion."[93] Since males, and particularly boys, were thought to be driven by aggressive, animal impulses, women's influence was welcomed as a moderating force. Avenues for expressing men's aggressive drives were still deemed necessary, but middle-class citizens increasingly saw kindness toward (some) animals as a means of developing impulse control and keeping aggression within acceptable bounds. By and large, humane moralists did not question the property status of animals; nor did they idealize life in the wild. Rather, they sought to encourage benevolence toward the domesticated animals who depended upon their human "masters."

Although humane moralists focused on the plight of domestic animals, they did at times extend their concern to wild animals. Despite differing motives, humane moralists and sport hunters were able to unite on a number of issues, including the prohibition of the trade in plumage and the protection of the wild bison. Appalled by the spectacle of thousands of dead buffalos scattered across the Great Plains, humane activists campaigned vigorously against the slaughter of buffalos. Ultimately, however, according to Isenberg, it was the "masculine ideology of the frontier conquest," not the "feminizing ideology of the SPCA," that succeeded in protecting the last remnants of the buffalos.[94]

## INTELLECTUAL ROOTS

With the advance of industrialization in the nineteenth century, gender roles also began to change. Large numbers of men left their farms and artisan businesses to join the corporate world, leaving women behind as the sole guardians of children. Entrusted with the task of moral education in the home, women also constituted the vast majority of teachers in schools. As a result of women's dominant role over young boys, men began to worry that boys were becoming overly feminized.[95]

Workplace changes also influenced the new views of gender. Rising numbers of women and immigrants had begun to enter the workforce, further threatening white middle-class men's sense of distinct identity. As a result, they felt a need to differentiate themselves from both women and the "lower classes." The repetitive work found in the new hierarchical corporate world added to their sense of loss of individuality and manliness.[96] The competitive ethos of the market economy also increasingly came to be seen as a reflection of the savage world of untamed nature. Within this context, the view of men as predatory animals, uniquely suited to the new competitive workplace, came to the fore. Women, by contrast, were viewed as ideally suited to the home—guardians of virtue or "angels in the house." While women's monopoly on virtue was still valued, a release from their restraining influence was increasingly sought.

Conceptions of manhood mirrored these changes. The combative spirit of the market economy produced the ideal of the Masculine Achiever, embodying traits of autonomy, striving, and aggression, and a new focus on self-advancement. The Masculine Achiever, in turn, inspired yet another ideal of manliness, the Christian Gentleman, a man of kindness, compassion, and self-mastery.

A third ideal of manliness, the Masculine Primitive, came to the fore later in the nineteenth century and emphasized man's animal nature. It was this ideal that most heavily influenced the nineteenth-century conservationists. The Masculine Primitive represented men as "savages," manifesting physical strength, powerful instincts, and personal force. Although this ideal predated Darwin's *Origin of Species*, ideas about men's animal nature received increased prominence after its publication.[97] Sport hunting presented the perfect means to personify the Masculine Primitive.

With the publication of *Origin of Species*, human beings' pride in their uniqueness was seriously eroded, and for the first time humans faced the prospect of being "reduced" to an animal state. In addition, the consolation previously found in a divinely ordered realm, leading toward a millennial, heavenly reward, was replaced by the idea of an evolutionary development governed by random laws of struggle and conflict.

One response to the prospect of an amoral universe was to acknowledge "man's animality," while placing it within a moral, teleological framework that sanctioned its controlled expression. "Man" might be an animal, but at least he could express his "animal" impulses in a rationally controlled and regulated manner.

The previous belief in the linear progression from "man's" sinful existence toward a heavenly reward was transformed into the notion of progress from a savage, animal state into a civilized society. The traditional boundary that had divided humans from other-than-humans became "reinterpreted in the West to involve not only differences in kind but also difference in *progress* along an evolutionary path."[98] Evangelical Protestantism also influenced the new vision of moral evolution through its emphasis on the efficacy of human will. The key to the attainment of progress in the new worldview resided not in competitive striving, but rather in the development of self-discipline and control over the beastly passions. And the passions that specifically concerned middle-class Americans were those of men.

The closing decades of the nineteenth century were a period of rapid urbanization and social transformation. Middle-class Americans became convinced that the "hectic pace and excessive stimuli of modern life" were taking a toll on the "advanced races," producing a medical condition called "neurasthenia."[99] Also known as "American nervousness," neurasthenia was conceived through the lens of market economics as a consequence of the improper expenditure of a valued commodity: human energy. As historian Tom Lutz writes, "People were assumed to have a certain amount of 'nerve force' or nervous energy, which was subject to a strict bodily economy. When the supply of nerve energy was too heavily taxed by the demands upon it, or when the available nerve force was not properly reinvested, nervous bankruptcy, or nervousness, was the result."[100] According to the beliefs of the age, sensitive individuals were particularly prone to the disease, although wasteful activities such as "masturbation, gambling, and other forms of illicit sexual or financial activity" were energy drains that could dissipate anyone's nervous energy.[101]

The cures for men and women, however, were diametrically opposed. Neurasthenia was viewed as a type of gender disorder, necessitating a return to gender-specific roles. Since exposure to the public domain was exhausting to women, "the rest cure" was prescribed, recommending seclusion, quiet, repose, force feeding, and abstinence from all writing. Avoidance of mental strain was designed to help women accept their natural femininity and adapt to their appropriate role in the family.[102]

The medical treatment for men, on the other hand, reflected different concerns. As citizens left their rural environments to move to the cities, opportunities for interaction with nature became increasingly rare. The middle classes worried that males, especially young boys, were becoming *overly* civilized, lacking outlets for their more primitive drives. Common correctives to this state of enervation included vigorous exercise, outdoor camping, and sport hunting. The "exercise cure" bolstered men's flagging virility, while helping them adapt their restored vigor to the predatory nature of the workplace.[103]

Thus, the animal passions that lurked in men needed to be allowed expression, but in a safe and cultivated manner. According to historian Gail Bederman, the meaning of the term "manliness" in the nineteenth century differed from subsequent ideas of "masculine" and "masculinity." Manliness held a moral connotation, signifying "honorable" and "high-minded." It "comprised all the worthy, moral attributes which the Victorian middle class admired in a man . . . sexual restraint, a powerful will, a strong character."[104] Manliness was not merely a descriptive category for individuals of the male gender; it was a *moral achievement*, attained through the proper exercise of rationality and will. The term masculine, on the other hand, only began to be used in the latter half of the nineteenth century, as cultural forces undermined the power of "manliness." This new term had an empty, fluid meaning, referring simply to having the attributes of men, as contrasted to women. Thus, one could have "masculine clothing" or a "masculine gait." The term masculine connoted men's innate, rather than achieved, difference from women.[105]

The new fields of natural science and biology also influenced definitions of manhood at the turn of the twentieth century. Since human beings were viewed now as a part of the natural world, they too could be studied with the same rigor increasingly applied to the rest of nature. Because humans were driven by animal impulses, these inner forces needed to be respected and controlled. A spate of journals and articles on the nascent science of childhood development emphasized the importance for men of rugged interaction with nature. Many childhood educators advocated hunting as an ideal way to develop the moral character of young boys. Since work no longer demanded the physical challenges of early pioneer life, another way had to be found to test men's character. Competitive sports such as boxing and football were valuable, but for many conservationists hunting was the ideal means for the attainment of skills as well as manly character. Robert Baden-Powell, the founder of the Boy Scouts movement, believed that "every young boy ought to learn to shoot and obey orders."[106] Paraphrasing Theodore Roosevelt, he also maintained that "the qualities that make a good scout are in large part the qualities that make a good hunter."[107]

Sport hunters and educators thus managed to adopt the Darwinian idea of struggle and fitness, while turning it on its head.[108] Man might be governed by the same drives that lurked within predatory animals, but at least he was capable of rising above his instincts by exercising self-control. Sport hunting, according to this model, allowed for the necessary expression of man's predatory nature, while moving it onto a higher, more civilized plane. As such, it was the ideal remedy for the overly civilized male struggling with his unruly "animal" instincts.

## THEODORE ROOSEVELT: MAN OF ADVENTURE

The naturalist Peter Matthiessen expresses a common perception when he writes that Roosevelt's inauguration "was one of the most auspicious and timely events in the history of American wildlife."[109] This belief persists despite the fact that Roosevelt was an avid sportsman who loved to hunt. Roosevelt's penchant for killing was typically accompanied by expressions of deep regard for the natural world. As the environmental historian Lisa Mighetto points out, frequently "Roosevelt's most sensitive nature prose was followed by his desire to kill an animal."[110] He loathed particular predators, denouncing the wolf as "an archetype of ravin, the beast of waste and desolation."[111] As Mighetto comments, "Roosevelt's portrayals of these animals could convey a striking lack of sympathy. After shooting one bear cub, he recorded that its skin was not 'big enough to use for anything but a doily.'"[112] Sport hunters in Roosevelt's day did not see the contradiction between a love for nature as a collectivity and the desire to extinguish individual lives.

Insight into the paradoxical juxtaposition of love and violence can be gained through an examination of the twin ideas of "manhood" and "adventure" in Roosevelt's life and philosophy. Born into a privileged family in New York City in 1858, Roosevelt was attracted to the world of adventure at a young age. A sickly child, plagued with recurring illnesses and asthmatic attacks, he appeared an unlikely candidate to become the champion of the manly life. Unable to engage in strenuous games and activities, he spent countless hours reading adventure novels, including many of the popular stories of the day: William Defoe's *Robinson Crusoe*, David Livingstone's *Missionary Travels and Researches in South Africa*, and Captain Mayne Reid's stories *The Boy Hunters*, *Afloat in the Forest*, and *Wild Life or Adventures on the Frontier*. Drawn to the world of nature, he developed a lifelong love for natural history. His interest was heightened when he discovered a dead seal whose skull provided the first specimen in what was to become his own natural history museum.[113] By the time he was a teen, "The Roosevelt Museum of Natural History," located in his bedroom, displayed a total of 250 dead animals, all preserved by the budding naturalist. Some, including birds and insects, were proudly killed and collected by Roosevelt himself.

His childhood diversions demonstrate the early juxtaposition of contradictory passions within Roosevelt: the young boy who claimed to love animals and the nascent scientist who surrounded himself with their dead bodies. The adventure stories further contributed to a conflation of excitement and fun with violence and death, a combination that was to follow him into his adult life.[114] The sense of conflict and struggle with "fierce" animals became integral components, in his mind, of a manly ethic. Describing his last and most dangerous expedition to Africa, he claimed, "I had to go. It was my last chance to be a boy."[115]

Roosevelt's battles with "wild" animals, chronicled in his voluminous writings,[116] mirror his lifelong battle against a more intimate adversary: his own body. Determined to transform his frail physique into his ideal conception of heroic manliness (especially in light of political aspirations), Roosevelt relinquished his life of privilege in pursuit of adventure on the Western frontier. After buying a cattle ranch in the Badlands of the Dakota Territory, he spent countless hours as a ranch hand, taking time off only to confront "fierce game" on hunting expeditions. After the untimely deaths of his mother and wife on the same day in 1884, he returned to the ranch, burying his grief in hard physical labor and hunting adventures. A few years later, the transformation was complete; Roosevelt, the Eastern urbanite, had attained his manly ideal, a product of the new frontier.

The connection between hunting and heroic adventure did not, of course, begin in the nineteenth century. In ancient Greece, Xenophon wrote that hunting was "the best training for war," fostering physical and mental skills to build "good soldiers and good generals."[117] But in the nineteenth century the relation between hunting and heroism was accentuated through its association with exploration and imperialism. Having subdued their own country, American men now turned their focus to other parts of the world. Once again, sport hunting played a central role. According to the historian John MacKenzie, the lure of hunting and exploitation of animals in distant lands was a "prime impulse of European expansion."[118] Imperial hunts fulfilled many functions: they provided a lucrative market for the trade in meat and animal parts, they enabled scientists to categorize numerous "exotic" species, and they were a symbolic act of dominance over colonial subjects whose "inferior" hunting methods the explorers supplanted.

Hunters also emphasized the enjoyable aspect of their sport, while seeking to legitimate it by linking it to nobler purposes. The study of natural history was one of these noble pursuits. Thus, while Roosevelt extolled the psychological benefits of hunting, he also conducted many of his hunting trips in the name of science. Some were authorized and paid for by institutions like the Smithsonian Institution in Washington and the National Museum in New York for the purpose of collecting prestigious museum pieces. In his zealous pursuit of "specimens," on one of these expeditions his party shot 512 "game animals." As MacKenzie comments,

> The true sportsman was a natural historian and a scientist. Killing was in a sense legitimated by his understanding of his quarry, its environment and its anatomy, and his knowledge of firearms and ballistics added an extra scientific dimension. The hunter had become a member of an exclusive club, its rules defined by Western technology and science.[119]

Whether framed within a moral, political, or scientific discourse, the logic of the hunting adventure always subordinated the killing of the animal to a larger moral framework. Describing this process, Roosevelt states:

> The finding and killing of the game is after all but a part of the whole. The free, self-reliant, adventurous life, with its rugged and stalwart democracy; the wild surrounding, the grand beauty of the scenery, the chance to study the ways and

habits of the woodland creatures—all these unite to give the career of the wilderness hunter its peculiar charm. The chase is among the best of all national pastimes; it cultivates that vigorous manliness for the lack of which in a nation as in an individual, the possession of no other qualities can possibly atone.[120]

Reflecting a similar theme, Baden-Powell, the founder of the Boy Scouts, argued:

All the fun of hunting lies in the adventurous life in the jungle, the chance in many cases of the animal hunting *you* instead of you hunting the animal, the interest in tracking him up, stalking him and watching all that he does and learning his habits. The actual shooting the animal that follows is only a very small part of the fun.[121]

In the same vein, the Spanish philosopher José Ortega y Gasset argues, "To the sportsman the death of the game is not what interests him; that is not his purpose. What interests him is everything that he had to do to achieve that death—that is, the hunt. Therefore what was before only a means to an end is now an end in itself. Death is essential because without it there is no authentic hunting. . . . To sum up, one does not hunt in order to kill; on the contrary, one kills in order to have hunted."[122] Following in his footsteps, the modern environmental author Michael Pollan maintains, "If one hunts one has to accept certain ultimate requirements without which the reality 'hunting' evaporates. Killing is one of those requirements." Thus, critiquing his first hunting expedition, he observes that, "having introduced a loaded gun in Act One" and then refraining from firing, he had "violated the Chekhovian dramatic rule."[123]

The narrative structure of hunting may be understood through an analogy with the sexual drive, with which hunting is often associated. Although sport hunters often downplay the final kill, none are willing to relinquish this as their ultimate goal. The narrative structure must entail the climax of the kill. The buildup of tension and excitement found in the "fore-play" of the chase only attains meaning when directed toward the final release attained in death. If the animal is at too great a disadvantage, the hunter is not able to demonstrate his prowess, and hunting loses its erotic appeal. Thus individual animals function as psychological instruments or props that facilitate a larger psycho-sexual experience.[124]

## WORK, SPORT, AND PLAY

Sport hunters in the late nineteenth and early twentieth centuries defined their activity through a series of oppositions: nature and culture, work and leisure, idle play and sport. The moral value of sport hunting for nineteenth-century Americans was typically seen to reside in its contrast to work.[125] It was a leisure activity, which by definition meant that its value lay in its opposition to the humdrum, workaday business world, devoid of novelty and adventure. Roosevelt reflects this attitude in his statement, "I am not disposed to under-value manly outdoor sports, or to fail to appreciate the advantage to a nation, as well as to an individual, of such pastimes; but they must be pastimes and not business, and they must not be carried to excess."[126] Conservationists such as Roosevelt, however, also sought to distinguish the American pastime of hunting from the overly civilized British tradition. For the American sportsman hunting was a form of leisure as well as "productive," arduous work, serving higher goals: "No form of labor is harder than the chase, nor so excellent as a training for war."[127]

While sport hunters were intent on disassociating their activity from the business world and defining hunting as a respectable leisure activity, they were equally intent on disputing the notion that hunting was a form of idle play. Although sport and play are both commonly defined by their nonproductive nature, their difference is thought to reside in the greater complexity of sport. According to the philosopher of sport Carolyn Thomas, "Sport has elements of play but goes beyond the characteristics of play in its rule structure, organization, and criteria for the evaluation of success."[128] In addition, although sport is believed to have its basis in play, Thomas observes that it has a second distinguishing feature: its agonistic or competitive quality. As sociologist Janet Lever points out, play, by contrast, is viewed as an inherently "cooperative interaction that has no explicit goal, no end point, and no winners."[129] Both play and sport are viewed as activities that are their own reward, unlike work, which is performed for external rewards.

Sport hunters in the early conservation movement believed that the rules and regulations they invoked elevated hunting from an irresponsible and nonproductive activity into a praiseworthy practice that contributed to the development of character, especially male character. They believed it served a psychological, rather than a crass biological utility. Play, associated with instincts, spontaneity, and the realm of random nature, was not what the young men of the nineteenth century needed. What was called for was an activity that involved competition and a *regulated* form of release of aggression—an organized sport symbolizing manly transcendence of the natural world.

The idea that hunting is a sport contains a number of conceptual flaws, which seemed to elude nineteenth-century hunters. Sport is typically conceived as a voluntary agreement among participants to follow mutually agreed upon goals. But the other-than-human "players" in this "game" do not consent to be competitors; nor do they have the same objectives. The sport is devoid of symmetry. The hunter sets the rules, including the goal to kill; the animals merely respond by attempting to flee. The forcible entry of other-than-human animals into this "game" renders the analogy with sport meaningless. The more appropriate analogy is with sacrifice or war.

As discussed in the previous chapter, developmental theorists like Lawrence Kohlberg contend that the ideal trajectory for ethical development moves from interpersonal affiliation toward a rational ethical code based on universal principles and abstract rules. The belief in the moral superiority of sport over play reflects a similar valuation. Play was relegated to the inferior realm of nonpurposeful nature, associated with instinct and emotion rather than rationally organized rules.

Roosevelt never fully relinquished his view of hunting as play, however. Hunting was a temporary reversion to the animal world and a playful reenactment of the lives of the earlier pioneers, whose sweat and blood had forged the greatness of the white race. By temporarily re-creating the pioneer experience according to more civilized rules, sport hunters were able to further advance not only themselves, but all of civilization. As Roosevelt argued, the conquest of the West

> is a record of men who greatly dared and greatly did; a record of wanderings wider and more dangerous than those of the Vikings; a record of endless feats of arms, of victory after victory in the ceaseless strife waged against wild man and wild nature. The winning of the west was the great epic feat in the history of our race.[130]

Historian John MacKenzie sheds light on this backward-looking aspect of hunting, observing that the love of the hunt always entails a quest to retrieve an idealized past. As long ago as ancient Greece, Xenophon praised hunting as a means of conferring on young men the virtues of their ancestors, which they possessed "by nature."[131] This atavistic aspect has been linked to the pursuit of adventure. As Martin Green observes, "adventure makes it seem possible for people to go back to an earlier social condition and revive the best part of the past—or the fiercest and grandest parts—in more favorable conditions."[132]

One of the "best parts" that Roosevelt hoped sport hunting would retrieve was the ideal of freedom: "The hunter is the arch-type of freedom."[133] Roosevelt's concern, however, was men's freedom. He viewed the pioneer and cowboy as the perfect antidote to the increasing enervation of the American male. As he writes, "he possesses, in fact, few of the emasculated, milk-and-water moralities of the pseudo-philanthropist; but he does possess, to a very high degree, the stern, manly qualities that are invaluable to a nation."[134]

Roosevelt's emphasis on the value of hunting as sport was also part of a larger military philosophy that endorsed warfare as a means for advancing American imperial designs. According to this worldview, violence has a regenerative power capable of producing peace. In his words, "It is only the warlike power of a civilized people that can give peace to the world."[135] The idea that hunting and warfare are regenerative activities and that warfare brings peace seems paradoxical. Yet this paradox reflects the contradictory drives that fueled masculine self-identity: the longing for connection and the desire for separation. Violence and death, through hunting, became the resolution to these opposing drives.

A popular form of entertainment also highlighted the connection between hunting and imperial designs. With the closing of the frontier, a playful re-creation of the conquest of the West became an international tourist attraction, lasting from 1883 to 1916. Based on the popular dime novels written by William (Buffalo Bill) Cody, Ned Buntline, and Prentiss Ingraham, these performances, called *The Wild West*, surpassed all previous forms of commercial entertainment in their size and success. Precursors to the modern western, they portrayed the various stages of the frontier conquest: The Primeval Forest, A Buffalo Hunt, and A Cattle Ranch, interspersed with Indian raids and assorted "Cowboy Fun," such as rodeo-style displays and exhibitions of other cowboy skills.

*The Wild West* managers proudly proclaimed the historical accuracy of their shows, which were *not* mere entertainment, but rather education. Moreover, their greatest contribution was the inculcation of important moral values, including the notion that violence and war were "instruments of American progress." The illusion of historical accuracy was accentuated by enlisting actual Indians and units from the U.S. cavalry.

*The Wild West* shows were not simply nostalgic reproductions of the past. By recapturing the frontier spirit and enlisting it for their cause, they were ideological props for imperial expansion. In order to advance their designs, the historical battle scenes of the frontier needed to be altered. Custer's Last Fight gave way to scenes of the Spanish-American war, with real soldiers included among the players. Called the World Congress of Rough Riders, these actors staged the "Battle of San Juan Hill," celebrating Roosevelt's conquests in the Philippines.[136] A historian of the West, Richard Slotkin, notes, "This substitution of an imperial triumph . . . completes the Wild West's evolution from a memorialization of the past to a celebration of the imperial future."[137]

## NATURE FAKERS

In the midst of his conquests in foreign lands, Roosevelt joined a group of naturalists in a heated battle against a band of storytellers. Many hunters in the nineteenth century considered themselves naturalists, claiming the study of nature as their prime motive in hunting. It was not enough to be a skilled marksman. It was equally important to have intimate knowledge of the animals that one killed. Theodore Roosevelt prided himself on his prowess as both a skilled hunter and a naturalist. According to Roosevelt, accurate knowledge of animals was important not only to ensure that appropriate species were killed in the appropriate manner, but because accurate knowledge fostered a desire to protect animals. By hunting, collecting, and studying other-than-human animals, young boys could gain an "objective" appreciation for nature.

The controversy that preoccupied Roosevelt concerned the factual validity of a number of popular animal stories. Why the president of the United States would take time away from his imperial machinations to criticize these children's stories can only be understood by examining their symbolic significance.

The stories under contention were written by several Canadian and American authors, including Ernest Thompson Seton, Jack London, and Charles G. D. Roberts, and William J. Long. Although they differed in important ways, they were all narratives about the lives of individual animals. Animal stories had been written previously (e.g., *Black Beauty* and *The Jungle Book*), but these earlier stories had anthropomorphized animals, or used them as a metaphor for human problems.[138] Now, however, naturalists were writing stories about wild animals, and readers were invited to understand the lives of animals from the animals' perspectives. The animals in these realistic stories "'lived for their own ends,' rather than for human ends."[139] Furthermore, the authors, for the first time, claimed factual authenticity.

The public dispute began in 1903 when John Burroughs, also a naturalist and author of wild animal stories, accused the authors of grossly distorting fact, conferring on them the name "Nature Fakers." A number of particular scenarios drew his vehement attacks: a woodcock who used mud and straw to construct a splint for a broken leg, a wolf who spun in circles to make the sheep watching him become dizzy, and a fox who escaped hunters by riding on the backs of sheep. But the stories that angered Burroughs the most depicted animals instructing their young in survival skills, a claim that he denounced was "ridiculous." The authors of these disparate stories shared an underlying belief that animals were capable of reasoning and were not simply driven by instinctual drives. The battle that ensued over the validity of these children's stories was, at its heart, a battle over humanity's unique claim to reason and individuality.

Roosevelt, who had been following this acrimonious debate in newspaper articles and magazines, became actively involved in 1907 when the stories were being incorporated into school curricula. Fearing that young children would be corrupted by sentimental feelings, thereby losing the requisite detachment that the rigorous study of nature required, he charged that, "As for the matter of giving these books to children for the purpose of teaching them the facts of natural history—why, it's an outrage."[140]

According to the wild animal story writer William J. Long, animals were individuals; each animal demonstrated unique behavior, which science could not predict. He wrote that there was "absolutely no limit to the variety and adaptiveness of Nature, even in a single species."[141] Furthermore, "Every animal has an individuality, however small or dim; that is certain."[142] He felt that sympathy, not rationality, was the proper way to acquire knowledge of animals. Invoking the philosophies of Hume and Descartes, Long argued that

> The nature student must seek from his own individuality which is the only thing that he knows absolutely . . . to interpret truthfully and sympathetically the individual before him. For this work he must have not only sight but vision; not simply eyes and ears and a notebook; but insight, imagination, and above all an intense human sympathy . . . by which alone the inner life of an animal becomes luminous, and without which the living creatures are little better than stuffed specimens.[143]

Similarly, Charles G. D. Roberts, a creator of the wild animal genre, argued that such stories have helped us to "come face to face with personality, where we were blindly wont to predicate instinct and automatism."[144] Summarizing their import, he writes,

> The animal story . . . is a potent emancipator. . . . It helps us to return to nature, without requiring that we at the same time return to barbarism. It leads us back to the old kinship of earth, without asking us to relinquish by way of toll any part of the wisdom of the ages, any fine essential of the "large result of time."[145]

Although the authors of the wild animal stories were not opposed to all hunting, their stories, which took the perspective of the animals, hardly painted hunters in an amiable light. Long expressly denounced sport hunting, admonishing that there was "no animal that naturally or instinctively goes out, as you do, and hunts for sport or pleasure."[146] The "Nature Fakers" also condemned the conventional methods of studying natural history, which killed countless animals for specimen collection. According to Long, this method of acquiring knowledge represented a "questionable slaughter of untold innocents in the acquisition of its superficial knowledge."[147]

The validity of the specific anecdotes under dispute is of less significance than the belligerence with which Roosevelt and Burroughs responded to Long, and their attempt to claim reason as a unique human attribute. Roosevelt was willing to admit that young animals might be capable of a modicum of learning, but both he and Burroughs painted a picture of wild animals governed primarily by instinct. Both feared that the "sentimental" depiction of nature by the "Nature Fakers" threatened to instill in humans a false sense of kinship with the rest of nature. In addition, the sympathies that the wild animal story encouraged might interfere with the unquestioned use of animals both in scientific study and in sport. Seton, in fact, argued that "since, then, the animals are creatures with wants and feelings differing in degree only from our own, they surely have their rights."[148] As Lutts comments, "the people mired in the Nature Fakery dispute were arguing over the value of science and sentiment in our effort to understand, appreciate, and protect wild animals."[149]

## CONCLUSION

Sport hunters of the nineteenth and early twentieth century claimed a common identity through a series of oppositions: nature/culture; animal/human; womanhood/manhood; savage/civilized; play/sport; and market or subsistence hunting/sport hunting. Rather than simply renouncing the first half of these dualisms, sport hunters sought to give many of them controlled, ethical expression. By instituting rules and regulations, idle play became adventurous sport, the savage became tame, the "animal passions" were civilized, and "effeminate" young men became mature gentlemen. Transforming these inferior traits into superior "gentlemanly" behavior, they claimed, benefited not only the individual sport hunter and wildlife, but the entire civilized world. According to this worldview, manhood was an accomplishment that followed a narrative structure, beginning in boyhood and passing into adulthood by means of internal struggle and conquest of the animal passions. Sport hunting was a central means for accomplishing this feat. By conserving animals, the sport hunters of the nineteenth century aimed to preserve their sport and the avenue to their manhood. Today's collective moral orientation toward nature and other-than-humans is their legacy.

## NOTES

1. Amy Forrest, "Hunting Heritage Starts at the Top," *Women in the Outdoors*, Spring 2004, 27.

2. "Bush Begins New Year by Bagging Quail," *Action News*, January 2, 2004.

3. Jimmy Carter, "A Childhood Outdoors," in *A Hunter's Heart: Honest Essays on Blood Sport*, ed. David Petersen (New York: Henry Holt and Company, 1997), 35.

4. Lois Romano, "Kerry Hunting Trip Sets Sights on Swing Voters," *Washington Post*, October 21, 2004.

5. Numerous versions of this incident have been written. Some claim that Roosevelt let the bear go, while others maintain that either the guides or Roosevelt shot the bear to end his suffering. Reports of the bear's size also vary drastically from six hundred pounds to a tiny cub. The incident, whether mythic or actual, inspired the creation of the cuddly "teddy bear" loved by millions of American children. For further discussion, see Paul Schullery, *The Bear Hunter's Century: Profiles from the Golden Age of Bear Hunting* (Silver City, N.Mex.: High Lone-Some Books, 1988), 213–219.

6. As Michael Messner elaborates, "With no frontier to conquer, with physical strength becoming less relevant in work, and with urban boys being raised and taught by women, it was feared that males were becoming 'soft,' that society itself was becoming 'feminized.'" Messner, *Power at Play: Sports and the Problem of Masculinity* (Boston: Beacon Press, 1992), 14.

7. In the nineteenth century the parallel between the dualisms male/female and culture/nature was complex. In their capacity as mothers, women were regarded as the inculcators of the civilizing virtues, and hence as guardians of civilization; one of their primary tasks was to subdue the animal nature that lurked within young boys. As sexual objects, however, women were viewed as the primary instigators of the animal passions in men and thus as closer to the natural world.

8. Roosevelt's understanding of Darwin, like that of many conservationists, was influenced by the social climate of industrial capitalism, with its emphasis on conflict and competition. Darwin never actually used the oft-quoted phrase "survival of the fittest." His emphasis was on the survival of the best adapted, due to random variations in nature. Although I sometimes refer to the "influence of Darwin" in this study, the reader should bear in mind that I am referring to this misinterpretation of his philosophy.

9. Elsewhere I have developed a six-fold typology of hunting, based upon the differing motives and narratives that hunters invoke. The first three, the *happy hunter*, the *holist hunter*, and the *holy hunter*, are forms of sport hunting. The happy hunter hunts for recreation and pleasure, the holist hunter for the sake of the environment or the "biotic whole," and the holy hunter for the purpose of spiritual communion. These hunters stand in contrast to another group, which hunts for utilitarian reasons and claims no moral discourse: the *hired hunter*, the *hungry hunter*, and the *hostile hunter*. The hired hunter hunts for the sake of commercial profit, the hungry hunter for food, and the hostile hunter for the purpose of eradicating "villainous" animals. Despite these distinctions, considerable overlap exists among the various types of hunters. For example, although happy hunters hunt for pleasure, they often invoke utilitarian reasons for the hunt. Thus, Arrian, a devoted follower of Xenophon who similarly valued hunting as preparation for war, enthused over the glorious entertainment of hunting hares, advising against premature capture, which lessened hunting's value as amusement. "Cynegetica," in *Xenophon and Arrian: On Hunting with Hounds*, ed. and trans. A. A. Phillips and M. M. Willcock (Warminster, UK: Aris and Phillips, 1999), 109, 113–115. In a similar vein, anthropologist Richard Nelson contends that Eskimo and Athabaskan subsistence hunters also "experience great pleasure and

something akin to adventure—if not adventure itself—as an integral element of hunting." Quoted in "A Letter from Richard Nelson, February 5, 1991," in *For Love of the World: Essays on Nature Writers*, Sherman Paul (Iowa City: University of Iowa Press, 1992), 176. My notion of the holy hunter also has affinities with what I refer to here as the "erotic hunt." Finally, both the pleasurable aspect of hunting and its association with manliness can be discerned in all six types. Marti Kheel, "License to Kill: An Ecofeminist Critique of Hunters' Discourse," in *Animals and Women: Feminist Theoretical Explorations*, ed. Carol J. Adams and Josephine Donovan (Durham, N.C.: Duke University Press, 1995), 85–125.

10. See, for example, William S. Laughlin, "Hunting: An Integrating Biobehavior System and Its Evolutionary Importance" in *Man the Hunter*, ed. Richard B. Lee and Irven DeVore (Hawthorne, N.Y.: Aldine De Gruyter, 1987), 304–320.

11. Plutarch, *Moralia*, vol. 12, trans. Harold Cherniss and W. C. Helmbold (Cambridge, Mass.: Harvard University Press, 1957), 321–323.

12. *The Latin Epigrams of Thomas More*, ed. and trans. Leicester Bradner and Charles Arthur Lynch (Chicago: University of Chicago Press, 1953), 27. Quoted in Matt Cartmill, *A View to a Death in the Morning: Hunting and Nature Through History* (Cambridge, Mass.: Harvard University Press, 1993), 77.

13. Raymond A. Dart, "The Predatory Transition from Ape to Man," *International Anthropological Linguistic Review* 1, no. 4 (1953): 209.

14. Raymond A. Dart with Dennis Craig, *Adventures with the Missing Link* (Philadelphia: Institute Press, 1967), 195.

15. Dart, *Adventures with the Missing Link*, 195–202.

16. Dart, "Predatory Transition," 207–208.

17. Dart, *Adventures with the Missing Link*, 202.

18. See *African Genesis: A Personal Investigation into the Animal Origins and Nature of Man* (New York: Dell, 1961); *The Territorial Imperative: A Personal Inquiry into the Animal Origins of Property and Nations* (New York: Atheneum, 1966); *The Social Contract: A Personal Inquiry into the Evolutionary Sources of Order and Disorder* (New York: Atheneum, 1970); and *The Hunting Hypothesis: A Personal Conclusion Concerning the Evolutionary Nature of Man* (New York: Atheneum, 1976).

19. Ardrey, *Hunting Hypothesis*. See also Lee and DeVore, *Man the Hunter*. For more recent discussions of "the hunting hypothesis," see Cartmill, *View to a Death;* Charles Bergman, *Orion's Legacy: A Cultural History of Man as Hunter* (New York: Dutton, 1997); Andrée Collard with Joyce Contrucci, *Rape of the Wild: Man's Violence against Animals and the Earth* (Bloomington: Indiana University Press, 1989); and Donna Haraway, *Primate Visions: Gender, Race and Nature in the World of Modern Science* (New York: Routledge, 1989).

20. Ardrey, *African Genesis*, 188–189. As he elaborates, "If this continent had indeed been the cradle of humankind, and had I been the first man, then I should have been born in fear."

21. Ardrey, *African Genesis*, 322. For further discussion of the impact of Ardrey's African experience on the development of his hunting hypothesis, see Boyce Rensberger, "The Killer Ape Is Dead," *Alicia Patterson Foundation Reporter* 12, no. 8 (December 1973): 1–7.

22. Haraway, *Primate Visions*, 217. As Haraway points out, scientific investigation of the hunting hypothesis spanned numerous disciplines, including paleontology, physical anthropology, cultural anthropology, psychology, and primate studies. For a detailed discussion of the history of the hunting hypothesis, focusing on the influence of Sherwood L. Washburn's functionalist approach to hunting, see 186–230.

23. Sherwood L. Washburn and C. S. Lancaster, "The Evolution of Hunting," in Lee and DeVore, *Man the Hunter*, 293. According to the authors, the more specific benefits of hunting include the development of reason, tool use, planning, sharing, and cooperation among males. Hunting was also credited with enabling male hominids to provide for and protect females and their offspring, thereby establishing the heterosexual nuclear family.

24. Laughlin, "Hunting: An Integrating Biobehavior System," in Lee and DeVore, *Man the Hunter*, 304.

25. New research into the importance of women's gathering practices for human development also contributed to a reevaluation of the hunting hypothesis. Beginning in the 1970s, feminist anthropologists proposed a model of "Woman the Gatherer" to dislodge "Man the Hunter" from his supremacy. Research showed that gathering has typically provided 60–80 percent of sustenance, and that women's technological inventions for food procurement, processing, and storage were critically important cultural developments. Adrienne L. Zihlman and Nancy Tanner, "Gathering and Hominid Adaptation," in *Female Hierarchies*, ed. Lionel Tiger and Heather Fowler (Chicago: Beresford Book Service, 1978), 163–194; Adrienne L. Zihlman, "Women in Evolution, Part II: Subsistence and Social Organization among Early Hominids," *Signs* 4, no. 1 (1978): 4–20; Frances Dahlberg, ed., *Woman the Gatherer* (New Haven, Conn.: Yale University Press, 1981); Autumn Stanley, "Daughters of Isis, Daughters of Demeter: When Women Sowed and Reaped," in *Women, Technology and Innovation*, ed. Joan Rothschild (New York: Pergamon Press, 1982); Sally Slocum, "Woman the Gatherer: Male Bias in Anthropology," in *Toward an Anthropology of Women*, ed. Rayna R. Reiter (New York: Monthly Review Press, 1975), 36–50. As Lewis Mumford summarizes, "Human existence was founded from the beginning on a collecting economy—and for 95 per cent of man's [*sic*] existence . . . man was dependent upon food-gathering for his subsistence. It was under these conditions that his curiosity, his ingenuity, his mental grasp were put to work." Mumford, "Man the Finder," *Technology and Culture* 6, no. 3 (Summer 1965): 375–381.

26. C. K. Brain, *The Hunters or the Hunted? An Introduction to African Cave Taphonomy* (Chicago: University of Chicago Press, 1981), 269. Also see C. K. Brain, "New Finds at the Swartkrans Australopithecine Site," *Nature* 225 (March 21, 1970): 1112–1119.

27. C. K. Brain, *Hunters or the Hunted,* 273–274.

28. See E. S. Vrba, "Some Evidence of Chronology and Palaeoecology of Sterkfontein, Swartkrans, and Kromdraai from the Fossil Bovidae," *Nature* 254 (March 6, 1975): 301–304; Pat Shipman, "Scavenging or Hunting in Early Hominids: Theoretical Framework and Tests," *American Anthropologist* 88, no. 1 (1986): 27–43; Donna Hart and Robert W. Sussman, *Man the Hunted: Primates, Predators, and Human Evolution* (New York: Westview Press, 2005); Barbara Ehrenreich, *Blood Rites:*

*Origins and History of the Passions of War* (New York: Henry Holt, 1997); and Lewis Binford, "Human Ancestors: Changing Views of Their Behavior," *Journal of Anthropological Archaeology* 4, no. 4 (1985): 292–327.

29. Haraway, *Primate Visions*, 217.

30. Cartmill, *View to a Death*, 233. According to a national survey by the U.S. Department of the Interior, in 1991 only 1 percent of females in the U.S. population of those sixteen years and older "enjoyed hunting." Fish and Wildlife Service, U.S. Department of Interior, and Bureau of the Census, U.S. Department of Commerce, *1991 National Survey of Fishing and Hunting and Wildlife Associated Recreation* (Washington, D.C.: U.S. Government Printing Office, 1993). Studying 175 societies, G. P. Murdock concluded that in 97 percent of his samples, hunting was performed only by men, and in the remaining 3 percent it was primarily a male pursuit. In 93 percent of the hunting societies, fishing was also solely or primarily men's work. G. P. Murdock, "World Ethnographic Sample," *American Anthropologist* 59 (1957): 664–687; and G. P. Murdock, *Ethnographic Atlas: A Summary* (Pittsburgh: University of Pittsburgh Press, 1967). On the cross-cultural preponderance of men as hunters, also see David D. Gilmore, *Manhood in the Making: Cultural Concepts of Masculinity* (New Haven, Conn.: Yale University Press, 1990). For a critique of hunting as a male activity, see Mary Zeiss Stange, who contends that women are equally capable of violence, and that hunting empowers women by helping them to reclaim their natural aggression. Stange, *Woman the Hunter* (Boston: Beacon Press, 1988). For a critique of Stange's book, see Greta Gaard's review in *Environmental Ethics* 22, no. 2 (Summer 2002): 203–206.

31. I use the terms "recreational hunting" and "sport hunting" here interchangeably. Although the term "sport hunting" does not appear in the ancient world, a similar opposition to subsistence hunting was made. Judith Barringer argues that "sport hunting" is misleading with reference to ancient Greek hunting since "sport implies a competitive aspect, which is absent from Greek hunting, *unless one views the hunter and his prey as competitors*" (emphasis added). Barringer, *The Hunt in Ancient Greece* (Baltimore, Md.: Johns Hopkins University Press, 2002), 7. Hunting in the ancient world, however, *did* entail the idea of a contest with the animal, even if it is a peculiar type of "game" in which one player conscripts an opponent, whom he then tries to kill. The terms sport hunting and recreational hunting do not imply that other, subsidiary purposes were not served by hunting, including procurement of food. As classical archaeologist J. K. Anderson points out, if sport is conceived as physical activity undertaken only for amusement, few of the ancients would be classified as sport hunters. *Hunting in the Ancient World* (Berkeley: University of California Press, 1985), xii.

32. Donald G. Kyle, *Spectacles of Death in Ancient Rome* (New York: Routledge, 1998), 191.

33. Barringer, *Hunt in Ancient Greece*, 7.

34. The notion of a contest with a wild animal has been central to most conceptions of hunting. Cartmill defines hunting as "the deliberate, direct, violent killing of unrestrained wild animals." *View to a Death*, 30. By contrast, it is often maintained that domesticated animals are always used for sacrifices. As Jonathan Z. Smith states,

"*animal sacrifice appears to be, universally, the ritual killing of a domesticated animal by agrarian or pastoralist societies*" (original emphasis). Smith, "The Domestication of Sacrifice," in *Violent Origins: Walter Burkert, René Girard, and Jonathan Z. Smith on Ritual Killing and Cultural Formation*, ed. Robert G. Hamerton-Kelly (Stanford, Calif: Stanford University Press, 1987), 197. However, historian Richard Bulliet observes that, although infrequent, sacrifice of "wild" animals does occur. The Ainu of northern Japan, for example, sacrifice young bear cubs, who are easy to "feed and control until the day of the sacrifice." Bulliet, *Hunters, Herders, and Hamburgers: The Past and Future of Human–Animal Relationships* (New York: Columbia University Press, 2005), 26.

35. Bergman, *Orion's Legacy*, 78.

36. J. K. Anderson, *Hunting in the Ancient World* (Berkeley: University of California Press, 1985), 31.

37. Plato, *Laws,* vol. 2, trans. R. G. Bury (Cambridge, Mass.: Harvard University Press, 1952), 121.

38. *Laws: Plato*, trans. Benjamin Jowett (Amherst, N.Y.: Prometheus Books, 2000), 179.

39. For a discussion of the connection between hunting, war, and masculine identity, see Ehrenreich, *Blood Rites*; Collard with Contrucci, *Rape of the Wild*; and Leo Barudy, *From Chivalry to Terrorism: War and the Changing Nature of Masculinity* (New York: Vintage, 2005). Although hunting is often conceived as a war, as Matt Cartmill points out, "it is a strange sort of war, in which the only side that can win is careful not to do so." Since the hunter wants to continue his "game" he must be careful not to deplete his "stock." Cartmill also notes, "throughout European history, hunters have tended to see themselves as enemies of the individual animals but friends of the animal *kinds*—and by extension as friends of the wild, nonhuman realm that the animals inhabit." *View to a Death,* 31.

40. *Aristotle's Politics*, trans. Benjamin Jowett (New York: Oxford University Press, 1967), 40.

41. Anderson, *Hunting in the Ancient World*, 18.

42. Barringer, *Hunt in Ancient Greece*, 11. Barringer clarifies that she uses the term initiation to refer to "a maturation procedure not necessarily ritualized in a formal pubic presentation . . . whose completion is socially acknowledged in some way." As she points out, theorists such as Jeanmair and Brelich, and subsequently many others, argue that "all types of hunting . . . [are] initiatory in character." *Hunt in Ancient Greece,* 12–13, 6. See Henri Jeanmaire, *Couroi et Courètes*, reprint edition (New York: Arno Press, 1975); and Angelo Brelich, *Guerre, Agoni, e Culti Nella Grecia Arcaica* (Bonn: R. Habelt, 1961) and *Paides e Parthenoi* (Rome: Edizioni dell' Ateneo, 1969).

43. The mastery entailed in this form of hunt historically has been juxtaposed to the commonplace use of traps, snares, nets, pitfalls, etc. Richard D. Taber and Neil F. Payne, *Wildlife, Conservation, and Human Welfare: A United States and Canadian Perspective* (Malabar, Fla.: Krieger Publishing Company, 2003), 30.

44. Pierre Vidal-Naquet, *The Black Hunter: Forms of Thought and Forms of Society in the Ancient Greek World*, trans. Andrew Szegedy-Maszk (Baltimore, Md.: Johns

Hopkins University Press, 1986), 3. Vidal-Naquet suggests that the solitary hunt of the epic heroes represents an adolescent precursor to the more formalized adult hunts practiced in groups.

45. Bergman, *Orion's Legacy*, 101–102.

46. Vidal-Naquet suggests that the solitary hunt recorded in Greek epics is an analogue of actual initiatory hunts undertaken by young adolescent males. Known as the "black hunt," because it took place at night, this hunt employed a net. By contrast, the prototypical adult hunt, the Calydonian boar hunt, took place during the day and employed weapons. *Black Hunter*, 118.

47. Bergman, *Orion's Legacy*, 86, 118. While hunting is typically associated with manliness in the ancient world, the Dionysian myths of female maenads and the later myths of Artemis as hunter illustrate a reversal of this association. Judith Barringer points out that it is "critical" to understand the distinction between "actuality and representation" in Greek art. *The Hunt in Ancient Greece*, 3. This applies equally to Greek myths and legends. There is no evidence that women hunted in the ancient world.

48. For further discussion of the relation between metaphor and hunting, see Bergman, *Orion's Legacy*, and Cartmill, *View to a Death*.

49. Bergman, *Orion's Legacy*, 175. For a history of hunting in the Middle Ages, also see Marcelle Thiébaux, *The Stag of Love: The Chase in Medieval Literature* (Ithaca, N.Y.: Cornell University Press, 1974), and Cartmill, *View to a Death*.

50. I use the pronoun "he" since myths most often portrayed a male pursuing a female. Homosexual pursuits are also found in myth and literature (female to female and male to male), but female pursuit of males was rare and inevitably followed by disastrous consequences. Barringer, *Hunt in Ancient Greece*, 127.

51. Thiébaux, *Stag of Love*, 93.

52. Bergman, *Orion's Legacy,* 129.

53. Claude Orrieux and Pauline Schmitt Pantel, *A History of Ancient Greece*, trans. Janet Lloyd (Malden, Mass.: Blackwell Publishing, 2006), 105.

54. *The American Heritage Dictionary of the English Language*, 4th ed., s.vv. "venison," "venery."

55. Bergman, *Orion's Legacy*, 129.

56. Bergman, *Orion's Legacy*, 113.

57. Bergman, *Orion's Legacy*, 114.

58. Bergman, *Orion's Legacy*, 102.

59. George Reiger, "Hunting and Trapping in the New World" in *Wildlife and America*, ed. Howard P. Brokaw (Washington, D.C.: Council on Environmental Equality, 1978), 42.

60. Gary G. Gray, *Wildlife and People* (Chicago: University of Illinois, 1993), 153.

61. The notion that drawing the first blood marks ownership of other-than-human animals bears a striking resemblance to the idea of marriage rights. Deflowering the bride and drawing the "first blood" has often been viewed as a symbol of ownership by a husband over his bride. Just as priests and royalty have historically enjoyed rights to draw blood (in sacrifice or hunting, respectively) so, too, royalty has been accorded the privilege to deflower brides. In ancient Ireland, the king not only had a right but a duty to deflower brides before handing them over to their husbands. See Joseph Lewis, *The Ten Commandments* (New York: Freethought Press Association, 1946).

62. Thomas R. Dunlap, "Sport Hunting and Conservation, 1880–1920," *Environmental Review* 12 (Spring 1988): 52.

63. Daniel Justin Herman points out that in the seventeenth century, less than one percent of the English population was allowed to hunt. Given the lack of experience, he argues that it is not surprising hunting did not become a primary mode of subsistence for New World colonists. Daniel Justin Herman, *Hunting and the American Imagination* (Washington, D.C.: Smithsonian Institution Press, 2001), 32.

64. Carolyn Merchant, *Reinventing Eden: The Fate of Nature in Western Culture* (New York: Routledge, 2004), 117. See also Annette Kolodny, *The Lay of the Land: Metaphor as Experience and History in American Life and Letters* (Chapel Hill: University of North Carolina Press, 1984).

65. According to the historian Thomas Babington Macaulay, Puritan qualms about hunting did not derive from compassion for animals but from concern over the excitement to the "passions" that this violent sport produced. Quoted in Keith Thomas, *Man and the Natural World: A History of the Modern Sensibility* (New York: Pantheon Books, 1983), 157. Thomas suggests that part of the reason for this aversion to blood sports was the belief that experiencing pleasure through the infliction of violence reduced one to the level of "beasts." The Puritans believed that the violence found in the natural world was a result of the Fall and evidence of "man's" sin. It should therefore be viewed as lamentable, not as a source of enjoyment. Although sex and hunting were viewed as necessary activities, they were best performed without exciting the "animal passions" and by focusing on the purpose for which they were performed, namely, procreation and procurement of flesh.

66. Frank Forester, *The Complete Manual for Young Sportsmen* (New York: Stringer and Townsend, 1856), 359.

67. Historians disagree on the extent of hunters' influence. John Reiger goes so far as to argue that hunters "spearheaded the early conservation movement." Reiger, *American Sportsmen and the Origin of Conservation*, rev. ed. (Norman: University of Oklahoma Press, 1986), 54. James A. Tober states that "the most significant force behind the passage of game legislation in the nineteenth century was exerted by sportsmen." Tober, *Who Owns the Wildlife: The Political Economy of Conservation in Nineteenth Century America* (Westport, Conn.: Greenwood Press, 1981), 181. In contrast, Samuel P. Hays argues that the conservation movement was a scientific movement whose leaders sprang from "such fields as hydrology, forestry, agrostology, geology, and anthropology." Hays contends that these scientists envisaged "a political system guided by the ideal of efficiency and dominated by technicians who could best determine how to achieve it." Hays, *Conservation and the Gospel of Efficiency: The Progressive Conservation Movement, 1890–1920* (Cambridge, Mass.: Harvard University Press, 1959), 2–3. Still other historians contend that since most adult men of that period were hunters, it is difficult to evaluate their direct influence as a group. See Alfred Runte's review of Reiger's *American Sportsmen and the Origins of Conservation* in *Journal of Forest History* 20 (April 1976): 100–101, and Dunlap, "Sport Hunting and Conservation." For Reiger's response, see *Environmental Journal* 12 (Fall 1988): 94–96.

68. William T. Hornaday, *Our Vanishing Wild Life: Its Extermination and Preservation* (New York: Charles Scribner's Sons, 1913), 54.

69. Hornaday, *Our Vanishing Wild Life*, 101, 94.

70. Hornaday, *Our Vanishing Wild Life*, 54.

71. Nicolas W. Proctor, *Bathed in Blood: Hunting and Mastery in the Old South* (Charlottesville: University of Virginia Press, 2002).

72. Proctor, *Bathed in Blood*, 61.

73. George Bird Grinnell, "The Book of the Boone and Crockett Club," *Forest and Stream* 30 (March 1888): 124, quoted in Reiger, *American Sportsmen*, 119.

74. Reiger, *American Sportsmen*, 29.

75. Herman, *Hunting and the American Imagination*, 6.

76. John MacKenzie, *The Empire of Nature: Hunting, Conservation and British Imperialism* (Manchester, UK: Manchester University Press, 1988), 22.

77. The contrast between the resource-based conservation philosophy and the aesthetic-based preservationist philosophy has been characterized in a number of other terms, for example, anthropocentric/nonanthropocentric and consumptive/nonconsumptive. See Roderick Nash, *Wilderness and the American Mind*, rev. ed. (New Haven, Conn.: Yale University Press, 1978).

78. Samuel P. Hays, *Conservation and the Gospel of Efficiency: The Progressive Conservation Movement, 1890–1920* (Cambridge, Mass.: Harvard University Press, 1959), 2.

79. Gifford Pinchot, quoted in Frank Graham Jr., *Man's Dominion: The Story of Conservation in America* (New York: M. Evans, 1971), 109.

80. John Muir, "Wild Wool," in *Wilderness Essays*, ed. Frank Buske (Salt Lake City, Utah: Peregrine Smith, 1980), 236.

81. Albert B. Hart and Herbert Ferleger, eds., *Theodore Roosevelt Cyclopedia* (New York: Roosevelt Memorial Association, 1941), 104.

82. Hart and Ferleger, *Theodore Roosevelt Cyclopedia*, 650.

83. John Muir, *The Yosemite* (San Francisco: Sierra Club, 1912), 192.

84. Even John Muir acquiesced in this linear vision of progress: "I suppose we need not go mourning the buffaloes. In the nature of things they had to give place to better cattle, though the change might have been made without barbarous wickedness." Muir, *Our National Parks* (Boston: Houghton Mifflin, 1901), 335, 364.

85. For a detailed discussion of the complex motives of the early preservationists, see Andrew C. Isenberg's analysis, which challenges the perception of preservationists as the "antithesis of resource exploitation." Isenberg, *The Destruction of the Bison: An Environmental History, 1750–1920* (Cambridge: Cambridge University Press, 2000).

86. Isenberg, *Destruction of the Bison*, 194.

87. Isenberg, *Destruction of the Bison*, 167.

88. John Muir is a partial exception to the above generalization. Muir argued for the importance of every individual being in nature. He also denounced hunting. However, as mentioned previously, Muir shared the common disdain among conservationists and preservationists for "tamed" animals.

89. Sarah Lucia Hoagland, *Lesbian Ethics: Toward New Values* (Palo Alto, Calif.: Institute of Lesbian Studies, 1989), 248.

90. Lisa Mighetto, *Wild Animals and American Environmental Ethics* (Tucson: University of Arizona Press, 1991), 42.

91. On the influence of pain on attitudes toward animals, see James Turner, *Reckoning with the Beast: Animals, Pain, and Humanity in the Victorian Mind* (Baltimore, Md.: Johns Hopkins University Press, 1980).

92. According to Sydney Coleman, women made up such a large part of the humane movement that "were the support of the women of America suddenly withdrawn, the large majority of societies for the prevention of cruelty to children and animals would cease to exist." Sydney Coleman, *Humane Society Leaders in America* (Albany, N.Y.: American Humane Association, 1924), 178.

93. Isenberg, *Destruction of the Bison*, 144.

94. Isenberg, *Destruction of the Bison*, 174. On the crucial contribution made by women to the conservation movement, see Carolyn Merchant, "The Women of the Progressive Conservation Crusade: 1900–1915," in *Environmental History: Critical Issues in Comparative Perspective*, ed. Kendall E. Bailes (Lanham, Md.: University Press of America, 1985), 153–170; Vera Norwood, *Made from This Earth: American Women and Nature* (Chapel Hill: University of North Carolina Press, 1993); and Glenda Riley, *Women and Nature: Saving the 'Wild' West* (Lincoln: University of Nebraska Press, 1999). As Riley sums up, "Clearly, women's efforts played a critical role in the conservation movement's development, as well as in the emergence of ecological awareness in the United States. From parlor to politics, conservation-minded women urged and lived environmentalism. In truth, women's efforts made it possible for such political leaders as Gifford Pinchot and Theodore Roosevelt to obtain the programs they sought." From "'Wimmin is Everywhere': Conserving and Feminizing Western Landscapes, 1870 to 1940," *Western Historical Quarterly* 29 (Spring 1998): 23.

95. Michael Kimmel, *Manhood in America: A Cultural History* (New York: Free Press, 1996), 121.

96. Kimmel, *Manhood in America*, 83–87.

97. Anthony Rotundo, "Learning About Manhood: Gender Ideals and the Middle-Class Family in Nineteenth-Century America," in *Manliness and Morality: Middle-Class Masculinity in Britain and America, 1800–1940*, ed. J. A. Mangan and James Walvin (New York: Saint Martin's Press, 1987), 35–51.

98. Jody Emel, "Are You Man Enough, Big and Bad Enough? Wolf Eradication in the US," in *Animal Geographies: Place, Politics, and Identity in the Nature-Culture Borderlands*, ed. Jennifer Wolch and Jody Emel (New York: Verso, 1998), 80.

99. Tom Lutz, *American Nervousness, 1903: An Anecdotal History* (Ithaca, N.Y.: Cornell University Press, 1992), 3–6. For early works on the neurasthenia, see neurologist George Miller Beard, *American Nervousness: Its Causes and Consequences* (New York: G. P. Putnam's Sons, 1881) and *A Practical Treatise on Nervous Exhaustion (Neurasthenia), Its Symptoms, Nature, Sequences, Treatment* (New York: William Wood, 1879).

100. Lutz, *American Nervousness*, 3.

101. Lutz, *American Nervousness*, 3–4.

102. Lutz, *American Nervousness*, 32–34. For representative advice to neurasthenic women, see Silas Weir Mitchell, *Fat and Blood and How to Make Them* (Philadelphia: J. B. Lippincott, 1878).

103. For typical recommendations for neurasthenic men, see Silas Weir Mitchell, *Camp Cure* (Philadelphia: J. B. Lippincott, 1877). For contemporary works on neurasthenia, see Anita Clair Fellman and Michael Fellman, *Making Sense of Self: Medical Advice Literature in Late Nineteenth Century America* (Philadelphia: University of Pennsylvania Press, 1981); George F. Drinka, *The Birth of Neurosis: Myth, Malady, and the Victorians* (New York: Simon and Schuster, 1984); Marijke Gijswijt-Hofstra and Roy Porter, eds. *Cultures of Neurasthenia from Beard to the First World War* (Amsterdam: Rodopi, 2001); and Barbara Will, "The Nervous Origins of the American Western," *American Literature* 70, no. 2 (1998): 293–316.

104. Gail Bederman, *Manliness and Civilization: A Cultural History of Gender and Race in the United States, 1880–1917* (Chicago: University of Chicago Press, 1995), 18.

105. Bederman, *Manliness and Civilization*, 18–19. Bederman states that "until 1890, literate Victorians rarely referred to individual men as 'masculine.'" After 1890, both "manliness" and "masculine" were used, although the noun "masculinity" was still rare in the 1890s.

106. Robert Baden-Powell, *Scouting for Boys: A Handbook for Instruction in Good Citizenship*, reprint of original 1908 edition (New York: Oxford University Press, 2004), 11, quoted in Michael Rosenthal, *The Character Factory: Baden-Powell and the Origins of the Boy Scout Movement* (New York: Pantheon Books, 1986), 128.

107. Rosenthal, *Character Factory*, 169.

108. Although Darwin's evolutionary philosophy was based upon the notion of random variations and adaptive fitness, not linear progression, *The Descent of Man* was interpreted as "the ascent of man."

109. Peter P. Matthiessen, *Wildlife in America* (New York: Viking, 1987), 178.

110. Mighetto, *Wild Animals*, 33.

111. Theodore Roosevelt, *Hunting the Grisly and Other Sketches* (Boston: Elibron Classics, 2000), 115.

112. Mighetto, *Wild Animals*, 37.

113. The feminist philosopher Donna Haraway argues that Roosevelt's childhood proclivity for collecting dead bodies expressed an early manifestation of a patriarchal orientation toward objectification and killing. Haraway, "Teddy Bear Patriarchy: Taxidermy in the Garden of Eden, New York City, 1908–1936," in *Primate Visions: Gender, Race and Nature in the World of Modern Science* (New York: Routledge, 1989), 26–58.

114. For an in-depth discussion of the connection between masculinity, adventure, play, and violence, see Martin Green, *The Adventurous Male: Chapters in the History of the White Male Mind* (University Park: Pennsylvania State University Press, 1993).

115. William Davidson Johnson, *T. R.: Champion of the Strenuous Life: A Photographic Biography of Theodore Roosevelt* (New York: Theodore Roosevelt Association, 1958), 138. John Muir once posed the question, "'Mr. Roosevelt, when are you

going to get beyond the boyishness of killing things . . . are you not getting far enough along to leave that off?' Taken aback, the President replied, 'Muir, I guess you are right.'" Quoted in Nash, *Wilderness and the American Mind*, 139.

116. Detailed descriptions of Roosevelt's hunting expeditions can be found in his nature trilogy, first published between 1885 and 1893. Theodore Roosevelt, *Hunting Trips of a Ranchman: Hunting Trips on the Prairie and in the Mountains* (New York: G. P. Putnam's Sons, 1885); *Ranch Life and the Hunting-Trail*, New York: Century Co., 1900; and *The Wilderness Hunter: An Account of the Big Game of the United States and Its Chase with Horse, Hound and Rifle* (New York: G. P. Putnam's Sons, 1893).

117. Xenophon, "Cynegeticus," in *Scripta Minora,* trans. E. C. Marchant (Cambridge, Mass.: Harvard University Press, 1968), 443, 445, quoted in Cartmill, *View to a Death,* 31.

118. MacKenzie, *Empire of Nature,* 304.

119. MacKenzie, *Empire of Nature*, 300.

120. Hart and Ferleger, *Theodore Roosevelt Cyclopedia*, 237.

121. Baden-Powell, *Scouting for Boys* (New York: Oxford University Press, 2004), 104.

122. José Ortega y Gasset, *Meditations on Hunting*, trans. Howard B. Wescott (New York: Charles Scribner's Sons, 1972), 96–97.

123. Michael Pollan, *The Omnivore's Dilemma: A Natural History of Four Meals* (New York: Penguin Press, 2006), 349.

124. On the link between hunting and sexuality, see Collard with Contrucci, *Rape of the Wild*; Brian Luke, "Violent Love, Heterosexuality and the Erotics of Men's Predation," *Feminist Studies* 24, no. 3 (1998): 627–655, and *Brutal: Manhood and the Exploitation of Animals* (Chicago: University of Chicago Press, 2007), 81-108; and Marti Kheel, "The Killing Game: An Ecofeminist Critique of Hunting," *Journal of the Philosophy of Sport* 23, no. 1 (May 1996): 38–40.

125. For further discussion of violence and adventure as a contrast to work, see Georges Bataille, *Erotism: Death and Sensuality*, trans. Mary Dalwood (San Francisco: City Lights Books, 1986). Bataille argues that ritual violence occurs in a liminal realm in which repressed or "wild" drives are permitted temporary expression.

126. Hart and Ferleger, *Theodore Roosevelt Cyclopedia,* 394.

127. Roosevelt, *The Winning of the West* (New York: G. P. Putnam's Sons, 1907), 147–148.

128. Carolyn E. Thomas, *Sport in a Philosophic Context* (Philadelphia: Lea and Febiger, 1983), 18.

129. Janet Lever, "Sex Differences in the Complexity of Children's Play and Games," *American Sociological Review* 43, no. 4 (1978): 481.

130. Johnson, *T. R.,* 209.

131. MacKenzie, *Empire of Nature*, 11.

132. Green, *Adventurous Male*, 68.

133. Roosevelt, *Ranch Life and the Hunting-Trail*, 83.

134. Roosevelt, *Ranch Life and the Hunting-Trail*, 56.

135. Johnson, *T. R.*, 209.

136. The term "Rough Riders," originally "skilled horsemen," was later applied to American troops in the Spanish-American war. Roosevelt, however, disavowed the theatrical origin of the term, claiming that it was spontaneously applied by U.S. citizens. Richard Slotkin, *Gunfighter Nation: The Myth of the Frontier in Twentieth-Century America* (Norman: University of Oklahoma Press, 1998), 83.

137. Slotkin, *Gunfighter Nation*, 83.

138. Ralph H. Lutts, ed., *The Wild Animal Story* (Philadelphia: Temple University Press, 1998), 1–3.

139. Lutts, *Wild Animal Story*, 1.

140. Edward B. Clark, "Roosevelt on the Nature Fakirs," *Everybody's Nature Magazine* 16 (June 1907): 770–774, quoted in Lutts, *Wild Animal Story*, 166.

141. William J. Long, "The Modern School of Nature-Study and Its Critics," *North American Review* 176 (May 1903): 687–696, quoted in Lutts, *Wild Animal Story*, 146–147.

142. Lutts, *Wild Animal Story*, 147–148.

143. Lutts, *Wild Animal Story*, 148.

144. Charles G. D. Roberts, *The Kindred of the Wild: A Book of Animal Life* (Boston: L.C. Page and Company, 1907), 2.

145. Lutts, *Wild Animal Story*, 29.

146. Quoted in Ralph H. Lutts, *The Nature Fakers* (Golden, Colo.: Fulcrum Publishing, 1990), 151.

147. From Long's "Brier-Patch Philosophy," quoted in Lutts, *Nature Fakers*, 148.

148. Ernest Thompson Seton, "Note to the Reader," in Lutts, *Nature Fakers*, 13.

149. Lutts, *Nature Fakers*, x.

# 4

## Thinking Like a Mountain or Thinking Like a "Man"?

> We abuse land because we regard it as a commodity belonging to us. When we see land as a community to which we belong, we may begin to use it with love and respect.
>
> Aldo Leopold
> *A Sand County Almanac and Sketches Here and There* (p. viii)

> Just short of the top I suddenly saw a large buck in a pine thicket about 50 yards up the hill, looking me over. I moved to avoid a bush, drew to the barb at point blank, and let fly. The unmistakable thud of the arrow striking flesh told me that I had hit.
>
> Aldo Leopold
> *Round River: From the Journals of Aldo Leopold* (p. 101)

### INTRODUCTION

Aldo Leopold has been hailed as the founding "father" of environmental ethics[1] and as a "prophetic" voice for a radically transformed orientation toward the natural world.[2] His famous book, *A Sand County Almanac*, first published in 1949, has sold over a million copies and is considered by many to be the bible of the environmental movement.[3] His praises are sung in Earth First! journals, hunting magazines, conservation textbooks, and books on environmental philosophy. The new *ecocentric* worldview that he espoused portrayed humans not as conquerors of the natural world, but as citizens of a biotic community that was deserving of love and respect.

In this chapter, I reassess the widespread view of Leopold. Did his ecocentric ethic demonstrate a genuine love and respect for *all* of life, or was Leopold's reverence reserved only for the larger biotic "whole" and the experiences that it produced? And did his philosophy represent a substantive break with the earlier ideas of the conservation movement, or, as I propose, was it merely a different manifestation of the masculinist orientation? In answering these questions, I argue that Leopold's lifelong love of hunting, with its masculine allure, was not incidental to his philosophy, but rather foundational to it.

## LEOPOLD'S EARLY YEARS

Aldo Leopold's environmental writings span the first half of the twentieth century and reflect his own intellectual development, as well as the historical changes that were occurring during his lifetime. Educated at the Forest School of Yale University, Leopold was deeply influenced by Gifford Pinchot, first chief of the U.S. Forest Service, whose remorseful timber baron father had endowed the new forestry school. Upon graduation in 1909, in the aftermath of Theodore Roosevelt's sweeping legislative changes increasing the regulatory power of the government, Leopold joined the Forest Service. He held various positions until 1928, actively advocating for reform in the areas of wilderness protection, "game management," and soil erosion. In 1933 he became chair of the nation's first game management department at the University of Wisconsin, where he taught until his death in 1948.

In his early years, Leopold espoused the prevailing utilitarian philosophy among conservationists: maximum production of "resources" to yield the most happiness for the greatest number of humans. In contrast to *preservationists*, who sought to minimize human impact on land, the Pinchot-inspired conservationists sought to produce as much lumber as possible, without endangering future supplies.[4]

The model of resource efficiency inspired the establishment of the first United States department of natural resources, the Division of Forestry. Reflecting the utilitarian approach, the department was placed under the jurisdiction of the Agriculture Department. It was this agricultural model of resource extraction and production that inspired Leopold's ideas about regulating another "resource": game.

Managing "game" for increased "production" of deer was commonplace in Leopold's day. What distinguished his early philosophy was the development of this notion into a rigorous science. According to the novelist and historian Wallace Stegner, Leopold was not one of those "throbbing nature lovers who, as he said, write bad verse on birchbark. He was a scientist, one of the first to profess the new science of ecology."[5] One of the major goals of this new discipline was the production of "game" for hunters' maximum enjoyment.

The prevailing attitude among conservationists was that predators were "varmints" or "vermin" that needed to be exterminated in order to produce more deer for sport hunting and public enjoyment. Leopold viewed predators as impediments to this utilitarian objective. As the young Leopold commented, there could be enough "for sportsmen or for varmints, but not enough for both."[6] His advocacy for wilderness areas inhabited by native animals did not extend to large predators. Summarizing the current attitude of the day, Leopold commented, "Predatory animals are the common enemy of both the stockman and the conservationist."[7] As the historian Susan Flader observes, "He possibly did not think of *varmints* as wildlife, much less as game."[8] Leopold himself later reflected, "I personally believed, at least in 1914 when predator control began, that there could not be too much horned game, and that the extirpation of predators was a reasonable price to pay for better big game hunting."[9]

Influenced by years in the Forest Service, Leopold came to believe that the same agricultural principles used to manage forests could be applied to the management of "game" animals. Summarizing successful conservation principles, Leopold maintained that game was to be a "major forest product."[10] Having defined animals as a crop, the "all-important question" for Leopold was "how to grow it."[11] Restrictions and protections for game animals by means of laws, refuges, and predator control, although valuable, were insufficient. This strategy of constraints, according to Leopold, needed to be supplemented by a policy of replenishment. Just as the Forest Service regarded timber as a renewable resource that could be managed to produce harvests on a sustained yield basis, Leopold argued that "wild" deer, like crops, could be similarly sustainably "harvested." As Susan Flader points out, Leopold compared

> protection against predatory animals and illegal kill to fire protection and timber trespass cases, breeding stock to growing stock, hunting demand to timber market, limitation of kill to limitation of cut, game laws and license fees to sale contracts and stumpage rates, natural increase and artificial restocking to natural reproduction and planting, and so on.[12]

The Department of Game Management, according to this model, should determine the carrying capacity of a designated area and calculate the quantity of deers that could be produced and harvested in a given range.[13]

In the early decades of the twentieth century, Leopold's advocacy for the establishment of refuges was also founded upon the agricultural paradigm. Today he is widely praised for having established the Gila refuge, one of the first wilderness preserves. But it is important to understand that a major motive for the preservation of this and other reserves was to create well-stocked hunting grounds. The game refuge, as he conceived it, was to be not so much a place for the protection of animals from hunters, but rather a breeding ground for producing an outflow of game for sport hunting. This was to be accomplished through the provision of food, plants, water, fences, and salt in carefully demarcated boundaries, which were established in such a way that the surplus "stock" would wander onto the hunting grounds that surrounded the refuges.[14] It was also to be free of "vermin."

Sport hunting was central to Leopold's ideas about game management and wilderness. Leopold viewed Park Service land, where hunting was prohibited, as a place where people came for the superficial experience of viewing pretty scenery. By contrast, he envisioned the national forests as recreational "play-grounds" or "shooting grounds" where all men could re-create the wilderness experience.[15] In describing his democratic goal for the creation of wilderness areas in the Southwest, he asserted his hope of establishing the last free "wilderness hunting ground" in the nation."[16] As Callicott notes, Leopold hoped to "preserve a few relics of the American frontier in which he and like-minded sportsmen might play at being pioneers."[17] Reflecting this perspective, one of his suggestions for a name for the Gila Wilderness Area was the "Gila National Hunting Ground."

## THINKING LIKE A MOUNTAIN OR THINKING LIKE A "MAN"

It is often maintained that Leopold had an early conversion experience which profoundly altered his attitudes toward hunting and predators. This belief is founded upon Leopold's account of an incident that occurred during a hunting expedition in the American Southwest. In a well-known essay entitled "Thinking like a Mountain," he described his encounter with a mother wolf at play with her grown pups. In his youthful exuberance, Leopold and his hunting companions shot randomly, wounding one pup and the mother wolf. As the mother wolf lay dying, she reached out for his rifle in a last act of defiance.[18] At that moment, Leopold writes that he had a sudden revelation:

> We reached the old wolf in time to watch a fierce green fire dying in her eyes. I realized then, and have known ever since, that there was something new to me in those eyes—something known only to her and to the mountain. I was young

then, and full of trigger itch; I thought that because fewer wolves meant more deer, that no wolves would mean hunter's paradise. But after seeing the green fire die, I sensed that neither the wolf nor the mountain agreed with such a view.[19]

Like the biblical story of Saint Paul's sudden conversion to Christianity, Leopold's hunting experience is often portrayed as an epiphanic "conversion" to ecological thought. Reflecting a common perception, Stephan Harding writes, "For Leopold, the experience was of sufficient intensity to trigger a total re-orientation in his life's work as a wildlife manager and ecologist."[20] And as Ruth Rosenhek writes, after this incident, "the 'hunter' was transformed to 'naturalist.'"[21]

These accounts of Leopold's transformation might give the impression that after that fateful day, Leopold laid down his rifle and never hunted again. The change in Leopold's thought, however, did not occur as an immediate metamorphosis, but rather as a slow evolution; moreover, the change in his attitude did not extend to all animals, but only toward predators. What Leopold fails to mention is that the event in question occurred some thirty years before he wrote about it, and that he continued to hunt for the rest of his life.[22]

Leopold goes on to describe his new attitude toward predators in what was to become a classic statement: "The cowman who cleans his range of wolves does not realize that he is taking over the wolf's job of trimming the herd to fit the range. He has not learned to think like a mountain. Hence we have dustbowls, and rivers washing the future into the sea." Leopold concludes, "I now suspect that just as a deer herd lives in mortal fear of its wolves, so does a mountain live in mortal fear of its deer."[23]

Nonetheless, Leopold continued to campaign vigorously against predators for many more years. According to Leopold's biographer Curt Meine, it was not until 1925, some sixteen years after his encounter with the dying wolf, that Leopold began to tentatively question his belief that the only good predator was a dead one, and even then he continued to refer to large predators as "vermin." Leopold's utilitarian focus on the production of "game" animals also persisted. As Meine comments, Leopold "would not rush to conversion."[24] As late as 1933 he wrote in his classic work on wildlife ecology and game management, "Game management is the art of making land produce sustained annual crops of wild game for recreational use."[25] And in 1934 he wrote in his submission to the Wisconsin regional plan report that the "acid test of the sufficiency of a conservation system" is the "production of a shootable surplus."[26]

Why then did Leopold use the story about hunting the wolves to imply a shift in his attitude? Historically, the narrative structure of "The Hunt" has lent itself to stories and myths of a journey into the wilderness, culminating in a dramatic confrontation.[27] In many cultures hunting stories serve as coming-of-age allegories. Typically, the death of the animal symbolizes the metaphorical annihilation of the young man, paving the way for rebirth into a mature identity, separate from the female world.[28] In a similar manner, hunting functions in Leopold's narrative as a death and rebirth into a new, mature philosophy. The "death" of his previous ego-centered worldview gives way to a broader regard for the ecological community. The actual death of the individual wolf is reduced to a psychological prop, a vehicle for the birth of his ecological philosophy.

The development of Leopold's ecological worldview, however, was far less dramatic than his hunting story suggests. His ecological awareness evolved over the course of many years, as he witnessed the failures of the predator control policies.[29] The real watershed events that appear to have influenced Leopold's final transition toward an ecological worldview took place more than twenty-five years after the death of the wolf.

In 1935 he went to Germany, where he saw the devastating impact of forest over-management. Lamenting the consequences of German "cubistic forestry," he noted that trees had been aligned in parallel rows, and creeks and rivulets had been straightened. An overpopulation of deers, caused by the "near extirpation of predators," had created additional degradation to the land.[30] As Leopold noted, "to the critical eye, there is something lacking," namely "wildness."[31] In 1936 and 1937 Leopold traveled to the Rio Gavilan region of Mexico. There he had the opportunity to see an ecologically intact landscape as yet undisturbed by human manipulation. Leopold was already familiar with the ecological problems produced by over-logging and overgrazing in the American Southwest. It was in light of these successes and failures in conservation management that Leopold's attitudes about predators and conservation practices gradually evolved. As Susan Flader points out in her detailed analysis of Leopold's changing attitudes toward predators, the impetus for his change in views emerged from practical considerations about the vital role of predators, not ethical concerns about their individual well-being.[32]

Nonetheless, the myth that Leopold underwent a dramatic transformation as a consequence of the hunting incident persists. Leopold's story has been interpreted as a confession of sin, followed by repentance and the adoption of a new faith. A number of Earth First! activists have made a moral fable of Leopold's hunting story, suggesting in their road shows and wilderness gatherings that the wolf calls out to humans to repent for their destructive activities and defend the Earth.[33] These followers of Leopold see in his story the intimation of a communication with wolves. What they fail to notice, however, is that Leopold assumes the perspective of the *mountain*, not that of the wolf. The lesson that Leopold learns from the hunting incident is neither empathy with the mother wolf nor compassion for the orphaned pups, but rather one about the importance of an ethic that transcends the individual inhabitants of the mountain community.

If Leopold, in fact, felt remorse for the death of the wolf that he killed in his youthful exuberance, he does not reveal it in his account. What emerges first and foremost in this oft-quoted essay is a concern for the prospect of a world devoid of the *species* "wolf." Although the hunting story hints at feelings of regret for killing the wolf, the lesson that Leopold draws from the incident is of a more detached, scientific nature.

In the latter part of "Thinking like a Mountain," Leopold describes his transformed worldview, using the image of a mountain to suggest an "objective" understanding. From the mountain's perspective, predators, such as wolves, are of vital importance for preventing overpopulation of deer. As he states poetically, "Only the mountain has lived long enough to listen *objectively* to the howl of the wolf" (emphasis added).[34] Although Leopold's use of poetic imagery implies an empathic connection with nature, once again a careful reading suggests another interpretation. Leopold does not call for an empathic identification with the wolf, but rather for an objective, long-range, species-based evolutionary view, which only the mountain can metaphorically "understand." He does not encourage the reader to *feel like* the wolf, or to *feel with* the wolf, but rather to *think like* a mountain. The pivotal message of the essay is not a plea for compassion for nature and, in particular, wolves, but rather a call for a more impartial ethic, symbolized by the mountain.

Leopold's imagery of mountains suggests a spiritual theme. Mountains are often used to reflect the religious motif of otherworldly transcendence.[35] From the apex of the mountain, one can look down upon all of creation with a God's-eye view of the earth. And from the earth, one can look toward the heavens and contemplate the soul's ascent. Both vantage points suggest the theme of transcendence that encompasses a greater "whole." Leopold uses the term "mountain" as synonymous with range, symbolizing the whole earth community. He might have called his essay "Thinking like a Range," or "Thinking like a Valley." However, these ecological communities did not lend themselves to his transcendent vision.

Leopold's exhortations about the importance of assuming the transcendent perspective suggests a parallel with the Jewish and Christian traditions' mandate to worship the Creator rather than the Creation. According to this directive, God is seen as the source of all life, so God should be worshipped rather than God's creations. Similarly, Leopold elevated the ecosystem over and above the individual inhabitants of the land, which he saw as its products.

Leopold's killing of the wolf also suggests another spiritual theme: animal sacrifice. As previously discussed, Nancy Jay argues that ritual sacrifice, which is universally performed by men, seeks to replicate the birthing process on a purportedly superior, spiritual plane. Men seek to transcend their own mortality through the act of killing, claiming allegiance to a timeless patrilineal brotherhood that connects them to past and future generations of men. Similarly, Leopold's killing of the wolf gives birth to a worldview that forges a cross-generational link with past and future generations of men, symbolized by the mountain.

The story behind the publication of Leopold's *A Sand County Almanac* provides insight into his beliefs about the process of developing ecological wisdom. The book was originally conceived as a series of thirteen topical essays to provide a forum for "ecological preachment." A former student and the prospective publishers of his book influenced him, however, to insert himself into his writings by adding personal anecdotes. The student suggested that Leopold's argument would be more powerful if he showed through personal narrative how his own attitude had changed. Leopold finally accepted the narrative approach after the publishing company Knopf rejected his book, urging him to use more narrative and less preaching.[36]

The final version was divided into three sections. The book began with personal stories, many about hunting in various seasons at his family retreat, a "shack" in "Sand" (actually Sauk) County. The second section contained discursive essays, set in various parts of North America. The final section was composed of four didactic pieces of a more personal nature on conservation, wildlife, and wilderness. Leopold originally intended "The Land Ethic" to be the first of the four final essays that would set forth his principles, from which the other essays were to follow. The editors who assembled the book posthumously, however, chose a more inductive approach. They placed "The Land Ethic" at the end, thereby giving the impression that his ecocentric worldview developed from his personal experiences. The repositioning of the essays also changed the final sentence of the book, which was to have been, "It is only the scholar who understands why the raw wilderness gives definition and meaning to the human enterprise."[37]

Leopold's preferred order for the chapters and his comments on the scholar suggest that he believed moral conduct toward nature emerged not from personal experience but from a conceptual understanding of one's environmental origins. As he explains, the scholar "appreciates that all history consists of successive excursions from a single starting point, to which man returns again and again to organize yet another search for a durable scale of values."[38] This "starting point," according to Leopold, was found in raw wilderness. It is out of this cognitive perspective that the land ethic emerges.

## THE HOLE IN LEOPOLD'S HOLISM

Leopold is frequently praised as the first environmental philosopher to argue for the "biotic rights" of all life. Most of these accolades, however, ignore his lifelong penchant for hunting. The discrepancy between Leopold's stated beliefs and his actions raises the question, to whom were these "rights" accorded? Before answering this question, it is helpful to review Leopold's holist philosophy. In his early writings, he espoused a form of holism inspired by the mystical ideas of the Russian philosopher Peter Ouspensky's *Tertium Organum*.[39] Ouspensky had advanced the idea of the earth as a conscious, living organism of interdependent parts. In a posthumously published essay Leopold writes, "Possibly, in our intuitive perceptions, which may be truer than our science and less impeded by words than our philosophies, we realize the indivisibility of the earth—its soil, mountains, rivers, forests, climate, plants, and animals, and respect it collectively not only as useful servant but as a living being."[40]

It was not until ten years later that Leopold wrote explicitly about the ethical dimension of conservation. This time, however, he expressed his holist ideas in the language of ecology. The spiritual holism that was implicit in Ouspensky's thought had been consistent with the prevalent view of ecology during Leopold's early years, in particular F. E. Clement's idea of a "climax community" which operated much like a living being. Callicott suggests that Leopold may have abandoned the organism analogy for the idea of nature as a community under the influence of ecologist Charles Elton's concept of nature as a community of producers and consumers. Possibly he turned to the community conception of nature because it was more consistent with Darwin's idea that the moral sense derives from social instincts.[41] Leopold's concept of the community, however, tended to emphasize its singular aspect, rather than the notion of an aggregation of individuals. As Callicott suggests, by the late thirties and forties Leopold's writings show the influence of British ecologist Arthur Tansley's model of nature as an energy circuit, coursing through a single "ecosystem." But whether he endorsed the model of the land as a single organism, a community of interdependent life forms, or a single ecosystem, Leopold's moral philosophy was directed toward the larger biotic community rather than to individual beings.

The belief that Leopold extended "rights" to all life stems from a few key passages in his writings. In his 1947 essay, "The Land Ethic," he wrote of soil, waters, plants, and animals that a land ethic "affirm[s] their right to continued existence, and, at least in spots, their continued existence in a natural state." Further, "a land ethic changes the role of *Homo sapiens* from conqueror of the land-community to plain member and citizen of it. It implies respect for his fellow-members, and also respect for the community as such."[42] An examination of Leopold's choice of terms, however, reveals that he did not believe in the right to life of all *beings*, but of all life *forms*.[43] The other-than-human "citizens" of his biotic community were species and eco-logical processes. Leopold collapsed individual beings into these larger, abstract constructs. Early in his career he explained that he referred to "timber, water, forage, farm, recreative, game, fish, and esthetic resources" as "The Forest."[44] Not only are individuals excluded from direct moral consideration in Leopold's land ethic, but their well-being can be sacrificed for the benefit of the whole. As Callicott remarks, "The land ethic, thus, not only has a ho-listic aspect; it is holistic with a vengeance."[45]

Leopold often referred to the importance of preserving "remnants" of all species. He wrote that "every remnant should be definitely entrusted to a cus-todian—ranger, warden, game manager, chapter, ornithologists, farmer, stockman, lumberjack."[46] Today, the idea of preserving "remnants" of all species is commonplace, codified in the 1973 Endangered Species Act. Leopold's early writings on this subject provide insight into some of its cen-tral psychological underpinnings. Species, for Leopold, had a symbolic value that transcended the physical realm. In his more philosophical discussions, he called wildlife "noumena," suggesting the influence of both Ouspensky and Kant. According to Callicott, Leopold's noumena differ from Kantian ideas in that they are "actual or physical (and, therefore, strictly speaking, phenome-nal)."[47] But it is the noumena, or species, that have "rights" in Leopold's phi-losophy, not individual beings. Thus, in a real sense, his worldview did not make room for individual beings. He regarded each species as symbolic of a deeper meaning, available only to those who were ecologically literate and could "read" the language of nature. For example, a crane had a special sig-nificance to a Wisconsin homesteader as a symbol of his untamable past and evolutionary history.[48]

Leopold summarized the holist foundations of his philosophy in a fre-quently cited 1948 article in *A Sand County Almanac*: "A thing is right when it tends to preserve the integrity, stability, and beauty of the biotic community. It is wrong when it tends otherwise."[49] Although the values of integrity and stability were consistent with the emerging field of ecological science, the idea that "beauty" should be a standard for assessing environmental conduct was novel within the scientific community of his time. Philosophers, histori-ans, and scientists have often praised Leopold for this emphasis on aesthetic concerns over a base economic view of nature. What most scholars fail to mention, however, is that for Leopold hunting itself was an aesthetic activity akin to art. Not only did sport hunting not detract from the "beauty, integrity, and stability" of the biotic community, it actually enhanced it. Leopold's core values were interconnected components that characterize a healthy *land*, not individual beings. By "health of the land," Leopold meant the "capacity of the land for self-renewal." As long as the larger ecosystem was able to renew itself, it met Leopold's standards of beauty. The capacity for "self-renewal" of particular, individual other-than-human animals had no bearing on his idea of beauty.

Leopold's views on respecting nature's capacity for self-renewal derived from his ideas about good agricultural and wildlife "husbandry" and the psychological benefits that such management would yield. While earlier conservationists emphasized the idea of manipulating nature's fertility for material gain, Leopold's definition of good husbandry reflects an appreciation for the nonmaterial qualities of nature, preeminently its regenerative capacity. Leopold often emphasized the idea that wildlife husbandry will reap its own psychological rewards. Focusing on the enjoyment derived from hunting, he states, "We foresters and game managers might logically pay for, instead of being paid for, our job as husbandmen of wild crops."[50] Though he denounced a materialistic orientation toward nature, Leopold never fully relinquished the utilitarian agricultural paradigm he learned in his years with the Forest Service. Other-than-human animals were a "crop," which with proper husbandry would yield psychological rewards. It is the quantity of lives taken and the manner in which they are killed that is morally relevant for Leopold, not individual beings themselves.

Leopold's agricultural model of wildlife husbandry is intimately tied to his notion of species preservation. Species must be preserved because they help to replenish the supply of wild game. If a species goes extinct, the wilderness loses part of its reproductive capacity.[51] As Leopold argues, "Wilderness areas . . . provide an opportunity to produce and hunt certain kinds of game, such as elk, sheep, and bears, which do not always 'mix well' with settlement."[52]

## SPORT HUNTING AND THE DEVELOPMENT OF THE ECOLOGICAL CONSCIENCE

Many of Leopold's ideas about sport hunting bear a striking similarity to those of Theodore Roosevelt, differing primarily in their emphasis. Some of these similarities include a belief in the value of sport hunting as a symbolic, Darwinian-styled contest with wilderness; its role as a passage into manhood; its value as a skill that contributes to the development of individual, national, and racial character; and its importance as a playful re-creation of the frontier experience. Leopold departed from his forerunner primarily in his ecological insights, as well as his greater emphasis on the insufficiency of an ethic based only upon rules and regulations designed to restrain aggressive conduct. Although he wrote about the value of hunting as sport, he also emphasized the idea of hunting as a form of play and artistic expression, both of which he viewed as vital components of the wilderness experience.

For Leopold the urge to hunt is both a biological drive and a natural means of expressing "man's" inherent aggression.[53] As he argues, the desire for hunting "lies deeper" than outdoor sport:

> The instinct that finds delight in the sight and pursuit of game is bred into the very fiber of the race. Golf is a delightful accomplishment, but the love of hunting is almost a physiological characteristic. A man may not care for golf and still be human, but the man who does not like to see, hunt, photograph, or otherwise outwit birds or animals is hardly normal. He is supercivilized, and I for one do not know how to deal with him.[54]

Leopold believed that this "natural" drive to hunt functioned as a safety valve for men's aggression. If suppressed, the "vacuum" created might be filled with something that was "not necessarily . . . better."[55] So convinced was Leopold of the instinctive nature of the hunting drive that he contends, "A son of Robinson Crusoe, having never seen a racket, might get along nicely without one, but he would be pretty sure to hunt or fish whether or not he were taught to do so."[56] Leopold therefore demands that "game and wild life be one of the normal products of every farm, and the enjoyment of it a part of the normal environment of every boy."[57] Saving wilderness, for Leopold, was thus a way of ensuring that his sons would have the opportunity to exercise this right. As he states, "I have congenital hunting fever and three sons . . . I hope to leave them good health, an education, and possibly even a competence. But what are they going to do with these things if there be no more deer in the hills, and no more quail in the coverts?"[58] As ecofeminist writer Chaone Mallory points out, however, two of Leopold's five children were female. Apparently, the "deer in the hills" were the birthright of only his sons.[59]

For Leopold, the opportunity to exercise the hunting instinct was a democratic right, not simply a "rich man's privilege."[60] And it was the purpose of game management to ensure that this prerogative was conferred. Just after Leopold discusses the inalienable right to the free exercise of the "normal" instinct to hunt, he goes on to lament that "the men who are destroying our wildlife are alienating one of these rights, and doing a terribly thorough job of it."[61] Wildlife must be conserved not because of the animals' right to life, but rather because of "man's" inalienable right to hunt and kill.

Leopold thus assumes the inherent right of humans (or, more particularly, men) to fulfill their aggressive drives through hunting. However, he also argues that ethical conduct is a matter of regulating this inherent right. Leopold expands on the idea of ethics as a form of restraint:

> An ethic, ecologically, is a limitation on freedom of action in the struggle for existence. An ethic, philosophically, is a differentiation of social from anti-social conduct. These are two definitions of one thing.[62]

For Leopold, however, sport hunting was not simply a matter of biological expression but also cultural expression. He viewed it as a cultural advance, which contributed to the moral improvement of the human race. As he writes,

> Physical combat for the means of subsistence was, for unnumbered centuries, an economic fact. When it disappeared as such, a sound instinct led us to preserve it in the form of athletic sports and games. Physical combat between men and beasts was, in like manner, an economic fact, now preserved as hunting and fishing for sport. Public wilderness areas are, first of all, a means of perpetuating, in sport form, the more virile and primitive skills in pioneering travel and subsistence.[63]

Inspired by Darwin's ideas on the evolutionary development of morality, Leopold argues that sport hunting was an evolutionary advance that contributed in positive ways to a land ethic or ecological conscience. Although Darwin is best known for his ideas of competition within nature and survival of the fittest, he also developed a theory of the origins of the "social instincts." It was this notion that seems to have had a formative influence on Leopold. According to Darwin, with the advance of civilization, humans developed an increasing capacity to extend their "social instincts" and "sympathies" to ever-expanding groups of people—first from tribes to nations, and finally to "men of all nations and races."[64] The shift to altruism is fully consistent with the struggle for existence in this view, since it represents awareness that cooperation fosters reproductive fitness.

The development of the social sympathies and the attendant expansion of ethical concern, according to Leopold, required that "man's" inherent aggressive drives have a means of expression, albeit in a restrained and regulated manner. "An individual's instincts prompt him to compete for his place in the community, but his ethics prompt him also to co-operate (*perhaps in order that there may be a place to compete for*)" (emphasis added).[65] Sport hunting thus was not only an ideal outlet for "man's" aggressive drives but also for his drive toward cooperation and self-control. He writes,

> Some can live without opportunity for the exercise and control of the hunting instinct, just as I suppose some can live without work, play, love, business, or other vital adventure. But in these days we regard such deprivations as unsocial. Opportunity for exercise of all the normal instincts has become to be regarded more and more as an inalienable right.[66]

Roderick Nash captures the idea of restraint in Leopold's philosophy, stating that for Leopold, "ethics applied to situations where a person who could have done a particular action held back because he knew that action was wrong."[67] But instinctual drives, according to Leopold, could not be repressed, only rechanneled in appropriate ways. What Leopold seems to be suggesting in the above passages is not only that the biotic community must be preserved in order to preserve the inalienable right to hunt, but that it *cannot* be preserved without the safety valve that hunting provides for "man's" aggression.

The conception of sport hunting as a matrix for the development of the social instincts is intimately tied to Leopold's notion of ecological conscience. The early conservationists relied on external laws and regulations to govern their conduct. But the true sportsman went beyond external constraints and relied on his "ecological conscience." According to Leopold, although it was "an honor" to attain a reputation as "a keen and successful sportsman," it was "a doubtful compliment at best" if it was founded upon always getting one's limit of game.[68] As he emphasizes, the hunter, who has only himself as an audience, "has no gallery to applaud or disapprove of his conduct" other than his conscience. Leopold argued that "it is difficult to exaggerate the importance of this fact."[69] Elsewhere he elaborates on the value of sport hunting for the development of this personal code of honor:

> Hunting for sport in its highest form is an improvement on hunting for food in that there has been added, to the test of skill, an ethical code which the hunter formulates for himself and must often execute without the moral support of bystanders. In these cases the surviving sport is actually an improvement on the receding economic fact.[70]

Leopold was deeply influenced by his father's hunting philosophy. As biographer Curt Meine notes, Carl Leopold adhered to a well-developed personal code of sportsmanship: never lose a "downed bird," never hunt after the sun goes down, and set your own bag limit, which sometimes meant foregoing a shot at a particular species.[71] Leopold learned from his father's example the importance of setting his own limits. Compassion for the animals he hunted, however, does not appear to be his foremost concern, but rather adherence to the sportsman's code, premised on the idea of a fair contest with the hunted animal. If the animal is shot indiscriminately, no moral value can accrue to the hunter. The moral and spiritual development of character *requires* self-limitations. By imposing limits on oneself, one achieves the greatest spiritual value, known only to the hunter and God.

Leopold argued that the sport hunter's reliance upon conscience produced a unique spiritual value—"the ethics of sportsmanship is not a fixed code, but must be formulated and practiced by the individual, with no referee but the 'Almighty.'"[72] This conceptualization of sport hunting as a form of spiritual communion with "the Almighty" or with one's higher power suggests the Protestant idea of individual communion with God. The good sportsman moves beyond reliance upon external forms of authority to engage in a personal communion with God, manifested as his conscience.

Leopold advances the idea of ecological conscience as a progressive development over previous attitudes, which relied only upon "the letter" of the sportsman's code. According to Leopold, "Nothing so important as an ethic is ever 'written.' Only the most superficial student of history supposes that Moses 'wrote' the Decalogue; it evolved in the minds of a thinking community, and Moses wrote a tentative summary of it for a 'seminar.'"[73] Similarly, Leopold argued that farmers should move beyond passive reliance upon government intervention by developing a personal relation to their land through the creation of their own "wilderness" areas. He admonished, "Subsidies and propaganda may evoke the farmer's acquiescence, but only enthusiasm and affection will evoke his skill."[74]

Leopold's emphasis on the importance of developing "enthusiasm and affection" suggests that he had moved beyond an instrumental relationship to nature. Once again, however, Leopold's understanding of emotional ties was limited. In the same address he underlines the importance of private land preservation for sport hunting, lamenting that one reason for "injured pride and family scrutiny" was the absence of a "coon hunt" in season on one's property.[75] Clearly, Leopold's ecological conscience did not extend to the individual animals whom he killed. It dictated only *how* sport hunting should be conducted.

## SPORT HUNTING AND THE RE-CREATION OF WILDERNESS

Leopold's early writings reveal that his motivation was not concern for ecology, but rather for a recreational experience found in the adventure of hunting. Like his predecessor Roosevelt, he valued wilderness as an arena for the enactment of a symbolic contestation with the "wild" and as a link with the American pioneering tradition. The word *wilderness* derives from the Old English *wilddeor*, meaning "wild beast."[76] Beneath Roosevelt and Leopold's efforts to preserve wilderness lurks the specter of the Wild Beast. For both conservationists, sport hunting represented the symbolic defeat of the menacing Beast, whose death ushered in "civilization." Just as Pinchotian foresters sought to maximize the amount of timber extracted from the forests, so too, the early Leopold sought to extract the maximum amount of sport hunting adventure from the wilderness.[77]

The possibility for reversion to an earlier "primitive" experience was what mattered most to Leopold. Small areas of "wilderness" were needed in the midst of more modernized regions to afford humans a chance to revert to their primeval roots. Just as masculine identity is established by means of a conceptual opposition to women, so too civilization is established through its opposition to the "wild." Without the contrast provided by our primitive roots, humans risk losing the raw material that makes human civilization possible. As Leopold writes in a 1925 article, Americans should

> preserve a sample of the Covered Wagon Life. For after all, the measure of civilization is in its contrasts. . . . And if, once in a while [the city man] has the opportunity to . . . disappear into the wilderness of the Covered Wagon Days, he is just that much more civilized than he would be without the opportunity. It makes him one more kind of a man—a pioneer.[78]

Part of the value of wilderness experience was found in its association with exploration and the "conquest" of "unknown places."[79] Leopold worried that with the vanishing number of unknown places, humans (and in particular, his white racial stock) would lose opportunities for adventure. In his later years, although Leopold increasingly emphasized the scientific value of wilderness areas, the association of wilderness with adventure can still be detected. Wilderness "laboratories" offered the same sense of adventure into the unknown that his hunting expeditions afforded. Preserving these laboratories was another way of safeguarding the adventure of the "wild."

Seeking to retain the primitive aspect of the wilderness experience, Leopold inveighed against an excessive reliance upon transportation to remote areas. He wished to protect the forests not from development, but from overdevelopment and, in particular, overmechanization. In Leopold's view, roads, motorized transport, hotels, cottages, and graded trails interfered with the aesthetic appreciation of nature. In a 1932 essay he explained, "When I go birding or hunting in my Ford, I am devastating an oil field, and re-electing an imperialist to get me rubber."[80] What Leopold failed to notice, however, is that when he was hunting in the wilderness, with or without his Ford, he was also devastating individual lives.

Leopold abhorred the over-reliance on machinery, which he viewed as an "adulteration" of sport hunting. In his later years he became an enthusiastic bow-hunter, believing that bow-hunting better approximated the primitive aspect of the hunting experience. Once again, however, Leopold failed to appreciate the impact of his actions on individual animals. Bow-hunting has been shown to inflict greater suffering on its targets, causing crippling and slow, agonizing deaths.[81]

In his later years, Leopold increasingly embraced a scientific approach, arguing that wilderness was also necessary as a "base-datum of normality, a picture of how healthy land maintains itself as an organism."[82] For Leopold, wilderness represented the "most perfect" norm of health, due to its long-range stability. Thus, each biome should have a wilderness preserve that could serve as a model of health; deviations from this norm then could be used as a "benchmark" for the "impact of land-use technologies."[83]

Leopold also increasingly emphasized the cultural value of preserving wilderness, pleading for "the preservation of some tag-ends of wilderness, as museum pieces, for the edification of those who may one day wish to see, feel, or study the origins of their cultural inheritance."[84] Like Theodore Roosevelt before him, Leopold believed that wilderness was a national heritage to be preserved for the welfare of future generations of Americans. But who, precisely, was to inherit this investment, and why was it important that they inherit it?

Leopold repeatedly answers these questions by underscoring the importance for young boys of recapturing the frontier experience through sport hunting, arguing that it provides a vital link between present day youth and their virile ancestors. The urge to revive the past is not just a matter of bringing the past into the present, but also a way of linking the past to the future. Leopold develops the notion of "revival" in his statement that "the trophy-hunter is the caveman reborn." He goes on to assert that "trophy-hunting is the prerogative of youth, racial or individual, and nothing to apologize for."[85] Thus, for Leopold, public wilderness areas provide an important means for accomplishing this transfer of manly virtues. They are essential for "allowing the more virile and primitive forms of outdoor recreation to survive the receding economic fact of pioneering."[86] Like sacrifice, sport hunting served to symbolically link a community of boys and men across the generations.

It was not *all* males who were to be linked into this community, however; rather only white Anglo-Saxon American men. Like Roosevelt, Leopold believed that the American frontier had helped to forge the unique American character. He writes that "coupled with . . . our racial stocks, it is the very stuff America is made of."[87] To destroy this environment was therefore tantamount to racial suicide. As he elaborates, "Anthropologists tell us that we, the Nordics, have a racial genius for pioneering, surpassing all other races in ability to reduce the wilderness to possession."[88] Susan Schrepfer observes that, by preserving wilderness, Anglo-American men were realizing a "racial imperative to emulate their fathers."[89] Sport hunting was the quintessential activity that symbolized this racial link with their forefathers.[90]

While Leopold believed that sport hunting's rules and regulations transformed its "primitive" aspect into a racially superior cultural activity, a number of theorists point to commonalities between the rules of sport hunting and the forms of traditional ritual.[91] As discussed earlier, hunting stories in many cultures have functioned as rebirth narratives. In addition, as Ingeborg Flügel pointed out in an early psychoanalytic journal, killing animals in a ritualized manner and in certain seasons is consistent with totemic thinking.[92] While killing a totem animal is typically considered taboo in tribal cultures, at designated times totem animals may be sacrificed in prescribed ways. In a comparable manner, sport hunting conservationists followed particular rules for how and when animals could be hunted.

The profession of "love" and "respect" in the context of killing the hunted animal also suggests the notion of a ritual sacrifice. Although Leopold's plea for sport hunting to move beyond formal laws implies that he rejected the mere ritualistic or formalistic aspect of sport hunting, his emphasis on the paramount importance of attitude suggests, rather, that the hunter's conduct concerning the kill be inspired from within. The rules and regulations were not to be abandoned, but rather internalized through an emotional connection to the "land." A disrespectful attitude, according to Leopold, desecrated the hunting experience, reducing it to an expression of base biological or economic motives.

Leopold recognized that sport hunting contained elements of both fantasy and play. He claimed that "along with the necessity for expression of racial instincts there happily goes that capacity for illusion which enables little boys to fish happily in wash-tubs. That capacity is a precious thing, if not over-worked."[93] For Leopold the creation of "wilderness playgrounds" was an important means for play-acting the early frontiersman's experience of the wilderness. Thus, in advocating the creation of the Gila Wilderness Area, he sought to provide boys with an opportunity for "reenacting American history." As he wistfully constructs the script: "a boy scout has tanned a coon-skin cap, and goes Daniel-Booneing in the willow thicket below the tracks. . . . A farmer boy arrives in the school room reeking of muskrat; he has tended his traps before breakfast. He is reenacting the romance of the fur trade."[94] The preoccupation with recreating the frontier experience helps to explain Leopold's acceptance of other uses of wilderness, including grazing in wilderness areas.[95] As he maintains, "Cattle ranches would be an asset from the recreational standpoint because of the interest which attaches to cattle grazing operations under frontier conditions."[96] Historian Paul Sutter observes that "grazing . . . was not a substantial threat to wilderness as [Leopold] then defined it."[97]

To be effective as fantasy, however, game management must be the "art which conceals art." As Leopold explains, "Most of our atavistic instincts, including hunting, find their exercise only through the frank acceptance of illusion."[98] Game management must create the illusion of wilderness without showing the mark of human interference. Leopold believed that the management of nature by humans was a necessity, but if over-managed, wilderness lost its aesthetic and recreational value. "The recreational value of a head of game is inverse to the artificiality of its origin, and hence in a broad way to the intensiveness of the system of game management which produced it. . . . Some but not too much management is good aesthetics."[99] The creation of "wilderness playgrounds" requires the realization that they cannot be artificially constructed. According to Leopold, "To artificially create wilderness areas would overwork the capacity for illusion of even little boys with washtubs."[100]

## THE HUNTING HERITAGE

In his famous essay "The Land Ethic," Leopold argued for the importance of moving beyond a conception of nature as property. Drawing on Darwinian notions of expanding moral concerns, he tells the mythical story of Odysseus, who, upon his return to Greece, hanged a dozen slave-girls accused of misbehavior in his absence.[101] As Leopold comments, "The girls were property. The disposal of property was then, as now, a matter of expediency, not of right and wrong."[102] He argues, "The first ethics dealt with the relation between individuals. . . . Later accretions dealt with the relation between the individual and society. . . . There is as yet no ethic dealing with man's relation to land and to the animals and plants which grow upon it. Land, like Odysseus' slave-girls, is still property."[103] In this essay, Leopold expresses his hope that over time humans eventually will evolve an ethic that will no longer view land as property.

In the prevailing Lockean concept of property, land had no value until it was mixed with human labor, after which human beings had "ultimate" and "absolute" rights over it, including the right to destroy it if they so desired.[104] Leopold challenged this amoral relation between humans and the land, arguing that the land was a living community that should be safeguarded for the benefit of future generations. In his view, "possession" denoted a living entity to be cherished in a joint custodial stewardship, while "property" was inanimate matter that could be used up and destroyed. Elsewhere, he also developed the idea of the biotic community as a "possession," proposing at one point the title "Great Possessions" for *A Sand County Almanac*.

For Leopold, both sport hunting and the land were clearly possessions to be passed on to future generations. Using the metaphors of economic investment to express this idea, he maintained that wildlife was a public investment

and that to exterminate "interesting species" was a "sin against future generations."[105] As for the primitive aspect of wilderness, he claimed that too many
roads in wilderness areas would "amortize the public investment."[106]

Leopold has often been praised for helping to establish a sound scientific
basis to environmental ethics. And yet, as mentioned, he also distinguished
himself through his emphasis on the ethical significance of aesthetics. Where
Roosevelt viewed hunting as an antidote to the over-feminization of young
men, Leopold stressed in addition that sport hunting was a vital form of artistic expression. According sport hunting a prominent place in his philosophy,
he argued that, in addition to all its other virtues, it had the ability to cultivate
a love and respect for the land through its aesthetic appeal to the senses, best
stimulated in a wilderness setting.[107] His views on the aesthetic allure of hunting are worth reviewing in greater detail since they underline the ways in
which an appeal to aesthetics and sensibility can coexist with violence toward
individual beings, as well as the ways it can camouflage violence.

Leopold compared nature's beauty to musical expression, equivalent to
"paid entertainment." Describing his visceral response to this beauty, he
states that he "tingled at the recollection" of "the sight of the big gander that
sailed honking into [his] decoys."[108] As he elaborates, "the duck-hunter in his
blind and the operatic singer on the stage, despite the disparity of their ac-
coutrements, are doing the same thing. Each is reviving, in play, a drama for-
merly inherent in daily life. Both are, in the last analysis, esthetic exercises."[109] The operatic metaphor implies that the hunter is both participant
and audience in the artistic expression of nature. Elsewhere, Leopold compares wildlife to theater, arguing that "only those able to see the pageant of
evolution can be expected to value its theater, the wilderness, or its outstand-
ing achievement, the grizzly."[110] As a theatrical experience, the evolutionary
drama required a proper scenery or backdrop to be fully appreciated. Ideally,
the setting would be as far from the trappings of human civilization as possible. Like earlier conservationists, Leopold invoked the primitivist theme of
harking back to a primitive frontier wilderness. He saw it as "a continuous
stretch of country preserved in its natural state, open to lawful hunting and
fishing, big enough to absorb a two weeks' pack-trip, and kept devoid of
roads, artificial trails, cottages, or other works of man."[111]

The value of sport hunting was realized, for Leopold, not only by inserting
oneself into a Darwinian "drama" of existence, but also by appreciating this
"drama" as a form of art. Hunting was a vital stage in a young boy's maturation process. Only in old age is it possible for men to find other substitutes for
this activity. As he states,

Hunting and nature study are merely the beginning and the end of a cycle normal to advancing age in each individual. Just as the evolution of the species is repeated in the pre-natural history of each individual, so the evolution of the nature-lover is being repeated in each boy keen for the hunt. It is conceivable that the hunting stage could be eliminated by educational pressure on the youth, but it seems equally probable that too much pressure of this kind might cut off or subvert the whole process, nature-lover included, and thus sever the last personal tie which binds the city dweller to the land.[112]

Although Leopold hints that as a young boy matures, he might replace his love of hunting with nature study, he never followed this maturational process in his own life. Nor did he ever go so far as to assert that sport hunting *should* be relinquished in one's adult years. His ideas on the relationship between sport hunting and maturity contrast with those of another well-known naturalist, Henry David Thoreau. Thoreau, too, believed that sport hunting was a natural part of a young boy's maturation, but he argued that waning interest in this blood sport was a mark of moral maturity.[113]

## CONCLUSION

One cannot dispute that Leopold made a significant contribution to environmental philosophy. He championed the concept of the earth as a community of interdependent beings, the idea of the fragility of the land, the importance of minimizing human interference, and the value of developing affective ties to the land. His writings also display a unique blend of scientific and aesthetic concerns. Despite these positive contributions, however, in this chapter I have challenged the view that Aldo Leopold made a decisive break with earlier views of nature. Although he moved beyond the previous generation's exclusive emphasis on the material benefits of conservation, his focus on the psychological and moral value of sport hunting perpetuates an instrumental view.

Further, Leopold's emphasis on the central importance of sport hunting reflects a masculinist orientation that "sacrifices" individual beings to a larger "objective" perspective, symbolized by the "land." Not only was the "beauty, integrity, and stability" of the land not marred by hunting, it was *enhanced* by it. Leopold's views on sport hunting reduced other-than-human animals to psychological props in a drama that reinforced the manly virtues. In short, he perpetuated a masculinist orientation that subordinates affective ties to individual beings to larger, more enduring constructs.

## NOTES

1. J. Baird Callicott, "Animal Liberation and Environmental Ethics: Back Together Again," in *In Defense of the Land Ethic: Essays in Environmental Philosophy,* ed. J. Baird Callicott (Albany: State University of New York Press, 1989), 15.

2. Wallace Stegner, "Living on Our Principal," *Wilderness* 48 (Spring 1985), reprinted in *Marking the Sparrow's Fall: The Making of the American West,* ed. Page Stegner (New York: Henry Holt, 1998), 149.

3. The first edition was published as *A Sand County Almanac and Sketches Here and There.* In 1966 Oxford University Press added eight essays from the Round River collection, and published the repackaged edition under the title *A Sand County Almanac with Essays from Round River.* In 1970 Ballantine republished it under the title *A Sand County Almanac.*

4. The utilitarian model of the Forest Service can be seen in their first manual, which states that the national forests existed "for the purpose of preserving a perpetual supply of timber for home industries, preventing destruction of the forest cover . . . and protecting local industries from unfair competition in the use of forest and range." Gifford Pinchot, *The Use of the National Forest Reserves: Regulation and Instructions,* U.S. Department of Agriculture, Forest Service, 1905, 7.

5. Stegner, "Living on Our Principal," 150.

6. Aldo Leopold, "Varmints," *Pine Cone,* no. 12 (January 1919): 1. A photo of this brief article may be seen in Susan L. Flader, *Thinking like a Mountain: Aldo Leopold and the Evolution of an Ecological Attitude toward Deer, Wolves and Forests* (Madison: University of Wisconsin Press, 1974), xxvi.

7. Aldo Leopold, "Wanted—National Forest Game Refuges," *Bulletin of the American Game Protective Association* 9, no. 1 (1920): 9.

8. Flader, *Thinking like a Mountain,* 61.

9. Aldo Leopold, "Review of Young and Goldman, *The Wolves of North America,*" in *The River of the Mother of God and Other Essays by Aldo Leopold,* ed. Susan L. Flader and J. Baird Callicott (Madison: University of Wisconsin Press, 1991), 322. Originally published in *Journal of Forestry* 43, no.1 (January 1945): 928–929.

10. Aldo Leopold, "Forestry and Game Conservation," in *River of the Mother of God,* eds. Susan L. Flader and J. Baird Callicott, 59. Originally published in *Journal of Forestry* 16, no. 4 (April 1918): 404–411.

11. Aldo Leopold, "Ten New Developments in Game Management," in *Aldo Leopold's Wilderness* eds. David E. Brown and Neil B. Carmony (Harrisburg, Pa.: Stackpole Books, 1990), 114. Originally published in *American Game* 14, no. 3 (7-8, 20).

12. Flader, *Thinking like a Mountain,* 67.

13. Leopold's scientific formulas for determining the "kill factor" for a given range were based on an analogy with the "steer factor" used in range cattle management. The steer factor, in turn, was derived from the Forest Service notions of sustained yield. Aldo Leopold, "Determining the Kill Factor for Blacktail Deer in the

Southwest," in *Aldo Leopold's Wilderness*, eds. David E. Brown and Neil B. Carmony, 87–91. Originally published in *Journal of Forestry* 18, no. 2 (February 1920): 131–134.

14. Aldo Leopold, "Game Management in the National Forests," in *Aldo Leopold's Wilderness*, eds. David E. Brown and Neil B. Carmony, 126–129. Originally published in *American Forests* (July 1930).

15. Aldo Leopold, "Wilderness as a Form of Land Use," in *River of the Mother of God*, eds. Susan L. Flader and J. Bairal Calliout, 140–141. Originally published in *Journal of Land and Public Utility Economics* 1, no. 4 (October 1925): 398–404.

16. Aldo Leopold, "A Plea for Wilderness Hunting Grounds," in *Aldo Leopold's Wilderness*, eds. David E. Brown and Neil B. Carmony, 158–159. Originally published in *Outdoor Life* 56 (November 1925).

17. J. Baird Callicott, "The Wilderness Idea Revisited: The Sustainable Development Alternative," in *The Great New Wilderness Debate: An Expansive Collection of Writings Defining Wilderness from John Muir to Gary Snyder*, ed. J. Baird Callicott and Michael P. Nelson (Athens: University of Georgia Press, 1998), 343.

18. The gun used by Leopold, still bearing the tooth marks left by the wolf, is on display at the University of Wisconsin–Madison's Department of Wildlife Ecology. According to Curt Meine, although never formally recorded, the story of the wolf's final stand is part of department lore. Email to author, February 13, 2007.

19. Aldo Leopold, "Thinking like a Mountain," in *A Sand County Almanac and Sketches Here and There* (New York: Oxford University Press, 1968), 129–130. Leopold's conservation ethic developed in large part out of this belief in the need to control the "trigger itch" that plagues the young or immature hunter. As he stated, "foregoing a sure shot" of a treed partridge was "my first exercise in ethical codes." *A Sand County Almanac and Sketches Here and There* (New York: Oxford University Press, 1968, 121. Roosevelt describes a similar evolution in thinking about the need for control of "buck fever," boasting that "the first two or three bucks I ever saw gave me buck fever badly, but after I had gained experience with ordinary game I never had buck fever at all with dangerous game. In my case the overcoming of buck fever was the result of conscious effort and a deliberate determination to overcome it." *Theodore Roosevelt: An Autobiography* (New York: Macmillan, 1914), 34–35. In a similar vein, a recent article in a popular hunting magazine offers advice on how to cope with the "performance anxiety" that accompanies buck fever. The author advises, "rather than damp down that incredible rush, what you want is to channel it, master it so it doesn't master you." Recommended techniques include breathing and meditation exercises, and repetition of mantras ("don't you dare use that word, because your buddies will ridicule you"). Bill Heavey, "This Is Your Brain on Bucks," *Field and Stream*, November 2006, 90, 105–106. For similar advice on how to transform the "adrenaline [surge]" that accompanies hunting into a "peak experience," see James A. Swan, *In Defense of Hunting* (New York: HarperCollins, 1995), 33–35.

20. Stephan Harding, "What Is Deep Ecology?" *Resurgence* 185 (November–December 1997): 14.

21. Ruth Rosenhek, "Nature as Faith," *Chain Reaction* 94 (July 2005): 21.

22. As Forrest Wood Jr. points out, Leopold wrote "Thinking like a Mountain" in 1944, looking back on "an experience that happened in New Mexico probably during the first year (1909) of his service with the Forest Service." *The Delights and Dilemmas of Hunting: The Hunting Versus Anti-Hunting Debate* (Lanham, Md.: University Press of America, 1997), 137.

23. Leopold, "Thinking like a Mountain," 132.

24. Curt Meine, *Aldo Leopold: His Life and Work* (Madison: University of Wisconsin Press, 1988), 242.

25. Aldo Leopold, *Game Management* (Madison: University of Wisconsin Press, 1986), 3. Originally published by Charles Scribner's Sons, 1933.

26. Aldo Leopold, "An Outline Plan for Game Management in Wisconsin," in *A Study of Wisconsin: Its Resources, Its Physical, Social and Economic Background; First Annual Report* (Madison: Wisconsin Regional Planning Committee, 1934), 250.

27. Charles Bergman, *Orion's Legacy: A Cultural History of Man as Hunter* (New York: Dutton, 1996), 266.

28. On the symbolic role of hunting throughout Western history, with a focus on its connection to masculine identity, see Bergman, *Orion's Legacy*; Andrée Collard with Joyce Contrucci, *Rape of the Wild: Man's Violence Against Animals and the Earth* (Bloomington: Indiana University Press, 1989); Merritt Clifton, "Killing the Female: The Psychology of the Hunt," *Animals' Agenda* 10, no. 7 (September 1990): 26–30, 57; Brian Luke, *Brutal: Manhood and the Exploitation of Animals* (Chicago: University of Illinois Press, 2007).

29. For an in-depth chronicle of Leopold's gradual evolution toward an ecological view of predators, see Flader, *Thinking like a Mountain*.

30. Aldo Leopold, "Wilderness," (transcribed speech) in *River of the Mother of God*, eds. Susan L. Flader and J. Baird Callicott, 227–228. Originally published in Stencil Circular 210, Extension Service, College of Agriculture, University of Wisconsin, Madison (February 1939).

31. Leopold, "Wilderness" (speech), 226.

32. Flader, *Thinking like a Mountain*, 93–96.

33. Bron Taylor, "Earth First! From Primal Spirituality to Ecological Resistance," in *This Sacred Earth: Religion, Nature, Environment*, ed. Roger S. Gottlieb (New York: Routledge, 1996), 550.

34. Leopold, "Thinking like a Mountain," 129.

35. H. Paul Santmire, "The Metaphors of Ascent and Fecundity," in *The Travail of Nature: The Ambiguous Ecological Promise of Christian Theology* (Philadelphia: Fortress Press, 1985), 18–21.

36. Lawrence Buell, *The Environmental Imagination: Thoreau, Nature Writing, and the Formation of American Culture* (Cambridge, Mass.: Harvard University Press, 1995), 171–172. For an in-depth history of the story behind the publication of *A Sand County Almanac*, see Dennis Ribbens, "The Making of *A Sand County Almanac*," *Wisconsin Academy Review* 28, no. 4 (1982), reprinted in *Companion to "A Sand County Almanac": Interpretive and Critical Essays,* ed. J. Baird Callicott (Madison: University of Wisconsin Press, 1987), 91–109.

37. Aldo Leopold, "Defenders of Wilderness" (essay), in *Sand County Almanac*, 200–201.

38. Leopold, "Defenders of Wilderness" (essay), in *Sand County Almanac,* 200.

39. Aldo Leopold, "Some Fundamentals of Conservation in the Southwest," *Environmental Ethics* 1, no. 2 (Summer 1979). Reprinted in *River of the Mother of God*, eds. Susan L. Flader and J. Baird Callicott, 86–97. Written in 1923, the article remained unpublished during Leopold's lifetime.

40. Leopold, "Some Fundamentals of Conservation," 95.

41. J. Baird Callicott, "The Conceptual Foundations of the Land Ethic," in *In Defense of the Land Ethic*, 89.

42. Aldo Leopold, "The Land Ethic," (essay) in *Sand County Almanac*, 204.

43. In a similar vein, Roderick Nash observes that "Leopold's concept of reverence-for-life was precisely that—for life in toto, and not so much for the individual players in the process." Nash, "Aldo Leopold's Intellectual Heritage," in Callicott, *Companion to "A Sand County Almanac,"* 82.

44. Aldo Leopold, "To the Forest Officers of the Carson," in *River of the Mother of God*, eds. Susan L. Flader and J. Baird Callicott, 41. Originally published in *Carson Pine Cone* 15 (July 1913).

45. Callicott, "Conceptual Foundations," in *In Defense of the Land Ethic,* 84.

46. Aldo Leopold, "Threatened Species: A Proposal to the Wildlife Conference for an Inventory of the Needs of Near-Extinct Birds and Animals," in *Aldo Leopold's Wilderness*, eds. David E. Brown and Neil B. Carmony, 193–198. Originally published in *American Forests* 42, no. 3 (1936): 116–199.

47. J. Baird Callicott, "The Land Aesthetic," in *Companion to "A Sand County Almanac,"* 167.

48. Callicott, "The Land Aesthetic," 167.

49. Leopold, "Land Ethic," (essay) in *Sand County Almanac,* 224–225.

50. Aldo Leopold, "Conservation Esthetic," (essay) in *Sand County Almanac*, 175.

51. It is worthy of note that the very concept of "species" as a biological entity is based on the capacity of animals to reproduce with beings of their own kind. Hence, the emphasis on regeneration is built into the very word itself.

52. Leopold, "Plea for Wilderness Hunting Grounds," 160.

53. Leopold's repeated use of the purportedly generic "man" makes it difficult at times to assess whether he felt that hunting was instinctive only to men or to all humans. However, his repeated references to what is natural for young boys suggest that he had men and boys in mind.

54. Aldo Leopold, "Goose Music," in *Round River: From the Journals of Aldo Leopold,* ed. Luna B. Leopold (New York: Oxford University Press, 1993), 167.

55. Leopold, *Game Management*, 391.

56. Leopold, *Game Management*, 232.

57. Aldo Leopold, "Game and Wild Life Conservation," in *River of the Mother of God,* eds. Susan L. Flader and J. Baird Callicott, 167. Originally published in *Condor* 34, no. 2 (March–April 1932): 103–106.

58. Leopold, "Goose Music," 173.

59. Chaone Mallory, "Acts of Objectification and the Repudiation of Dominance: Leopold, Ecofeminism, and the Ecological Narrative," *Ethics and the Environment* 6, no. 2 (2001): 73.

60. Leopold, "Plea for Wilderness Hunting Grounds," 156.

61. Leopold, "Goose Music," 167.

62. Leopold, "Land Ethic," 202.

63. Leopold, "Wilderness for Recreation" (essay), in *Sand County Almanac,* 192.

64. Charles Darwin, *The Descent of Man and Selection in Relation to Sex,* reprint edition (New York: Barnes and Noble, 2004), 102.

65. Leopold, "Land Ethic," 203–204.

66. Leopold, "Goose Music," 167.

67. Nash, "Aldo Leopold's Intellectual Heritage," 79.

68. Aldo Leopold, "On Killing the Limit," *Pine Cone* (July 1917): n.p., quoted in *Aldo Leopold: His Life and Work,* Meine, 163.

69. Aldo Leopold, "Wildlife in American Culture" (essay), in *Sand County Almanac,* 178.

70. Leopold, "Wilderness as a Form of Land Use," 137–138.

71. Meine, *His Life and Work,* 18 (as recalled by Leopold's brother, Frederic).

72. Leopold, "Goose Music," 172.

73. Leopold, "Land Ethic," 225.

74. Aldo Leopold, "The Farmer as a Conservationist," in *River of the Mother of God,* eds. Susan L. Flader and J. Baird Callicott, 258.

75. Leopold, "Farmer as a Conservationist," 263.

76. *The American Heritage Dictionary,* 4th ed., s.v. "wilderness."

77. Some writers have argued that Leopold's endorsement of hunting in wilderness areas (later called "primitive areas" by the Forest Service and "wilderness" by the Park Service) was motivated by pragmatic concerns. It is suggested that he recognized that he would garner more support for his cause if he emphasized the utility of wilderness areas for hunting. Leopold was intent on countering the notion that wilderness was an empty vacuum, serving no use. His purpose was to point to the recreational benefits to be found in these seemingly unused areas. See, for example, "Wilderness as a Form of Land Use," 134–142. Some also point to the competition between the Forest Service and the Park Service for public land designation as an additional motive. Since the Park Service prohibited hunting, Forest Service promoters could use hunting as a competitive edge over their Park Service counterparts. They could also argue that their roadless wilderness areas were less expensive to maintain and that they were in a better position than the Park Service, which allowed tourists, to preserve wilderness. Daniel J. Philippon, *Conserving Words: How American Nature Writers Shaped the Environmental Movement* (Athens: University of Georgia Press, 2005), 169.

78. Aldo Leopold, "Conserving the Covered Wagon," in *River of the Mother of God,* eds. Susan L. Flader and J. Baird Callicott, 129. Originally published in *Sunset Magazine* 54, no. 3 (March 1925): 21, 56.

79. Aldo Leopold, "The River of the Mother of God," in *River of the Mother of God,* eds. Susan L. Flader and J. Baird Callicott, 123–124. Originally published in *Sunset Magazine* 54, no. 3 (March 1925): 21, 56.

80. Leopold, "Game and Wild Life Conservation," 165.

81. For information about the suffering that bow-hunting inflicts, see Aaron N. Moen, "Crippling Losses," *Deer and Deer Hunting* 12, no. 6 (1989): 64–70; and Al Hofacker, "On the Trail of Wounded Deer: The Philosophy of Waiting," *Deer and Deer Hunting* 10, no. 2 (1986): 65–85 and 104.

82. Aldo Leopold, "Wilderness as a Land Laboratory," in *River of the Mother of God*, eds. Susan L. Flader and J. Baird Callicott, 288. Originally published in *Living Wilderness* 6 (July 1941): 3.

83. Flader and Callicott, introduction, *River of the Mother of God*, 27.

84. Leopold, "Wilderness" (essay), in *Sand County Almanac,* 188.

85. Leopold, "Conservation Esthetic," 176.

86. Leopold, "Wilderness as a Form of Land Use," 138.

87. Leopold, "Wilderness as a Form of Land Use," 137.

88. Aldo Leopold, "Pioneers and Gullies," in *River of the Mother of God*, eds. Susan L. Flader and J. Baird Callicott, 106.

89. Susan R. Schrepfer, *Nature's Altars: Mountains, Gender, and American Environmentalism* (Lawrence: University Press of Kansas, 2005), 160.

90. In "Wilderness as a Land Laboratory," Leopold further reveals his views on Native Americans while describing the wilderness landscape of the Sierra, commenting that it "retains its full fauna and flora (save only the wild Indian)," 289.

91. On the theme of hunting as a form of ritual sacrifice, see Walter Burkert, *Homo Necans: The Anthropology of Ancient Greek Sacrificial Ritual and Myth*, trans. Peter Bing (Berkeley: University of California Press, 1983), 12–22.

92. Ingeborg Flügel, "Some Psychological Aspects of a Fox-Hunting Rite," *International Journal of Psycho-Analysis* 12 (1931): 487.

93. Leopold, "River of the Mother of God," 125.

94. Leopold, "Wildlife in American Culture," 177–178.

95. Paul S. Sutter, "'A Blank Spot on the Map': Aldo Leopold, Wilderness, and U.S. Forest Service Recreational Policy, 1909–1924," *Western Historical Quarterly* 29, no. 2 (Summer 1998): 208.

96. Aldo Leopold, "The Wilderness and Its Place in Forest Recreational Policy," in *River of the Mother of God,* eds. Susan L. Flader and J. Baird Callicott, 81. Originally published in *Journal of Forestry* 19, no. 7 (November 1921): 718–721.

97. Sutter, "'Blank Spot on the Map,'" 208.

98. Aldo Leopold, "Game Methods: The American Way," in *River of the Mother of God*, eds. Susan L. Flader and J. Baird Callicott, 163.

99. Leopold, "Game Methods," 158, 159.

100. Leopold, "River of the Mother of God," 126.

101. Roderick Nash argues that Leopold at times comes very close to plagiarizing Darwin's ideas of an expanding ethic. Nash, "Aldo Leopold's Intellectual Heritage," 80. Callicott, in turn, points out that Darwin's conception of ethics is indebted to Hume, who argued that ethical behavior depends upon and is motivated by "the moral sentiments." See Callicott, "Hume's *Is/Ought* Dichotomy," in *In Defense of the Land Ethic*, 118.

102. Leopold, "Land Ethic," 201.

103. Leopold, "Land Ethic," 202–203.

104. Eugene C. Hargrove, *Foundations of Environmental Ethics* (Englewood Cliffs, N.J.: Prentice Hall, 1989), 70.

105. Leopold, "Forestry and Game Conservation," 59.

106. Leopold, "Wilderness as a Form of Land Use," 139.

107. Reflecting upon the importance of hunting to Leopold's land ethic, Callicott states, "[Leopold] may even have harbored the belief—however troubling and paradoxical it may seem—that a genuine and deep 'love and respect' for nature is possible only through a specific form of direct physical experience with nature: hunting. Hunting was the portal through which Leopold himself embarked on his romance with nature and it was the kind of experience that led to his mature environmental attitude and values, including his land ethic." In "Turning the Whole Soul: The Educational Dialectic of *A Sand County Almanac*," *Worldviews* 9, no. 3 (2005): 366.

108. Leopold, "Goose Music," 168–169.

109. Leopold, "Conservation Esthetic," (essay) in *Sand County Almanac,* 168.

110. Leopold, "Wilderness" (essay), in *Sand County Almanac,* 199.

111. Leopold, "Wilderness and Its Place in Forest Recreational Policy," 79.

112. Leopold, "Social Consequences of Conservation," undated manuscript, quoted in Meine, *Aldo Leopold: His Life and Work*, 296. Meine states that Leopold was groping to reconcile the "wild-lifers" and the "gunners" in this passage. It is interesting to note that Leopold believed that scientific study of nature might function as a substitute for sport hunting for men in their advanced years, despite his continued pursuit of it.

113. Thomas L. Altherr, "'Chaplain to the Hunters': Henry David Thoreau's Ambivalence Toward Hunting," *American Literature* 56, no. 3 (1984): 345–361.

# 5

## The Ecophilosophy of Holmes Rolston III

In my opinion, the greatest scandal of philosophy is that, while all around us the world of nature perishes—and not the world of nature alone—philosophers continue to talk, sometimes cleverly and sometimes not, about the question of whether this world exists.

Karl Popper
*Objective Knowledge* (p. 32)

### INTRODUCTION

**W**hile debate over the existence of the world continues to preoccupy many philosophers, in the postmodern world a new breed of philosophers have turned their energies to another realm: the existence of values in nature. Is value an objective quality that inheres in nature, or do some humans merely attribute value to it? Modern nature ethicists have sought to resolve this debate, and Holmes Rolston III believes that he has found the answer.

Rolston is widely regarded as a pioneer in the development of the field of nature ethics and as one of its leading philosophers. Recipient of numerous accolades, including the prestigious Templeton Prize for Progress or Discoveries about Spiritual Realities, and the renowned Gifford Lectureship, he is widely cited in books and courses on nature ethics. Although Rolston's writings are more abstract than those of Roosevelt and Leopold, they raise many of the same themes and provoke similar questions. What is the place of individual animals in the biotic whole? What role is played by feelings of care? What obligations do humans have to nature? And to what extent do Rolston's views reflect a masculinist orientation, which values reason over emotion, humans over other-than-human animals, spirit over matter, and the "whole" over individual beings?

## PHILOSOPHICAL BACKGROUND

Since David Hume published *A Treatise of Human Nature*, most philosophers have agreed that humans project their evaluative feelings of right and wrong onto nature. In Hume's formulation, good and evil are not objective qualities of the external world, but rather feelings of approbation or disapprobation that arise in humans upon the contemplation of some action or object. Hume characterized the fallacy of misplaced attribution of value as the "is/ought" dichotomy.[1] It is this dichotomy that Rolston seeks to address.

Rolston speaks of himself as a "wilderness guide" mapping the "unexplored theoretical ground" of environmental ethics, leading his readers on an uncharted journey from the realm of nature to the realm of morality, from the "is" to the "ought."[2] Echoes of the sense of adventure that Roosevelt and Leopold derived from hunting can be discerned in Rolston's description of the path to ecological morality: "[it requires] the daring, and caution, of a community of scientists and ethicists who can together map both the ecosystem and the ethical grammar appropriate for it."[3] Although humans "go in the track of our surroundings," responding to natural values, when we develop our appreciative experience of nature we are "trailblazing" our way into an "ethical frontier."[4] He brings a formidable background to the task of building the bridge between nature and moral theory. With undergraduate degrees in physics and math, a doctorate in theology and religious studies, and a master's degree in the philosophy of science, Rolston was first drawn to physics by its "harmony, symmetry, universal law, beauty, elegance," as well as its potential to transform the world.[5] He became disenchanted with physics, however, because it reduced the Earth to a "speck of dust" and humans to "nothing but matter in motion." Moving on to biology, he had occasion to take a class taught by an entomologist, who impressed Rolston with his ability to "[see] things that nobody else was seeing." Under the binocular microscope Rolston learned that you could see things that you "did not catch in cloud chambers." Ultimately, though, Rolston, the son of a Presbyterian minister, pursued theology, hoping to find answers to his questions about the nature of nature. As he reasoned, "Why not study what nature really was—creation—and that meant learning about the Creator."[6]

Rolston worked as a pastor for ten years in southwestern Virginia where he also took biology classes and explored the southern Appalachian Mountains.

Just as he had earlier yearned for a metaphysic to complement his physics, Rolston came to feel the need for a philosophy to go with his biology. Discouraged by fellow theologians in his interest in a theology of nature, he turned to philosophy. He was disappointed to discover that the proponents of the positivist vogue in philosophy did not welcome his quest for a philosophy of nature. As he comments,

> These hard naturalists were worse humanists than the theologians. Nonhuman nature was value-free, nothing but a resource for the satisfaction of human desires, abetted by the skills of science. Value was entirely in the eye of the beholder, assigned by the preference of the valuer.[7]

Rolston ultimately found an academic niche as a professor of philosophy at Colorado State University, where he currently teaches classes in environmental ethics.

Rolston attributes his belief in the objective value of nature to several influences: the "disgraceful" deforestation and strip-mining in his favorite forests and mountains near his birthplace in Virginia; his interest in mosses, impressive for their ability to flourish with complete indifference to philosophers and theologians; and the philosophy of Aldo Leopold, especially Leopold's emphasis on the moral value of the ecosystem.[8] Inspired by these influences, Rolston wrote his famous essay, "Is There an Ecological Ethic?" published in 1975 in the journal *Ethics*.[9] The appearance of this article in a mainstream journal of academic philosophy gave credibility to the emerging field and helped pave the way for a specialized journal devoted to philosophical discussion of environmental ethics.[10]

Rolston has written five books and over seventy articles challenging the prevailing anthropocentric view that denies nature a value independent of human needs. It has been equally important to Rolston to avoid subjectivism, which defines environmental ethics as a matter of human preference or choice.[11] According to Rolston, the natural world has value apart from human awareness, but when humans "discover" this value, new values arise, along with corresponding duties. Thus, humans "are not so much lighting up value in a merely potentially valuable world as they are psychologically *joining* an ongoing defense of biological value."[12]

Rolston's belief in nature's objective value is a minority position among nature ethicists. Yet his focus on the idea of "value" is not. Since the inception of the field of nature ethics, philosophers have debated the validity of attributing intrinsic or inherent value to nature. The debate was significantly shaped by the publication of an article by Richard Routley in 1973. Routley asked his readers to entertain a thought experiment in which a lone survivor of a catastrophic event sets out, with malevolent design, to destroy a redwood grove. He invites his readers to consider whether a moral wrong can be perpetrated upon nature if no humans exist who care about nature's fate.[13] The deeper question posed by Routley's piece was whether nature had nonanthropocentric or intrinsic value.

In arguing for the value of nature, environmental theorists hope to provide a reasoned defense against the aggressive and predatory ethos toward nature prevalent in the modern world.[14] Ironically, the debate has acquired an aggressive aspect of its own. The "hunt" for environmental ethics has come to resemble a competitive sport in which nature theorists act as judges of which natural entities can "play" the game. They assign "scores" or "values" to the different entities of nature that are allowed to compete. There are winners and losers. The "winners" are usually those believed to resemble humans in the possession of qualities such as "sentience," "consciousness," "rationality," and "autonomy." The losers, thought to lack these traits, become objects devoid of interests or rights. Routley's article asks us to consider what would happen if the "judges" in the competition were disqualified for (anthropocentric) bias.

Rolston believes that he has found the solution to Routley's thought experiment as well as to the "is/ought" dilemma. The judges need not be recalled; rather, the rules for judging need to be reformulated. Since Rolston maintains that nature has value apart from human beings, it is therefore not accurate to say that human beings *bring* value to nature. Nor is it valid to claim that nature has no objective value without human valuers. Human beings *join* in an ongoing natural process, which is continuously producing objective instrumental and intrinsic values. The "judges," therefore, need not be dismissed for lack of impartiality; they need only accept their participatory role.

Rolston thus sets out to objectively identify the distinct values that exist in nature, along with the appropriate duties they are owed. He perceives three kinds of values in nature: instrumental, intrinsic, and systemic. Instrumental value means something is appreciated as a means to an end. Thus, insects value plants for the energy they provide and warblers value insects for their protein.[15] Humans reflect this instrumental view of nature when they ask, "What is it good for?" The term intrinsic value, by contrast, is used to characterize an entity that is regarded as "worthwhile in itself without necessary contributory reference."[16] According to this approach, one "appreciates a forest" as more than "just board feet of timber."[17] Organisms have both instrumental and intrinsic value. The ecosystem, however, has neither simply an instrumental, nor exactly an intrinsic value, since it cannot value itself in the way that an organism can. As the "productive process" or "source" of all value, it merits a new term: systemic value.

Rolston locates intrinsic value in the struggle of all organisms to preserve their own integrity, as an end in itself. Every organism in nature has a *telos* or "good-of-its-kind." The attempt to "defend" their lives demonstrates biologically that all organisms "care" about what happens to them. Rolston believes that "if we attach value to life defended (rather than to human preferences), then we must attach value to plants, because plants defend their lives as good-in-themselves."[18] Instrumental and intrinsic values are intermeshed with one another in the ecosystem in the sense that no organism is a mere instrument, for each has its integral intrinsic value. Nevertheless, when one life is "sacrificed" for another, "its intrinsic value collapses, becomes extrinsic, and is in part instrumentally transported to another organism."[19]

All natural entities do not have equal value, according to Rolston, and hence equal rights and equal consideration are inappropriate. In *Environmental Ethics*, Rolston constructs a hierarchy of values for various categories of nature that, in turn, impose corresponding duties. Humans have the greatest intrinsic value, followed by animal life (in proportion to phylogenetic or neural complexity), then plant life, and finally, microbes.[20] Rolston contends that higher organisms have greater intrinsic value than plants because they "realize a greater range of values" and represent a greater evolutionary achievement.[21] However, Rolston reserves the "cardinal value" in nature for the ecosystem, which holds systemic value. "The individual is programmed to make more of its kind," he explains, while "the system is making more kinds."[22] It is therefore a source for multiple values. Humans have duties to the system "that projects and protects, regenerates and reforms all these member components in the biotic community." In Rolston's holistic philosophy, duties to the ecosystem will almost always come before duties toward individuals: "Perhaps on some occasions duties to the products will override duties to the system that produced them, but—apart from humans who live in culture as well as in nature—this will seldom be true."[23]

Rolston posits the idea of a distinct moral status for humans, based on their unique mental capabilities. While other organisms treat one another instrumentally, only humans can appreciate the intrinsic value of nature. This capacity to see beyond their self-interests gives humans the special obligation to be evaluators and care-takers for the natural world. "The task of environmental ethics," then, is to "identify and adjudicate" the intertwined interests of plants, animals, and humans.[24]

## VALUING METAPHORS

Rolston employs numerous metaphors which appear at odds with his intentions. Many of these metaphors reflect a masculinist orientation, elevating mind over matter, spirit over nature, and the conscious over the unconscious. Rolston commonly refers to ecosystems as a "productive process" or compares them to "market economics."[25] Individual organisms are "programmed to make more of [their] kind," species are "a cybernetic achievement," and "randomness" in nature functions as a "values generator, a value transformer."[26] As the most "sophisticated product" of the "productive process," humans "have the highest per capita intrinsic value."[27] According to Rolston, "value appreciates (increases) with humans," who "cash in on, and spend, what is naturally given."[28] Interests in nature are "investments in a bigger corporation,"[29] and humans "ought not to spend biological capital without a resolute effort to engineer an alternative."[30] The ecosystem is "an economy in which the many components have been naturally selected for efficient fitness in a prolific system."[31] In the ethical sphere, "the moral sense then becomes a new form of cybernetic control."[32]

Rolston also uses fertility metaphors to suggest that nature is not *fully* complete without the fertilization that human consciousness brings. The ecosystem is valued for its "fertility" and "generative capacity."[33] It is the "womb of life" and a "pregnant Earth."[34] For Rolston, "the most impressive feature of Earth" is its "fecundity" and "creativity."[35] And although humans do not create nature's value, the "objective roots of value" are described by Rolston as achieving their "fruits" in human "subjectivity."[36] Human beings culminate the productive process by bringing their "subjectivity to intense focus to complement objectivity."[37] Rolston describes human valuing as a kind of "internal excitation" and argues that environmental ethics "consummates" the evolutionary ethic, generating new values.[38] The relation between humans and nature is also viewed as an attraction of opposites. As both "mother and wife," "nature is . . . the bosom out of which we have come, and she remains our life partner, a realm of otherness for which we have the deepest need."[39] Elsewhere, Rolston comments, "human valuation of nature, like our perceptions, is drawn from environmental intercourse."[40]

Rolston's emphasis on nature as the generating matrix of value is designed to counter the low regard for nature that is prevalent in modern society. However, his use of the metaphors of fertility and production perpetuates a masculinist view of nature as the feminine raw material out of which the superior realm of spirit and ethical values emerges.

## THE DISCOVERY OF HUMAN SUPERIORITY

Rolston concedes that human superiority does not derive from biological usefulness, since humans have none. Yet one finds repeated references to human superiority throughout his work. These assertions reflect an orientation based on an opposition between culture and nature, spirit and matter, reason and emotion, the conscious and the unconscious, and transcendence and immanence. According to Rolston, humans are superior "cognitively," "ethically," "critically," and "culturally."[41] They are the "ablest form of life," as well as its "most sophisticated product."[42] Humans have "wonderful brains." Their minds are "the most interesting and, presumably, the rarest thing in the universe."[43] Humans are also the "wise species," who are alone in having "personality" and in doing things with "self-conscious design."[44] The moral significance of this superior cognitive capacity is that they can appreciate the ecological "whole" or global story. Only humans can stand outside of themselves and appreciate the intrinsic value of nature: "Humans are spectacular because they emerge to see the spectacle they are in."[45]

Rolston contrasts this capacity for transcendence with the self-centered orientation of other organisms in the natural world. From the perspective of individual organisms,

> interactions . . . are nothing but struggle. Each is out for itself, pitted against others in predation and competition. Carnivores kill herbivores, who consume the grasses and forbs. Every living thing pushes itself through the world and grabs resources.[46]

Rolston corrects this predatory view, adding that modern biology prefers the model of adaptive fitness, which can moderate the competition. Nevertheless, individual organisms are "aggrandizing unit[s] in the hunt for instrumental value," unable to appreciate the larger order that emerges at the level of the ecosystem or "productive process."[47] With the evolutionary appearance of human subjective awareness, "wildness as a jungle of exploitation becomes a theater of adventure and improvisation."[48] According to Rolston, only human beings have the capacity to

> take a sustained interest in sectors of the environment not their own. . . . For the first time, a form of life values something outside its own niche, cares intensively or comprehensively beyond its own pragmatic sector. . . . We meet this creature who can value at a distance.[49]

In transcending survival values, human beings attain "an almost supernatural altruism, unprecedented on the planet."[50] He concludes that "they are superior in loving the other, perhaps even as themselves."[51]

This flattering depiction of human beings has a number of conceptual problems. Rolston attributes human superiority to the ability to move beyond a self-centered worldview. Yet this assertion of superiority hardly sounds like genuine, non-self-centered love. Rolston also claims that human superiority is based in part upon the human *capacity* to love the parts of nature. However, capacity and actuality are two distinct phenomena. Rolston does not clarify whether the mere capacity to love the rest of creation is *sufficient* grounds for human superiority, or whether only those who are "self-realized" are superior. What happens to Rolston's environmental ethic if most of humanity fails to "discover" nature's value? Rolston concedes that most people will not be capable of comprehending the metaphysical implications of natural history. By and large, however, he appears to be so intent on praising human *capacities* that he fails to acknowledge *real* human conduct toward the natural world. It is, perhaps, more accurate to argue that human beings are unique in our capacity to soil our own nest and in our unparalleled violence toward our own species as well as others.[52]

## THE GLOBAL OVERSEER: THINKING LIKE THE ECOSYSTEM

Rolston rarely makes direct reference to religious ideas in his best-known work, and most commentators overlook this dimension of his thought.[53] One can, however, detect a religious subtext to his writing in notions of spiritual transcendence, human stewardship, the redemptive value of suffering, and the idea of God's presence in history.[54] Although never explicitly stated, Rolston's depiction of the ecosystem as the "source" suggests the traditional image of the Jewish and Christian God who brings order out of chaos. As the "generating matrix" of all life, the ecosystem is the "cardinal value" to which individual organisms are subordinated.

Similarly, Rolston's ideas of human stewardship of nature parallel the Jewish and Christian notion of human beings' special role as care-taker of Creation. As the sole species which can grasp the order and intrinsic value of nature and "link up" its interests with "the whole natural Earth," humans are conferred dominion, by evolutionary history, over the rest of the natural world. They must not dominate nature for their own self-interests, however. Genuine transcendence entails an "overarching care for others."[55]

Although Rolston does not invoke the idea of a divine sanction for human guardianship over nature, he believes that people are adapted by evolution to be stewards and have "a dominion involving genuine transcendence."[56] As he elaborates, "Several billion years worth of creative toil, several million species of teeming life, have been handed over to the care of this late-coming species in which mind has flowered and morals have emerged."[57] Human superiority gives us an "aristocratic responsibility for the natural world."[58] Rolston contends, "Although humans are 'citizens' within nature, it may well be that the role of man [*sic*]— at once 'citizen' and 'king'—is to govern what has hitherto been the partial success of the evolutionary process. . . . This permits interference with and rearrangement of nature's spontaneous course. It enjoins domestication."[59] For Rolston, domestication is simply a "natural" expression of the "capture of value" for humans and therefore something that should be pursued.

Rolston's development of the idea of nature's evolutionary story also parallels the Jewish and Christian emphasis on history. Judaism and Christianity differed from earlier worldviews in the belief that life on earth follows a divine historical rather than cyclical development. In a similar vein, Rolston seeks to replace the notion of nature as endless repetition with one of nature as storied achievement. Evolution is a grand adventure, an epic drama, awaiting the "last chapter" which humans alone can provide.[60]

Rolston's views on the unique role of humans in understanding nature resembles Teilhard de Chardin's philosophy that humans "complete" the Creation through their ability to "admire" it.[61] Rolston perceives the natural world as an evolutionary drama, deserving of aesthetic appreciation. As Rolston comments, "one human role is to admire and respect the ecosystems they culminate."[62] According to this view, evolution is an unfolding story that "comes to a head in humans," the only species able to comprehend and admire it. He reasons, "The systemic source cannot reflectively evaluate what it has produced; only we can." Moreover, when humans learn to value this larger story, they "become nobler spirits."[63] When they fail this task, they "act like beasts."[64] Although human beings are cognitively superior to nature, they demonstrate their *moral* superiority only through their ability to value things outside of themselves.[65]

Rolston depicts the human ascent out of the "beastly realm" as human destiny. In the "climb to humanity . . . 'natural man'—and woman—need to become the spiritual man and woman; they need their broken spirits inspired by the divine spirit (*pneuma*, 'wind,' in-spiring), divine inspiriting elevating the mere biology."[66]

Rolston conceptualizes this human ascent to spirit as a second and superior birth. As he writes, "This genesis of spirit, recompounded from nature, requires the second birth superimposed on the first, transcending natural possibilities."[67] Rolston also equates this transcendence of our purely biological existence with the expansive awareness found in Maslow's theory of self-actualization. He draws from Maslow,

> Self-actualizing people are more able to perceive the world as if it were independent not only of them but also of human beings in general. This also tends to be true of the average human being in his highest moments, i.e. in his peak experiences. He can then more readily look upon nature as if it were there in itself and for itself, and not simply as if it were a human playground put there for human purposes.[68]

The other organisms, by contrast, are mired in the realm of immanence, unable to focus on anything other than their own survival. Other-than-human animals have a "gastrocentric view (centering on food), a self-centered view (protecting its kind)" and "a species-centered view (propagating its kind)."[69] Only human beings can see beyond such self-centered needs. When human beings stand back and appreciate the "wild" drama of existence, they become more human and help to create a "more sophisticated storied achievement."[70]

Rolston's formulations often reflect the transcendental notion that nature veils a divine presence which only human beings can decipher: "The landscape is a text to be interpreted, as surely as the cultural heritage recorded in our libraries."[71] The divine spark of creation is not equivalent to nature, but is contained within it. The inherent inventiveness of the "productive process" "throws up" values, the "critical value" being "survival." God's transcendence, however, is reflected first and foremost in nature's regenerative capacity. Like Leopold, Rolston refers to the idea of plenitude, which he locates in nature's fertility. As he states, "Earth is a fertile planet, and in one sense, fertility is the deepest value category of all, one classically reached by the category of creation." But according to Rolston, such fecundity, which underlies all life, is best understood as "divine creativity." As he elaborates, the divine spirit expresses itself in and through the systemic process. This enthralling creativity "leads and lures us along available routes of Earth history."[72]

Acknowledging the creative spark within nature, Rolston rejects the deontological analogue of divine command. We should respect nature not because it is God's command, nor because it is an ethical imperative. Rather, he argues, humans are encouraged to *adapt* their conduct to the creative, the natural processes that ecosystems project.[73] In contrast to the traditional Jewish and Christian conception of God as history's omnipotent architect, Rolston argues that "God is not molding . . . craftsman-like."[74] Rolston's God acts from below and

> microscopically creates the energetic, pro-life material which bubbles up trials. "From above," systematically and environmentally, God coaxes forth living organisms via selectivity intrinsic in the processes and God selects the best adapted via natural selection.[75]

Like Leopold, Rolston defines ecological understanding as the basis of a transcendent view that leads to caring for the larger community. Rolston further spiritualizes the idea, viewing it as an awareness of divine creativity, a transcendent realm that transforms purely biological nature. Concurring with Leopold on the evolutionary development of the ecological conscience, Rolston asks if there would not be something "magnificent about an evolution of conscience that circumscribed the whole."[76] From this God-like vantage point, human beings develop a reverence and respect for all of life. Thus, reverence, empathy, and feelings of compassion spring from a scientific understanding of ecology and metaphysics. Rolston compares the experience of astronauts to the experience of biologists who study natural history: "Viewing the fertile Earth, they get in space something of the experience that biologists get in time—a glimpse of divinity."[77] But does this scientifically inspired, God-like view include care for individual other-than-human animals?[78]

Rolston considers animal suffering within the context of his views on ecological maturity. The "typically modern man" sees only an arena of random struggle and conflict, feeling "afloat on and adrift in an indifferent, if not a hostile universe." The mature "ecological man," who has an awareness of ecological science, feels at home because he is aware of belonging to "a community of value."[79] As Rolston explains, "like business, politics and sports, ecosystems thrive on competition."[80] Moreover, he contends, "life is a suffering through to something higher, which, seen from an earthly side, seems to be random chance, but seen from a godward side, is divine creativity."[81] This view of maturity leads Rolston to respond to the concern over animal suffering by asking, "Is nature at the level of sentient life a passion play?"[82]

Rolston's pronouncements on the beneficial function of suffering in nature reflect the traditional Christian belief that suffering is valuable as a vehicle for spiritual ennoblement. Rolston perceives animal suffering as a "sacrifice" that conforms to this Christian ideal. It is nature as a whole that is advanced by sacrifice, not individual beings. As he states, "Each of the suffering creatures is delivered over as an innocent sacrificed to preserve a line, a blood sacrifice perishing that others may live."[83] Rolston explicitly compares this tragic aspect of nature to the "sacrifice of the Son of God," who is "led to slaughter" and then produces "new life."[84] He argues that "there is a necessary element of tragedy in the drama of creation, the blood sacrifice on which sentient life is founded, which both *is* and *ought to be*."[85] Acceptance of this redemptive aspect of life demonstrates a mature moral and spiritual understanding.

## THE CAPTURE OF ANIMALS IN VALUES

Rolston's arguments about human duties to other-than-humans are the weakest part of his philosophy, revealing a masculinist orientation that subordinates empathy and care to an abstract conception of value. He acknowledges that his attitude toward animals "will disappoint animal activists. . . . I eat animals and leave them to perish in the wild. I kill goats to save a few endangered plants. I tolerate hunting, under ecosystemic conditions. I accept some wildlife commerce as a management tool. I seem to have no mercy."[86] He defends these practices because he believes that they are consistent with the capturing of values that occurs in the natural world, as exhibited by predators who consume what they need. But while Rolston's theory may capture values in nature, his values also function to capture animals.[87]

Rolston's views about animals contain a number of inconsistencies. Although he places animals above plants in moral value, due to their higher consciousness, he argues that duties to other-than-human animals are less stringent than those owed to plants, since plants serve a greater instrumental good in the ecosystem.[88] Obligations owed to plants are governed by what Rolston refers to as the principle of the "nonloss of goods." As he reasons, although plants do not experience pain, each organism is a center of life and deserves respect for its struggle to maintain that life. The goods that humans achieve in life must outweigh those that plants "sacrifice" for human well-being. Thus, the aesthetic appreciation derived from picking a bouquet of flowers must be greater than "the goods of the flowers destroyed."[89]

Duties to other-than-human animals follow the "homologous principle" and the "non-addition principle," both of which judge ethical conduct toward animals relative to a benchmark found in the ecosystem. The former states that humans have a duty to "not cause inordinate suffering, beyond those orders of nature from which the animals were taken. . . . Culturally imposed suffering must be comparable to ecological functional suffering."[90] In other words, it must serve a similar ecological function or "logic." Killing and eating animals is therefore seen as comparable (i.e., homologous) to predation. The nonaddition principle further posits that humans should not *amplify* the suffering that already exists in nature. Thus, although animal suffering must not be "pointless," it is acceptable as long as it does not augment what might have occurred in the ecosystem.

Rolston, however, weakens the homologous principle through his strained understanding of "ecological suffering," condoning the use of animals for medical experimentation and agricultural production of food, neither of which are found in the ecosystem. He further stretches the homologous principle by maintaining that humans "*may substitute variant forms in their interests*" (emphasis added).[91] Furthermore, although humans should not amplify the cruelty in nature, he pointedly adds, "*certainly not without showing that greater goods come of doing so*" (emphasis added).[92] Thus, humans have only to proclaim that greater goods will ensue from the infliction of animal suffering to make it acceptable. The homologous principle receives a final blow in his statement that duties to animals may be superseded by "basic human interests," since "in culture there are necessities unknown in nature."[93] Thus, what begins as an attempt to follow nature ends by allowing humans to use animals in ways that do not exist in the natural world.

As philosopher Ned Hettinger points out, Rolston's principles for the treatment of other-than-human animals allow for the loss of values, while his principles for the treatment of plants conserve values:

> Although Rolston's theory includes a strong consequentialist principle that must be satisfied before one can take a plant life, viz., the values achieved as a result of our behavior must at least equal the values lost, his principles protecting animals are weaker deontological ones, requiring only that we act in the right sort of way and for the right reason. In general, the two principles protecting animals . . . are compatible with behavior that causes an overall loss of value in human interaction with animals, which Rolston prohibits in comparable interaction with plants.[94]

Rolston justifies his greater consideration for plants on ecological grounds. He argues that since collectively plants have a greater instrumental value to the ecosystem than animals, other-than-human animals may be sacrificed to preserve the health of an ecosystem. Moreover, plants should be given greater consideration than other-than-human animals if they are endangered, since biological diversity is a good of the ecosystem, the cardinal value.

Rolston's primary justification for conceding to the sacrifice of other-than-human animals stems from what he believes is natural within human culture. However, he establishes a distinct set of rules for what is natural for humans, arguing that humans are both a part of nature and a part of culture. Thus a naturalistic ethic, according to Rolston, needs to recognize (1) what humans share with animals, (2) the nature of humans, and (3) how culture differs from nature.[95] While human culture should try to conform to the workings of the natural world, humans must recognize what is distinctly natural to them within this realm.

Rolston's formulation that human beings should pursue activities that are natural for them *within the realm of culture* functions as an escape clause for his principle that humans should cause no more harm than already exists within the natural world. Thus, he argues that it is natural for humans to exploit nature. Humans should not prohibit this relation, since to do so would be forbidding all culture.[96]

One of Rolston's primary justifications for the use of animals is that it is "homologous" with predation in nature. Thus meat-eating for humans is "analogous to predation" and a "natural component of ecosystems, one to which we do not object."[97] Some of the necessities that Rolston cites as basic human interests include the "natural" use of animals for the manufacture of shoes, wool, and insulin. These are examples of the natural "capture of value" or the "hunt" for value in which all organisms are engaged. Rolston concedes that these activities are unknown in nature, and that this argument stretches the homologous logic beyond food chains.[98] Nonetheless, he contends that since they serve "basic human needs," there are no grounds for objecting to them. Rolston appears to overlook the lack of consensus concerning what is natural and necessary, or basic, for humans. In addition, his focus on the "naturalness" of meat-eating overlooks the cultural context within which meat-eating occurs, and in particular its long historical association with class, prestige, privilege, and masculine identity.

In his homologous principle, Rolston fails to appreciate the distinct context in which "natural" functions are performed. Hunting and animal agriculture may appear to be similar when only one function—the procurement of food—is considered. However, when the manner in which this procurement occurs is considered as well as the motives, the analogy breaks down. Rolston overlooks the glaring lack of similarity between the use of animals for the production of food, clothing, or medicine, and predation in the other-than-human world. Almost without exception, no species other than humans subjects other species to a life of confinement and suffering for the provision of food, clothing, and medicine.[99]

Rolston contends that domestication follows the principles of ecosystems in "capturing agriculturally the values in a cow," and that "there is nothing undignified in this event, even though the once natural values in the cow, like those in the gazelle, have to be destroyed by the predator." He furthermore argues that a cow *cannot* be treated with indignity, since in contrast to a gazelle, who is "pure wild grace," a cow is "a meat factory, pure and simple . . . cows cannot know they are disgraced."[100] Rolston supports his dismissal of animal welfare concerns with the argument that "domestic animals are only partly natural;" they are "bred to be eaten."[101] But if domestic animals are only partly natural, are not humans responsible for making them so? The argument for dismissing their suffering becomes circular. Because they are degraded to begin with (not natural), it is acceptable to treat them as objects or as "meat-machines." Rolston's views on domestic animals seem a far cry from his eloquent arguments for the intrinsic worth of nature.

Paradoxically, Rolston's views on hunting are at once more grounded in naturalistic philosophy and more spiritualized than those of Roosevelt or Leopold. Rolston condemns trophy hunting and hunting *merely* for sport. Similarly, he decries the killing of elephants to make ivory piano keys and the killing of animals for fur. None of these activities, according to Rolston, are "natural." But he considers sport hunting acceptable if the hunter eats the flesh of the animal he kills, since this conforms to survival values.[102] In a similar vein, Rolston denounces the religious sacrifice of animals but argues that he "can tolerate such sacrifice where animals are eaten (as Jews and Muslims do)."[103] When the flesh of animals is eaten in hunting and animal sacrifice, there is a "natural component."[104]

Like Roosevelt and Leopold, Rolston believes that hunting is a natural activity for humans when conducted in appropriate ways. And like his predecessors, he praises hunting for its playful reenactment of "the primordial hunt."[105] Similarly, he finds the value of sport hunting in its sublimation of drives that would otherwise threaten civilization. It therefore has instrumental value for civilization that transcends its value as mere sport. Thus, he states, "the sport hunt sublimates the drive for conquest, a drive without which humans could not have survived, without which we cannot be civilized."[106]

Rolston compares the urge to hunt to the sexual drive: "Perhaps the hunting drive, like the sexual urge, is dangerous to suppress and must be reckoned with."[107] Rolston uses the sexual analogy to underscore the importance of allowing the hunting urge free expression. But the comparison with the sexual urge is problematic, as can be seen by extending his analysis into the human realm. Sex is both a biological drive and a socially constructed activity. A man who rapes a woman cannot credibly defend his actions by saying the rape provided a much-needed outlet for his sexual energy. Nor can he claim that it fulfilled a necessary ecological role in perpetuating the species. Rape is wrong because it is a violation of another living being.

This analysis pertains equally to sport hunting. Rolston's analysis of the analogous benefits of hunting to sexual expression elides the reality of the violent manner in which this expression occurs. It also fails to explore other motives that may underlie the violent expression of "natural" drives. The literature on rape disputes the idea that sexual violence is a mode of sexual gratification, arguing that rapists are not motivated by the urge to fulfill a sexual drive, nor are they out of control. On the contrary, rape is an attempt to establish men's dominance and control.[108] Similarly, hunting may be seen as a mode of sexual violence that entails the assertion of masculine dominance and control over the natural world.[109]

Rolston further supports sport hunting by arguing that it is a valuable lesson in predation and in ecology. "In ways that mere watchers of nature can never know, hunters know their ecology," he maintains. "The hunter's success is not conquest but submission to the ecology. It is an acceptance of the way the world is made."[110] Thus, it is "no embarrassment" that "men enjoy skilled hunting, mixed with unease about killing. After all the tiger enjoys her kill, necessary as this is."[111] He buttresses his defense of sport hunting by suggesting that it is not really sport, but "a sacrament of the fundamental, mandatory seeking and taking possession of value that characterizes an ecosystem and from which no culture ever escapes."[112] Once again, Rolston emphasizes the supposed psychological benefits that accrue to men who hunt, while overlooking the violent manner in which these benefits are obtained.

Rolston elevates ethical principles and guidelines for the treatment of other-than-human animals over empathy and compassion for their plight. His formulation of the homologous functions that humans and animals share shows little appreciation for the analogous nature of human and animal experience, especially suffering.[113] He has harsh words for those who "sympathize with the pains of animals and wish to eliminate these pains," perceiving such people as "not biologically sensitive but insensitive."[114] According to Rolston, the acceptance of the ecological necessity of killing is a mark of moral maturity realized in the activity of hunting. As he explains, "the ecological ethic, which kills in place, is really more advanced, more harmonious with nature, than the animal rights ethic, which, in utter disharmony with the way the world is made, kills no animals at all."[115] Pain is a "pervasive fact of life, not to be wished away by a kindly ethic either in natural systems or in cultural overlays on these systems. Suffering is a necessary evil, a sad good, a dialectical value."[116]

Rolston concedes that humans have a duty to avoid the "pointless" infliction of pain upon animals "as far as possible," not out of "justice," but out of benevolence.[117] Any concern beyond the "benchmark" of pain provided by ecology, however, is a "hedonist concern" that defies the laws of ecology.[118] He contends that

> Sentience in nature and sentience in culture are not really the same thing, despite their common physiology and origin. Sentience in nature belongs with food chains and natural selection; sentience in culture has been transformed into another gestalt, that of self-reflective personality and moral agency. . . . Eating a person would disrupt personal life as set in a cultural pattern; it would reduce personal life to the level of animal life in an ecology. It insults persons to treat them as food objects by the criteria of animal ecology; persons may and must treat nonhuman lives as food objects, but it *respects* animals to treat them so (emphasis added).[119]

According to Rolston, respect for nature enjoins humans not only to hunt other-than-human animals, but to raise and kill animals for food.

Rolston further defends the suffering of domestic animals, arguing that although they may experience "physical pain" from confinement and impending death, their inferior cognitive capacities prevent them from suffering *affliction*. Affliction, for Rolston, requires the ability to anticipate the future. Thus, he argues that in contrast to humans, "chickens can live in ignorant *bliss* of their forthcoming slaughter" (emphasis added).[120] Anyone who has seen or heard of the horrific treatment of animals on factory farms would find Rolston's quibble over the distinction between affliction and suffering highly questionable. It sharply contrasts with his praise of humans for the capacity to stand outside of themselves and care for others.

## TRANSCENDENCE AND SPECIES

Rolston's holism consists in the position that it is "more important to protect" the "integrity" and "individuality" of species than to protect "individual integrity."[121] He explains, "a lost individual is always reproducible; a lost species is never reproducible."[122] Although species do not have a "self," according to Rolston, they do have a "biological identity" and to cause the extinction of a species is to shut down a "unique story."[123] Rolston attaches a higher value to species because they are integral "players" in the larger story, carried forward by the formative process. To be concerned over species extinction is not simply an instrumental concern about saving "the sinking ark." It is akin to a concern over "tearing pages out of an unread book."[124] Extinction, according to Rolston, "shuts down the generative processes." It is more important than killing individual beings since it "kills 'essences' beyond 'existences,' the 'soul' as well as the 'body.'"[125]

Rolston evokes Leopold's idea of "noumena" when he argues that "the individual represents (re-presents) a species in each new generation. It is a token of a type, and the type is more important than the token."[126] He maintains that "a duty to a species is more like being responsible to a cause than to a person. It is commitment to an *idea*" (Rolston's emphasis).[127] Rolston also regards species as a link across the generations. As he states, a species is "a specific form of life [that] unfolds an intergenerational narrative."[128] It is this narrative lifeline or "living drama" that humans are bound to respect, not its individual "actors." Rolston goes so far as to claim that "When we move to the level of species, we may kill individuals for the good of their kind."[129] The sensitivity that is absent in Rolston's discussion of individual animals is present in his discussion of species. Thus, "what is offensive in the impending extinctions is not merely the loss of rivers and resources, but the maelstrom of killing and insensitivity to forms of life and the forces producing them."[130] Yet despite Rolston's professed commitment to a noninstrumental conception of nature, he falls back on the language of utility. Species have value "as process, product, and instrument in the larger drama, toward which humans have duties instanced in duties to species."[131]

## LOCAL STORIES

Near the end of his major work, *Environmental Ethics*, Rolston softens his emphasis on the significance of human transcendence, arguing for the value of local stories. He acknowledges that the "role of historical overseers . . . may seem to require too advanced a reconstruction of natural history, too much scientific education, skill in environmental interpretation well past the capacities of most of Earth's residents." He concludes that "only a minority of humans have had, or can have, such a global overview."[132] Human limitations, it would seem, are such that the global story needs to be supplemented by local stories: "we need an art of life to go with the science of natural history."[133] Thus, we need to fit our environment not just systemically, but ideographically through embedded stories. He explains that in "complementing now the global oversight considered earlier, we seek a local view, not as ideal observers looking on from some original position, but as living participants in stories of our time and place. We must complement transcendence with immanence."[134]

Rolston maintains that an ethic must be "formal, general, universal, applicable without regard to time and place, true all over Earth." However, he continues, these abstractions are "only a skeleton."[135] He contends, "ethics is also a creative act, not simply the discovery and following of rules and duties."[136] An ethic "has an environment, a niche to inhabit. . . . Ethics evolve, as do species, and have storied development."[137]

Rolston's emphasis on the ethical significance of local stories, which tie humans to particular times and places, recalls Leopold's idea of not simply following external rules, but rather developing an emotional bond to the land. Rolston draws this parallel himself when he argues that Leopold's land ethic, which argued for maintaining the "integrity, stability, and beauty of the biotic community,"[138] was embedded in his love for the Wisconsin sand counties. As he states, "Leopold's biographical residence is the personal backing to his ethic."[139]

The focus on local stories and emotional attachments to the land is one of the most intriguing aspects of Rolston's work. While his ideas on objective value have sparked the greatest interest among theorists, a number of nature ethicists, including some ecofeminists, have embraced his ideas on narrative. Jim Cheney perceives Rolston's discussion of narrative as suggestive of a feminist sensibility,[140] and for Christopher Preston it demonstrates the common ground between Rolston's philosophy and that of ecofeminists.[141] However, even within Rolston's local perspective, emotional attachments are still directed to larger phenomena, like "species" and the "ecosystem," not individual beings.[142] In addition, Rolston reserves the capacity for lived story lines only for humans, maintaining that from an objective perspective, plants and animals have stories, but they cannot know their own stories: "plants and animals are historical beings objectively but do not know this subjectively. . . . Humans are the only historical subjects in a historically objective world."[143] Rolston appears to believe that the human capacity to *consciously* plan for the future makes human story lines unique. As he states, "A principal characteristic of human life is to develop into biography. . . . Humans want a storied residence in nature where the passage of time integrates past, present, and future in a meaningful career."[144] By contrast, Rolston argues that nature "runs automatically and, within her more active creatures, instinctively, or perhaps in rudimentarily cognitive ways. But persons do things by self-conscious design, which is different."[145]

Rolston's characterization of animals as instinctive and without subjective story lines recalls the "Nature Faker" debate in which Roosevelt and Burroughs objected to the depiction of animals in children's stories. Both decried the idea that an animal could be the subject of a life, motivated by conscious choice, rather than following mere instinct. Human superiority is found in the capacity to transcend the unconscious (instinctive) biological realm in favor of a self-conscious perspective capable of objectively viewing and assessing one's own story lines as well as the larger "whole."

The depiction of animals as driven by instinct and of humans as uniquely capable of being governed by conscious deliberation does a disservice not only to other-than-humans, but to human beings as well. Many of us whose plans are ill-defined, and who do not believe, along with Rolston, that we "always act deliberately," may wonder if we qualify, according to such philosophical standards, as full-fledged human beings.

## CONCLUSION

Rolston's environmental philosophy is an ambitious attempt to chart a new direction for environmental philosophy. He takes the position that humans do not bring value to a valueless world, but rather "discover it." Yet, at the end of his long philosophical journey, Rolston arrives full circle, reinforcing the traditional masculinist dualisms: conscious/unconscious, rational/nonrational, human/other-than-human, and spirit/nature. When human beings add their global awareness to the natural world, the "hunt" for value, he asserts, rises to a higher, nonbiological plane. "Survival value" becomes "divine creativity," "predation" becomes "sacrifice" or "sacrament," and the "jungle" becomes a garden on Earth. While other organisms remain mired in immanence and the self-centered hunt for instrumental value, only human beings have the capacity to grasp the divine creativity within nature.

Rolston is convinced that by understanding the grand drama of evolutionary history, one will learn to care for nature. Yet he limits his own concern to the larger "players" in the drama, dismissing those who care for the suffering of other-than-human animals as "insensitive."[146] The highest form of compassion, in his view, is a byproduct of metaphysics, not a direct expression of empathy. Despite Rolston's efforts to underline the idea of human interdependence and nature's value, his epistemological vision reflects a masculinist orientation that values the universal over the particular, consciousness over unconsciousness, and objective (ecological) awareness over care for individual beings.

## NOTES

1. David Hume, *A Treatise of Human Nature* (Oxford: Clarendon Press, 1960), bk. 3, pt. 3, sec. 1. For a reappraisal of the relevance of Hume's ideas to an environmental ethic, see J. Baird Callicott, "Hume's *Is/Ought* Dichotomy" in *In Defense of the Land Ethic: Essays in Environmental Philosophy*, ed. J. Baird Callicott (New York: State University of New York Press, 1989), 117–127.

2. Holmes Rolston III, *Environmental Ethics: Duties to and Values in the Natural World* (Philadelphia: Temple University Press, 1988), xi–xiii.

3. Holmes Rolston III, "Is There an Ecological Ethic?" *Ethics: An International Journal of Social, Political, and Legal Philosophy* 85, no. 2 (January 1975): 109.

4. Rolston, *Environmental Ethics: Duties and Values*, 213.

5. This biographical sketch is drawn from Holmes Rolston III, "Respect for Life: Christians, Creation, and Environmental Ethics," *Center for Theology and the Natural Sciences Bulletin* 11, no. 2 (Spring 1991): 1.

6. Rolston, "Respect for Life," 2.

7. Rolston, "Respect for Life," 3.

8. Rolston, "Respect for Life," 3.

9. Rolston, "Is There an Ecological Ethic?" 93–109.

10. Eugene Hargrove, "From the Editor: After Twenty Years," *Environmental Ethics* 20, no. 4 (Winter 1998): 339–340.

11. The debate within environmental ethics over whether nature has value apart from human valuing has given rise to numerous books and articles. The writings of Holmes Rolston III and J. Baird Callicott are the best known on this subject, and are widely cited for their opposing views. Callicott takes the position that values in nature are subjective, although he argues that they are formulated in response to objective facts. Callicott maintains that his view does not assert the anthropocentric source of values in nature, but rather their anthropogenic origin. For this discussion and Rolston's response, see J. Baird Callicott, "On the Intrinsic Value of Nonhuman Species," in *In Defense of the Land Ethic*, 129–155. For a critique of Callicott's views on the subjective nature of values, see Holmes Rolston III, "Are Values in Nature Subjective or Objective?" in *Philosophy Gone Wild: Essays in Environmental Ethics* (Buffalo, N.Y.: Prometheus Books, 1986), 91–117.

12. Rolston, *Environmental Ethics: Duties and Values*, 112.

13. Richard Routley, "Is There a Need for a New, an Environmental Ethic?" in *Proceedings of the 15th World Congress of Philosophy*, September 17–22, 1973, Varna Bulgaria, vol. 1., Philosophy and Science, Morality and Culture, Technology and Man, ed. Bulgarian Organizing Committee (Sophia, Bulgaria, Sophia Press, 1973), 205–210. After 1985, Richard Routley was known as Richard Sylvan.

14. The word "value" derives from the Latin *valere*, meaning "to be strong, hence well." It also derives from the same root word as "valiant" and "valor." The common use of the word in nature ethics reflects the suggestion of a search for a strong (valiant) defense of the natural world. Eric Partridge, *Origins: A Short Etymological Dictionary of Modern English* (New York: Macmillan, 1958), 760.

15. Rolston, *Environmental Ethics: Duties and Values*, 186.

16. Rolston, *Environmental Ethics: Duties and Values*, 186. Rolston points out that he uses the term "intrinsic value" in a "truncated sense," since it is misleading to suggest that intrinsic value can exist without a beholder. A more accurate word, he states, would be "extrinsic value," the prefix "ex" suggesting the external role of humans in "coagulating" nature's preexisting value. Humans merely subjectively reflect back what is already objectively there in unrealized form. *Environmental Ethics: Duties and Values*, 115.

17. Rolston, *Environmental Ethics: Duties and Values*, 226.

18. Holmes Rolston III, "On Behalf of Bioexuberance," *Garden Magazine* 11, no. 4 (July–August 1987): 3.

19. Rolston, *Environmental Ethics: Duties and Values*, 222.

20. Rolston, *Environmental Ethics: Duties and Values*, 120.

21. Rolston, *Environmental Ethics: Duties and Values*, 68.

22. Rolston, *Environmental Ethics: Duties and Values*, 187–188.

23. Rolston, *Environmental Ethics: Duties and Values*, 188.

24. Rolston, *Environmental Ethics: Duties and Values*, 125.

25. Rolston, *Environmental Ethics: Duties and Values*, 188, 155.

26. Rolston, *Environmental Ethics: Duties and Values*, 187, 149, 207.

27. Rolston, *Environmental Ethics: Duties and Values*, 188, 73.

28. Rolston, *Environmental Ethics: Duties and Values*, 116, 4.

29. Rolston, *Environmental Ethics: Duties and Values*, 302.

30. Rolston, "Engineers, Butterflies, Worldviews," *Environmental Professional* 9 (1987): 300.

31. Rolston, "Engineers, Butterflies, Worldviews," 299.

32. Holmes Rolston III, "The River of Life: Past, Present, and Future," in *Philosophy Gone Wild*, 70.

33. Holmes Rolston III, *Genes, Genesis and God: Values and Their Origins in Natural and Human History* (New York: Cambridge University Press, 1999), 296.

34. Rolston, *Environmental Ethics: Duties and Values*, 187, 225.

35. Holmes Rolston III, *Conserving Natural Value* (New York: Columbia University Press, 1994), 181.

36. Rolston, *Environmental Ethics: Duties and Values*, 116.

37. Rolston, *Environmental Ethics: Duties and Values*, 339.

38. Rolston states that "valuing requires . . . an internal *excitation* . . . that brings emoting, and we may be tempted to say that the marriage of a subject to its object gives birth to value." Since value exists within nature before human awareness, he says instead that "human valuing of nature generates new values." *Environmental Ethics: Duties and Values*, 28.

39. Holmes Rolston III, "Can and Ought We to Follow Nature?" *Environmental Ethics* 1, no. 1 (Spring 1979): 28.

40. Holmes Rolston III, "Philosophical Aspects of the Environment," in *Philosophy Gone Wild*, 59.

41. Rolston, *Environmental Ethics: Duties and Values*, 71.

42. Rolston, *Environmental Ethics: Duties and Values*, 73.

43. Rolston, *Environmental Ethics: Duties and Values*, 26, 24.

44. Rolston, *Environmental Ethics: Duties and Values*, 345, 336, 34.

45. Rolston, *Environmental Ethics: Duties and Values*, 339.

46. Rolston, *Environmental Ethics: Duties and Values*, 162.

47. Rolston, *Environmental Ethics: Duties and Values*, 187.

48. Rolston, *Environmental Ethics: Duties and Values*, 221.

49. Holmes Rolston III, "Values Gone Wild," in *Philosophy Gone Wild*, 141.

50. Rolston, "Values Gone Wild," 141.

51. Rolston, *Environmental Ethics: Duties and Values*, 72.

52. Even if Rolston's characterization of humans as the only non-self-centered species is correct, this would not constitute grounds for our "objective" superiority. Humans typically select those qualities that they value most and then claim that they constitute the basis for their objective superiority. Perhaps if birds could convey what they felt was the most important attribute of an animal, they would tell us it is the ability to fly.

53. For exceptions to this generalization, see Judith N. Scoville, "Value Theory and Ecology in Environmental Ethics: A Comparison of Rolston and Niebuhr," *Environmental Ethics* 17, no. 2 (1995): 115–133, and Francisco Benzoni, "Rolston's Theological Ethic," *Environmental Ethics* 18, no. 4 (Winter 1996): 339–351.

54. Direct references to religious ideas can be found in Rolston's *Science and Religion: A Critical Survey* (New York: Random House, 1987); "Respect for Life," 1–8; and "Genes, Genesis, and God in Natural and Human History," *Center for Theology and the Natural Sciences Bulletin* 11, no. 2 (Spring 1991): 9–23.

55. Rolston, *Environmental Ethics: Duties and Values*, 337.

56. Rolston, *Environmental Ethics: Duties and Values*, 338.

57. Holmes Rolston III, "Duties to Endangered Species," *Bioscience* 35, no. 11 (December 1985): 725. Reprinted in *Philosophy Gone Wild*.

58. Rolston, *Environmental Ethics: Duties and Values*, 336.

59. Rolston, "Is There an Ecological Ethic?" 106.

60. Holmes Rolston III, "In Defense of Ecosystems," *Garden* 12, no. 4 (July–August 1988): 32.

61. Although Rolston does not refer to Teilhard de Chardin directly, his environmental philosophy parallels de Chardin's idea of admiring nature, with the important addition that admiration of nature needs to be accompanied by responsibilities.

62. Rolston, *Environmental Ethics: Duties and Values*, 72.

63. Rolston, "Values Gone Wild," 141.

64. Rolston, *Environmental Ethics: Duties and Values*, 337.

65. Rolston's views on human superiority mirror those of Leopold, who also claimed that humans' ability to mourn the loss of another species is "evidence of our

superiority over the beasts." Aldo Leopold, in "Wisconsin," *A Sand County Almanac and Sketches Here and There* (New York: Oxford University Press, 1968), 110.

66. Holmes Rolston III, "Does Nature Need to Be Redeemed?" *Zygon* 29, no. 2 (June 1994): 222.

67. Rolston, "Does Nature Need to Be Redeemed?" 223.

68. Abraham Maslow, *Toward a Psychology of Being*, 2nd ed. (Princeton, N.J.: Van Nostrand, 1968), 76, quoted in Rolston, *Conserving Natural Value*, 166.

69. Rolston, *Environmental Ethics: Duties and Values*, 72.

70. Rolston, "Values Gone Wild," 141.

71. Holmes Rolston III, "The Human Standing in Nature: Fitness in the Moral Overseer," in *Values and Moral Standing*, ed. Wayne Sumner, Donald Callen, and Thomas Attig (Bowling Green, Ohio: Bowling Green State University, 1986), 100.

72. Rolston, "Genes, Genesis, and God," 21.

73. The ethicist Judith Scoville posits that this emphasis on human adaptation to a divine process parallels H. Richard Niebuhr's idea of "fitting" one's action to a situation in response to the question, "What is going on here?" The ethicist Francisco Benzoni also finds similarities between Rolston's idea of nature's divine creativity and process thought. Scoville, "Value Theory and Ecology," 126; Benzoni, "Rolston's Theological Ethic," 348.

74. Rolston, "Genes, Genesis, and God," 21.

75. Rolston, "Genes, Genesis, and God," 20. Elsewhere, Rolston clarifies how his own ideas diverge from that of process thought. Although Rolston concurs that God operates by "creative persuasion where this is appropriate," he contends that the notion of allurement does not adequately acknowledge God's omnipotence within the "imperatives of the causal order." He argues that at the "lower structural levels," such as rocks and stars, persuasion is of no relevance. Rolston therefore proposes the idea of "God as 'influence' on the natural process." Turning to the animate forms of life, Rolston furthermore maintains that the process concept of God does not adequately acknowledge the relative autonomy and integrity of "creatures," who are empowered by God to be "independent active selves." Thus, in place of "divine lure" he postulates a "storied history" in which a personal God acts as a divine Presence within nature, spinning "this marvelous story of the universe and its projects." *Science and Religion*, 322.

76. Rolston, "Is There an Ecological Ethic?" 109.

77. Rolston, "Genes, Genesis, and God," 22.

78. For a critique of the extraterrestrial whole Earth image, see Yaakov Jerome Garb, "Perspective or Escape? Ecofeminist Musings on Contemporary Earth Imagery" in *Reweaving the World: The Emergence of Ecofeminism* (San Francisco, Calif.: Sierra Club Books, 1990), 264–278.

79. Rolston, "Is There an Ecological Ethic?" 107.

80. Rolston, "In Defense of Ecosystems," 4.

81. Rolston, "Genes, Genesis, and God," 21.

82. Rolston, *Environmental Ethics: Duties and Values*, 93.

83. Rolston, "Does Nature Need to Be Redeemed?" 219.

84. Rolston, "Does Nature Need to Be Redeemed?" 220.

85. Rolston, *Conserving Natural Value*, 125.

86. Holmes Rolston III, "Treating Animals Naturally?" *Between the Species: A Journal of Ethics* 5, no. 3 (Summer 1989): 131.

87. Rolston appears to have some misgivings about the apparent "lack of mercy" for other-than-humans that ensues from the application of his theories to practical situations. As he concedes, "I am less than confident in applying my theory to the examples that I cite." "Treating Animals Naturally?" 131.

88. This point is made by Ned Hettinger in a sympathetic critique of Rolston's views on animals. Hettinger, "Valuing Predation in Rolston's Environmental Ethics: Bambi Lovers versus Tree Huggers," *Environmental Ethics* 16, no. 1 (Spring 1994): 3–19.

89. Rolston, *Environmental Ethics: Duties and Values*, 120.

90. Rolston, *Environmental Ethics: Duties and Values*, 61.

91. Rolston, *Environmental Ethics: Duties and Values*, 61.

92. Rolston, *Environmental Ethics: Duties and Values*, 59.

93. Rolston, *Environmental Ethics: Duties and Values*, 85.

94. Hettinger, "Valuing Predation," 8.

95. Rolston, "Treating Animals Naturally," 132.

96. Rolston, "Treating Animals Naturally," 134.

97. Rolston, *Environmental Ethics: Duties and Values*, 79.

98. Rolston, *Environmental Ethics: Duties and Values*, 85.

99. Apart from humans, the closest example of the use of one species by another for food is found in the insect world. Some species of ants raise aphids to obtain a supply of a sweet sap that is secreted from their alimentary canals. The ants release the sap by stroking the aphids with their antennae. The ants also build mud shelters for the aphids and move them to new plants as the old ones decay.

100. Rolston, *Environmental Ethics: Duties and Values*, 83.

101. Rolston, *Environmental Ethics: Duties and Values*, 80.

102. Rolston, "Treating Animals Naturally," 136.

103. Rolston, "Treating Animals Naturally," 135.

104. Rolston, "Treating Animals Naturally," 135.

105. Rolston, *Environmental Ethics: Duties and Values*, 90.

106. Rolston, *Environmental Ethics: Duties and Values*, 90–91.

107. Rolston, *Environmental Ethics: Duties and Values*, 90.

108. See Diana E. H. Russell, *The Politics of Rape: A Victim's Perspective* (New York: Stein and Day, 1975), 260; Susan Brownmiller, *Against Our Will: Men, Women and Rape* (New York: Simon and Schuster, 1975), 15; and Anthony R. Beech, Tony Ward, and Dawn Fisher, "The Identification of Sexual and Violent Motivations in Men Who Assault Women: Implication for Treatment," *Journal of Interpersonal Violence* 21, no. 12 (December 2006): 1635–1653.

109. On the connection between hunting and male dominance, see Andrée Collard with Joyce Contrucci, *Rape of the Wild: Man's Violence against Animals and the Earth* (Bloomington: Indiana University Press, 1988); Brian Luke, "Violent Love, Heterosexuality and the Erotics of Men's Predation," *Feminist Studies* 2, no. 3 (1998): 627–653, and *Brutal: Manhood and the Exploitation of Animals* (Chicago: University

of Illinois Press, 2007; Merritt Clifton, "Killing the Female: The Psychology of the Hunt," *The Animals' Agenda* 10, no. 7 (September 1990): 26–30, 57; Marti Kheel, "License to Kill: An Ecofeminist Critique of Hunters' Discourse," in *Animals and Women: Feminist Theoretical Explorations*, ed. Carol J. Adams and Josephine Dono-van (Durham, N.C.: Duke University Press, 1995), 85–125; and Charles Bergman, *Orion's Legacy: A Cultural History of Man as Hunter* (New York: Dutton, 1997).

110. Rolston, *Environmental Ethics: Duties and Values*, 92.

111. Rolston, *Environmental Ethics: Duties and Values*, 93.

112. Rolston, *Environmental Ethics: Duties and Values*, 91.

113. The continuity between the emotional life of humans and other-than-human animals was first noted by Darwin. "The lower animals, like man, manifestly feel pleasure and pain, happiness and misery. . . . Terror acts in the same manner on them as on us, causing the muscles to tremble, the heart to palpitate, the sphincters to be re-laxed, and the hair to stand on end." Charles Darwin, *Descent of Man and Selection in Relation to Sex*, reprint ed. (New York: Barnes and Noble, 2004), 56. For recent discussions of the similarities between the emotions of humans and animals, see Frans de Waal, *Good Natured: The Origins of Right and Wrong in Humans and Other Animals* (Cambridge, Mass.: Harvard University Press, 1996) and Jeffrey Moussaieff Masson and Susan McCarthy, *When Elephants Weep: The Emotional Lives of Animals* (New York: Delacorte Press, 1995).

114. Rolston, *Environmental Ethics: Duties and Values*, 60.

115. Rolston, *Environmental Ethics: Duties and Values*, 91.

116. Rolston, *Environmental Ethics: Duties and Values*, 60.

117. Rolston, *Environmental Ethics: Duties and Values*, 60–61.

118. Rolston, *Environmental Ethics: Duties and Values*, 61.

119. Rolston, *Environmental Ethics: Duties and Values*, 82.

120. Rolston, *Environmental Ethics: Duties and Values*, 80.

121. Rolston, *Environmental Ethics: Duties and Values*, 151.

122. Rolston, *Environmental Ethics: Duties and Values*, 145.

123. Rolston, *Environmental Ethics: Duties and Values*, 151, 145.

124. Rolston, "Duties to Endangered Species," 718.

125. Rolston, "Duties to Endangered Species," 723.

126. Rolston, "Duties to Endangered Species," 722.

127. Rolston, *Environmental Ethics: Duties and Values*, 144.

128. Rolston, *Environmental Ethics: Duties and Values*, 145.

129. Rolston, *Conserving Natural Value*, 114.

130. Rolston, "Duties to Endangered Species," 720.

131. Rolston, *Environmental Ethics: Duties and Values*, 157.

132. Rolston, *Environmental Ethics: Duties and Values*, 345–346.

133. Rolston, *Environmental Ethics: Duties and Values*, 346.

134. Rolston, *Environmental Ethics: Duties and Values*, 350–351.

135. Rolston, *Environmental Ethics: Duties and Values*, 342.

136. Rolston, "Human Standing in Nature," 95.

137. Rolston, *Environmental Ethics: Duties and Values*, 342.

138. Aldo Leopold, "The Land Ethic," in *Sand County Almanac*, 224–225.

139. Rolston, *Environmental Ethics: Duties and Values*, 352–353.

140. See Jim Cheney, "Eco-Feminism and Deep Ecology," *Environmental Ethics* 9, no. 2 (Summer 1987): 144–145.

141. Preston notes that, like Rolston, some ecofeminists look to evolutionary and ecological narratives as a source of guidance for ethical interaction with nature. Christopher J. Preston, "Intrinsic Value and Care: Making Connections through Ecological Narratives," *Environmental Values* 10 (2001): 251. Ynestra King, for example, sees ecological science as a source of a non-hierarchical ethic that affirms "unity in diversity." "Toward an Ecological Feminism and a Feminist Ecology," in *Machina Ex Dea: Feminist Perspectives on Technology*, ed. Joan Rothschild (New York: Pergamon, 1983, 124).

142. In a similar vein, Preston notes that Rolston overemphasizes the larger scientific narratives of evolutionary history and ecology, paying "little more than lip service" to individual narratives. Rolston's own ethic, however, according to Preston, contains the seeds of a more balanced view, which recognizes the ethical impact of human stories on the creation of value. Thus, even "objective intrinsic value" is only made visible through a relational event—the encounter between humans and non-human nature. Preston, "Intrinsic Value and Care," 255, 258.

143. Rolston, *Environmental Ethics: Duties and Values*, 343.

144. Rolston, *Environmental Ethics: Duties and Values*, 351.

145. Rolston, *Environmental Ethics: Duties and Values*, 34.

146. Rolston, *Environmental Ethics: Duties and Values*, 60.

# 6

## The Transpersonal Ecology of Warwick Fox

Through the wider Self every living being is connected intimately, and from this intimacy follows the capacity of identification and as its natural consequences, the practice of non-violence.

Arne Naess
"Self-Realization" in *The Deep Ecology Movement* (p. 22–23)

To hunt is to experience extreme oneness with nature. . . . The hunter imitates his prey to the point of identity.

Randall Eaton
*The Hunter as Alert Man* (p. 9)

### INTRODUCTION

Supporters of "deep ecology" have proposed the idea that an all-encompassing sense of self, "Self-realization," is an essential aspect of mature ecologically grounded identity, ineluctably leading toward compassion for all forms of life.[1] But as the above examples suggest, identification can be expressed in myriad ways, including through violence.

In this chapter, I examine the concept of "Self-realization" advanced by supporters of deep ecology, focusing on one of its prominent spokespeople, Warwick Fox. I selected Fox for closer scrutiny because his views on Self-realization represent the most explicit expression of holist philosophy among theoreticians of deep ecology and because they underscore the pitfalls of an overly abstract concept of self. The questions that I bring to bear on Fox's philosophy parallel those asked in previous chapters: To what extent do his

concepts of self-realization, ecocentric philosophy, and cosmological identification perpetuate the masculinist theme of devaluing personal, affective
ties? To what degree do these constructs exclude other-than-human animals?
Finally, does the use of gender-neutral language obscure differences in how
women and men attain self-realization?

Before turning to Warwick Fox's philosophy, it is instructive to examine
the historical and philosophical context in which it emerged. Fox formed his
theories as part of a critical dialogue with the literature on deep ecology, and
in particular Arne Naess's writings on Self-realization. Deep ecology itself
developed as part of a broad movement in environmental philosophy away
from the study of *ethics* and toward an *ecophilosophical* approach. To accurately situate Fox's philosophy, I shall begin by summarizing deep ecology
within the context of this new movement, and then examine the contributions
of humanist philosophy and transpersonal psychology to Fox's perspective.

## THE ECOPHILOSOPHICAL SHIFT

The majority of philosophers in the field of modern nature ethics have been
preoccupied with a metaphorical "hunt" for abstract principles and universal
rules to govern human conduct toward the natural world. In the 1970s, a number of nature theorists took a different direction. Dissatisfied with the focus
on abstract value theory and universal norms, they began to search for an
ethic (more often called a "consciousness") that emphasized experience and
worldviews. The writings of deep ecology theoreticians, ecofeminists, and
other late twentieth-century radical ecologists all reflected the new orientation. This area of investigation was referred to as "ecophilosophy" to indicate
its divergence from the value theory focus of "environmental ethics." At its
broadest level, ecophilosophy is defined as "the study of . . . problems common to ecology and philosophy."[2] More specifically, Bill Devall argues that
ecophilosophy seeks "a new metaphysics, epistemology, cosmology, and environmental ethics of person/planet."[3] Holmes Rolston III lies midway between the earlier, axiological approach and the newer, ecophilosophical orientation in that he retains the concepts of duties to nature and "objective
intrinsic worth," while emphasizing the importance of human experience in
the "discovery" of values in nature.

The followers of deep ecology culminated the ecophilosophical shift, relinquishing abstract principles and universal rules in favor of a consciousness
that identifies with the "cosmos" or universe. As Fox explains, "deep ecologists agree with Birch and Cobb's insight that 'human beings are more deeply
moved by the way they experience their world than by the claims ethics
makes on them.'"[4] Thus, according to Fox, "deep ecology is ultimately

grounded in *sensibility* (i.e., an openness to emotions and impressions) rather than a *rationality* (i.e., an openness to data 'facts' and logical inference)."[5] The sensibility that most often interested philosophers of deep ecology was that of a mature human identity, alternatively named "ecological conscious-ness," "Self-realization," or the "expanded Self."[6]

This focus on the concepts of self-identity and self-realization was novel in the modern field of nature philosophy. Yet, it was not without precedent. Leopold, Roosevelt, and Rolston all advanced an embryonic form of self-real-ization. For Roosevelt and Leopold, moral maturity was embodied in Manliness and The Good Sportsman. In addition, Leopold praised the moral maturity of those who perceived themselves as "citizens of a biotic community." And for Rolston, maturity was found in the "human overseer" who discovered the "ob-jective value" of nature. Each man regarded his form of moral maturity as an *evolutionary advancement*, demonstrating human superiority over the rest of the natural world, which he, like his society, conceived as mired in mere survival.

Despite this foreshadowing of the deep ecological concept of Self in the writings of Roosevelt, Leopold, and Rolston, the notion of self-realization differed from its predecessors. Although these men often decried an instru-mental orientation toward nature, at times each invoked utilitarian justifica-tions for valuing his transcendent constructs over and above individual be-ings. And all three subscribed to the idea of the evolutionary superiority of humans. By contrast, followers of deep ecology embraced a nonanthropocen-tric view, which ostensibly rejected the notions of human superiority and eco-logical consciousness as products of evolutionary history. Nonetheless, many endorsed their own version of evolutionary development, expressed in the ideal of human maturation or Self-realization as the most evolved form of identity. As I discuss below, this conception of an evolved Self contains its own forms of anthropocentrism, or more specifically, androcentrism.[7]

## THE DEEP ECOLOGICAL MOVEMENT

The core principles of the deep ecological movement were first articulated in the English-speaking world by Arne Naess in a 1973 article, "The Shallow and the Deep, Long-Range Ecology Movement: A Summary."[8] Since then, numerous publications have developed and assessed the merits of "deep ecol-ogy," and it has become a commonplace term among academic philosophers and grassroots activists. Naess, however, never used the term "deep ecology" in his 1973 article, and later expressed regret over its adoption. His purpose, as expressed on numerous occasions, was not to proclaim a unitary philoso-phy, but rather to develop an approach for dealing with the current environ-mental crisis through a process of deep questioning of fundamental values.

Naess contrasted the "deep ecological movement" with the "shallow ecological movement," concerned only with pollution and resource depletion as they affect human health and affluence in the developed countries. The shallow movement was characterized by an instrumental orientation, which focused on short-term technical solutions for advancing human well-being. Followers of the deep ecological movement, on the other hand, embraced a relational view of nature that sought long-term solutions based on respect for all of life.

The deep ecological movement moved beyond the reformism of the shallow movement in asking deep questions to expose the core premises and beliefs underlying environmental policies. Once brought to the surface, these premises and beliefs and their corresponding policies could then be evaluated and revised in light of their impact. For Naess, it was above all this *methodological* approach of deep questioning about sustainable ecology that distinguished the deep ecological movement. His purpose, therefore, was not to delineate two opposing camps, one of which was "deep." As he states, "let me repeat what I have always tried to make clear: the words 'deep' and 'shallow' are NOT applied to people, but to argumentation patterns."[9]

Naess's background in skepticism and Gandhian nonviolence influenced his philosophical approach. Unwilling to assert an unchanging objective truth, or universal moral rules, he sought to develop broad principles upon which people from diverse cultural, philosophical, and religious backgrounds could agree. His primary purpose was not to develop an abstract philosophical system, but to facilitate the growth of a broad-based ecological movement.

Naess proposed seven core principles as characteristic of the deep ecological movement. The first two have been widely regarded as the most important: (1) "Rejection of the man-in-environment image in favor of *the relational total-field image*," and (2) "*biospherical egalitarianism* in principle."[10] The first principle refers to the idea that organisms are "knots in the biospherical net or field of intrinsic relations."[11] As he explained, the "total-field model dissolves not only the man-in-environment concept, but every compact thing-in-mileu concept—except when talking at a superficial or preliminary level of communication."[12] The second principle, *biospherical egalitarianism*, is a corollary to the total field image. If everything is viewed as part of an interconnected web of life, one experiences a desire, "in principle," to respect the "universal right to live and blossom . . . for all life forms."[13]

On a 1984 camping trip, Arne Naess and George Sessions sought to further broaden the deep ecological movement through the development of a platform statement, designed to unite people across a range of cultures, religions, and philosophies.[14] Once again, their major purpose was not to compel ad herence to a particular philosophy, but rather to inspire cross-cultural collective actions for all those who agreed with their tentative principles. The following eight points were proposed:

Basic Principles of Deep Ecology[15]

1. The well-being and flourishing of human and nonhuman Life on Earth have value in themselves (synonyms: intrinsic value, inherent value). These values are independent of the usefulness of the nonhuman world for human purposes.
2. Richness and diversity of life forms contribute to the realizations of these values and are also values in themselves.
3. Humans have no right to reduce this richness and diversity except to satisfy *vital* needs.
4. The flourishing of human life and cultures is compatible with a substantial decrease of the human population. The flourishing of nonhuman life requires such a decrease.
5. Present human interference with the nonhuman world is excessive, and the situation is rapidly worsening.
6. Policies must therefore be changed. These policies affect basic economic, technological, and ideological structures. The resulting state of affairs will be deeply different from the present.
7. The ideological change is mainly that of appreciating life quality (dwelling in situations of inherent value) rather than adhering to an increasingly higher standard of living. There will be a profound awareness of the difference between big and great.
8. Those who subscribe to the foregoing points have an obligation directly or indirectly to participate in the attempt to implement the necessary changes.

## "DEEP ECOLOGY": FORMAL AND PHILOSOPHICAL MEANINGS

With the publication of Bill Devall and George Sessions's 1985 book, *Deep Ecology: Living as If Nature Mattered*, the term "deep ecology" was increasingly used to refer to not only a popular movement but also a philosophical field. The widespread interest in these writings is in part attributable to the broad manner in which "deep ecology" is defined. This looseness of definition has given rise to heated debates not only over the merits of deep ecology but also about what it actually is.[16] To resolve this controversy, Warwick Fox set out to clarify the basic tenets of deep ecology, and to identify the most valuable part.[17]

According to Fox, Naess's philosophy of deep ecology has three central meanings: the "popular," the "formal," and the "philosophical."[18] The first is concerned with the popular movement of deep ecology, as expressed in the eight-point platform statement. It pertains to the most general views shared by supporters of the deep ecological movement. The formal level of meaning is based upon the methodological approach of deep questioning. Lastly, the philosophical level is founded upon Naess's notion of Self-realization, ecosophy T, attained through identification with a larger Self.

While Naess believes that the process of deep questioning is the core of deep ecology, Fox finds the philosophical level to be the most valuable. As he reasons, the popular level, based on the eight-point platform statement, merely proposes a nonanthropocentric viewpoint, a distinction made by any number of other ecophilosophies. Since advocacy of nonanthropocentrism is not a unique feature of deep ecology, it cannot be meaningfully used to characterize deep ecology.

Turning to what he characterizes as Naess's formal level, Fox argues that it, too, should be dismissed, since it yields contradictory results that fail to meet Naess's claims. According to Naess, the process of deep questioning begins with particular evaluative statements or "ultimate norms." These norms are "prescriptions or inducements to think or act in certain ways" that are apprehended through intuition and cannot therefore be deduced.[19] Some common sources of these norms are religious and philosophical beliefs, as well as scientific worldviews, particularly the study of ecology.[20]

Once ultimate norms are identified, according to Naess, deep ecological philosophies are then derived through a series of hypotheses or descriptive statements which in turn produce other ultimate norms.[21] Naess contends that it is the questioning process from these ultimate norms that characterizes the deep ecology movement, "not so much the *answers* that are given to deep questions."[22]

Whereas Naess argues that the process of deep questioning would yield deep ecological policies, regardless of the premises with which one started,[23] Fox disputes the inevitability of a connection between unspecified premises and deep ecological policies. He points out that "it is just as easy to derive anthropocentric views from fundamentals (such as 'Obey God!' and 'Further the ends of evolution') as it is to derive ecocentric views, and further, that it is at least as plausible to believe that anthropocentrists do in fact derive their views from fundamentals as it is to believe that ecocentrists derive their views in this way."[24] According to Fox, "The startling corollary to this . . . consequence of defining deep ecology in a purely formal way is that even an environmentally destructive view must be characterized as a deep ecological philosophy if it is derived from fundamentals."[25] Fox maintains that although

Naess only refers to the deep questioning process in some of his published papers, and often in passing, the prominence it holds for him can be detected in all of his writings.[26] Fox, by contrast, considers this formal aspect of deep ecology to be the most problematic. According to Fox, the only viable understanding of deep ecology consists in the philosophical level, represented by Naess's personal ecosophy T.

Naess had used the letter T to imply that his view was just one among many possible formulations of deep ecophilosophy, since the ultimate premises from which one can derive an ecophilosophy are multiple. As he admits, "it is to some degree arbitrary which norms are chosen as basic, ultimate or most fundamental in the sense of not being logically derivable from any others."[27] Naess expresses his ecosophy T as a syllogism, beginning with the ultimate norm of *Self-realization*. The syllogism further develops by combining this norm with particular hypotheses (or tentative statements) in order to produce further "precisations" (or new formulations). The precisations are increasingly precise statements or subsets of the preceding statements. As he outlines his syllogism, he presents norms as the letter N, followed by an exclamation point, and hypotheses as the letter H. The word *Self* is capitalized to distinguish it from the narrowly conceived lowercase *self*, which he perceives as representing only personal self-interests. Naess expresses his most recent version of ecosophy T in the following way:

> N1: Self-realisation!
>
> H1: The higher the Self-realisation attained by anyone, the broader and deeper the identification with others.
>
> H2: The higher the level of Self-realisation attained by anyone, the more its further increase depends upon the Self-realisation of others.
>
> H3: Complete Self-realization of anyone depends on that of all.
>
> N2: Self-realisation for all living beings! . . .
>
> H4: Diversity of life increases Self-realisation potentials.
>
> N3: Diversity of life!
>
> H5: Complexity of life increases Self-realisation potentials.
>
> N4: Complexity!
>
> H6: Life resources of the Earth are limited.
>
> H7: Symbiosis maximizes Self-realisation potentials under conditions of limited resources.
>
> N5: Symbiosis![28]

Despite Naess's admonition that ecosophy T should not be viewed as representative of deep ecology, it is this psychologically grounded norm of Self-realization that Fox believes should serve as the foundation of deep ecology. Having found what he considers the best meaning for "deep ecology," however, Fox proceeds to find shortcomings in the use of the term.

## TRANSPERSONAL ECOLOGY:
## FOX'S EXPANSION OF "DEEP ECOLOGY"

According to Fox, the term "deep ecology" does not properly convey Naess's philosophical approach, which he believes is rooted in a widened interpretation of transpersonal psychology. To more accurately characterize this orientation, he proposes a new name, "transpersonal ecology." As Fox analyzes Naess's ideas about the process of Self-realization, he finds support for the transpersonal psychological approach. Naess draws upon certain psychological presuppositions about the natural unfolding of the Self. According to Naess, the first seven years of life are characterized by an egocentric view. Then, until puberty, the sense of self is extended to family and friends. In the post-pubescent period, one develops an ecosophical outlook according to which "one experiences oneself to be a genuine part of all life."[29] At this stage, one is able to enlarge one's identity from the narrowly conceived "self" to a wider concept of Self.

Fox further develops Naess's ideas on moral maturity, positing that differing concepts of self correspond to particular environmental orientations. Utilizing the well-known and widely accepted tripartite understanding of human psychology or the self, Fox contends that each aspect of self manifests in a particular environmental approach.[30] In the tripartite view, the self consists of (1) "a *desiring-impulsive* aspect," (2) "a *rationalizing-deciding* aspect," and (3) "a *normative-judgmental* aspect."[31] The desiring self is the "lower," "primitive," "childlike," or "animal" self, which seeks immediate fulfillment of its desires without any regard for others or for the constraints imposed by reality. The "higher," judgmental self is the moralistic, parental, or idealistic self. Like the lower self, the higher self is "irrational" or at least "nonrational," in that it seeks to impose unrealistic demands. The rationalizing-deciding self is the "locus of control" and arbiter that mediates between the demands of the desiring-impulsive self and the normative, judgmental self. As the adult aspect, the rationalizing-deciding self takes into account the demands of the other two, as well as the constraints imposed by reality.[32]

Fox contends that the rationalizing decision-making self "sees itself as the 'I' or the central core around which all psychic activities revolve." In its role as the decision-maker, this self guards its self-image by disowning unacceptable actions or seeking to rationalize them. It is this self that "specializes in explanations or justifications," such as "I didn't know what came over me" or "I couldn't help myself."[33]

According to Fox, all three aspects of the self correspond to traditional attitudes toward nature and their respective environmental philosophies. Thus, the lower or "animal" self corresponds to the "unrestrained exploitation and expansionism" that has characterized our relations with the other-than-human world. The rationalizing-deciding self corresponds to "resource conservation and development and resource preservation." And the normative-judgmental or parent-like self, which issues statements of "ought," corresponds to intrinsic value theory in general.[34] Together, these are the most common approaches to ecophilosophy.

Transpersonal psychology "emphasizes a fundamentally different kind of self." The difference is that the Self of transpersonal psychology is expanded beyond its self-perceived needs. As Fox explains, "whatever their qualitative differences, the desiring-impulsive self, the rationalizing-deciding self, and the normative-judgmental self all refer to a narrow atomistic, or particle-like conception of self whereas the transpersonal Self refers to a wide, expansive, or field-like conception of self."[35] Even the seemingly selfless, idealistic, normative self is concerned with demands that "this particular self should do better than it has done (or than other selves have done)."[36] The idealistic self is misguided in conceiving of itself in an overly isolated sense and unrealistically depicting the relation between moral demands and human choice.

Fox's transpersonal ecological Self is not driven by unrestrained, "animal" appetites. Nor does it conform to moral dictates. Like Naess, Fox argues that the expanded Self includes a wider sphere of identification with "family and friends, other animals, physical objects, the region in which I live, and so on." As a consequence of its more embracing identification, the realized Self experiences "physical or symbolic violations of the integrity" of the things with which one identifies as "violations of my self." Thus, "ethics (conceived as being concerned with moral 'oughts') is rendered superfluous!" Fox describes the ethical relationship with other beings that results from this sense of self-realization with language that suggests a natural relation, rather than one born out of a sense of duty or responsibility. He writes, "(assuming that one is not self-destructive), one will *naturally* (i.e., spontaneously) protect the *natural* (spontaneous) unfolding of this expansive self (the ecosphere, the cosmos) in all its aspects" (emphasis added).[37] The expanded Self is thus an instinctive maturational unfolding of one's potential.

## TRANSPERSONAL PSYCHOLOGY: HISTORICAL ROOTS

The core concept that Fox adapts from transpersonal psychology is the ideal of transcending one's biological existence. This transpersonal ideal first developed from humanistic psychology, which in turn was based upon humanistic philosophy. The term "humanism" derives from the word *humanitas* and in ancient Rome referred to "the education of man as such and what the

Greeks called *paideia*: the education favored by those who considered the liberal arts to be instruments, that is, disciplines proper to man which differentiate him from the other animals."[38]

Humanism, which emerged as a philosophy in the Renaissance, was premised upon the belief that human beings alone were individual, rational beings, distinct from other beings in the natural world. The idea of human beings as unique individuals stood in contrast to the understanding in the medieval period, in which humans were associated primarily with their social roles. The late medieval view regarded the "self" as "something to be denied in favor of God and all he represented."[39] The word "self" took on its modern meaning of a "permanent subject of successive and varying states of consciousness" in the latter part of the seventeenth century.[40] The discovery of historical perspective was central to an understanding of the self as an autonomous center that organizes the various aspects of life.[41] The new, historically oriented narrative structure placed the individual at the center of meaning, rather than in a wider context of God, society, or nature. The individual came to be seen as "adventurer, genius, and rebel."[42] The Romantics in the eighteenth century further emphasized individual human uniqueness by focusing on unique "potential." The link between individuality and personality was only fully formed in the nineteenth century, when a focus on personal narratives emerged as a major form of creative expression for the autonomous self.[43] The notion of novelty of expression has been a central legacy of humanism and an integral part of the modern concept of the self: "Unique individual expression requires novelty, and modern persons are groomed to be innovators, experimenters, and pioneers."[44]

This new concept of self was significant in developing the claim that humans are autonomous, free, and rational, and that these are uniquely human traits.[45] However, far from positing a genuine notion of autonomy, the modern humanist notion of self has relied on other-than-human animals as a contrast against which to construct the self. As the psychologist Kenneth Shapiro observes, "animals are employed as a categorical foil representing precisely the absence of reason and relative autonomy, hallmarks of individuality."[46] Just as men, under patriarchal society, view women as their antithesis in the quest for masculine self-identity, so too humans have often viewed animals as a foil for the establishment of human identity.

In the late nineteenth and early twentieth century, two schools of psychology, Freudian psychology and behaviorism, threatened to dislodge humans from their newly acquired sense of rationality and freedom. According to Freudian psychology, humans were governed by irrational "animal" drives that could be sublimated or repressed but never eliminated. Behaviorism, on the other hand, believed human behavior could be explained by a mechanistic stimulus-response model, previously reserved for other-than-human animals. Humanist psychology arose in the 1960s as a middle ground or Third Force, designed to rescue people from these pessimistic, deterministic views by emphasizing the potential within healthy humans.

Like the earlier classical philosophy of humanism, humanist psychology defined itself in opposition to the animal world. Abraham Maslow, its originator, argued that the norms of health needed to be expanded beyond the satisfaction of "deficiency needs" or "instinctive needs." Maslow viewed the fulfillment of basic needs as a "lower" form of existence that humans shared with the animal world. Unlike deficiency needs, satisfied by reducing tension, growth needs are met by exercising human freedom and "self-actualization" of human perfection.[47] Maslow gave the name "peak experience" to the "being values," or a sense of the perfection that self-actualizers experience.

By the late 1960s, however, Maslow and other humanistic psychologists began to feel the limitations of the theory of self-actualization. As Fox notes, the self-actualized self was still "conceived as a skin-encapsulated ego, as a separate 'I'-sense."[48] Maslow suggested a new category of human self-actualizers who were not "merely healthy," but were "individuals who have transcended self-actualization."[49] These "transcenders" could rise above the narrowly conceived ego or the self to achieve a sense of embeddedness within the larger cosmos. Maslow states,

> I consider Humanistic, Third Force Psychology to be transitional, a preparation for a still "higher" Fourth Psychology, transpersonal, transhuman, centered in the cosmos rather than in human needs and interests, going beyond humanness, identity, self-actualization, and the like.[50]

Drawing upon seventeenth-century philosopher Baruch Spinoza's vocabulary of living "under the aspect of eternity" and the Taoist idea of "living in harmony with the nature of things by allowing them to develop or unfold in their own way," humanistic psychology and transpersonal psychology espoused a more encompassing concept of the human than did the classical humanistic ideal.[51] Self-actualizers and transcenders realized *all* of their potentials, not merely their reasoning powers. Despite this broadened conception, which included emotional experiences, the dichotomy between human and other-than-human animals remained intact. Where the earlier humanists accorded rationality only to humans, the new humanism of psychology appended "imagination, creativity and spirituality" to the list of uniquely human traits. As Shapiro argues, this arrangement is "structurally similar to the human/animal, reason/unreason dichotomized hierarchy of classical humanism."[52] Thus, a presumed dualism between humans and animals continues to be reflected in the belief that only humans are uniquely individual, autonomous beings. Whether they attain their "potential" through the exercise of reason or through the unfolding of their spiritual natures, human beings alone possess the ability to transcend mere (animal) instincts and survival needs.

## FOX'S TRANSPERSONAL ECOLOGY

Warwick Fox argues that transpersonal psychology, notwithstanding its anthropocentric legacy, provides the best foundation for the deep ecological notion of Self-realization. He contends that since the psychological foundation is deep ecology's most important aspect, and the formal meaning of "deep ecology" is conceptually untenable, it should be replaced with the more accurate term "transpersonal ecology." Fox, while recognizing an anthropocentric bias within transpersonal psychology, believes it is possible to extract its positive aspects without incorporating this orientation.

Fox also criticizes the spiritual orientation of some transpersonal psychologists who posit "God, the Absolute, or the Ultimate as 'pure consciousness,'" and see humans as superior to other-than-humans because they participate "more in this ideal than other beings."[53] He cites the example of the transpersonal theorist Ken Wilber, who views humans as completing an evolutionary consciousness, in contrast with plants and animals, which have the lowest level of consciousness.[54] Similarly, Fox criticizes Maslow for positing that the expanded self of self-actualizers is extended to the "limit" of an "identification with the human species."[55] He suggests, however, that Maslow's ideas *point* in [a] non-anthropocentric, naturalistic, ecological-cosmological direction."[56] Fox also criticizes the idea of a linear evolution that develops toward completion in humans, arguing instead that "evolution has to be thought of as a luxuriously branching bush, not as a linear scale that is filled in by greater and lesser examples of some ideal end point."[57]

Despite his renunciation of a hierarchical interpretation of evolutionary history, Fox erects his own hierarchy with respect to consciousness. He posits an ascending scale of three forms of identification, with the widest, cosmological view being the most mature and advanced. The lowest form is *personal identification*. According to Fox, personal identification is the everyday way in which we identify with others. It consists of experiences of "commonality with other entities that are brought about through personal involvement with these entities."[58] At the concrete level this is our involvement with "members of our family, our friends and more distant relations, our pets, our homes, our teddy bear or doll," and at the more abstract level with things such as "our football or basketball club."[59] As Fox explains, "we experience these entities as a part of 'us,' as part of our identity."[60] At this level of *personal* attachment, a genuine *transpersonal* perspective has not been achieved.

At the next level of awareness, a transpersonal perspective is achieved through an *ontological identification* with all that exists. Ontological identification "refers to experiences of commonality with all that is that are brought about through deep-seated realization of the fact *that* things are."[61] Fox describes this level of awareness as the most laborious to reach and the most difficult to express. It is the level achieved by those who are prepared to "undertake arduous practice of the kind that is associated with certain kinds of experientially based spiritual disciplines," such as Zen Buddhism.[62] Achieving ontological awareness, according to Fox, one becomes impressed with "the astonishing fact that things *are*." When this occurs, "all that exists seems to stand out as a foreground from a background of nonexistence, voidness, or emptiness—a background from which this foreground arises moment by moment." As a consequence, "'the environment' or 'the world at large' is experienced not as a mere backdrop against which our privileged egos and those entities with which they are most concerned play themselves out, but rather as just as much an expression of the manifesting of Beings (i.e., of *existence per se*) as we ourselves are."[63]

The third level of identification, *cosmological identification*, is the most comprehensive form. In this consciousness, we experience "commonality with all that is . . . brought about through deep-seated realization of the fact that we and all other entities are aspects of a single unfolding reality." It comes about through the "empathic incorporation of *any* cosmology" that depicts the world as a "single unfolding process." Whereas ontological awareness typically finds its source in religious traditions, cosmological awareness is most likely to arise out of science. According to Fox, the scientific basis of cosmological awareness is the most "viable" one for many people in the modern world.[64] Although there are any number of paths leading to an awareness of the unitary nature of existence, deep ecologists emphasize the path of cognition. As Fox states, "the deep ecologist (as philosopher) emphasizes 'mental-phenomenological inquiry.'"[65]

Fox's idea that maturity consists in *joining* the process of nature's unfolding has some resemblance to Rolston's idea of joining the ongoing evolutionary story of the Earth and Leopold's idea of joining the "drama" of evolutionary history, although in general Rolston and Leopold place more emphasis on its Herculean aspect. However, Fox's notion of *ontological awareness* does show some evidence of a similar heroic, arduous struggle. Residual traces of a sense of the drama can be detected in the definition of Self-expansion as a process that transcends the biological world in search of novel forms of expression.

Although Fox does not claim that cosmological awareness is a naturalistic evolutionary advance, he does suggest that it is a spiritual improvement or maturational development. According to Fox, modern science evokes a model of the world as a branching tree developed from a "single seed of energy . . . that has been growing for fifteen billion years, becoming infinitely larger and infinitely more differentiated in the process."[66] All existing entities may be compared to leaves on the tree, but at the upper limits of consciousness (ontological or cosmological), humans can learn to identify with the entire tree. Fox contrasts this "impartial" awareness with personally-based identification, claiming that it does not "cling or cloy but rather gives the recipient 'room to move,' room to be themselves."[67] Echoing Rolston, Fox argues that cosmological awareness and personally based identification operate in reverse directions. Whereas personally based identification begins with those entities that are closest to oneself and moves outward, cosmologically-based awareness proceeds from an identification with the cosmos and works inward toward a sense of commonality with particular entities.[68] Kinship ties have a place in this advanced awareness, but only within the larger global context. As Fox states, transpersonal ecologists simply want to put personally-based identification in what they see as its "appropriate place" within the "overarching context" provided by "ontologically and cosmologically based identification."[69]

Cosmological and ontological identification, thus, according to Fox, function to restrain the negative tendencies he attributes to personally-based identification, which he links to putting "*my* self first, *my* family and friends next, and so on." He maintains that these tendencies to "egoisms, attachments, and exclusivities find personal, corporate, national and international expression in possessiveness, greed, exploitation, war, and ecocide." These "poisons" are "costing us the earth."[70]

Fox believes that cosmological awareness will *inevitably* lead in the direction of caring actions toward others. However, he never fully explains how this progression to caring conduct will occur. He posits that the tendency toward Self-realization is a natural maturational process by which "the self can and does grow/develop/mature . . . over time."[71] Fox is adamant in rejecting value theories that assign worth to nature, based on particular rational, moral criteria, arguing that they are premised on the idea of dictating correct moral conduct to "a narrow, atomistic, or particle-like volitional self."[72] Transpersonal ecologists *invite* readers or listeners to see themselves as "bound up with the world around them."[73] Once one attains the realistic awareness of interconnectedness, "it becomes more or less impossible to *refrain* from wider identification (i.e., impossible to refrain from the this-worldly realization of a more expansive sense of self)."[74] Similarly, Fox argues that with a deep understanding of the way things are, one "*will* (as opposed to should)" care for nature.[75]

Fox's most significant claim is that the caring conduct ensuing from a cosmological awareness is superior to the caring that occurs in a "this-worldly" orientation. Just as Roosevelt and Leopold argued that sport hunters express natural drives in a superior (controlled) manner that takes into account the well-being of the "species" or the "land," so too transpersonal ecologists maintain that they are expressing natural (caring) instincts on a superior, transpersonal plane. However, Fox's conviction that caring action inevitably flows from cosmological worldviews which embrace an expanded sense of self is contradicted by even the most cursory observation of the real world.

The failure of cosmological identification to produce caring conduct and attitudes is exemplified by two figures frequently cited by Naess and other followers of deep ecology as inspirations for the idea of Self-realization: Baruch Spinoza and Mohandas Gandhi.[76] Spinoza is praised for advancing a nonanthropocentric philosophy in which all beings are modes of a single whole conceived as "Substance," "God," "Nature," and "Being." For Spinoza, the effort to persist in one's own being (*conatus* or "self-preservation") is the basic motivation underlying the essence of all things. When, through the cultivation of reason, humans realize their true essence, an attitude of reverence, love, and humility for all of nature will ensue. But how far do these feelings and attitudes extend?

Spinoza's philosophy clearly demotes humans from their supposed privileged position at the center of the universe, viewing humans as part of a larger whole. Yet he also believed, "it is plain that the law against the slaughtering of animals is founded rather on vain superstition and womanish pity than sound reason."[77] Bill Devall and George Sessions concede that Spinoza held contempt for other-than-humans, but argue that this was "anomalous."[78] Naess similarly argues that Spinoza's harsh statements about animals contradict the most fundamental aspects of his system. As he concludes, "Spinoza was personally what we today call a speciesist, but his system is not speciesist."[79] But can Spinoza's contempt for other-than-human animals be so readily dismissed as aberrant? Are we to overlook his characterization of compassion for animals as "womanish pity," a designation that epitomizes the masculinist ideal of devaluing women, other-than-human animals, and emotions?[80]

Mohandas Gandhi's life and philosophy also display a way in which the cosmological self can exclude caring conduct.[81] Gandhi's notion of self-realization entails the idea that the central purpose of life is to strive after perfection, which he defined as becoming "like unto God." He also believed that the realization of the "Self" and the realization of "Truth" are intimately bound together, and that self-enlightenment could not exist apart from the enlightenment of others.[82]

Fox presents Gandhi's dedication to the path of "selfless" (i.e., nonegoic) action as exemplifying the expanded Self. However, both he and Naess overlook the degree to which Gandhi's path of selflessness entailed callousness toward his wife and son. Gandhi's concept of self-realization was founded upon self-restraint, conceived as conquering the "animal passions" associated with personal attachments and desires. At thirty-seven, he renounced sex with his wife, remaining celibate for the rest of his life. He believed that work must always be placed before family ties. According to his biographer, Louis Fischer, "from young manhood, he was sweet and kind toward everybody except his wife and sons. . . . He never quite learned to be a father to his sons," toward whom he had "an ungandhian coldness."[83]

The examples of Spinoza and Gandhi suggest that an expanded concept of Self does not ineluctably produce caring conduct. Fox and other followers of deep ecology recognize the insufficiency of grounding ethical conduct toward nature on rational injunctions, yet by and large they fail to see that human behavior is not primarily motivated by rational metaphysical insights and conceptual analysis. While Fox acknowledges that it is important for people to feel the awareness of unity at an experiential level, he gives no indication of how this awareness might be attained in practice, particularly with reference to individual beings.

Insights into possible motivating factors for transforming one's self-identity into a larger Self also appear to be lacking in much of the literature on deep ecology. Supporters of deep ecology vacillate between suggesting that the expanded Self results from a gradual process of maturation, or from a sudden conversion experience. In either case, there is little exploration of the process. Naess does propose one significant avenue for conversion to widened identification, that of witnessing animal suffering.[84] Fox, on the other hand, simply asserts that the transpersonal experience of ecology provides the necessary motivation to respect the realization of other forms of life. As he explains,

> [transpersonal ecologists invite] readers or listeners . . . to experience themselves as intimately bound up with the world around them . . . to such an extent that it becomes more or less impossible to *refrain* from wider identification (i.e., impossible to refrain from the this-worldly realization of a more expansive self).[85]

However, Fox gives no explanation of what produces the transpersonal experience of ecology in the first place. As Jonathan Maskit comments, "for those who do not share [the intuition of expanded awareness] . . . what is needed is something like a conversion experience."[86] Similarly, process theologian John Cobb suggests that "to a theologian [the position of deep ecologists] sometimes seems analogous to Christian pietests who argue that individual conversions will ultimately solve all problems of social evil."[87]

Deep ecology supporters openly refer to the religious dimension of the conversion to the widened Self. As Naess states, "insofar as this conversion, these deep feelings, are religious, then deep ecology has a religious component."[88] Fox also likens transpersonal awareness to a religious worldview. Notwithstanding his recognition of diversity and plural perspectives, Fox's greater emphasis is on a single, unitary form of identification, much like a monotheism that leaves limited room for lesser gods, or an imperial ruler who allows his colonial subjects a limited autonomy. Fox attributes the greatest value to the most abstract forms of awareness, bringing to mind the Biblical admonishment to worship the Creator and not the creation. He, along with supporters of deep ecology, praises the cosmological orientation of the poet Robinson Jeffers. Explaining his poem "The Tower Beyond Tragedy" Jeffers writes,

> Orestes, in the poem, identifies himself with the whole divine nature of things; earth, man, and stars, the mountain forest and the running streams. . . .This perception is his tower beyond the reach of tragedy; because, whatever may happen, the great organism will remain forever immortal and immortally beautiful. Orestes has "fallen in love outward" not with a human creature, nor a limited cause but with the universal God.[89]

Elsewhere, Jeffers states more emphatically,

> I believe that the universe is one being, all its parts are different expressions of the same energy, and they are all in communication with each other . . . therefore parts of one organic whole. . . . It seems to me that *this whole alone* is worthy of the deeper sort of love (emphasis added).[90]

Like the previously studied theorists, Fox conceives of this expansive identity as a "community" not of individual beings but rather of "species" and "ecosystems." He maintains that this "community" is more important than individual beings:

> In terms of the wider identification approach, then, it can be seen that there is a strong sense in which the community (e.g., the species or the ecosystem) is even more important than the individual expressions that constitute it since the community itself constitutes an entire *dimension* of the world with which I identify, i.e., of my Self.[91]

Despite Fox's claim that the expanded sense of Self does not imply superiority over other species, the presumption of human superiority underlies his entire philosophy. Disclaimers about human superiority cannot eradicate the larger psychological framework that Fox inherited from transpersonal psychology, wherein humans reach their highest potential only when they transcend their biological (animal) natures. Although Fox does not argue, as does

Rolston, that the human ability to assume a global perspective is grounds for human superiority, he establishes criteria for attaining the highest form of awareness that only humans can meet. Lawrence Kohlberg's previously discussed cognitive psychology reflects a similar type of exclusionary bias. Although Kohlberg did not argue that the impartial mode of moral thinking of boys was superior to that of girls, his contention that impartiality represented the most advanced form of moral thinking *functioned* to establish the superiority of young boys. In a similar vein, Fox's concept of psychological and spiritual maturity functions to exclude the other-than-human world.

Fox repeatedly refers to "letting entities unfold," yet provides no clues as to what that unfolding might entail for other-than-human beings. Recalling Rolston's view, Fox perceives humans as progressing toward a spiritual consciousness, inspired by an awareness of the global unfolding of the universe, while the rest of nature is entrapped in a material unfolding dictated by self-centered needs.

A number of critics have similarly argued that the deep ecological notions of transcendence and Self-realization are inherently anthropocentric. As John Cobb contends, "the focus is on human experience and how it can be changed. . . . But there is little consideration of any point of view other than the human one."[92] "Deep green" theoretician Richard Sylvan further argues that "[the goal of self-realization] emerges direct from the humanistic Enlightenment; it is linked to the modern celebration of the individual human, freed from service to higher demands, and also typically from ecological constraints."[93] And according to philosopher Eric Katz, "all three of the core distinguishing ideas of deep ecology—identification, Self-realization, and holistic ontology—are deeply embedded in a human-centered worldview. . . . The preservation of nature is justified . . . because it furthers the process of Self-realization, a process that includes the further realization of the narrow self of the human ego."[94]

Coming to the defense of deep ecology, George Sessions argues that Naess has a broadened sense of Self-realization that extends beyond humans. Contrasting this perspective with Fox's transpersonal ecology, he argues, "as I interpret Naess he means by Self-realization the realization of Gaia and even the cosmos—everything—*the system*—is realizing itself. Thus, if humans were not here anymore, there would still be Self-realization. To turn this into a form of human psychology, i.e., 'transpersonal psychology' seems to restrict this to humans." He concludes, "to me then, transpersonal psychology—the ecological self—is *part* of deep ecology—concerning *human* potential, but it doesn't speak to the potential of the nonhuman." Thus, according to Sessions, it is transpersonal ecology, not deep ecology, that perpetuates anthropocentrism.[95]

Whether or not Sessions is accurate that Naess intends Self-realization to apply to the cosmos, he does appear to extend it to other-than-humans by trying to understand, for example, what it might mean for a praying mantis. Just as the attainment of pleasure is not the basis for Self-realization in humans, neither would it be for animals. Thus, the male praying mantis, who is driven to mate even though he will be eaten in the act of copulation, may not experience pleasure, but he is Self-realized.[96]

Responding to Sessions's criticisms, Fox maintains that the accusation that "transpersonal ecology is anthropocentric because it focuses on the human capacity for identification" is a misunderstanding of the term "anthropocentrism." He argues this

> is as perverse a use of this term as it is to say that a group such as Men Overcoming Violent Emotions (MOVE) is sexist simply because it focuses on men. Rather, just as MOVE is wholly directed toward *overcoming* domestic violence in particular and sexist behavior in general, so transpersonal ecology is wholly directed toward *overcoming* the various forms of human chauvinism and domination. . . . Seen in this light, it should be clear that transpersonal ecology's focus on the human capacity for, and experience of, wide and deep identification is not remotely anthropocentric in the intended, evaluative sense of that term (italics in original).[97]

Fox is correct in his assertion that the focus on human beings is not necessarily anthropocentric. Since people are the ones who have plundered the planet and reduced the rest of nature to instruments for their use, it is appropriate (and nonanthropocentric) that they focus on their own conduct and experience, including their perceptions of the natural world. The emphasis on human subjectivity, however, does reinforce anthropocentrism if it obscures the subjective identity of other beings. John Cobb makes this point, referring to the characteristic "lack of interest" among deep ecology supporters in the subjective experiences of other-than-human animals, and their "contempt for humane societies and animal rights activists."[98] As he elaborates, "We do not want a new sensibility that undercuts our sensitivity to suffering, and this suffering is always individual. To overcome anthropocentrism is precisely to recognize that other creatures also have their points of view, which are just as valid as ours, that their suffering is just as real as ours."[99]

## ECOFEMINIST CRITIQUES OF THE EXPANDED SELF

Fox's endorsement of the most transcendent form of identification as the highest form of maturity echoes the traditional masculinist emphasis of philosophies that subordinate kinship ties and care for individuals to a more global awareness. Although Fox argues for an important role for experience and intuition, the experiences and intuitions he values most are those that bypass direct, unmediated ties with other living beings.

An altogether different approach is taken by many feminist theorists who believe that the path toward caring need not (and should not) take a detour through abstract metaphysics. They have argued that identification with others is a hazardous basis for feelings of care. These theorists instead emphasize the paramount importance of recognizing differences. The feminist philosopher Sara Ruddick, for example, argues that even "the idea of empathy, as it is popularly understood, underestimates the importance of knowing another *without* finding yourself in her."[100] In contrast, "Attention lets difference emerge without searching for comforting commonalities, dwells upon the *other* and lets otherness be."[101] Carol Gilligan and Grant Wiggins also believe that even empathy "implies an identity of feeling—that self and other feel the same." Instead, they propose the word "co-feeling," since it suggests that "one can experience feelings that are different from one's own."[102] Co-feeling "depends on the ability to *participate* in another's feelings (in their terms), signifying an attitude of engagement rather than an attitude of judgment or observation."[103] Gilligan and Wiggins argue that the term "co-feeling" has the merits of including a wider range of feelings than the word "compassion," which has its etymological roots in the notion of suffering ("suffering with"). Paraphrasing a passage from Milan Kundera's novel *The Unbearable Lightness of Being*, they contrast "compassion" with terms used in other languages, such as Czech, Swedish, and German, in which a similar prefix is combined with the root meaning "feeling" rather than suffering. As Kundera elaborates, "to have compassion (co-feeling) means not only being able to live with the other's misfortune but also to feel with him [*sic*] any emotion—joy, anxiety, happiness, pain."[104] These examples of caring for others while recognizing differences are a far cry from Fox's depiction of a realized Self that incorporates the other. The emphasis of feminist theorists is on expanding one's capacity to care for others, rather than expanding one's identity.

Fox's Self-realization suggests a trajectory of consciousness in which one proceeds from the outermost limits of the ecosphere downward toward individual entities. The philosopher Maria Lugones proposes another kind of "world-traveling." Lugones is concerned with the ways that white/Anglo women fail to identify with women across racial and cultural boundaries. She relates how she was unable to identify with her own mother, viewing her with the racial bias of the dominant culture.[105] Lugones develops the notion of playful "world-traveling," according to which we can learn to journey into different worlds and realities, so that "we can understand *what it is to be them and what it is to be ourselves in their eyes.*"[106] Fox's expanded Self, on the other hand, travels to distant entities, incorporates them, and remains there. There is no suggestion of Lugones's idea of traveling back and forth in one's identifications.

Fox also fails to acknowledge the multiple forces that limit or impinge upon our ability to identify with others. He focuses exclusively on the limitations imposed by an anthropocentric worldview. But gender, race, class, and sexual orientation also influence our perception of others. Fox's contention that one can achieve an impartial ontological worldview that encompasses the "reality" of the world not only ignores the force of these contingent factors, but fails to appreciate that there is no single attainable God's-eye view of reality.

The idea of an abstract, expanded "Self" has also been the focus of a series of ecofeminist critiques. Although some are directed against deep ecology in general, they are especially applicable to Fox, who has argued most explicitly against the feminist emphasis on particularity, care, and recognition of difference. The Australian philosopher Ariel Salleh was one of the first feminists to criticize the expanded concept of Self. In a 1984 article in Environmental Ethics, she argued that the deep ecology idea of Self-realization is a product of men's alienation; it is "the self-estranged male reaching for the original androgynous natural unity within himself."[107] She suggests that "if on the one hand, the search seems to be stuck at an abstract cognitive level, on the other, it may be led full circle and sabotaged by the ancient compulsion to fabricate perfectibility."[108] Salleh perceives that some of the rationalist and technist recommendations of deep ecology (such as the call for an artificial, externally imposed limitation of the human population) resemble the age-old male quest for domination. Salleh also criticizes deep ecologists for their use of "the generic term *Man* in a case where use of a general term is not applicable,"as well as for their failure to look at women's lived experience "as a social basis for the alternative consciousness that [they are] trying to formulate and introduce as an abstract ethical construct."[109] Finally, she asserts that only when deep ecologists rediscover and love "the woman inside themselves," and when women are "allowed to love what we are," will we be able "to make a better world."[110]

In a subsequent article, Salleh focuses her critique on the lack of materialist analysis within deep ecology, urging adherents to "become more reflexively aware of the sociohistorical grounding of their discourse."[111] Salleh maintains, in particular, that analyses of deep ecology supporters have ignored the treatment of women as "a sexual, reproductive and labor 'resource.'"[112] Commenting on the eclipse of "half of humanity" from the "total field," she states that "men's self-realization by expanded self does nothing to alter the ongoing invisibility and 'non-identity' of Woman=Nature."[113]

The philosopher Jim Cheney enlarges upon Salleh's charge that the quest for Self-realization reflects a state of alienation. In an article entitled "The Neo-Stoicism of Radical Environmentalism," Cheney perceives a "subtext" in the deep ecologists' call for an expanded Self. He argues that the idea of Self-realization suggests male alienation from nature and community.[114] Cheney claims that the longing to identify with an abstract conception of the whole is analogous to the Stoic notion of identification with the "logos" of the universe. Just as Stoicism was a by-product of the break-up of the city-state and the consequent loss of ties to a local embedded community, so too is deep ecology an expression of modern-day estrangement from social context and place. The subtext of the idea of Self-realization, according to Cheney, is the "containment of the other, of difference, rather than genuine *recognition* of the other, genuine acknowledgment and embracing of the other."[115] The search for fusion is fueled by "feelings of alienation born of an atomistic worldview in which all relations are external."[116] The result of this approach is that "rather than an ethical voice emergent from existential encounter, from genuine relationship, we get an ethical voice grounded in the authoritarian impersonal truth of metaphysics, of internalized vision."[117]

The Australian philosopher Val Plumwood adds another voice to the critique of the abstract nature of the expanded Self. Plumwood suggests three major forms of deep ecological identification: (1) a self that is indistinguishable from others, (2) an expanded self that incorporates others, and (3) a self that transcends others.[118]

The first understanding of self that Plumwood critiques is the "indistinguishable" self, so named because all boundaries between self and nature are dissolved. She observes that deep ecologists view this self as a corrective to the radical dualism between humans and nature. John Seed expresses the notion of the "indistinguishable self" in his statement, "I am part of the rainforest protecting myself."[119] While Seed suggests that this form of identity will result in rainforest protection, Plumwood argues that "one could equally well take one's own needs for [the rainforest's]."[120] Thus, the deep ecological solution to the duality separating humans and nature is a self that fails to recognize the distinct identity and interests of others.

The second construction of self that Plumwood critiques is the notion of an expanded identity. While supporters of deep ecology view this enlarged Self as a corrective to the rational egoism that characterizes the nonenlightened self, Plumwood argues that in reality, enlargement of the Self merely extends egoism by incorporating the other into oneself, appending the other's interests to one's own. The implication is that humans will only protect nature out of self-concern. She sees evidence of this egoistic orientation in Fox's statement that "in this light" environmental protection or "ecological resistance is simply another name for self-defense."[121] Thus, according to Plumwood, although the larger Self allows for a wider set of concerns, it continues to operate on "the fuel of self-interest (or Self interest)."

The third deep ecological self that Plumwood critiques is "the transpersonal self." The transpersonal self seeks to overcome personal attachments and individual needs and desires by transcending the realm of particularity. Plumwood focuses her critique on Fox's ontological and cosmological concepts of Self and his negative views of "personal identification." As she argues, this devaluing of the personal realm "inherits the rationalistic preoccupation with the universal and its account of ethical life as oppositional to the particular."[122]

Since the realm of particularity has traditionally been associated with women, Plumwood argues that "'transpersonal ecology' represents a significant increase in theoretical masculinization over and above the earlier form of deep ecology."[123] Quoting Carol Gilligan, she argues that it also "breeds moral blindness or indifference—a failure to discern or respond to need."[124] In addition, it paradoxically denies "the deep and highly particularistic attachment to place which has motivated both the passion of many modern conservationists and the love of many indigenous people for their land (which much of deep ecology inconsistently tries to treat as exemplifying its model)."[125]

Plumwood finds all three forms of identification inadequate in that they fail to critique the underlying structure of the concepts of "human" and the "self." As she argues, the notion of "human" has been integrally linked with the notion of rationality and the public sphere, and held in contrast to the female and animal realms and their attendant associations with emotionality and unreason. The concept of "human" has also been integrally linked to a self defined by an instrumental, dominating relation to that which is considered outside the human realm. Plumwood argues that "what is missing from the accounts of both the ethical philosophers and the deep ecologists is an understanding of the problem of discontinuity as created by a dualism linked to a network of related dualisms."[126] Only when the dualistic foundation of conceptions of the human and the self in relation to nature is challenged will it be possible to develop the richer notion of a "self-in-relationship."[127] In this formulation,

> Respect for the other results neither from the containment of self nor from a transcendence of self, but is an *expression* of self in relationship, not egoistic self as merged with the other but self as embedded in a network of essential relationships with distinct others.[128]

In a similar vein, Karen Warren contrasts "notions of an indistinguishable, expanded, or transpersonal self" with an ecofeminist sensibility that sees relationships as self-defining. Rather than making "otherness or difference a problem to overcome," she argues, an ecofeminist sensibility acknowledges "dependencies and bonds of care and responsibility" while leaving "selves intact."[129]

The foregoing critiques have in common the belief that the expanded Self not only fails to counter deep-seated masculinist urges, but masks their expression. What are the practical consequences of this failure to identify and critique the masculine construction of the self?[130] Fox and other followers of deep ecology describe the narrowly conceived "self" and the larger "Self" in gender-neutral language. However, there are significant differences in how the identities of men and women are constructed in Western patriarchal society. As discussed in chapter 2, young girls are more likely to preserve a sense of continuity with the mother figure as they mature, whereas boys tend to develop their self-identities by severing ties with their mothers and the entire female world. According to some feminist theorists, the need to sever such connections extends to all that is associated with women, including the natural world.[131]

What happens, then, when one expands a (masculine) self that is constructed in opposition to others? One answer can be found in the writings of nature philosophers who invoke the language of "self-realization" and "spiritual communion" in support of hunting.[132] Thus, Bill Devall and George Sessions cite hunting, along with surfing, sailing, sunbathing, and bicycling, as one of a number of "especially useful" activities that, with the "proper attitude," can help encourage "maturity" of the self.[133] In a similar vein, Paul Shepard, regarded as an "architect of deep ecology,"[134] points to the critical importance of hunting for male maturation and bonding with other males.[135] Lamenting the passing of the hunter-gatherer stage of evolution, he maintains that hunting and killing are "a singular expression of our identity with natural processes."[136]

Although these and other writers invoke the deep ecological notion of identification and expanded awareness, this awareness may nonetheless provide a context for the expression of hostile behavior. What first appears to be a transpersonal or beyond-the-ego experience is, upon further examination, merely the familiar, heroic struggle to establish the masculine self. The animal is still the "other," a necessary prop for establishing a seemingly transegoic state. The evolved Self supposedly transcends the dualism of self and other, but in reality the ego has merely assumed another form. Where hunters such as Roosevelt and Leopold established their masculine self-identity through sport hunting, the "spiritually mature" Self renames the same act of violence as "spiritual communion with nature."

The romanticization of hunting as a means of realizing a mature male identity illustrates, once again, the absence of concern for the subjective experience of other-than-humans. The morally mature Self perceives a connection with other "life forms" or "wildlife" but not with individual animals. Deep ecology supporters, for example, do not realize their larger Selves through identification with an animal imprisoned in a laboratory. Nonetheless, as Cobb reports saying to Shepard in a personal conversation about hunting, "all the respect shown to the prey, even when it [*sic*] was regarded as sacred probably [makes] very little difference with regards to its suffering." Cobb goes on to say that Shepard was startled by his comments and recalls Shepard saying that "he had never come across any expression of concern for the animal as subject. It was what the animal meant in the experience of human beings that preoccupied him."[137]

Arne Naess argues that the expanded Self is the product of a "deepened perception of reality and our self."[138] He believes that "care flows naturally" from this ecological Self, *"assuming that you need no moral exhortation to show care . . . provided you have not succumbed to a neurosis of some kind, developing self-destructive tendencies or hating yourself"* (emphasis added).[139] But the notion that male (and female) gender identities constructed under a sexist society are currently healthy presumes too much. Since masculine identity is founded upon an attempt to annihilate an integral aspect of oneself, it is not surprising that self-expansion may follow a similar path of destruction.

The reliance upon a gender-neutral concept of an expanded Self contains additional problems with respect to women's constructed identities in patriarchal society. The psychology underlying the deep ecological concept of expanded identification resembles the Golden Rule: Those who identify with a larger Self will do unto others as they would have others do unto them. But existing differences in gender identity make such facile generalizations problematic. Women's socialization into caring practices and putting the needs of others first may require a modification of the standard precept. As Gloria Steinem observes, "the traditional sequence assumes a healthy self-esteem and asks for empathy. . . . But for many people whose self-esteem has been suppressed, the revolution lies in reversing it."[140] As she elaborates elsewhere, "the Golden Rule, written by and for men, needs reversal to be valuable to many women. . . . For us women the challenge is to treat ourselves as well as we treat others."[141]

Although overlooking the subliminal influence of gender-identity on the process of Self-realization, deep ecology supporters do acknowledge the influence of some nonrational modes of consciousness, including religious worldviews and cosmologies. Naess stipulates that the process of deep questioning must seek to uncover "deep psychological and social motivations as well as logically basic norms and hypotheses."[142] He also compares the process of deep questioning to a form of "community therapy" which heals "our relations to the widest community, that of all living beings."[143] Despite these allusions to psychological factors, more often he and other supporters of deep ecology focus on a cognitive paradigm for addressing environmental problems. As Naess states, environmental problems are the "result of thoughtlessness, rather than thought," implying that resolution of the ecological crisis can be achieved through cognition.[144] Naess also believes that "if we ask deeply enough, our questions will require us to make a radical shift . . . what some people have called a paradigm shift."[145] But do his questions and those of other supporters of deep ecology delve deeply enough?

While the notion of deep questioning is a worthy endeavor, success will not be attained if current conceptions of gender identity remain outside the orbit of questioning. By ignoring the gendered nature of self-identity in patriarchal society, deep ecology supporters overlook the potential influences of alienation, hostility, and fear, which may affect the Self-realization process. Focusing on a larger, abstract Self merely allows these repressed feelings an acceptable arena for expression.

An ecofeminist ecosophy, based on recognition of the distinct ways in which gender has been constructed in patriarchal society, might ask very different questions about environmental problems. Rather than employing a cognitive approach, it might delve more deeply by asking, Why do men commit more acts of violence against nature than women do? What fears drive their actions? What can be done to stop violence against women and nature? And how could current constructions of gender identity be transformed? Through a process of deep questioning about these and other issues particular actions may present themselves, such as the need to transform the child-rearing practices that contribute to this violent conduct.

In "The Deep Ecology–Ecofeminism Debate and Its Parallels," Fox defends deep ecology against some of the charges of masculinist bias.[146] However, he demonstrates little understanding of the ecofeminist positions, which he reduces to arguments over semantics. Fox insists that ecofeminists mistakenly claim that androcentrism is the source of environmental problems, whereas he and other followers of deep ecology understand that anthropocentrism subsumes androcentrism. Since both women and men dominate nature and subscribe to the presumption of human superiority, he maintains, it is inaccurate to accuse men of a disproportionate responsibility for the domination of nature. Furthermore, since the followers of deep ecology believe in respect for the unfolding of all entities, opposition to sexism is implicit in their formulations. Fox fails to understand Plumwood's point that positing the "human" as an autonomous, rational being is a gendered construct. Thus, even when the word "human" is employed, masculinist values in opposition to women and the natural world are inscribed in it.

A number of ecofeminist writers have sought to distinguish among adherents to deep ecology, arguing that the views of some, particularly Naess, are compatible with ecofeminist philosophy. Ariel Salleh, who led the early critique, has since softened her position, perceiving a move toward materialism by Naess and other supporters of deep ecology. She praises their focus on "sensory experience of habitat" and "self-realization, based on rootedness in place as a prerequisite to right ecological action."[147] Commenting approvingly on Naess's more recent writings on internal relations, she states that "it is now clear how this approach to deep ecology might marry with an embodied materialism."[148]

Naess's 1973 article, "The Shallow and the Deep, Long-Range Movement: A Summary," had raised concerns among feminists and others about the status of individuals within his holist philosophy. Naess had characterized the deep ecological movement as embracing a "relational, total-field" model that "dissolves not only the man-in-environment concept, but every compact thing-in-milieu concept—except when talking at a superficial or preliminary level of communication."[149] Furthermore, in the original eight-point platform statement which he coauthored with George Sessions, no mention is made of the "intrinsic worth" of individual beings. It is "the flourishing of human and nonhuman *life on earth*" that is recognized as having "intrinsic worth," and life *forms* that are viewed as having "independent value" (emphasis added). Since then, Naess has sought to correct a potential misreading which infers that his holist ontology eclipses individual beings. In *Ecology, Community, and Lifestyle*, Naess states that "identification with living beings individually" is the first field of research within ecosophy T.[150] Elsewhere he writes that "at any level of realization of potentials, the individual egos remain separate. They do not dissolve like individual drops in the ocean. Our care continues ultimately to concern the individuals, not any collectivity. But the individual is not and will not be isolatable, whatever exists has a gestalt character."[151] Naess also declares emphatically that deep ecological views "are incompatible with the kind of holism which obliterates individuality."[152] In an effort to reinforce this point, he states that he is "in favor of letting point 1 of the 8 points refer only to individuals: 'Every living being has intrinsic value.' Point 2 will then concern richness and diversity."[153]

Karen Warren acknowledges that "there are significant differences between Naess, on the one hand, and his leading American and Australian followers, on the other."[154] Agreeing with the critiques of deep ecology advanced by Cheney and Plumwood, she argues that the philosophies of Fox, Sessions, and Devall reflect patriarchal assumptions through their "erasure of difference and individuality" and the "merging of self-with-Self."[155] In contrast, she argues that Naess avoids the totalizing tendencies found among other supporters of deep ecology through his emphasis on the importance of individual beings and "ecosophical pluralism."[156] His deep ecology position, therefore, is or "could be compatible with ecofeminism."[157]

Warren points out that Naess's ecosophical pluralism recognizes the spontaneous and emotional realm of experience as a source of knowledge and reality, thereby permitting a wide variety of norms and respect for the concerns of others, including those in the third world. The total view that Naess advocates, according to Warren, is both a personal worldview and a "personal medium for interpersonal exchange and discussion" among a plurality of people. Similarly, the deep ecology platform statements are designed to "function as mid-level statements where the total views of many *intersect.*"[158]

Despite praising statements of respect for individuals in Naess's philosophy, Warren expresses concern over the absence of "an explicit acknowledgement and fostering of the plurality of voices *within* (as well as *among*) individuals." She grants that Naess would likely agree with her misgivings, citing his personal communication to David Rothenberg in which he states, "Actually there is a lot to say about too tightly integrated characters. Not enough room for inconsistencies, spontaneity, play."[159]

Christian Diehm suggests that with some revisions Naess's philosophy can support the ecofeminist emphasis on respect for differences.[160] Diehm addresses the three types of Self which Plumwood attributes to deep ecologists: the *transpersonal*, the *expanded* and the *indistinguishable*. Considering the *transpersonal* Self, Diehm defends Naess against the charge that the deep ecological Self transcends personal identifications, arguing that for Naess, they are "the very fabric of the universal." As Diehm points out, "for Naess . . . self-realization is a process that follows the vectors of the emotional charges of the particular, and this undermines the attempt to classify his position as trans-personal in Fox's sense."[161]

Turning to the *expanded* Self, Diehm agrees with Warren that Naess differs from other supporters of deep ecology, in that he does not view the expanded Self as a remedy for the isolation of the individual ego. He argues that the relational field Naess writes about is not something that the individual achieves as a *means* of overcoming alienation; nor is it about "losing oneself in a collective." Since Naess's notion of the self is always in relation, it is rather about "finding oneself and others through positive forms of relation." Identification merely "*realizes,* brings to life and fulfillment, the internal relations already constitutive of the self."[162]

Thus, according to Diehm, Naess's expanded Self is not a continuation of egoism (the lonely isolated self seeking to aggrandize itself through incorporating the other); rather, it is based on the *intermingling* of self-interests, since "self and other are essentially intertwined."[163] Naess's gestalt ontology does *not* imply the egoistic notion that one will only work for others if they are viewed as extensions of oneself. Rather, it suggests that a self-realized person will come to understand that her well-being is *allied* with the well-being of others.

However, Diehm does find some validity in Plumwood's critique of the indistinguishable Self, concurring with her statement that "Naess's vision . . . ultimately draws on sameness and identity as the basis of respect."[164] Thus, for Naess, empathy is achieved through seeing others as "like oneself."[165] Diehm maintains that as long as "the bonds between self and other are fostered and enriched by a process of identification alone, the interests of others will always be understood by reference to one's own."[166] He acknowledges that Naess avoids the idea of a merging of interests, as evidenced by the statement that "even in identification one must recognize that self and other are 'different individuals.'" However, although Naess recognizes the *ontological* distinctness of individual selves and avoids the notion of *identical* interests, nonetheless, Diehm argues, Naess's notion of Self-realization does not adequately acknowledge *dissimilar* interests. He therefore risks excluding those with whom one cannot readily identify or "assuming that the same sorts of things that are good for oneself are also the sorts of things that are good for others."[167]

Diehm concludes by affirming Plumwood's assertion that "relationships cannot flourish without the recognition that others are relatively distinct beings with potentially dissimilar interests, for in the absence of this others are lost or annihilated." He suggests an alternative ecofeminist vision in which difference is seen as a starting point that sparks an ongoing dialogue in which people "attempt to find a way to articulate ourselves properly to others, a way of recognizing and assuming responsibility, of being responsive." Identification in this conception would then be viewed as "*one mode* of an ongoing dialogue in which we attempt to find ways to articulate ourselves properly to others" (emphasis added). Thus, Self-realization, conceived as the "making real of the self as relational being, would have to be seen as a function of our dialogue with the differences of the world."[168]

As Cheney, Warren, and Diehm suggest, Naess does appear to demonstrate more concern for individuals than other adherents of deep ecology do. Nonetheless, most followers of deep ecology disregard the limited applicability of their expanded identity ideas with regard to the nonideal reality in which the average human being resides. For example, the emphasis among deep ecology supporters on merged or identical selves or interests ignores the experiences of those whose boundaries have been violated. An abused woman would not benefit from identifying with her abuser; she would do better to affirm her *distinct* identity and interests. Her self-realization, therefore, requires *dis*-connecting from her abuser.

Ecofeminists have also directed their critiques at the deep ecological concept of biospherical egalitarianism advanced by Naess in "The Shallow and the Deep, Long-Range Ecology Movement."[169] Listed as second of the seven core characteristics of the deep ecological movement, *biospherical* (or *biocentric) egalitarianism* refers to the "right to blossom of all living beings—in principle" and the "intrinsic value" of all life. The notion of biospherical egalitarianism is widely praised in deep ecological literature, and frequently critiqued. One of the objections the concept often elicits is that it is atomistic. Thus, Jim Cheney objects to it because it suggests that ethical norms are based upon rights, and hence that ethical value resides in individual forms of life rather than in relations.[170] A consequence of this atomistic conception, according to Cheney, is that it structures conflict into the moral situation, without providing a means for resolving it.[171] In a similar vein, Karen Warren argues that biospherical egalitarianism attributes rights to "*relators*," in contrast to an ecofeminist ethic, which considers context and hence "the nature of the *relationship*." Warren maintains that an ecofeminist ethic recognizes that "*care* and *justice-through-care* and *appropriate reciprocity* and *friendship* attach primarily to relationships," not simply abstract "relators" (emphasis in original).[172]

Naess responds to this criticism by emphasizing that he uses the terms "rights" and "intrinsic value" in an "everyday [sense] as in you have no right to eat your little sister's food!"[173] As he explains in his original formulation, "the 'in principle' clause is inserted because any realistic praxis necessitates some killing, exploitation and suppression."[174] Since then Naess has gone to great lengths to distance himself from a normative, deontological understanding of "rights," providing practical suggestions to guide people in cases of conflict with the other-than-human world. He posits that "a vital need of the nonhuman living being A overrides a peripheral interest of the human being B."[175] Still later he proposes that priority should be given to those who are "nearer to us."[176] Ultimately, Naess expresses regret over his use of the term, maintaining "total egalitarianism" is impossible between humans and other-than-humans.[177] Nevertheless, Naess argues that even if the metaphorical sense of biospherical egalitarianism allows some forms of killing, it is not based upon a notion of human superiority. All life can still be said to have the "same sort of value, namely inherent value."[178]

Naess's attempt to soften the absolutist connotations of biospherical egalitarianism is echoed in Fox's discussion of the concept. According to Fox, biospherical egalitarianism "refers to the attitude underlying specific ethical decisions and practices," rather than to a doctrine that can be applied according to objective criteria.[179] He argues that a literal interpretation of biospherical egalitarianism would lead to the conclusion that one "might as well eat meat as vegetables since all organisms possess equal intrinsic value." In his critique of this perspective, Fox appears to reflect the ecofeminist sensitivity to feelings and intuitions, as well as context, emphasizing the importance of intuition in evaluating such situations. Quoting Alan Watts, who stated that he is a vegetarian "because cows scream louder than carrots," Fox writes this is "the view, I'm sure, that deep ecologists tend to adopt *in practice*."[180] In a similar vein, Fox writes that "deep ecologists *are* 'willing to trust their inner voices.'"[181] Fox, however, goes on to endorse a hierarchical worldview in defense of these intuitions, arguing that "some forms [of life] are more significant expressions of pure consciousness than others," citing in support that "the notion of a hierarchy of states of mind/being, with greater value being ascribed to the higher states, is central to all mystical traditions."[182]

Despite seeming similarities between ecofeminist ethics and Fox's emphasis on feelings and intuitions, significant differences exist. The feelings and intuitions that are valued most in his transpersonal ecology are those which result from or reinforce abstract worldviews. As he states, "the deep ecologist (as philosopher) emphasizes mental-phenomenological inquiry."[183]

Fox continues his universalistic orientation when he critiques the word "life" in the phrase "the equal right of all life to blossom." Naess has also tried to clarify his usage. As he explains, "the term 'life' is used here in a comprehensive nontechnical way to refer also to things that biologists may classify as nonliving: rivers (watersheds), landscapes, cultures, ecosystems, 'the living earth.'"[184] To dispel confusion over the inclusion of nonliving systems within "biocentric" ethics, Fox proposes that the term be replaced, in popular usage, with "ecocentric." Fox contends that "ecocentric" is both more inclusive and appropriate, since the "motivation of deep ecologists depends more upon a profound sense that the earth or ecosphere is *home* than it does upon a sense that the earth or ecosphere is necessarily alive."[185]

For philosophical usage, Fox proposes yet another term, "autopoietic ethics," which is even more abstract and all-encompassing. Autopoietic derives from the Greek words *auto* (self) and *poiein* (to produce). According to Fox, "autopoiesis" is an all-inclusive term that refers to the self-regenerating capacities of both living organisms and living processes. All self-generating entities and systems are morally relevant or "ends in themselves." They have interests, in the sense that what happens to them matters to them.[186] Thus, Fox claims that the criterion of self-regeneration moves beyond the inclusion of only biological organisms and "opens the door for the inclusion of ecosystems and the ecosphere (Gaia)." In addition, Fox argues that it

presumably opens the door for the inclusion of more abstract kinds of entities such as species (or at least gene pools) and social systems (human and nonhuman), and perhaps opens the door for the inclusion of many other, quite different kinds of entities as well (e.g., cognitive processes considered in their own right).[187]

Just as the expanded Self is conceived as an all-embracing identity that incorporates other entities into itself, autopoietic ethics is conceived as an all-embracing ethical framework that incorporates all self-regenerating entities into a single system.

Fox presents autopoietic ethics as an answer to the critiques directed against other holist systems, such as Gaian ethics and ecosystem ethics. He argues that these perspectives, often referred to as *ethical holism*, are misunderstood to mean the subordination of individual forms of life to the larger whole. According to Fox, autopoietic ethics better captures the intention of these systems since it does not suggest that only ecosystems and the ecosphere deserve moral consideration, but rather that "all autopoietic systems" are "worthy of moral consideration." He believes that the underlying idea of ecosystem ethics and ecosphere ethics is not that the "good of the ecosystem or the ecosphere should rigidly dictate the lives of individual biological organisms but only that these considerations should set certain limits on the otherwise *diverse* behavior of such organisms."[188] Fox never explains, however, what those limitations are and who is to determine them.

Thus, where Rolston attributes the highest value in nature to the ecosystem, due to its reproductive capacity, Fox moves the level of abstraction even further by using self-regeneration as the basis for moral considerability. In addition to displaying no consideration for the moral difference between individuals and systems, he dismisses the relevance of the distinction between "biological entities" and "nonbiological entities," arguing that it is a criterion "of no moral consequence."[189]

## CONCLUSION

Warwick Fox, who set out to distill the most worthwhile aspect of deep ecology, locates it in an expanded version of transpersonal psychology. His interpretation of transpersonal ecology depicts the Self as reaching its highest potential when it achieves identification with the cosmos. Although Fox is aware of the limitations of transpersonal psychology, he believes he can expand the field to incorporate a respect for all of life. Yet transpersonal psychology's legacy of humanism, inextricably rooted in androcentrism and devaluation of the natural world, is not so easily shed. Fox concedes that self-realization extends to all entities but insists that other-than-human entities within nature realize themselves merely on a material plane. And only human beings achieve the most mature form of realization, which transcends the physical realm, encompassing the cosmos.

Unlike Roosevelt and Leopold, Fox does not extol the virtues of hunting for moral maturity, yet his transpersonal philosophy shows a similar lack of concern for individual animals. Animals exist only as a collective backdrop to the transpersonal, not as individual beings with subjective experiences.

Like his predecessors, Fox views affiliative ties as a lower form of awareness that impedes a more evolved form of identity. His widened sense of identification moves beyond the inferior "cloying" aspect of personal attachment. The most expansive form of awareness replicates the natural processes that occur in the material world, but in a purportedly superior manner. Thus, feelings of care do exist but on a higher, spiritual plane, as a byproduct of metaphysics rather than biology. Similarly, "communities" exist, but they consist of abstractions, such as "ecosystems" and "species," not individuals. Yet as ecofeminists have argued, the danger in widening one's identification to these larger wholes is that one may widen it beyond the scope of individual beings. Fox's transpersonal ecology, as well as his ecocentric and autopoietic ethics, reflects this flaw. Taken together, they demonstrate the familiar masculinist quest to escape the unpredictable world of particularity for something more distant, enduring, and abstract.

## NOTES

1. A note about my usage of terms is warranted. I follow Naess in using the phrase "supporters of deep ecology" or "supporters of the deep ecological movement," rather than the term "deep ecologists," which Naess believes is unnecessarily divisive due to the derogatory connotations of its implied opposite, "shallow ecologists." Naess coined the term "deep ecological" in 1973 to refer to a worldwide grassroots movement, unified by broad platform principles and aims. It is this movement that Naess sought to characterize with the term "deep ecological." However, despite Naess's original intention, "deep ecology" is widely viewed as a philosophy, or cosmology, united by several core ideas. Peter C. van Wyck comments, "in a sense, Naess's message seems to have been inverted" in that deep ecology has been reified as a concept and foundational program. *Primitives in the Wilderness: Deep Ecology and the Missing Human Subject* (Albany, N.Y.: SUNY Press, 1997), 37. Eric Katz argues that the three central ideas commonly associated with deep ecology comprise Naess's ideas on Self-realization, the process of identification, and a holistic relational ontology. Katz, "Against the Inevitability of Anthropocentrism," in *Beneath the Surface: Critical Essays in the Philosophy of Deep Ecology*, ed. Eric Katz, Andrew Light, and David Rothenberg (Cambridge, Mass.: MIT Press, 2000). In light of this widely held definition of deep ecology, I acquiesce in using the term "deep ecology" to refer not only to a movement but to a field of philosophical investigation broadly pertaining to

the above ideas. See also the section entitled *"Deep Ecology": Formal and Philosophical Meanings*, later in this chapter. It should also be noted that, following Naess, deep ecology supporters employ the term "Self" rather than the lower-case "self" to refer to a larger identity that extends beyond one's individual self-interests.

2. Arne Naess, *Ecology, Community, and Lifestyle: Outline of an Ecosophy*, trans. and rev. David Rothenberg (New York: Cambridge University Press, 1989), 36.

3. Bill Devall, "The Deep Ecology Movement," in *Ecology*, ed. Carolyn Merchant (Atlantic Highlands, N.J.: Humanities Press, 1994), 125.

4. Warwick Fox, "On Guiding Stars to Deep Ecology: Warwick Fox Answers Naess's Response to Fox," *Ecologist* 14 (1984): 203–204. Reprinted with minor revisions as "On Guiding Stars of Deep Ecology: Warwick Fox's Response to Naess's Response to Fox," in *Philosophical Dialogues: Arne Naess and the Progress of Ecophilosophy*, ed. Nina Witoszek and Andrew Brennan (Lanham, Md.: Rowman & Littlefield, 1999), 173. Page numbers for "On Guiding Stars" in this chapter refer to *Philosophical Dialogues*. Fox quotes from Charles Birch and John B. Cobb Jr., *The Liberation of Life: From the Cell to the Community* (Cambridge: Cambridge University Press, 1981), 177.

5. Warwick Fox, "Environment, Ethics and Ecology Conference, Australian National University, August 26–28, 1983," *Ecophilosophy* 6 (May 1984): 12.

6. Bill Devall and George Sessions use the term "ecological consciousness" to refer to the processes of deep questioning and the "expanded Self," developed by Naess. See, for example, Bill Devall and George Sessions, *Deep Ecology: Living as If Nature Mattered* (Salt Lake City, Utah: Gibbs M. Smith, 1985), 66.

7. For the view that deep ecology expresses a form of anthropocentrism, see Katz, "Against the Inevitability of Anthropocentrism," 17–42. For the view that "anthropocentrism has historically functioned as androcentrism," see Karen Warren, "Ecofeminist Philosophy and Deep Ecology," in Witoszek and Brennan, *Philosophical Dialogues*, 257. Also see Val Plumwood, *Feminism and the Mastery of Nature* (New York: Routledge, 1993), 24–27.

8. "The Shallow and the Deep, Long-Range Ecology Movement: A Summary" was adapted with minor revisions from a lecture given the previous year at the World Future Research Conference, Bucharest, September 3–10, 1972. It was published in *Inquiry* 16 (1973): 95–100. It has also been included in recent anthologies, such as *The Deep Ecology Movement: An Introductory Anthology*, ed. Alan Drengson and Yuichi Inoue (Berkeley, Calif.: North Atlantic Books, 1995). Page numbers cited in this chapter refer to the *Inquiry* article.

9. Arne Naess, "Response to Peder Anker," in Witoszek and Brennan, *Philosophical Dialogues*, 444.

10. The complete list of characteristics of the deep ecology movement, cited by Naess in his 1973 article, are: (1) rejection of the man-in-the-environment image in favor of the relational, total-field image, (2) biospherical egalitarianism in principle, (3) principles of diversity and of symbiosis, (4) anti-class posture, (5) fight against pollution and resource depletion, (6) complexity, not complication, and (7) local autonomy and decentralization. Naess, "Shallow and the Deep," 95–98.

11. Naess, "Shallow and the Deep," 95.

12. Naess, "Shallow and the Deep," 95.

13. Naess, "Shallow and the Deep," 96. Naess explains that the words "in princi-ple" are used as a concession to the necessity for "some killing, exploitation and sup-pression." "Shallow and the Deep," 95. For further discussion of the idea of the "uni-versal right to live and blossom . . . for all life forms," see Naess, *Ecology, Community, and Lifestyle*, 166–169.

14. Naess subsequently suggests that the choice of the terms "principles" and "platform" was "perhaps unfortunate" in suggesting a rule-bound philosophical posi-tion. Naess explains his intention was to "present an attempt to formulate what might be accepted by the great majority of the supporters of the movement at a fairly gen-eral and abstract level." Arne Naess, "The Deep Ecology 'Eight Points' Revisited," in *Deep Ecology for the 21st Century: Readings on the Philosophy and Practice of the New Environmentalism*, ed. George Sessions (Boston: Shambhala, 1995), 214, 220.

15. Devall and Sessions, *Deep Ecology*, 69–70. A number of slight revisions have been made to the original platform statement over the years. Naess's most recent ver-sion appears in Arne Naess, *Life's Philosophy: Reason and Feeling in a Deeper World* (Athens: University of Georgia Press, 2002), 108–109.

16. For Naess, the process of deep questioning represents the "essence" of deep ecology, while for Andrew McLaughlin the platform statement about the deep eco-logical movement constitutes its defining characteristic. Stephan Bodian, "Simple in Means, Rich in Ends: An Interview with Arne Naess," in Sessions, *Deep Ecology for the 21st Century*, 27; Andrew McLaughlin, "The Heart of Deep Ecology," in Ses-sions, *Deep Ecology for the 21st Century*, 90. For Bill Devall, on the other hand, deep ecology's commitment to anti-anthropocentrism is "the central concern," whereas for Fox, "Naess's philosophical sense of deep ecology" (which Naess labeled "ecosophy T") represents the "most interesting and significant" sense of deep ecology. Bill De-vall, *Simple in Means, Rich in Ends: Practicing Deep Ecology* (Salt Lake City, Utah: Gibbs M. Smith, 1988), 57; Warwick Fox, *Toward a Transpersonal Ecology: Devel-oping New Foundations for Environmentalism* (Boston: Shambhala, 1990), 145.

17. The core principles outlined in Naess's 1973 article and the eight-point plat-form statement contain the rudiments of Naess's personal philosophy, ecosophy T, as well as his methodological approach to deep questioning. Although Naess had writ-ten about both of these approaches early in his career, they became widely available to the English-speaking world when his work was translated into English by David Rothenberg in 1989. See Naess, *Ecology, Community, and Lifestyle*. It is toward the philosophical ideas presented in this book that Fox directs his critique.

18. The reader should bear in mind that Fox's tripartite typology of deep ecology reflects his particular analysis, not that of Naess. Fox also uses the phrase "deep ecol-ogists," arguing that it is an accurate label that does not imply a pejorative evaluation of its opposite, "shallow ecologists."

19. Naess, *Ecology, Community, and Lifestyle*, 42.

20. Deep ecology supporters regard a wide variety of religious and philosophical traditions as sources of inspiration for ultimate norms. Bill Devall and George Ses-sions contend that Taoism, Buddhism, process thought, new physics, perennial phi-losophy, and the literary schools of naturalism and pastoralism are all possible stim-uli for a new non-anthropocentric ethic. Devall and Sessions, *Deep Ecology: Living*

*as If Nature Mattered*, 79–108. Naess also cites the impact on deep ecology of the philosophies of Whitehead, Spinoza, Hegel, Schelling, Bergson, Heidegger, and Wittgenstein. Arne Naess, "The Encouraging Richness and Diversity of Ultimate Norms," in *The Selected Works of Arne Naess*, ed. Harold Glasser and Alan Drengson (New York: Springer, 2005), 10:239.

21. Naess proposes a four-level process for deriving deep ecological philosophies or ecosophies from ultimate norms. They include: "(1) verbalized fundamental philosophical and religious ideas and intuitions; (2) the platform of the deep ecology movement; (3) more or less general consequences derived from the platform—lifestyle and general policies of every kind; and (4) concrete situations and practical decisions made in those situations." Unity is only required at level two. "The Apron Diagram," in Glasser and Drengson, *Selected Works of Arne Naess*, 10:76, 77.

22. Arne Naess, "Deepness of Questions and the Deep Ecology Movement," in Sessions, *Deep Ecology for the 21st Century*, 210. Elaborating upon the distinguishing feature of deep ecology, Naess states that the strength of deep ecology is that it "asks 'why' insistently, and consistently, taking nothing for granted! . . . [It] is therefore 'the ecology movement which questions deeper'" (subquotes in original). Arne Naess, "The Deep Ecology Movement: Some Philosophical Aspects," in Sessions, *Deep Ecology for the 21st Century*, 75–76.

23. Naess later expressed his preference for the Germanic *problematizing*, with its "profound existential" connotations, over the term "*deep questioning*." Referring to this process of problematizing, Naess originally stated, "it is my hypothesis that any systematic contemporary philosophy will, if it takes a stand on the ecological crisis, support the Deep Ecology movement." Naess, "Deepness of Questions," 205. Naess later clarified that "it would be very naïve to state that if you question deeply enough you inevitably end joining the deep ecology movement," explaining that the "relevant problematizing is conducted within the ecological movement itself." Naess, "Response to Peder Anker," 445.

24. Warwick Fox, "The Meanings of Deep Ecology," *Trumpeter* 7, no. 1 (Winter 1990): 49.

25. Fox, *Toward a Transpersonal Ecology*, 95.

26. Fox, *Toward a Transpersonal Ecology*, 92.

27. Naess, *Ecology, Community, and Lifestyle*, 42.

28. Naess, *Ecology, Community, and Lifestyle*, 197–200.

29. Naess, *Ecology, Community, and Lifestyle*, 174.

30. Fox, *Toward a Transpersonal Ecology*, 204–215.

31. Fox, *Toward a Transpersonal Ecology*, 204.

32. Fox, *Toward a Transpersonal Ecology*, 205–206.

33. Fox, *Toward a Transpersonal Ecology*, 207.

34. Fox, *Toward a Transpersonal Ecology*, 206.

35. Fox, *Toward a Transpersonal Ecology*, 215.

36. Fox, *Toward a Transpersonal Ecology*, 216.

37. Fox, *Toward a Transpersonal Ecology*, 217.

38. Nicola Abbagnano, "Humanism," trans. Nino Langiulli, in *The Encyclopedia of Philosophy*, vol. 4, ed. Paul Edward (New York: Macmillan and Free Press, 1967), 70.

39. Ann Carolyn Klein, *Meeting the Great Bliss Queen: Buddhists, Feminists and the Art of the Self* (Boston: Beacon Press, 1995), 27.

40. *The Oxford English Dictionary*, 2nd ed., s.v. "self." The first literary usage of this meaning of the self noted in the *OED* was in 1674 by the poet Traherne.

41. Abbagnano, "Humanism," 71.

42. Richard Tarnas, *The Passion of the Western Mind: Understanding the Ideas That Have Shaped Our World View* (New York: Ballantine Books, 1991), 227.

43. Klein, *Meeting the Great Bliss Queen*, 28.

44. Klein, *Meeting the Great Bliss Queen*, 28.

45. Kenneth Shapiro, "Animal Rights versus Humanism: The Charge of Speciesism," *Journal of Humanistic Psychology* 30, no. 2 (1990): 9–37.

46. Shapiro, "Animal Rights versus Humanism," 10.

47. Abraham Maslow, *Toward a Psychology of Being*, 2nd ed. (New York: Van Nostrand, 1968), 21–29.

48. Fox, *Toward a Transpersonal Ecology*, 292.

49. Abraham Maslow, *The Farther Reaches of Human Nature* (New York: Viking Press, 1971), 282.

50. Maslow, *Toward a Psychology of Being*, iii–iv.

51. Maslow, *Farther Reaches of Human Nature*, 269–295.

52. Shapiro, "Animal Rights versus Humanism," 27–28. Shapiro makes this point in relation to humanistic psychology, but it applies equally to transpersonal psychology.

53. Fox, *Toward a Transpersonal Ecology*, 199.

54. Fox, *Toward a Transpersonal Ecology*, 199–200. Fox cites Wilber's book *Eye to Eye: The Quest for the New Paradigm* (Garden City, N.Y.: Anchor Books, 1983), 100, and his article "Odyssey: A Personal Inquiry into Humanistic and Transpersonal Psychology," *Journal of Humanistic Psychology* 22, no. 1 (1982): 57–90. For a critique of Wilber, see Michael Zimmerman, "Possible Political Problems of Earth-based Religiosity," in Katz, Light, and Rothenberg, *Beneath the Surface*, 178–191.

55. Maslow, *Farther Reaches of Human Nature*, 272.

56. Fox, *Toward a Transpersonal Ecology*, 202.

57. Fox, *Toward a Transpersonal Ecology*, 200.

58. Warwick Fox, "Transpersonal Ecology and the Varieties of Identification," *Trumpeter* 1 (Winter 1991). Reprinted in Drengson and Inoue, *Deep Ecology Movement*, 136.

59. Fox, *Toward a Transpersonal Ecology*, 249.

60. Fox, *Toward a Transpersonal Ecology*, 250.

61. Fox, *Toward a Transpersonal Ecology*, 250.

62. Fox, *Toward a Transpersonal Ecology*, 250–251.

63. Fox, *Toward a Transpersonal Ecology*, 251.

64. Fox, *Toward a Transpersonal Ecology*, 252.

65. Warwick Fox, "Deep Ecology: A New Philosophy of Our Time?" *Ecologist* 14, nos. 5-6 (1984): 197.

66. Fox, *Toward a Transpersonal Ecology*, 255–256.

67. Fox, *Toward a Transpersonal Ecology*, 257.

68. Fox, *Toward a Transpersonal Ecology*, 258.

69. Fox, *Toward a Transpersonal Ecology*, 267.

70. Fox, *Toward a Transpersonal Ecology*, 267.

71. Warwick Fox, "An Overview of My Response to Richard Sylvan's Critique of Deep Ecology," *Trumpeter* 2, no. 4 (Fall 1985): 18.

72. Fox, *Toward a Transpersonal Ecology*, 244.

73. Fox, *Toward a Transpersonal Ecology*, 244.

74. Fox, *Toward a Transpersonal Ecology*, 244–245.

75. Fox, *Toward a Transpersonal Ecology*, 247.

76. See for example, George Sessions, "Spinoza and Jeffers on Man in Nature," *Inquiry* 20, no. 4 (1977): 481–525; Arne Naess "Environmental Ethics and Spinoza's Ethics: Comments on Genevieve Lloyd's Article," in Witoszek and Brennan, *Philosophical Dialogues*, 91–99; Naess, "Spinoza and Ecology," *Philosophia* 7, no. 1 (1977): 45–54. Also see Naess, *Gandhi and Group Conflict: An Exploration of Satyagraha* (Oslo: Universitetsforlager, 1974), 34–37, and Naess, "Self-Realization: An Ecological Approach to Being in the World," in Drengson and Inoue, *The Deep Ecology Movement,* 22–25.

77. *Philosophy of Benedict de Spinoza*, trans. R. H. M. Elwes (New York: Tudor Publishing, 1933), 217.

78. Devall and Sessions, *Deep Ecology: Living as If Nature Mattered*, 240.

79. Naess, "Environmental Ethics and Spinoza's Ethics," 99.

80. Spinoza's views on other-than-human animals have been the subject of debate among a number of deep ecology adherents. The philosopher Genevieve Lloyd contends that Spinoza's philosophy denies other-than-humans intrinsic worth, since he believed that they may be utilized in any way that is beneficial to humans. She concedes that certain excesses of human exploitation would probably be prohibited by his non-anthropocentric philosophy, although their exclusion would not be due to compassion, but rather due to their endorsement of a false belief about humanity's elevated place in nature. As she explains, "Spinoza cannot say: 'Things (such as butterflies, whales, rain forests) are good, or have value, or have rights, independently of man.' But he can say: 'It is *good for man* to perceive things . . . as they really are. It is good for man to perceive things truly'" (emphasis in original). Genevieve Lloyd, "Spinoza's Environmental Ethics," in Witoszek and Brennan, *Philosophical Dialogues*, 85–86. Caring conduct toward other-than-human animals, therefore, is a by-product of the quest for truth rather than the result of direct feelings of empathy and care for other-than-humans. Naess concedes that although other-than-human animals cannot be citizens in Spinoza's philosophy, they can be members of "'life communities' on a par with babies, lunatics, and others who do not cooperate as citizens but are cared for in part for their own sake." Although Spinoza's philosophy is not one of morals, Naess elaborates, it is nonetheless "one of generosity, fortitude, and love." As Naess explains, "the more we act from our essence alone, the more we act out of love and generosity." Naess concludes, "There is no indication in the system that love is only possible, or realized, in relation to a tiny subset of particular beings, namely humans." Naess, "Environmental Ethics and Spinoza's Ethics," 92–96.

81. Unlike Spinoza, Gandhi displayed profound compassion for other-than-humans, as evinced by his lifelong commitment to vegetarianism. Nonetheless, his concept of self-realization entailed a view of human superiority based on the human capacity to conquer the "animal passions" such as sex, hunger, emotions, and material cravings. Gandhi's vegetarianism was premised on his belief that meat eating was a reversion to the violence of the animal world as well as an indulgence in these base appetites.

82. Fox suggests that what attracted Naess to Gandhi was his rejection of traditional Hinduism, and his exemplification of the Mahayana (or northern Buddhist) tradition of the bodhisattva. Fox, *Toward a Transpersonal Ecology*, 111. While Hinayana Buddhism focuses on individual salvation, Mahayana's worldview emphasizes an interdependent model, which strives for the self-realization of all beings.

83. Louis Fischer, *The Life of Mahatma Gandhi* (New York: Harper and Row, 1950), 71.

84. Naess, quoted in Bodian, "Simple in Means, Rich in Ends," 30. For the argument that "suffering is perhaps the most potent source of identification," see Arne Naess, "Identification as a Source of Deep Ecological Attitudes," in *Deep Ecology*, ed. Michael Tobias (San Diego, Calif.: Avant Books, 1985), 264.

85. Fox, *Toward a Transpersonal Ecology*, 244–245.

86. Jonathan Maskit, "Deep Ecology and Desire: On Naess and the Problem of Consumption," in Katz, Light, and Rothenberg, *Beneath the Surface*, 223.

87. John Cobb Jr., "Deep Ecology and Process Thought," *Process Studies* 30, no. 1 (2001): 130.

88. Naess, quoted in Bodian, "Simple in Means, Rich in Ends," 30.

89. Quoted in George Jean Nathan, *The Theatre Book of the Year, 1950–1951: A Record and an Interpretation* (New York: Alfred A. Knopf, 1951), 137.

90. From a letter to Mary James Power, published in her book *Poets at Prayer* (Freeport, N.Y.: Books for Libraries Press, 1977), 60. Quoted in Devall and Sessions, *Deep Ecology: Living as If Nature Mattered*, 101.

91. Warwick Fox, *Approaching Deep Ecology: A Response to Richard Sylvan's "Critique of Deep Ecology"* (Hobart, Australia: University of Tasmania, 1986), 83.

92. Cobb, "Deep Ecology and Process Thought," 126.

93. Richard Sylvan and David Bennett, *The Greening of Ethics* (Tucson: University of Arizona Press, 1994), 154.

94. Katz, "Against the Inevitability of Anthropocentrism," 33, 38.

95. George Sessions, personal correspondence with Warwick Fox, March 8, 1989. Quoted in Fox, "On the Interpretation of Naess's Central Term 'Self-Realization,'" *Trumpeter* 2 (Spring 1990): 98.

96. Naess, "Self-Realization: An Ecological Approach," 29.

97. Fox, *Toward a Transpersonal Ecology*, 242.

98. Cobb argues that the main difference between Whiteheadian theorists and deep ecology supporters resides in "the locus of intrinsic value." For deep ecology proponents, intrinsic value lies in the notion of the "collective well-being and flourishing . . . [of] the biosphere as a whole and the ecosystems that make it up." For Whiteheadians,

on the other hand, it resides in "the experiences of the individual entities that are involved." Cobb believes, however, that sensitivity to the suffering of animals requires some hierarchical ranking of intrinsic value, based on a being's relative richness of experience, or in Whitehead's terms, its "strength of beauty." Cobb further maintains that some judgment of relative intrinsic value is "implicit in Naess's practice and attitude" in that he acquiesces to trampling upon thousands of plants when high mountain trekking, but would undoubtedly feel compunction if he were killing "thousands of rabbits or deer." Cobb's hope is that the Whiteheadian approach "can contribute to overcoming the animosity that still sometimes separates deep ecologists from animal rights activists." Cobb, "Deep Ecology and Process Thought," 116–123. See further discussion of biospherical egalitarianism and intrinsic value later in this chapter. For a discussion of a non-hierarchical ecofeminist approach, which also includes sensitivity to animal suffering, see chapter 7.

99. Cobb, "Deep Ecology and Process Thought," 121. Notable exceptions to the lack of concern for animal suffering among deep ecology supporters include Alan R. Drengson and Arne Naess. Drengson critiques the "fear, hatred, and . . . fanaticism" that are projected onto other-than-humans, decrying the loss of the "capacity to sense the feelings of another." Drengson, "Social and Psychological Implications of Human Attitudes toward Animals," *Journal of Transpersonal Psychology* 12, no. 1 (1980): 64, 71. In his more recent work Naess expresses concern for animal suffering, alluding to his ability to identify with a dying flea. As previously mentioned, Naess believes that empathy with the "death struggle" of other-than-human animals can precipitate the process of Self-realization. Naess, "Self-Realization: An Ecological Approach," 15. Both Drengson and Naess also diverge from other deep ecology supporters in their concern for domesticated animals. Rejecting the notion that "the [domestic] sheep is a less developed, 'dumb' animal compared to the superbly intelligent and beautiful wolf," Naess contends that wolf reintroduction programs must consider the well-being of both sheep and wolves. Naess, however, also accepts the practice of human ownership of captive animals, arguing that the cultural institution of sheep-herding should also be protected. Arne Naess and Ivar Mysterud, "Philosophy of Wolf Policies (I): General Principles and Preliminary Exploration of Selected Norms," in Witoszek and Brennan, *Philosophical Dialogues*, 349.

100. Sara Ruddick, *Maternal Thinking: Toward a Politics of Peace* (Boston: Beacon Press, 1989), 121.

101. Ruddick, *Maternal Thinking*, 122.

102. Carol Gilligan and Grant Wiggins, "The Origins of Morality in Early Childhood Relationships," in *Mapping the Moral Domain*, ed. Carol Gilligan, Victoria Ward, and Jill McLean Taylor with Betty Bardige (Cambridge, Mass.: Harvard University Press, 1988), 122.

103. Gilligan and Wiggins, "Origins of Morality," 122.

104. Milan Kundera, *The Unbearable Lightness of Being* (New York: Harper and Row, 1984), 20, quoted in Gilligan and Wiggins, "Origins of Morality," 121.

105. Maria Lugones, "Playfulness, 'World-Traveling' and Loving Perception," *Hypatia* 2, no. 2 (1987): 5.

106. Lugones, "Playfulness," 17.

107. Ariel Salleh, "Deeper Than Deep Ecology: The Ecofeminist Connection," *Environmental Ethics* 6, no. 4 (1984): 344.

108. Salleh, "Deeper Than Deep Ecology," 345.

109. Salleh, "Deeper Than Deep Ecology," 340.

110. Salleh, "Deeper Than Deep Ecology," 345.

111. Ariel Salleh, "Class, Race, and Gender Discourse in the Ecofeminism/Deep Ecology Debate," in Witoszek and Brennan, *Philosophical Dialogues*, 236; originally published with slight differences in *Environmental Ethics* 15 (Fall 1993). The charge that supporters of deep ecology lack a materialist analysis has been made by a number of other commentators. The most vociferous critique was mounted by social ecologist Murray Bookchin. See Bookchin, "Social Ecology versus Deep Ecology: A Challenge for the Ecology Movement," in Witoszek and Brennan, *Philosophical Dialogues*, 281–301. For a third world critique of the focus on wilderness preservation and the lack of concern among deep ecologists for how these policies affect people in third world communities, see Ramachandra Guha, "Radical American Environmentalism and Wilderness Preservation: A Third World Critique," and "Radical American Environmentalism Revisited," in Witoszek and Brennan, *Philosophical Dialogues*, 313–324 and 473–479. Alan Drengson and Yuichi Inoue maintain that "these positions are not incompatible with the broad deep ecology movement." *Deep Ecology Movement*, xxvi. Naess also responds by affirming "*the necessity of a substantial change in economic, social, and ideological structures*" (emphasis in original). Naess, "Deepness of Questions," 211. Additionally, he claims that the wilderness idea is not "a necessary component of the deep ecological stance." Naess, "Comments on Guha's 'Radical American Environmentalism and Wilderness Preservation: A Third World Critique,'" in Witoszek and Brennan, *Philosophical Dialogues*, 327. Questions remain about the relative priority of materialist factors in producing ecological problems and bringing about social change. Michael Zimmerman represents a common view in the literature of deep ecology supporters, maintaining that the present exploitation is due to "epistemology, metaphysics and ethics." Zimmerman, "Feminism, Deep Ecology and Environmental Ethics," *Environmental Ethics* 9, no. 1 (1987): 44. In a similar vein, Fox states that "deep ecologists place their primary emphasis upon changing our 'underlying perception of the way things are' (i.e., changing our ontology)." Fox, "On Guiding Stars," 173.

112. Salleh, "Class, Race, and Gender," 237.

113. Ariel Salleh, "In Defense of Deep Ecology: An Ecofeminist Response to a Liberal Critique," in Katz, Light, and Rothenberg, *Beneath the Surface*, 119.

114. Jim Cheney, "The Neo-Stoicism of Radical Environmentalism," *Environmental Ethics* 11, no. 4 (1989): 293–326.

115. Cheney, "Neo-Stoicism," 302.

116. Jim Cheney, "Ecofeminism and Deep Ecology," *Environmental Ethics* 9, no. 2 (1987): 124.

117. Cheney, "Neo-Stoicism," 311.

118. Val Plumwood, "Nature, Self and Gender: Feminism, Environmental Philosophy, and the Critique of Rationalism," *Hypatia* 6, no. 1 (1991): 12. For further critique of the denial of difference within deep ecology, see Plumwood, *Feminism and the Mastery of Nature*, 165–189.

119. John Seed, "Beyond Anthropocentrism," in *Thinking like a Mountain: Towards a Council of All Beings*, ed. John Seed, Joanna Macy, Pat Fleming, and Arne Naess (Philadelphia: New Society Publishers, 1988), 36.

120. Plumwood, "Nature, Self and Gender," 13.

121. Fox, "Approaching Deep Ecology," 60, quoted in Plumwood, "Nature, Self and Gender," 14.

122. Plumwood, *Feminism and the Mastery of Nature*, 181.

123. Plumwood, *Feminism and the Mastery of Nature*, 182.

124. Carol Gilligan, "Moral Orientation and Moral Development," in *Women and Moral Theory*, ed. Eva Feder Kittay and Diana T. Meyers (New York: Rowman & Littlefield, 1987), 24, quoted in Plumwood, *Feminism and the Mastery of Nature*, 181.

125. Plumwood, *Feminism and the Mastery of Nature*, 182.

126. Plumwood, "Nature, Self and Gender," 17.

127. Plumwood, "Nature, Self and Gender," 20.

128. Plumwood, "Nature, Self and Gender," 20.

129. Warren, "Ecofeminist Philosophy and Deep Ecology," 266–267.

130. Portions of the following analysis are drawn from Marti Kheel, "Ecofeminism and Deep Ecology: Reflections on Identity and Difference," in *Covenant for a New Creation: Ethics, Religion and Public Policy*, ed. Carol S. Robb and Carl J. Casebolt (Maryknoll, N.Y.: Orbis Books, 1991), 141–164.

131. See Dorothy Dinnerstein, *The Mermaid and the Minotaur: Sexual Arrangements and Human Malaise* (New York: Harper and Row, 1967), and Elizabeth Dodson Gray, *Green Paradise Lost* (Wellesley, Mass.: Roundtable Press, 1979).

132. Examples of environmental writers who invoke the language of self-realization and spiritual communion in relation to hunting include Gary Snyder, Barry Lopez, Holmes Rolston III, Paul Shepard, Bill Devall, and George Sessions. For an ecofeminist critique of the narratives of these hunting advocates, see Marti Kheel, "License to Kill: An Ecofeminist Critique of Hunters' Discourse," in *Animals and Women: Feminist Theoretical Explorations*, ed. Carol J. Adams and Josephine Donovan (Durham, N.C.: Duke University Press, 1995), 85–125.

133. Devall and Sessions, *Deep Ecology: Living as If Nature Mattered*, 188.

134. Bron R. Taylor and Michael Zimmerman, "Deep Ecology," in *The Encyclopedia of Religion and Nature*, ed. Bron R. Taylor (New York: Continuum, 2005), 456.

135. Shepard often extols the benefits of hunting for "humans," although he periodically specifies that he means only men and boys. He asserts that women are biologically drawn to gathering, while "the male of the species is genetically programmed to pursue, attack and kill for food. To the extent that men do not do so they are not fully human." Shepard, *The Tender Carnivore and the Sacred Game* (Athens: University of Georgia Press, 1998), 122–123. Shepard furthermore argues that the value of hunting for men parallels women's experience of giving birth: "What is important is to have hunted. It is like having babies; a little of it goes a long way." Shepard, "Post-Historic Primitivism," in *The Wilderness Condition: Essays on Environment and Civilization*, ed. Max Oelschlaeger (San Francisco: Sierra Club Books, 1992), 86. Deep ecology supporters often praise Shepard's critique of modernity as contrasted to the idyllic "Paleolithic" mode of existence. See, for example, George Sessions's introduction to *The Tender Carnivore*.

136. Paul Shepard, *Man in the Landscape: A Historical View of the Esthetics of Nature* (New York: Alfred A. Knopf, 1967), 211.

137. Cobb, "Deep Ecology and Process Thought," 123.

138. Naess, "Self-Realization: An Ecological Approach," 27.

139. Naess, "Self-Realization: An Ecological Approach," 26, 24.

140. Gloria Steinem, *Revolution from Within: A Book of Self-Esteem* (Boston: Little, Brown and Company, 1992), 186.

141. Gloria Steinem, commencement speech (Wellesley College, Wellesley, Mass., May 28, 1993).

142. Naess, *Ecology, Community, and Lifestyle*, 44.

143. Naess, "Self-Realization: An Ecological Approach," 27.

144. Naess, "Deepness of Questions," 205.

145. The statement was suggested by Stephan Bodian and endorsed by Naess in an interview. Bodian, "Simple in Means, Rich in Ends," 28.

146. Warwick Fox, "The Deep Ecology–Ecofeminism Debate and Its Parallels," *Environmental Ethics* 11, no. 1 (Spring 1989): 5–25.

147. Salleh, "In Defense of Deep Ecology," 109.

148. Salleh, "In Defense of Deep Ecology," 117.

149. Naess, "Shallow and the Deep," 95.

150. Naess, *Ecology, Community, and Lifestyle*, 181.

151. Naess, *Ecology, Community, and Lifestyle*, 195.

152. Arne Naess, "The Ecofeminism versus Deep Ecology Debate," in Witoszek and Brennan, *Philosophical Dialogues*, 272.

153. Naess, "Ecofeminism versus Deep Ecology Debate," 272.

154. Warren, "Ecofeminist Philosophy and Deep Ecology," 263.

155. Warren, "Ecofeminist Philosophy and Deep Ecology," 258.

156. Warren, "Ecofeminist Philosophy and Deep Ecology," 264.

157. Warren, "Ecofeminist Philosophy and Deep Ecology," 255.

158. Warren, "Ecofeminist Philosophy and Deep Ecology," 264–265.

159. Warren, "Ecofeminist Philosophy and Deep Ecology," 265.

160. Christian Diehm, "Arne Naess, Val Plumwood, and Deep Ecological Subjectivity: A Contribution to the 'Deep Ecology–Ecofeminism Debate,'" *Ethics and the Environment* 7, no. 1 (Spring 2002): 24–38.

161. Diehm, "Arne Naess, Val Plumwood," 26–27.

162. Diehm, "Arne Naess, Val Plumwood," 28.

163. Diehm, "Arne Naess, Val Plumwood," 29.

164. Val Plumwood, "Comment: Self-Realization or Man Apart? The Reed-Naess Debate," in Witoszek and Brennan, *Philosophical Dialogues*, 207, quoted in Diehm, "Arne Naess, Val Plumwood," 33.

165. The reference is adapted from Naess's account of an incident of children's empathy with the suffering of injured insects, arising from their ability to see the insects as "like themselves." Naess, *Ecology, Community, and Lifestyle*, 172.

166. Diehm, "Arne Naess, Val Plumwood," 33.

167. Diehm, "Arne Naess, Val Plumwood," 33.

168. Diehm, "Arne Naess, Val Plumwood," 34.

169. Naess, "Shallow and the Deep," 95–100.

170. Cheney, "Ecofeminism and Deep Ecology," 115–145.

171. Cheney, "Ecofeminism and Deep Ecology," 140.

172. Warren, "Ecofeminist Philosophy and Deep Ecology," 266.

173. Naess, "Deep Ecology 'Eight Points' Revisited," 217.

174. Naess, "Shallow and the Deep," 95.

175. Arne Naess, "A Defense of the Deep Ecology Movement," *Environmental Ethics* 6, no. 3 (Fall 1984): 267.

176. As Naess elaborates, "human beings are closer to us than animals," and "we have . . . a greater obligation to that which is nearer to us." Naess, *Ecology, Community, and Lifestyle*, 170–171.

177. Naess's expression of regret over his statement that some exploitation was "inevitable" was made in an article responding to Ariel Salleh's criticism of this position. Naess explained that he was referring only to the inevitability of exploitation between humans and other-than-humans, not intra-human relations. Naess, "Ecofeminism versus Deep Ecology Debate," 271; Salleh, "Class, Race, and Gender," 236–237.

178. Arne Naess, "An Answer to William C. French: Ranking, Yes, but the Inherent Value is the Same," in Witoszek and Brennan, *Philosophical Dialogues*, 146. For a discussion of Naess's changing views on biospherical egalitarianism and an argument against the use of the term, see William C. French, "Against Biospherical Egalitarianism," in Witoszek and Brennan, *Philosophical Dialogues*, 127–145.

179. Fox, "On Guiding Stars," 174.

180. Fox, "Deep Ecology: A New Philosophy," 198.

181. Fox, "Deep Ecology: A New Philosophy," 196. Fox is responding to Donald Worster's claim that since the eighteenth century proponents of ecological ethics have tended to look to science to corroborate their own intuitions. Donald Worster, *Nature's Economy: The Roots of Ecology* (San Francisco: Sierra Club Books, 1977), 336–337.

182. Fox, "Deep Ecology: A New Philosophy," 199.

183. Fox, "Deep Ecology: A New Philosophy," 197.

184. Naess, *Ecology, Community, and Lifestyle*, 29.

185. Fox, *Toward a Transpersonal Ecology*, 117–118.

186. Fox, *Toward a Transpersonal Ecology*, 172.

187. Fox, *Toward a Transpersonal Ecology*, 172.

188. Fox, *Toward a Transpersonal Ecology*, 178.

189. Fox, *Toward a Transpersonal Ecology*, 176.

# 7

## Ecofeminist Holist Philosophy

> "Control of nature" is a phrase conceived in arrogance, born of the Neanderthal age of biology and philosophy, when it was supposed that nature exists for the convenience of man.
>
> Rachel Carson
> *Silent Spring* (p. 297)

### INTRODUCTION

In the preceding chapters I argued that the form of holism endorsed by Roosevelt, Leopold, Rolston, and Fox presents a vision of ethical maturity defined by abstract constructs or "wholes" that transcend empathy and care for individual beings. I postulated that this focus on larger abstract constructs represents a masculinist perspective, which reinforces traditional dualisms between nature/culture, unconscious/conscious, emotional/rational, female/male. What, then, is the nature of a feminist, and in particular, ecofeminist philosophy? What role do empathy and care play in it? What is the moral status of individual other-than-human animals? And finally, is there a place for holism in an ecofeminist ethical orientation toward nature?

In this chapter, I will outline an alternative understanding of holist philosophy that incorporates care and respect for individual beings as well as larger ecological processes. Using the model of holistic health, I propose investigating the factors that promote (and impede) the development of empathy and care. Rather than attempting to craft a rationally compelling argument for why people *should* care about other animals, I ask why such feelings fail to arise to begin with. I do not claim to present a comprehensive theory or philosophy for grounding human ethical conduct toward nature, nor do I aspire to speak for all ecofeminists. My intention is to offer a preliminary direction that may inspire further study into the ecology of care.

Ecofeminist theorists often advocate a holistic awareness as an alternative to the dualistic and atomistic worldview of Western patriarchal society.[1] Many embrace the relational worldview inherent in holism as more realistic and compassionate. One might conclude that ecofeminists and the authors examined in this study endorse a similar concept of holism. In this chapter, I explore and challenge this presumption. Although areas of convergence exist, ecofeminism as I conceive it is premised upon a distinct view of human nature and moral maturity.

In the analysis that follows, I argue for an ecofeminist holist philosophy that emphasizes six themes: (1) an attempt to understand the current domination of women and nature in its varying social, political, and historical contexts; (2) an acknowledgment of the role of unconscious influences, and in particular the role of gender identity, in shaping attitudes toward nature; (3) an appreciation of the potential of metaphors to facilitate and impede ethical consciousness; (4) a recognition of the importance of appropriate feelings of care and acts of attention in promoting ethical conduct and thought; (5) an affirmation of the moral significance of both individuals *and* larger "wholes"; and (6) support for the practice of veganism as an important means of expressing care toward other animals.

## ROCKING THE FOUNDATIONS

Most ecofeminists agree that ecofeminism is not a single philosophy, but a loosely knit philosophical and practical orientation that examines and critiques the historical, mutually reinforcing devaluation of women and nature.[2] Many contemporary ecofeminists have further broadened this analysis from a focus on the parallel *situations* of "women" and "nature" to an emphasis on the shared *ideologies* that support multiple forms of domination, including those based on race, class, age, ethnicity, and sexual orientation. Carol Adams compares this common mentality to the foundation of a house supporting various forms of oppression.[3]

While ecofeminists pursue diverse paths, many have turned to historical analysis. In contrast to most nature theorists, who have focused on developing abstract theories and constructs for grounding moral conduct, ecofeminists have sought to situate the oppression of women and nature in its social and historical contexts. Although the former approach attempts to construct a universal moral foundation, the latter seeks to uproot the ideological substructures that thwart the growth of an alternative orientation and consciousness toward nature.[4]

One goal of placing the exploitation of women and nature in historical context is to provide a basis of hope for change in existing attitudes. If domination has historical roots, the argument for its inevitability is called into question. Ecofeminists thus delve beneath surface actions and ideas to challenge the prevailing assumptions about human nature that underlie modern Western society. While most theorists in the modern Western ethical tradition presume the inevitability of egoistic impulses and then offer abstract principles and constructs to control them, for many ecofeminists the overriding ethical question is, rather, how and why compassion and moral conduct toward nature have failed to be sustained. Philosopher Alison Jaggar speculates on what would occur if liberals were to rethink their assumptions about human nature: "Instead of community and cooperation being taken as phenomena whose existence and even possibility is puzzling, and sometimes even regarded as impossible, the existence of egoism, competitiveness and conflict . . . would themselves become puzzling and problematic."[5]

Ecofeminists, of course, are not unique in their interest in the origins of the current domination of nature. Since the 1967 publication of Lynn White's influential article critiquing the Judeo-Christian tradition for its contribution to destructive environmental attitudes and practices, nature philosophers have become increasingly interested in historical influences.[6] Ecofeminists share a concern about many of the same social, cultural, and intellectual origins. However, their overriding focus is on understanding the role that gender plays within these influences, and how it intersects with other forms of domination. Yet, despite this shared interest in understanding the conceptual foundations of abuse, by and large ecofeminists have overlooked the influence of the unconscious as a factor.[7]

## RATIONAL DESIGN OR UNCONSCIOUS INFLUENCE?

Ecofeminists have employed a number of terms to characterize the underlying mentality that supports nature abuse, such as "androcentric," "dualistic," "patriarchal," and "masculinist." Karen Warren subsumes these notions under the more general construct, a *logic of domination*, which she argues is the "most important characteristic of an oppressive conceptual framework."[8] According to Warren, this system of thought

> assumes that superiority justifies subordination. A logic of domination is offered as the moral stamp of approval for subordination, since, if accepted, it provides a justification for keeping Downs down. Typically this justification takes the

form that the Up has some characteristic (e.g., in the Western philosophical tradition, the favored trait is "mind," reason, or rationality) that the Down lacks and by virtue of which the subordination of the Down by the Up is justified.[9]

In a similar vein, the Australian philosopher Val Plumwood uses the terms "mastery" and "rational design" to characterize the conceptual system that underlies the abuse of nature, women, and other marginalized humans in the Western world.[10] The "master subject," according to Plumwood, is associated with rationality and autonomy, and defined in radical opposition to the material realm, which is conceived as lacking in agency. According to the "logic of mastery," nature is *"instrumentalised* as a mere means to human ends via the application of a moral dualism that treats humans as the only proper objects of moral consideration and defines 'the rest' as part of the sphere of expediency" (original emphasis).[11] With the rise of capitalism, a new form of mastery came into prominence, defining "rationality as egoism, and sociality as an instrumental association driven by self-interest."[12] As Plumwood explains, the "logic of instrumental reason . . . is the dominant logic of the market and the public sphere."[13]

While these analyses have been enormously helpful in the development of ecofeminist philosophy, the rational connotations of the term "logic" may inadvertently suggest that oppression derives primarily from a conscious ideology, thereby obscuring the unconscious influences that contribute to nature abuse. Plumwood does point out that the "aggressive colonising and instrumentalising logic of the master rationality and the maximising logic of the Rational Economy emerge as profoundly unintelligent, even irrational, as ecological and survival strategies." However, her repeated references to reason and instrumentalism suggest an overriding emphasis on conscious design. The focus on rational mastery also leads Plumwood to employ cognitive language to describe her solution to the dominating practices of the master, namely, a new version of "rationality."[14]

Although Plumwood identifies the important role played by the notions of reason and instrumentality in the oppression of women and nature, she is less successful in explaining conduct that does not readily fit the instrumental paradigm.[15] For example, as a number of feminist and other theorists argue, a man does not rape a woman simply because she is a means to a rationally conceived goal, such as sexual gratification. Rather, as Diana Scully and Joseph Marolla contend, "rapists view the act as an end in itself."[16] The primary "end," in their view, is not simply sex, but revenge or punishment directed at women, as "a class, a category, not as individuals."[17] As sociologist Diana E. H. Russell states, rape is "an extreme acting out of qualities that are regarded as supermasculine in this and many other societies: aggression, force, power, strength, toughness, dominance, competitiveness."[18] Beneath this hatred, according to object relations theorists, lie deep feelings of fear and the conflicting yearning for connection.[19]

Some feminists, like the philosopher Seyla Benhabib, recognize the role of unconscious influences on our actions and thoughts. Criticizing the cognitive-developmental model of moral reasoning, she posits that the dynamic between "self and social structure . . . may involve learning as well as resistance, internalization as well as projection and fantasy." She stipulates that it is important to recognize that "our affective-emotional constitution, as well as our concrete history as moral agents, ought to be considered accessible to moral communication, reflection, and transformation."[20] Similarly, the philosopher Diana Meyers underlines the moral relevance of "dissident speech," which she defines as the "activity of giving benign figurative expression to nonconscious materials that would otherwise distort moral judgment."[21] Still other theorists have emphasized the positive role played by the unconscious in moral conduct and thought. Thus, Sarah Hoagland argues for the importance of "dreaming, imagination, humor, psychic faculty, playfulness, and intuition in the development of an ethical being."[22]

The acknowledgment of the impact of the unconscious has profound implications for ecofeminist philosophy. One inference is that logical argumentation with the perpetrators of abuse against nature may be of limited use. If hunting, animal experimentation, and other forms of nature abuse stem from men's feelings of alienation and their unconscious attempt to (violently) forge connections, then these processes must be identified and challenged if violence is to be stopped. As Catherine Roach notes, "before we celebrate our interconnectedness, or along with it, we should plumb the reality and motivations of our disconnections, for therein lies the real problem."[23] It may be that abuse of nature, women, and other marginalized humans has an unconscious cathectic charge that no amount of proscription and logical analysis can eradicate by itself.

## IMAGES OF TRANSFORMATION

Many ecofeminists implicitly acknowledge the impact of the unconscious through their focus on the role of metaphorical modes of thought. In order to identify the historical roots of oppression, ecofeminists examine the negative images and symbols with which patriarchal society has sought to represent nature, women, and other subordinated humans. Ecofeminists, however, have explored not only the historically oppressive influence of metaphors but also their liberatory impact. Carolyn Merchant's analysis of the changing historical images of women and nature in Western society illuminates the dual role played by metaphorical images.[24]

According to Merchant, two distinct metaphors influenced Western society's attitudes toward nature, one promoting protection and the other abuse. Merchant describes the beneficial impact of the pre-modern perception of the Earth as a living being, dating back to Ancient Greece:

> The image of the earth as a living organism and nurturing mother has historically served as a cultural constraint restricting the actions of human beings. One does not readily slay a mother, dig into her entrails for gold, or mutilate her body. . . . As long as the earth was considered to be alive and sensitive, it could be considered a breach of human ethical behavior to carry out destructive acts against it. [25]

Yet, although the ancient Greek image of nature as a living being promoted respect for nature, Merchant contends that it also harbored the seeds of more destructive configurations. The image of nature as a living, active, female-imaged organism inspired the idea that nature is wild, uncontrolled, and evil, while the perception of nature (and women) as passive was interpreted to mean that nature functioned like a machine. According to Merchant, the earlier perception of nature as a living organism functioned as a "restraining ethic," thereby mitigating excessive exploitation of the natural world. With the rise of capitalism and the emergence of commercial and technological innovations, the organic notion was replaced by the image of nature as a machine, thereby facilitating exploitive practices hitherto restrained.

Merchant rejects an idealist analysis of the transition to a mechanistic worldview, pointing to the complex, dialectical relation between images and ideas on the one hand and material factors on the other. She argues that the appeal of mechanistic images was their adaptability to the social, economic, ecological, and intellectual crises in sixteenth- and seventeenth-century European culture. As Merchant states, "Because it viewed nature as dead and matter as passive, mechanism could function as a subtle sanction for the exploitation and manipulation of nature and its resources."[26] With the new values, the double-edged image of nature as female was "turned upside down," thereby "sanctioning the rape . . . of the Earth."[27]

Merchant does not overlook the negative influences within earlier Western philosophies, particularly the Greek and Christian notions of dominion over the Earth. Yet, her overall emphasis is on the beneficial effect of the organic aspect of Greek and pagan philosophies. By contrast, other feminists have identified the dualism between mind and matter in Greek philosophy as the conceptual basis for violence toward women and nature.[28] Still others believe that patriarchal modes of conduct and thought originated long before either the scientific revolution or Greek philosophy, when earlier matriarchal (or matrifocal) societies were overrun by Indo-European warrior bands.[29] Even accepting Merchant's sympathetic view of the Greek-inspired notion of organicism, one might question the merit of a worldview that lent itself so easily to subversion.

While providing valuable insights, Merchant's analysis illustrates the frequent neglect among ecofeminists and other nature philosophers of any explicit acknowledgment of psychological influences. In particular, it fails to examine the contributing role of social constructions of masculine identity in violence against nature, women, and other devalued humans. She thus looks to images and metaphors that *restrain* human aggression, rather than attempting to understand its deeper roots.

Although ecofeminists have emphasized the influence of particular images in the ongoing oppression of women and nature, most have not concluded that metaphorical modes of thought are inherently oppressive. On the contrary, many theorists propose alternative metaphors for characterizing both nature and preferred models of human relations with nature. Some of the images that have been proffered by ecofeminists are that of nature as a "web," the Earth (or Gaia) as a living being or a "mother," ethical conduct toward nature as a "partnership," and respect for nature's "charm."[30]

The four theorists in this study also employ metaphorical modes of thought to express their ideas. Like ecofeminists, they sometimes invoke the idea of a "web" to convey a sense of holistic awareness. Other metaphors that frequently appear in their works include that of nature as an "evolutionary story," a "drama," a "biotic community," a "branching tree," "the land," or a "productive process." Nature ethics, moreover, is conceived as "trailblazing" for a new consciousness, a journey into a new "ethical frontier," or the "expansion" of a transpersonal Self.

I have argued that an unstated, guiding metaphor that underlies many nature philosophies, including those of the holists in this study, is that of a "hunt" for a theory or form of consciousness that can compel moral conduct. For Theodore Roosevelt and Aldo Leopold, ethical consciousness toward nature arose in the actual activity of sport hunting, which functioned as a symbolic birth into a superior, virile identity. Leopold also conceived of hunting as a means of inserting oneself into the larger drama of evolutionary history. Although neither Rolston nor Fox argue for the central importance of hunting, their philosophies nevertheless "sacrifice" other animals to larger constructs. Rolston explicitly uses such terminology, arguing that individual beings are "sacrificed" to larger ecological processes; Fox conceptually sacrifices individuals through the construct of an expanded Self that transcends the "animal" drives as well as direct ties of affection to individual beings. For both theorists, individual beings are submerged into the larger ecological drama or Transpersonal Self.

In recent years, linguists and cognitive scientists have identified the central role of metaphor in all thought, including abstract concepts and ethical ideas. Since metaphors operate largely at a level beneath cognition, recognition of their importance entails a concomitant acknowledgment of the impact of the unconscious. The linguist George Lakoff and philosopher Mark Johnson, for example, state that one of the major findings of cognitive science is that "thought is mostly unconscious."[31] Johnson goes further, asserting that it is "inconceivable to think of moral reasoning without reference to metaphor."[32] While the deliberate attempt to cultivate images that positively influence ethical conduct toward nature is a welcome development, metaphors should not be considered a conceptual *foundation* for a nature ethic. Metaphors are fluid and easily manipulated for multiple ends.[33] They also cannot be grafted onto people's consciousness if the emotional "soil" has not been adequately tilled. Although the conscious focus on metaphors can encourage caring conduct toward nature, it is not a substitute for a genuine, deep-rooted sense of connection.[34] With these caveats in mind, I offer the following thoughts on ecofeminist metaphors.

If, as I have argued, the metaphors of hunting and sacrifice may be characterized as masculinist, what images might ecofeminists draw on to inspire their own nature philosophy? Perhaps the most frequently invoked metaphor for ecofeminist theorizing has been the image of a quilt, suggesting that ecofeminism is not a single philosophy, but rather a coming together of myriad ideas and experiences. As Warren explains, the quilt metaphor reflects the diverse social and historical contexts in which quilts are made, as well as the act of quilt-making as an ongoing activity.[35] Warren also develops the notion of ecofeminist theorizing as a fruit bowl in which particular fruits represent different ecofeminist principles. While the choice of fruits varies depending upon circumstances, certain practices and ideas are inadmissible.[36] Part of the work of ecofeminist theorists, then, is to identify what practices and ideas are appropriate for either the quilt or the fruit bowl. Warren proposes certain "necessary conditions." As she explains, "nothing that is knowingly, intentionally, or consciously naturist, sexist, racist or classist—which reinforces or maintains 'isms of domination'—belongs on the quilt."[37] Similarly, while ecofeminist philosophy may draw upon a variety of ethical traditions to form a particular fruit bowl, one "that does not make any room for emotional intelligence, particularly the importance of caring about oneself and others, in ethical reasoning and conduct will not qualify" for selection.[38]

In contrast to the metaphor of the hunt, another possible metaphor for ecofeminist philosophy may be gathering, or foraging. Like the metaphor of the quilt, gathering suggests an ongoing group activity, in particular "the collecting of food that grows wild."[39] Another meaning of "gathering" is "to come together in a group," thereby forming *a* gathering.[40] Ecofeminism may thus be understood as the *act* of gathering, which involves the collection of life-sustaining practices and ideas, and additionally as *a* gathering, a coming together of multiple voices. The etymological roots of the two words underline their contrasting significance. Gathering derives from the Germanic *gath*, meaning "bring together,"[41] whereas hunting evolved from the Old English *hentan*, meaning "to try to seize."[42] Gathering suggests a communal, life-giving undertaking, in sharp contrast to hunting, the violent capture and obliteration of another living being.

Roosevelt and Leopold convey the drama of the hunt, describing the buildup of tension and excitement leading toward the climax found in the kill. Both hunt out of a desire for this experience, not out of need.[43] Just as many men assume that the act of sex must culminate in intercourse and male orgasm,[44] so too the narrative structure of hunting necessarily culminates in the attempt to kill another animal. The "fore-play" of the chase only has meaning if directed toward the final death.[45] Gathering, by contrast, is devoid of climactic violence.

The metaphors of quilting and gathering both suggest an experience of joining or "coming together." Although hunters often depict their activity as a "coming together" with nature, or immersion in the natural world, clearly it is a "communion" with a difference. The "game" of hunting involves the conquest and death of an "other." When the animal is killed, the competition is complete. Gathering, by contrast, pertains to the realm of cyclical, non-violent, repetitive activities, typically devalued in the Western world.

The metaphor of play as contrasted with sport also helps illuminate the distinctive spirit of ecofeminist philosophy.[46] By and large, nature philosophy is conceived as a sport in which nature philosophers adjudicate the competing values of the natural world, declaring winners and losers. Although the theorists in this study reconfigure the rules of the "game," individual other-than-human animals (and in particular domestic animals) remain the losing "players." Non-competitive play, by contrast, suggests a more reciprocal form of interaction with nature. Play is an activity that is shared by many animals, performed for sheer delight rather than for instrumental reasons. As authors Jeffrey Masson and Susan McCarthy comment, "Play, laughter, and friendship burst across the species barrier."[47] This joyful, ostensibly useless, cross-species activity evokes the non-instrumental orientation that is so often discussed by nature philosophers as an abstraction.

Play also involves the ability to imaginatively create another world for the sole purpose of inhabiting this self-creation.[48] It is this playful "world-traveling" aspect of imagination that feminist Maria Lugones identifies as a basis of empathy.[49] Voyaging to other worlds has particular relevance in our human interactions with other-than-human nature. As Sara Ebenreck suggests, "awareness of imaginative activity may be especially important for environmental ethics, in which the guidelines for action have to do with response to others who are not human, for whom respectful attention may require of us the probing work of imaginative perception."[50]

Modern Western culture has achieved an unprecedented alienation from nature. For many, the urge to reconnect is experienced as a deep spiritual or psychological need. Killing is not the best way, however, to fulfill this need, and certainly not the most compassionate. Play as a social activity connects individuals together in a joyful, imaginative realm. The cooperative play of young girls may provide a more mature and compassionate model for attaining intimacy with nature than hunting. The Council of All Beings workshops, developed by John Seed and Joanna Macy, are an example of playful connection with other animals which resembles the cooperative nature of girls' play.[51] In these councils, participants are asked to imaginatively enter into the world of another species and to bring their experience back to the group. Participants express profound feelings of empathy, grief, and rage when they realize the impact of deforestation, factory farming, and hunting for other-than-humans. Given the opportunity to express and share such feelings, people can be motivated to engage in a larger context of action.

Still another transformational image for ecofeminist philosophy may be found in the model of holistic health. Throughout history, women have practiced what is now called "alternative medicine."[52] This ecological approach to health recovery presumes that illness begins when the body's natural recuperative powers have been compromised. The goal then is to provide the body with the opportunity to heal by trusting natural processes and by learning the larger "story" underlying the dis-ease. Working with plants, herbs, and the body's own regenerative powers, women have sought to fortify health, rather than to "attack" illness. Their approach has been to understand why ailments occur in order to understand the measures necessary to promote healing. The patient's symptoms are viewed as messengers from the body that need to be understood, not simply suppressed. Modern Western allopathic medicine, by contrast, conceives of illness as a malfunctioning of the body machinery caused by alien organisms (viruses, bacteria, and malignancies) that attack the human body. The appropriate response to invading organisms is to return the affront with a counterattack. Not surprisingly, the two primary treatments for "battling" cancer—chemotherapy[53] and radiation—were developed from weapons of war.[54]

Heroic allopathic medicine is characterized by a lack of interest in prevention or knowing the etiology behind illnesses. The medical establishment thus spends most of its time, money, and resources on battling emergency situations and advanced stages of disease. Millions of dollars are spent on organ transplant research, for example, ignoring simpler measures for preventing disease in the first place, such as exercise and eating a diet richer in plant foods. Similarly, "allopathic ethics" has become a heroic battle against the aggressive impulses that invade the social "body." Rather than exploring the social, historical, and psychological factors that create ethical problems, Western "allopathic ethics" approaches moral dilemmas at an advanced stage of their development, treating the symptoms of patriarchy (its dilemmas and conflicts), rather than the disease inherent in its worldview. Ecofeminist philosophy, by contrast, follows a holistic model, exploring the worldview and mentality that underlie existing conflicts, while simultaneously working to promote an environment in which appropriate care can flourish.

Thus a holistic ecofeminist philosophy, as I conceive it, focuses less on how to deal with aggressive conduct and more on how to preempt aggressive practices before they arise.[55] One of the most direct ways to prevent violence toward women and nature is to reach young children (especially boys) before the cultural conditioning to accept and engage in violence becomes entrenched. This entails addressing the current construction of masculine identity in schools, the media, and homes. The men's studies theorist John Stoltenberg encourages men to "refuse to be a man."[56] As his work suggests, however, it would be even more effective to ensure that a young child is not raised "to be a man" in the first place. There are many small ways to help challenge masculine identity in childhood. It could be as simple as not encouraging boys to engage in competitive sports,[57] or showing disapproval when a child crushes insects with relish or keeps them in captivity. Significantly, Tenzin Gyatso, the fourteenth Dalai Lama, when asked the most important lesson to teach children, responded, "Teach them to show kindness to insects."[58] Social transformation, however, is a matter of changing not only ideas, but also the institutions and industries that derive from masculine norms—the military, sports, government, religions, and economic structures.[59] The culture of masculine violence must also be challenged in the industries that support abuse of other-than-human animals: hunting, animal agriculture (or "animal husbandry"), and animal experimentation.

If masculine identity operates largely within the realm of the unconscious, how is it possible to effect change through conscious acts? Some investigators of the unconscious roots of patriarchy believe, in fact, that there is little basis for optimism. In his analysis of the neurotic foundations of social order under patriarchy, the legal scholar J. C. Smith argues that:

> Seeking to change society through rational planning and organized enforcement invites pathology. Thus, hope for social change leads eventually to despair, and

despair to inertia. . . . From the political perspective, postmodernism commences with the realization that conscious acts of the human will cannot produce the kind of radical change that is required to alter the substantial course of history.[60]

Other theorists, however, have found encouragement in the idea of transforming social and cultural practices and, in particular, current child-rearing practices in the nuclear family. Chodorow's and Dinnerstein's early analyses suggest that change is possible when and if fathers assume a role as caretakers of children. While agreeing with some of the major insights of object relations theorists, I do not share their belief that the inclusion of fathers in parenting will necessarily end boys' violence. Only broad social, cultural, and economic transformation can accomplish this objective. The presumption that an active father figure is necessary to produce nonviolent males is countered by numerous examples of well-adjusted children raised in all-female household.[61] Miriam Johnson further contends, "In this society, equal parenting will solve nothing; indeed, it will reinforce male dominance unless husband and wife are more truly equal."[62]

Outside the field of ecofeminism most nature philosophers continue to ignore the relevance of gender to destructive practices toward nature. A holistic ecofeminist philosophy, in contrast, begins by naming this reality. It seeks to identify not only the dualistic ideologies that perpetuate the abuse of nature, women, and marginalized others, but the ways in which those ideologies are intertwined with psychosocial identities. Ecofeminists must also turn their critical analysis to the field of nature ethics, remaining alert to residues of masculinism within other nature philosophies. Although identifying the influence of gender on moral conduct and thought will not eliminate masculinism, it can provide a first step toward destabilizing its influence.[63]

## ECOFEMINIST REFLECTIONS ON AN ETHIC OF CARE

Throughout this study, I have criticized the individuals under study for their emphasis on abstract, transcendent constructs and their failure to recognize the importance of empathy and care for individual beings. Since the 1980s, feminist ethicists have sought to counter this orientation toward abstraction by reevaluating feelings of care. Since Carol Gilligan's insight about the "different voice" that tends to characterize women's morality, a heated discussion has ensued over the relative merits of an ethic of care in ethical conduct and thought.[64]

Carol Gilligan is often mistakenly accused by feminist and other critics of espousing an ethic of care over an ethic of rights. In fact, her thesis has been that the two forms of ethical thought (care and justice) are inextricably inter-twined: the "two views of morality . . . are complementary rather than se-quential or opposed."[65] Her ideas on how these ethical viewpoints are com-bined, however, have evolved over the years. There is some suggestion in Gilligan's early work that recognition of the previously neglected care ethic would lead to a new, alternative standard for evaluating moral maturity for both women and men.[66] However, her predominant focus has been on the ways in which an ethic of care can be integrated with an ethic of equality or rights. According to Gilligan, women's moral development typically grows from a concept of self-sacrificial care to one that incorporates the ideal of equality. Men, on the other hand, move from a detached notion of justice and rights to an ideal of equity which incorporates the contextual nature of all re-lations, as well as the importance of intimacy and care. In other words, women come to appreciate the value of equality, whereas men come to ap-preciate the importance of affiliation.

In some respects Gilligan appears to follow moral psychologist Lawrence Kohlberg in positing a progression of moral development based on what peo-ple report about their decision-making process. Gilligan's final stage of women's moral development—adherence to the ideal of "truth"— employs some of the same language used to portray the traditional ideals of objectiv-ity that she critiques.[67] But Gilligan might just as easily have labeled it a ma-ture stage of "integrated care." It is the capacity to care for themselves that women develop at this stage of moral development, not a detached notion of justice or objective "truth."[68]

A great deal of confusion surrounds Gilligan's research, partly due to the development of her own views since her original work.[69] Contrary to popular understanding, Gilligan does not insist that care and justice are respectively unique to women and men. In fact, Gilligan's research demonstrated consid-erable overlap in men and women's moral orientation. Two-thirds of the sub-jects of three samples adopted both the perspectives of justice and care. How-ever, among those with only one perspective, care, "although not characteristic of all women, was almost exclusively a female phenomenon,"[70] while there was a "virtual absence of Care Focus dilemmas among men."[71]

Despite this clarification, Gilligan's readers may remain confused about how, precisely, the ethics of justice and care are to be integrated. A recurring theme in Gilligan's work is the image of a "marriage" between the two ap-proaches.[72] Neither justice nor care as traditionally defined is complete in and of itself. Each must be "fertilized" by the other to become whole. But does this mean that one whose moral framework remains oriented toward care can-not fully mature? At times, she suggests that the integration of care and jus-tice is an ideal—only when the two ethics are brought together do they constitute a complete whole. However, she also refers to the "integrity of the two disparate modes of experience."[73] Gilligan also suggests that each ethic lacks integrity until it is "tempered" by its opposite.

In her subsequent research, Gilligan abandons the model of a marriage between the two ethics, framing the two perspectives as *moral orientations*, rather than opposing views.[74] She uses this term to underline a common tendency to focus on one or the other moral framework. In other words, Gilligan is not so much interested in men's and women's abilities as in the moral choices they make and the way they explain them. Gilligan invokes the idea of a gestalt image which may look like either a rabbit or a duck, depending on how it is viewed. As she comments, "What makes seeing both moral perspectives so difficult is precisely that the orientations are not opposites nor mirror images or better and worse representations of a single moral truth. The terms of one perspective do not contain the terms of the other."[75] Thus, "one perspective may overshadow or eclipse the other, so that one is brightly illuminated while the other is dimly remembered."[76] According to this view, gender differences between women and men in moral reasoning do not reflect distinct capacities, but rather differing frameworks or emphases. How moral problems are perceived reflects varying concepts of self. If one's sense of self is premised upon an emphasis on connection, then fear of abandonment becomes the overriding concern; conversely, if a need for separation from others predominates, then aversion to connection becomes the guiding motivation.

Still later, Gilligan reframed the relation between justice and care through an analogy to music, suggesting that different moral perspectives blend together as a harmonic whole. As she elaborates,

> The polyphony of voice, as well as the ever-changing or moving-through-time quality of the sense of self and the experience of relationship, has led us to shift the metaphoric language psychologists traditionally have used in speaking of change and development from an atomistic, positional, architectural, and highly visual language of structures, steps and stages to a more associative and musical language of movement and feeling that better conveys the complexity of the voices we hear and the psychological processes we wish to understand.[77]

Feminist theorists have challenged Gilligan's thesis concerning gender differences in "voice" on a number of counts, including her methodology. Theorists point to flaws in her sampling, which was based on white middle-class girls. Some have argued that if race and class are controlled, the distinctive notion of a women's ethic of care disappears, while others note that it is not only women and girls who demonstrate the care perspective.[78] Yet, as previously mentioned, Gilligan's research was never intended to be conclusive. As she explains, "the argument was not statistical," but rather "interpretative . . . [hinging] on the demonstration that the examples presented illustrated a different way of seeing."[79] Thus, as she maintains, "to claim that there is a voice different from those which psychologists have represented, I need only one example—one voice whose coherence is not recognized within existing interpretive schemes."[80]

Perhaps the most frequent criticism, as noted in chapter 2, is that Gilligan's analysis promotes essentialist ideas of women's distinct nature, ignoring the role of socialization in creating the differences that she describes.[81] Thus, Bill Puka argues that Gilligan ignores the extent to which caring conduct and thought represent "a set of coping strategies for dealing with sexist oppression."[82] He claims that "care levels bear a strong resemblance to patterns of attitudinal assimilation and accommodation commonly observed among poor and oppressed groups, or in oppressive situational contexts."[83] In addition, Puka maintains that Gilligan gives no indication of what triggers moral progression in women, thereby implying that women's progression through moral stages "seems spontaneous."[84] A similar point is made by Tronto, who argues

> insofar as caring is a kind of attentiveness, it may be a reflection of a survival mechanism for women or others who are dealing with oppressive conditions, rather than a quality of intrinsic value on its own. The idea of "attentiveness," which entails anticipating the wishes of one's superiors, may, therefore, be appropriate only for those in a "subordinate social position."[85]

Tronto also faults the ethic of care for neglecting the public realm, arguing that as long as political life is identified with the more valued public sphere, caring will always be viewed as "beyond (or beneath) political concern."[86]

Still others warn of the danger of over-romanticizing women's care-taking capacities.[87] Indeed, John Broughton accuses Gilligan of a "crude romanticism" that "rejects rationality," and Alison Jaggar points to the ways in which research on sex differences can be used to rationalize inequality.[88]

Although there is some truth in the charges against Gilligan, typically they distort her position. It is unfair to claim that she ignored the role of socialization and sexism in women's moral development;[89] Gilligan repeatedly points out that women conform to a self-sacrificial ideal of caring because they believe that they have no choice.[90] Gilligan also acknowledges societal influences on the development of women's moral thinking. She points to the influence of women's rights ideology in the 1970s as a critical factor creating the climate for women's maturation beyond the notion of self-sacrifice.

In the introduction to the revised edition of *In A Different Voice*, Gilligan clarifies that she uses the term "voice" to convey the "possibility for resistance, for creativity, or for a change."[91] By voice, she means the "core of the self."[92] Since voice consists of both nature and culture, it sidesteps rigid dichotomies between the two. Gilligan's "core of self" is comparable to what other writers label "agency," and much of her book may be seen as an effort to help women regain a sense of their own agency by learning to listen to their inner voices.

Despite its flaws, Gilligan's work laid important groundwork for further discussion of the meaning of feminist ethics. It signaled a warning about the dangers of an unqualified praise of "women's experience." At the same time, her work highlighted the importance of exploring differences between women and men, irrespective of their origins. As Gilligan and the psychologist Grant Wiggins argue, "empirically sociologists point to striking sex differences in both incidence and forms of antisocial behavior, manifest at the extreme in the statistics on violent crime."[93] Reversing the traditional burden of explanation, Gilligan contends that "the burden of proof would seem to rest with my critics to give a psychologically coherent explanation of why the sex differences they mention make no difference to moral development or self-concept."[94]

Few of Gilligan's critics have risen to this challenge. Most either ignore or minimize her major findings on gender differences in aggression, choosing to disclaim gender differences in moral *thinking* rather than examine differences between women and men in *actual conduct*. Fearing the repercussions of identifying gender differences, many theorists have overlooked the greater harm that can result from ignoring the differences that clearly do exist. As the psychologist Janie Victoria Ward comments, "it is senseless to discuss morality without looking more closely at the issue of violent behavior. . . . We can no longer discuss violence without immediately acknowledging sex differences in this frightening social phenomenon."[95] In a similar vein, I believe that it is senseless to discuss moral conduct toward nature without acknowledging these same gender differences in violence toward nature.

Most feminist ethicists have focused on reframing the relation between an ethic of justice and rights. The most common perspectives fall into four major categories: (1) those who extend or elaborate on the ethic of care, arguing that although it is valid, it must be refined or enlarged in particular ways; (2) those who consider care to be an inadequate basis for an ethic, at least as a universal ideal; (3) those who argue that ethics of care and justice both overlook other important qualities or activities, such as the act of "attention" (Ruddick, Hoagland), "trust" (Baier), "female agency and integrity" (Hoagland and Card), "care respect" (Dillon); and (4) those who attempt to join an ethic of care to an ethic of justice or rights.[96]

The predominant strategy among feminist theorists is to join the two ethics. However, they disagree over the following questions: Should justice or care be given priority? Are the two ethics distinct, operating in "separate but equal" spheres? Do they overlap, and if so, in what way (i.e., are they intertwined in ongoing mutual support, dialectically related, in interactive tension, or ideally complementary)? Do they constitute a synthetic whole expressing similar or identical concerns, merely using different vocabulary to express the same ideas, or does one subsume the other? And finally, do gender differences correspond to the two ethical positions?

As previously mentioned, in the post-Enlightenment Western tradition, care has been relegated to the realm of personal relations, distinct from the "more important" public sphere which is the province of moral theory. Acts of "beneficence" may be admirable, but they lack the conceptual force of universal law or reason, and hence do not qualify for the status of ethical theory. Conceived as a natural capacity, care is thought to be voluntarily given, as opposed to justice and rights, which can be enforced by a rational moral authority. An ethic of care therefore is consigned to the realm of a supererogatory or imperfect duty, closely allied with the notion of women's emotional work.

Many theorists have argued that an ethic of care can, in fact, "make it" in the world of justice and rights, if only it is admitted into the public realm. Like the stereotypical role-polarized couple who argue over chores and whether the wife can work outside the home, these theorists appear to be quarreling over whether care or justice does the disproportionate amount of labor and whether an ethic of care can, in fact, "work" outside the home. Some have concurred with the traditional paradigm that allows care to enter the "ethical workforce," but only as a volunteer who can provide additional moral "income." Only justice/rights in this conception is capable of earning the "wages" of respect.

There is no disputing that feminist ethicists have shed important light on the subject of ethics. The focus on how care can and does operate outside the private realm balances the overemphasis on abstract rational constructs in Western ethical theory. The relevance of the justice perspective for family situations is similarly valuable, acknowledging that personal relations do not escape the realm of moral scrutiny. Nonetheless, the preoccupation with forging a new (and liberated) union between an ethic of justice and care has served, in my opinion, to distract many feminists from investigating the deeper dimensions of the care perspective in its own right. Whereas philosophers have had centuries to ponder the merits of the justice perspective, the ethic of care, a relative newcomer on the philosophical block, has barely been explored.

A number of feminists note that caring relations are not always ethically desirable. Maintaining relations is not an ethical ideal, for example, in abusive relations, as discussed in chapter 6. On the contrary, for many women, *severing* relations with an abusive partner may be the first step on the path to liberation and healing. A woman who has been abused must learn to focus her care on herself, rather than on her abuser. Thus, as feminists have argued, an ethic of rebellion may at times be a more important ethical ideal for women who experience oppression. Some feminists have sought to characterize an ethic of rebellion against oppression as "feminist" and an ethic of care as "feminine." According to these theorists, the "feminine" approach to ethics reinforces and normalizes the existing oppression of women by positing an essential notion of women as the primary caregivers in society.[97] But the care approach to ethics can also be feminist. Clearly what is needed is not care as a universal norm, but *appropriate* care.

Kathy Davis points out that Gilligan's critics have confounded method-ological and political critiques. On the one hand, they denounce Gilligan's re-search for its potentially detrimental effect on women, and on the other, they use methodological arguments to dismiss it in the name of scientific "objec-tivity."[98] But the potentially harmful effects of her research are a separate is-sue from its validity. Davis contends that the intense scrutiny directed toward Gilligan's admittedly modest study camouflages a political standpoint which is fueled by a dislike of her findings. What is more important than the objec-tive truth of Gilligan's research, according to Davis, is the ongoing interest it continues to generate. Rather than trying to deny her claims, Davis suggests that feminist theorists "[put] our fascination to productive use . . . letting it lead the way to uncovering what it is about the project of a female morality of care that is so attractive or frightening to feminists at this particular junc-ture in history."[99]

Other feminists propose alternatives to an ethic of care, most notably the idea of *attention*. "Attentive love" was first proposed by Simone Weil and subsequently developed by Iris Murdoch. For Weil, attentive love is a pure, receptive, perceiving act, whereby one asks of the other, "What are you go-ing through?" As originally developed, it was viewed as a contrast to egois-tic perception. For Weil, attentive love was also intimately tied to the pursuit of God.[100] Murdoch secularized Weil's ideas, aligning attentive love with the pursuit of "Good," rather than the pursuit of God. She retains the idea of a selfless love, however, and an emphasis on not allowing our fantasies, fears, or needs to interfere with our capacity for clear, loving attention to others. She argues that when one directs a "patient, loving regard" upon a "person, a thing, a situation," the will is presented not as "unimpeded movement," but as "something very much more like 'obedience.'"[101] In this alternative vision of ethics, empathetic imagination is more critically important than conscious reasoning and choice.

More recently, feminists have posited the importance of the act of attention for both maintaining and dismantling oppressive structures. Most theorists have emphasized "attentive love" from the perspective of the perceiver. Marilyn Frye, by contrast, is concerned primarily with the effects of unloving or arrogant perception on the person or object that is beheld. Like Gilligan and Ruddick, Frye stresses the importance of respecting the distinct individuality of the one that is perceived. Contrasting arrogant and loving perceptions, she states,

> one who sees with a loving eye is separate from the other whom she sees. There are boundaries between them; she and the other are two; their interests are not identical; they are not blended in vital parasitic or symbiotic relations, nor does she believe they are or try to pretend they are.[102]

Those with an "arrogant eye," in contrast, "organize everything seen with reference to themselves and their own interests."[103]

Sarah Hoagland further develops the notion of attention through an examination of the role of "agency" and "integrity" in maintaining and dismantling oppressive structures. According to Hoagland, these qualities are involved in making choices. She argues that values flow from the choices that we make and the things we choose to focus upon.[104] Most important for Hoagland are the choices made by those who live under oppression (in particular, lesbians). Patriarchal ethics, according to Hoagland, attempts to undermine agency and integrity through social organization and control, relying on the ideas of "justice" and "obligation." As she explains, the concept of justice "exists to sort out competing claims within a system that has as its axis dominance and subordination."[105] Rights are conferred upon subordinates by those who have power; in contrast, empowering *choices* are made by those who live under oppression.[106]

Using the Wittgensteinian notion of an axis held in place by what surrounds it, Hoagland advocates dismantling the foundations of patriarchal thought.[107] Thus, she focuses neither on justice and obligation, nor on an abstract conception of "care"; her primary interest lies in discovering what it is that promotes female agency and integrity. She states:

> In my opinion, the heart of ethical focus, the function of ethics, and what will promote lesbian connection, is enabling and developing individual integrity and agency within community. I have always regarded morality, ideally, as a system whose aim is, not to control individuals, but to *make possible*, to encourage and enable, individual development (emphasis in original).[108]

Rather than proving false a patriarchal framework that revolves around dominance and subordination, Hoagland argues that "our strategy can be one of transforming perceptions so that existing values cease to make sense." In the new paradigm that she calls for, "rape, pogroms, slavery, lynching, and colonialism are not even conceivable."[109]

Although attentive love is frequently discussed in the context of an ethic of care, and may be seen as an elaboration or refinement of it, the emphasis on perception moves the discussion of ethics into the realm of epistemology and "moral vision." As Marilyn Frye observes, Hoagland thereby "[shifts] the language of the modern tradition of ethics—from knowing what is right or good to deciding what to pay attention to."[110]

The four holist perspectives studied in the earlier chapters also challenged the traditional understanding of ethics. All are to be commended for appreciating the importance of changing one's internal perceptions of nature, rather than relying on externally imposed rules and regulations. Roosevelt suggests the idea of a perceptual shift when he compares nature's beauty to a "Gothic cathedral." And Leopold advances this idea by exhorting farmers to develop a personal relation to the land, rather than relying on government intervention. Rolston argues that ethics is a creative act and not simply "the discovery of and following of rules and duties."[111] And Fox criticizes the idea of grounding ethical conduct toward nature on rational injunctions, arguing that cosmological awareness promotes a "natural (i.e. spontaneous) unfolding of potentialities."[112] Clearly, the authors' philosophies include a place for creativity and feelings, not simply rational rules. However, for all four authors, "undistorted perception" entails directing these feelings toward larger, impartial constructs that constitute larger "wholes."

## ATTENDING TO OTHER-THAN-HUMAN ANIMALS

The effort to adapt an ethic of care to our interactions with the natural world challenges our traditional conception of care, which typically has been tied to personal, dyadic relations. Some feminist theorists, such as Nel Noddings, argue that care requires a direct "response" to the one cared for.[113] However, although this may be an apt definition for some forms of caring in the "civilized" or "domesticated" realms of our world, it is ill-suited for our dealings with other-than-human nature, particularly "wild" or "untamed" nature.[114] Often the most caring thing we can do for other-than-human animals is to leave them alone. What is needed, first and foremost, in our interactions with nature is not an abstract, universal ethic of care, but appropriate or *contextualized* care.[115]

The four authors in this study all fail to show evidence of such care for individual and domestic animals. In their philosophies, other-than-human animals function as props for attaining a desired psychological state. For Roosevelt and Leopold, sport hunting is a symbolic confrontation with animals that bolsters manhood; saving species and the wilderness is an investment for future generations of men. While individual animals may sometimes captivate their imaginations, it is the continued existence of species that concerns them, not individual lives. Roosevelt feared that the "wild animal" stories would impede the detachment requisite for hunting animals and using them for experiments. Similarly, Rolston and Fox contend that human maturity requires transcending personal ties of affection, as well as our self-centered "animal" natures, in favor of a more expansive awareness, encompassing species, the land, the ecosystem, or the larger "Self." For Rolston, this entails renouncing "sentimental" ties to other-than-human animals, who may be appropriately hunted for sport or raised and eaten by an ecologically mature individual.

Ecofeminist philosophy, as I conceive it, proposes an alternative understanding of caring that affirms the integrity of individual other-than-human animals, both domestic and wild. It begins with the simple observation that other animals are individual beings with feelings, needs, and desires. Nature philosophies can then be evaluated for their capacity to incorporate this awareness. When nature ethicists underline the importance of caring for nature, it is helpful to ask, who is the recipient of care? Are individual beings included in their concept of "nature," or only larger wholes? Similarly, when people call for "saving tigers and lions," do they mean individual beings, or only species? The philosopher Margaret Urban Walker also suggests that we evaluate moral values by asking "Who's kept quiet?" and "What's left out?" in the telling of lives.[116] These are important questions for assessing our interactions with nature.

Caring for other-than-human animals can only flourish with the aid of empathy. Empathy, in turn, can be seen as the culmination of many small acts of attention. Cumulatively, these acts of attending can help us to appreciate other-than-human animals as individual beings with subjective identities, rather than merely part of a larger backdrop called "the biotic community," "the ecosystem," or "the land."[117] By pooling our small acts of attention we can exert a powerful influence on one another. For example, Lourdes Arguelles recounts how, as a child, she observed the slight wince that crossed the face of her grandfather when the animals on their farm were killed. Although he never explicitly shared his feelings of abhorrence, she regards her perception of his distress as a major factor in her subsequent adoption of a vegetarian diet.[118] In this example, a small, nonverbal communication was the catalyst for change, not an abstract norm or rule.

The connection between the act of attention and caring can be discerned in the use of the words "careless" and "careful." When we say that someone has acted "carelessly," we mean that they have failed to pay attention to a particular situation or thing; on the other hand, when we admonish someone to "be

careful," we are, in effect, telling them to pay more attention to their surroundings. As a society, our social and cultural institutions have tended to
promote carelessness, rather than care, for other animals.

Josephine Donovan further develops the notion of paying attention to other-
than-humans in her discussion of dialogical ethics and standpoint theory. According to standpoint theory, oppressed groups have an epistemic privilege
that gives them access to more complete knowledge than that of their oppressors. Donovan draws on Georg Lukács's understanding of class consciousness
as workers' awareness of possessing "a qualitative core" that surpasses their
status as reified objects in the minds of their oppressors.[119] In a similar vein,
Donovan argues that other-than-human animals also have a sense of themselves as more than commodities, a perception that caring humans are obliged
to express on their behalf.[120] By engaging in empathic conversations with
other animals about their species-specific situations, Donovan contends that
we can "[listen to them], paying emotional attention, taking seriously—*caring
about*—what they are telling us."[121] As she elaborates elsewhere, "We should
not kill, eat, torture, and exploit animals because they do not want to be so
treated, and we know that. If we listen, we can hear them."[122]

A growing number of humanistic psychologists have sought to enlarge the
definition of wellness to include empathy for other animals. As Melanie Joy
argues, "In an inclusive humanistic paradigm, empathy and unconditional
nonviolence will be considered central to psychological wellness."[123] For Joy,
this expansive empathy extends to all "sentient beings."[124]

The presumption of these psychologists is that humans will naturally develop empathy unless thwarted by external forces. But if empathy is a natural response to suffering, why then does it so often fail in our relations to
other-than-human animals? Many care theorists have noted that ideological
conditioning plays a major role in blocking the natural pathways to compassion. As Donovan notes, "To a great extent . . . getting people to see evil and
to care about suffering is a matter of clearing away ideological rationalizations that legitimate animal exploitation and cruelty."[125]

Brian Luke examines four personal and collective strategies which people
use to block their empathy for other-than-human animals: (1) "denying personal responsibility," (2) "denying the harm done," (3) "denying animal subjectivity," and (4) "overriding sympathies for exploited animals."[126] Social
and cultural beliefs are powerful contributors to these forms of evasion. Luke
cites the biblical mandate giving humans "dominion over all the earth" (Genesis 1:26) and God's divine decree, "Every moving thing that lives shall be
food for you" (Genesis 9:3). In another arena, propaganda from animal agriculture and food industries, in cooperation with the U.S. government, stifles
feelings of empathy by convincing people that exploitation of other-than-hu-

man animals is a prerequisite for leading a healthy life.[127] Behind these social and cultural forces, however, as I have suggested, lies a deeper ideological construct that blocks empathy: masculine identity.

According to a growing number of theologians and philosophers, the biblical teachings cited by Luke do not condone human beings' role as dominators of nature, but rather their position as care-takers. Yet, caring for and about other-than-human animals is not the same as care-taking or stewardship. Stewardship, as a tradition, has been interpreted as an obligation that humans have to manage the rest of nature. In the philosophies of Roosevelt, Leopold, and Rolston, stewardship reflects this managerial ethos, softened by an emphasis on care-taking. Although they view care-taking as a corrective to a domineering ethos, they nonetheless perpetuate the idea that humans are entitled to govern the rest of the natural world. This form of care-taking focuses on human responsibility for the proper functioning (as defined by humans) of the whole of nature, not on the well-being of individuals who may be sacrificed for the whole.

## ATTENDING TO INDIVIDUALS AND WHOLES

What, then, of the larger wholes, including ecosystems, species, and evolutionary processes, that concern Roosevelt, Leopold, Rolston, and Fox? Do these concepts have a place in an ecofeminist holist nature philosophy? And is there a role for science? The theorists in this study all accord science a central role in the proper functioning of wholes. In their world views, science is both a tool for management and an inspiration for a transcendent perspective. Clearly, scientific understanding can help us evaluate the impact of human interactions on the natural world. It can teach us how to minimize our negative influence upon the rest of nature and how to support natural habitats. It may also give us biological and ecological knowledge of particular "species" that can help us understand the needs of individuals within those species. However, it cannot teach us empathy and understanding for individual beings.

The holists in this study contend that the science of ecology provides the lesson that all living beings are interconnected. Although this is an important insight, how interconnection is achieved is equally important. For Roosevelt and Leopold, connection with nature is achieved through sport hunting and the re-creation of an idealized past. For Rolston it is achieved through identifying with the forces of evolutionary and natural history. And for Fox it is attained through the development of an expanded Self. In these formulations, an embodied sense of connection with the cycles of nature gives way to a connection with larger historical, evolutionary, or metaphysical narratives.

Ecofeminists also often invoke ecology's lesson of interdependence as a basis for an ecofeminist ethic. Yet they frequently emphasize the importance of avoiding the totalizing tendencies within holism. Chris Cuomo, for example, embraces a modified version of Leopold's dictum, "a thing is right when it tends to promote the integrity, stability, and beauty of the biotic community."[128] In an effort to broaden Leopold's focus, Cuomo argues that his formula need not be restricted to the biotic community. As she asks, "Are these criteria of health and flourishing not applicable to individuals, groups, and species as well as biota?"[129] In a similar vein, Karen Warren proposes a "care-sensitive" ethic in which the "health (well-being, flourishing) of the particular is viewed as intimately connected with the health (well-being, flourishing) of the general."[130]

Science and technology often function to give humans an inflated sense of their power. Although human society wreaks untold damage on the world, we are led to believe that with scientific knowledge, we can rectify this abuse. Efforts to save endangered species illustrate this sense of omnipotence. "Saving" endangered species in "breeding programs" or zoos merely perpetuates the same managerial ethos that brought "species" to the brink of extinction in the first place. Humans save "endangered species" because of their remorse for human actions and their desire to have ongoing access to the threatened species, or at least the knowledge of their existence. It is distressing to see a particular manifestation of nature pass from history. However, it is important to acknowledge that moral problems do not (and should not) always have a technological fix.

The focus on saving "endangered species" has served as an important tool for protecting natural habitat. But it becomes problematic when efforts are directed toward removing individual beings from their natural habitat for the benefit of the "species," or preserving animals in zoos. I, for one, mourned when the last condors were removed from the wild to be placed in a breeding program for the purpose of producing offspring for future release. Breeding programs are not motivated by consideration for the well-being of the individuals who are wrenched out of their environment and subjected to human manipulation and control of their food, shelter, and sexuality. Similarly, heroic efforts to breed animals in zoos for release into the "wild" perpetuate the sacrificial mentality that I have critiqued throughout this book. Keeping an animal in captivity in order to display her or his "species," or for the purposes of breeding future representations may please the human onlooker, but it harms the individual animals incarcerated for such purposes. The concept of "species" is a mental construct, akin to the notion of race.[131] It is the living beings who matter, not the human abstractions. A more compassionate and effective use of the money spent on these programs would be to protect the natural homeland of the animals who remain in the wild.

In a similar vein, the effort to preserve the genetic makeup of "wild" animals in gene "banks" in order to repopulate areas where particular "species" are considered threatened illustrates the agricultural model of animal husbandry now extended to the wild. Wildlife "husbandry," of course, is not a novel idea. As previously discussed, Aldo Leopold was an early advocate of the agricultural paradigm in the development of the new field of "game management." Significantly, "wildlife" was placed under the Department of Agriculture and animals were "harvested" as "crops." Gene banks that house endangered species of animals are merely the culmination of this long history of reproductive control. Just as marriage has granted a husband legal license to his wife's sexual and reproductive services, the model of animal husbandry grants agribusiness and wildlife managers access to the bodies and reproductive services of other-than-human animals.[132] But humans are not husbands of nature, and nature is not our wife. Animal husbandry is long overdue for divorce.[133]

The theorists in this study urge humans to see themselves as part of a larger natural community or "household." They argue that feelings of compassion for all parts of this larger "family" are the latest and most mature expression of human evolutionary development. But as feminists have shown, the family or household is hardly a haven of safety. On the contrary, domestic violence is a routine occurrence. So, too, the extended "family" praised in the tradition of the land ethic harbors acts of violence against individual other-than-human animals. Just as shelters for battered women are havens from men's violence, (some) parks and refuges are havens against the violence of human hunters. The violence that exists outside of these refuges, however, goes unnamed. Clearly, awareness of kinship with other animals or a larger conception of "family" does not necessarily elicit compassion.

The coexistence of feelings of love and respect for the larger whole with a devaluation of "domestic" animals and of all other-than-human animals as individuals finds a parallel in the dualism between the public and private realms. Just as the public realm is seen as the generating matrix for economic values, the ecosystem or the larger whole is the place where moral values are formed. The moral "worth" of individual and domestic animals is conceptually erased in the "ecological economy." Moral regard for species follows the laws of scarcity in economics: when a "species" is rare, its value is enhanced; when it is abundant, its value falls. The functioning of the "productive process" is the overriding goal.

The authors in this study reflect this low regard; none extend their sympathies to the plight of domestic animals. Rolston goes so far as to assert that a "cow is a meat factory. . . . Cows cannot know they are disgraced."[134] Leopold valued and accepted cattle ranching so utterly that he did not believe it detracted from the wilderness setting he esteemed so highly.[135] As Roderick

Nash notes, "[Leopold] expressed no interest in opposing vivisection or easing the lot of domestic animals."[136]

Ecofeminist philosophy, by contrast, affirms the importance of both "domestic" and "wild" animals. Many other-than-human animals have been taken out of their natural habitats and are therefore dependent upon humans for their well-being. This dependency raises difficult moral dilemmas. The domestication of dogs and cats, for example, has resulted in an enormous overpopulation of companion animals that requires unnatural solutions (spaying and neutering) to rectify an unnatural situation. Ecofeminist philosophers can honor other-than-human animals in the domestic sphere by providing them with homes, while simultaneously advocating a world in which other animals no longer live in captivity. At a practical level, this is not as difficult as it may at first appear. It requires only that domesticated animals not be allowed to be mate. The practice on factory farms, in which animals typically are "bred" through artificial insemination, simply would have to end. The difficulty lies in influencing the industries that support these practices. However, it was not so long ago that many people in the United States supported slavery. Is it too much to believe that the subjugation of other animals may one day be eliminated as well?

Often the well-being of individuals is viewed as conflicting with the well-being of the "whole." Rules for governing our interactions with nature are invoked to resolve the ensuing conflicts. However, Elizabeth Dodson Gray expresses how sensitivity for individual beings is compatible with care for the "whole" through an analogy with the family. As she explains:

> The point is that we parents continually find some ground for making our decisions, grounds other than ranking our children in some hierarchy of their worth. What we perceive instead is that our children have differing needs, differing strengths, differing weaknesses. And occasions differ too. It is upon the basis of some convergence of all these factors that we make our decisions. And our decisions are always made within the overriding imperative that we seek to preserve the welfare of each of them as well as the welfare of the entire family.[137]

The analogy with the notion of family is not intended to suggest that humans should act toward the natural world as parents. Nor, as previously suggested, does it imply that families are always havens from violence. The significance of the analogy lies in the advocacy of the kind of sensitivity that a parent (more often a mother) has for each of her offspring as an individual and as part of a larger unit. Indeed, the philosopher Mary Midgley has argued that the mother-infant bond is the basis of all morality.[138] As Midgely points out, kinship-based ethics can extend beyond the realm of the human family to other-than-human animals.

The authors in this study exemplify a distinct mode of establishing connections. As previously discussed, Roosevelt and Leopold regarded hunting as a form of male bonding, linking past and future generations of men and boys. For Rolston hunting was "a sacrament," demonstrating a mature relation to the life cycles of the ecosystem.[139] Whereas hunters often experience feelings of connection through the infliction of death, many women have similar experiences through a life-*giving* act: giving birth (O'Brien, Ruddick, Spretnak).[140] Still other ways of forging connections with future generations can be found. In contrast to the prototypical male hero who aspires to live on in people's memories through acts of conquest, one can perform simple acts of kindness that take on lives of their own.

## VEGAN PRACTICE: CONTEXTUALIZING CARE

Nature philosophers (including ecofeminists) frequently call for greater respect for the natural world without elucidating concrete practices that express this respect. I propose that veganism[141] is a practice that ecofeminists can support as a natural expression of caring. While holist philosophers focus on maintaining the functioning of larger abstract wholes, my hope is that ecophilosophers will *narrow* their focus to acknowledge the pain and suffering currently experienced by many other-than-human animals, including those who are raised to be eaten. My additional desire is that ecofeminists will embrace veganism as an important means for reducing that suffering and for contributing to the overall well-being of the natural world.

Ecofeminist theorists of vegetarianism often differentiate their approach from that of theorists who employ abstract philosophical constructs to ground moral consideration for other animals.[142] Although sympathetic to the underlying goals of animal advocacy philosophers, ecofeminists critique the deontological approach of Tom Regan and the utilitarian orientation of Peter Singer.[143] They argue that, despite differences, both orientations reinforce the very dualisms that have relegated other-than-human animals to a subordinate status in the first place (i.e., reason over emotion, self-conscious awareness over mindless instinct). In both philosophies, duties are derived from the recognition of particular qualities that other animals are thought to share with humans—for Regan, the capacity for subjective awareness, and for Singer, the ability to experience pain. "Rights" or "interests" are based upon abstract principles, not relations of care.[144] Correct moral conduct, therefore, entails applying rules to concrete situations. By contrast, ecofeminist vegetarian theorists typically focus on the importance of relationships, particularly those based on care. Rather than ranking other animals by means of abstract constructs they are thought to share with humans, ecofeminist theorists focus on both commonalities and differences.

A number of ecofeminists situate the notion of care within a broader conceptual framework, *contextual vegetarianism*.[145] Instead of advocating a universal injunction to be vegetarian based on abstract, atomistic criteria, the contextual approach seeks to understand vegetarianism as a response to particular social and cultural networks of relations. As Deane Curtin summarizes this thinking, "A distinctively ecofeminist defense of moral vegetarianism is better expressed as a core concept in an ecofeminist ethic of care. . . . The caring-for approach responds to particular contexts and histories. It recognizes that the reasons for moral vegetarianism may differ by locale, by gender, as well as by class."[146]

The holists in this study also dissent from the model of rights; and they, too, propose philosophies that incorporate feelings of care for the natural world. Yet, as previously argued, the care that they advocate is for larger ecological processes, such as ecosystems and species, not individual beings. Ethical vegetarianism is, therefore, either absent in their moral theories or the object of critique. For example, for Rolston, meat eating is a natural component of the ecosystem, and those who sympathize with the plight of animals raised for food *lack* sensitivity.[147] The suffering is morally condoned, as long as it does not exceed that which theoretically would occur in the natural world.[148]

Ecofeminist proponents of contextual vegetarianism have sought to differentiate their approach from the abstract individualism of mainstream animal rights theorists as well as the holists' emphasis on supra-individual constructs. Karen Warren proposes a midway position. While recognizing the importance of the ecological relationships within which dietary practices occur, she argues that the focus on larger wholes must be balanced by an appreciation for relations of care. As she explains,

> The position on vegetarianism I defend is critical of both ecologically holistic views that do not adequately respect the individual status of nonhuman animals as sentient, cognitive beings, and radically individualistic animal welfarist views that do not adequately respect the ecological status of animals (human and non-human) as members of an ecological community. I go between the horns of this "holism versus individualism" dilemma by defending a view of contextual moral vegetarianism that recognizes human and nonhuman animals as both discrete individuals and co-members of an ecological community.[149]

Warren concludes that "although universal moral vegetarianism is not required by ecofeminist philosophy . . . ecofeminist philosophy does provide moral constraints on how earth others—nonhuman animals and the nonhuman natural environment—are conceptualized and treated."[150] Thus, "a care-sensitive approach prohibits eating practices in contexts that maintain or per-petuate Up-Down relationships of unjustified domination, rather than prohibit the consumption of animals in context-independent, universal terms of ani-mal rights."[151] Deane Curtin suggests a guideline for ecofeminist philosophy: "The injunction to care, considered as an issue of moral and political devel-opment, should be understood to include the injunction to eliminate needless suffering wherever possible, and particularly the suffering of those whose suffering is conceptually connected to one's own."[152]

The contextual, care-based approach to vegetarianism has important in-sights, emphasizing the relevance of the distinct circumstances in which meat eating occurs. While agreeing with this focus on differences, I nonetheless propose that advocating vegetarianism or veganism as an *ideal* is fully con-sistent with the contextual ecofeminist approach. Although my personal hope is that ecofeminists will view veganism as an integral part of the ecofeminist "gathering" or "quilt," I do not attempt to impose this position as a universal *injunction*.[153] My avoidance of universal claims does not detract from my heartfelt adherence to veganism as an ethical ideal, or from my desire that others share it. Nor does it diminish my wish to convince others of the ethi-cal and health benefits of a vegan diet. I do not, however, aspire to construct a rationally convincing argument that will compel people to adopt veganism through its conceptual force. Rather than attempting to build a logically com-pelling foundation for veganism, I prefer to shed greater awareness on the so-cial and cultural structures upon which meat eating rests. Thus, I reverse the onus of justification, asking those who consume animals and their products to explain the rational foundation of *their* dietary choice. Many of the arguments in defense of an animal-based diet are based on misinformation or lack of knowledge. When people are presented with new facts, the structural supports for their animal-based consumption may be weakened.[154] However, it is the context of meat eating and its socio-cultural, psychological supports that are my primary focus, not simply arguments *for* vegetarianism or veganism.

My reluctance to develop a rational foundation for my ethical commitment has a notable parallel in the realm of intra-human ethics. Most people do not offer rational arguments to explain why they refrain from killing other hu-mans. They avoid killing because they feel, intuitively, that it is wrong, de-terred by empathy for others and an aversion to causing them harm. While people may invoke religious and philosophical beliefs to explain why killing humans is wrong (such as "humans are made in the image of God" or they have the attribute of "reason"), these are non-provable convictions which support intuitions about respecting other humans.

For centuries, the combined forces of religion, philosophy, science, and in-dustry have promoted meat consumption as natural, healthy, and sanctioned by God. Thus, vegetarianism has been dismissed as inadequate and meat eating has been reinforced as a compulsory norm. Those who resist the pressure to conform have been reviled as heretics,[155] zealots, and homosexuals.[156] In modern Western society, they are more likely to be considered eccentrics or extremists. Despite some evidence of increasing tolerance for vegetarians today, the pressure to comply with the norm of meat eating still operates as a powerful cultural and economic force.

The norm of compulsory meat eating is analogous to the norm of *compulsory heterosexuality*. According to feminist author Adrienne Rich, in patriarchal society heterosexuality is not truly a choice or preference, but rather a compulsory institutional norm, "imposed, managed, organized, propagandized, and maintained by force." The purpose of this enforcement is to maintain "male right of physical, economic and emotional access" to women.[157] The norm of meat eating functions similarly in Western culture to ensure male-dominated society's access to other-than-human animals and to their flesh.

Before exploring the role of masculinism in the perpetuation of meat-eating, it may be helpful to address some of the arguments that frequently arise when vegetarianism or veganism are proposed. Three of the most common theoretical challenges to vegetarianism pertain to: (1) cultural practices, (2) predation within ecology, and (3) concern for the suffering of plants.

Dietary choice is intensely personal and emotional, touching on issues of class, race, and cultural identity. Some critics of veganism perceive it as an accoutrement of privileged, middle-class life that may be acceptable to people in the developed world, but when advanced as a universal ideal is disrespectful of other cultures and may even smack of racism.[158] Vegetarianism as a cultural practice, however, is a tradition in its own right that has been espoused by dominant, counter-cultural, and subcultural populations for thousands of years. Many Buddhists and Hindus advocate vegetarianism, yet they are not charged with cultural insensitivity. Thich Nat Hanh, for example, endorses vegetarianism as an embodiment of the ideal of nonviolence, but no one, to my knowledge, argues that he is guilty of cultural imperialism.[159]

Meat eating is often condoned when it is embedded in cultural traditions and conducted with "respect."[160] However, not all cultural practices are morally defensible. Most people in the modern world agree that slavery and clitoridectomy, practices deeply embedded in some cultures, are immoral. There is nothing inherently oppressive in encouraging vegetarianism or veganism as ideals, while recognizing that there may be environmental and climatic factors that make them difficult in some cultures. Advocating ideals is not the same as seeking to impose one's beliefs on other people and other cultures.[161]

Alice Walker emphasizes the importance of renouncing one's personal participation in oppressive cultural practices and describes the difficulties that this often entails. She relays her personal struggle to become vegetarian in light of her Southern upbringing, in which meat was the "mainstay of her diet."[162] Explaining her motivations, she states that "slavery was an intrinsic part of Southern heritage. Propertied white people loved having slaves. That was something they were all used to and they even fought a war to keep them. But that view did not take into account the desires of the slaves, who didn't want to be slaves. In the same way, animals don't want to be eaten."[163]

In a similar vein, defenders of meat eating often point to indigenous peoples who said prayers before killing animals. If native people killed and consumed animals in a spirit of gratitude, it is contended, others can emulate their example and eat meat too.[164] In this argument, native cultures are treated as if they are a monolithic block, overlooking the differences that exist among particular tribes.[165] But some tribes of native peoples killed animals indiscriminately, with little or no regard for either conservation or animals' suffering.[166] In addition, wrenching a narrative out of the context of one culture and grafting it onto another is not only disrespectful and self-serving, it is an act of violence in its own right.[167]

A second criticism of vegetarianism is the contention that meat eating is a *natural* predatory activity that is fully consistent with ecology. According to Holmes Rolston III, while "it insults humans to treat them as food objects by the criteria of animal ecology; persons may and must treat nonhuman lives as food objects."[168] However, the modern practice of confining animals on factory farms for the purpose of breeding and consuming them is almost unparalleled in the natural world. According to biologist Stephan Lackner, predators represent only 20 percent of animals. Disregarding those slaughtered by humans, "only five percent of all animals are killed by other animals. . . . Ninety-five percent of all animal lives are terminated without bloodshed: by old age, sickness and exhaustion, hunger and thirst, changing climates, and the like."[169] Rather than using herbivorous animals as a model for themselves, humans cite the relatively scarce example of carnivores to support their exploitative practices. Those animals who do eat flesh foods do so out of biological necessity. Cats, for example, can develop serious health problems, including blindness, when they are deprived of animal-derived nutrients.[170]

Val Plumwood further develops the ecological argument against "universalizing" forms of vegetarianism or veganism by arguing that they reinforce a neo-Cartesian mind/body dualism.[171] According to Plumwood, whereas the dominant culture associates humans with mind and the rest of nature with matter, "ontological vegetarians" merely include other-than-human animals in the realm of mind, continuing to relegate all other aspects of the natural world to the realm of mindless matter. Thus, by ontologizing other animals as "non-edible," animal advocates deny the ecological contexts in which humans can and do eat other animals in morally acceptable, non-instrumentalizing ways. Plumwood argues that there is nothing wrong with killing other animals for food; what is morally problematic is the reduction of other-than-human animals to *nothing more than* "meat." Humans, according to Plumwood, are embedded in ecology, and thus we must accept that we too will become someone else's food.

While Plumwood's emphasis on the moral problems entailed in instrumentalizing other living beings is commendable, her contention that the ideal of vegetarianism perpetuates a mind/body dualism fails to recognize that many vegetarians are motivated by a visceral repugnance to the suffering and death of other animals, hardly a disembodied neo-Cartesian stance. Often, it is the ability to put oneself into the bodies of other animals, rather than abstract philosophical thought, that motivates people to become vegetarian. We do not dismiss feelings of abhorrence toward inter-human killing as anti-ecological. So, too, we can evaluate our feelings of empathy for other animals using criteria other than ecology.[172]

Plumwood's ecological critique is linked to a third challenge to vegetarianism, often posed as a question: What about plants? Don't plants also suffer? Isn't pulling a carrot out of the ground as violent as killing an animal? Although some people raise the possibility of feelings in plants in all sincerity, many use it as an attempt to exonerate their practice of meat eating. It is tempting to respond by falling back on scientific arguments about the existence of a central nervous system in animals, and its absence in plants, to support greater moral obligations to animals over plants. As I have argued throughout this study, however, science provides insufficient and shaky ground for a nature philosophy. Scientific arguments may mask deeper feelings. Thus, those who rely upon scientific studies about plants often seem to be using this data to silence their own intuitive awareness that other animals do, in fact, experience pain. Although it is also tempting to invoke the language of "rights" or concepts such as "inherent value" or "inherent worth" to defend other-than-human animals, these constructs bring one group of beings into the orbit of moral concern by excluding the rest of nature. Animal advocates, for example, routinely invoke the "rights" of "sentient" or "self-conscious" animals, but few argue for the rights of rivers, mountains, and streams. The notion of rights, thus, places a conceptual wedge between the concerns of animal rights proponents and environmentalists.[173]

Eschewing the concept of rights, however, does not mean abandoning all distinctions. A number of theorists have argued that the notion of differing "needs" is more helpful than that of rights in providing guidance in human interactions with nature. Each part of nature has particular needs, which we as humans can strive to respect. As Ted Benton argues, "Basic interests in bodily development, sustenance, health and reproduction, and in the ecological conditions of these, can be recognized as shared features of human and animal life."[174] For Benton, needs include that which is necessary "not simply for survival, but for well-being, or flourishing, as a being of a certain kind."[175] In a similar vein, Martha Nussbaum advocates a "capabilities approach," arguing that "animals are entitled to a wide range of capabilities to function, those that are most essential to a flourishing life, a life worthy of the dignity of each creature. . . . The entitlements of animals are species-specific and based upon their characteristic forms of life and flourishing."[176] Ethological research can provide practical assistance in identifying some of these factors, such as what types of vegetation an animal or plant requires to flourish. We need not always rely on science, however. As humans, we are also emotionally equipped to comprehend some of these needs through our capacity for empathy. We typically know, for example, when an animal is in pain. Our sensory-emotional experience informs us that the suffering of other animals is much like our own. As Josephine Donovan argues, extrapolating from our own emotional experiences is an important component in ethical relations with other-than-human animals.[177]

Animal advocates have been criticized for devoting their time and energy to animals, rather than human beings. At the same time, they are reproached for their failure to care for plants. In both instances caring is viewed as a finite resource that cannot encompass diverse groups. Foregrounding the plight of individual other-than-human animals, however, does not exclude recognition of the individual integrity of plants. I wince when I encounter bonsai trees, and have serious moral qualms about keeping plants in pots. Although it is not the basis for my veganism, I find comfort in knowing that my diet helps to reduce suffering, since far fewer plants are required to feed a person on a vegan diet than one who eats animal-based foods.[178] My own commitment to eat plants rather than other animals, however, springs from deep-seated feelings that cannot be reduced to formulae or rules. It begins with the anguish that I first experienced when I learned about the treatment of animals on factory farms. Although I do not reduce ethical conduct to feelings of aversion and attraction, I believe these are a good place to begin. Dialogue with others can also help us to deepen our initial moral responses.

Just as caring for plants and caring for other-than-human animals need not be mutually exclusive, so too the practice of veganism or vegetarianism exemplifies how concern for individuals and concern for the whole need not be (and frequently are not) counterposed. A vegan diet helps alleviate the suffering of animals, contributes to human health,[179] and reduces the human impact on the natural world. According to an exhaustive 2006 United Nations FAO (Food and Agriculture Organization) report on the impact of the livestock industry on the environment, "livestock production accounts for 70 percent of all agricultural land and 30 percent of the land surface of the planet." The livestock industry is responsible for "18 percent of greenhouse gases" worldwide and, "in the United States, with the world's fourth largest land area, livestock are responsible for an estimated 55 percent of erosion and sediment, 37 percent of pesticide use, 50 percent of antibiotic use, and a third of the loads of nitrogen and phosphorus into freshwater resources." It is furthermore "the major driver of deforestation, as well as one of the leading drivers of land degradation, pollution, climate change, overfishing, sedimentation of coastal areas and facilitation of invasions by alien species." As the report concludes, the livestock industry is "one of the top two or three most significant contributors to the most serious environmental problems, at every scale from local to global. . . . The impact is so significant that it needs to be addressed with urgency."[180]

The quotidian decision to continue to eat meat is often made in ignorance of its larger social context. "Meat" typically arrives on the human dinner plate at the end of a long narrative of violence. As Carol Adams points out, the animal that once existed becomes the "absent referent" in the social construction of meat. The once-living being is now referred to as "meat." The term "meat" functions as a mass construct, submerging the individual identities of other-than-human animals.[181] It can refer to any number of beings. Thus, when people consume other animals, they eat a disembodied "product." As Adams notes, if, when referring to "meat," people were to speak of "*her* breast" or "*his* leg," it might help restore the "absent referent." By piecing together these truncated narratives of our culture, people can make more conscious ethical choices.[182]

In the modern Western philosophical tradition, moral dilemmas are generally weighed on an abstract plane. The mind/body dualism that has been an integral part of Western philosophy is thereby reproduced each time we consider moral dilemmas in this manner. An embodied approach to decision-making, however, may lead to very different conclusions than detached deliberation. We might, for example, decide on an abstract plane that it is morally acceptable to eat meat, but if we were to see, hear, and smell the conditions of the animals who are raised and slaughtered for meat, we might conclude otherwise. If we feel horror or discomfort at seeing their pain, we might question the ethics of indirectly supporting these practices through our financial and dietary choices.[183]

Simone de Beauvoir's account of her visit to a slaughterhouse during her 1947 visit to the United States illustrates the power of firsthand accounts of suffering.[184]

I will not leave Chicago without also seeing the slaughterhouses. I know that from all over America, live animals flow into this great center, and they are then sent back across the whole country in the form of canned or frozen meat. The slaughterhouses are quite far from the center of town, and the elevated railway runs for miles and miles above a plain that's filled with corrals where the cattle are kept. From morning to night, they pour out of the trains that bring them from the West or the South, and cowboys on horseback guide the herds into the lanes of this enormous concentration camp. The smell of blood, gamy and rancid, drifts everywhere, even into the railway cars. When I climb down the station stairs, it catches in my throat, and even though I tried to harden my heart in advance, nausea sweeps over me with every breath. I haven't eaten lunch, and I ask where the restaurant is. I'm shown a large building that stands above wooden sheds; the restaurant is on the top floor. The place is filled from top to bottom with offices where typewriters are clacking away. The smell does not penetrate into this place. Here, the meat and blood are converted into abstract numbers that are written on clean paper in a carefully controlled environment. The offices of La Salle Street and Wall Street don't smell of oil and sweat either, but the gap that separates the world of profit from the world of work is more obvious here than elsewhere because the smell that infests the dungeon is so close at hand. . . . On the walls, there are photographs of cows and sheep glowing with health. You also see marvelous roast beefs and sliced hams pictured in mouth-watering, lying colors—reassuring images in which the triumph of man over nature is achieved.

I am going to witness the intermediate stage of the drama. After my meal, I ask what time the visit begins, and I'm told that a "tour" is leaving in five minutes from a nearby building. I go down, walk through the stench, and then go up to an office where five or six people are waiting. The guide opens the door; it's as though we were going to visit a museum. But at the end of the long wooden gallery where the floor rises and falls in inclined planes, a sign warns us, "Faint-hearted people should stay at the door." Everyone goes in.

Slaughterhouses are private enterprises. There are large ones and modest ones; I think that this is one of the most extensive. Wooden platforms, built purposely for tourists, wind around the vast halls, halfway between the ground and the ceiling. From this elevated position, we can see the animals' agony and the human labor from a distance but in detail. Large numbered signs explain the different phases of the operations to us, like the road signs that recount American history or the posters that describe the monuments of Florence and Rome to the GIs—this country has a definite pedagogical streak. These large butchering factories have been described too many times for me to repeat it all here—the shrieking pigs, the spurting blood. Already by the fifth sign, the animals have been disemboweled, decapitated, scalded, and are only pliable matter, like squared-off planks of wood. Before they are cut up, they spend twenty-four hours hanging from hooks in the huge refrigeration rooms. This seems to me more like a sacred rite than an operation with a useful purpose; it's the night-watch before a battle, the initiation that transfigures a carnal being, rooted in na-ture and filled with murky discharges, into a human conquest that has its place and its role in society. The animal that just bellowed and spit its blood becomes a piece of food that a civilized individual can eat for nourishment with peace of mind. In the same way, marriage transforms a woman of the poisonous sex into a chaste wife. In the big open storerooms beside the refrigerators, hams rolled in cellophane have the color of ripe corn or toasted bread; the crusty gold of the sausages has kept the purity of the flames, and the spell of flesh and blood has been conjured away. I would eat a piece of bacon without a second thought.

Even though the death of the cattle is less spectacularly ghastly than the sight of the pigs having their throats cut, and even though the animal is hidden behind a wooden fence when the executioner's mallet strikes its head, this enormous palace of butchery nevertheless makes the strongest impression. In the hot smell of blood, in the dull light of the hall where iron knives gleam, two dramas are superimposed: man against animals and men among themselves. It's no accident that the bloody arms carving up the carcasses are nearly all black arms under their red-stained gloves. Slaughterhouse work is arduous, and the history of the slaughterhouses is one of the darkest chapters in the history of American labor—a story of strikes and racial battles. . . . The bosses profit from the wretched sit-uation of blacks, who are allowed to enter only a few professions and who are used systematically against union workers. This maneuver is unfortunate for both the white workers and the blacks themselves, who, identified as enemies, find themselves utterly dependent on their employers with no support among their own class.

I watch the cattle, felled by the mallet and still shuddering, roll through a trap-door onto the tile floor. A hook grabs them and hoists them up, and an arm wielding a knife severs their artery and their life. They are decapitated and their legs draped in a large white cloth; carts carry away enormous blue entrails and buckets of foaming blood. Basins of water are emptied onto the tiles, and the metal gleams with murderous reflections against the red ground. This colossal slaughter is the visible tragedy, but it's only the symbol of another, crueler, deeper tragedy. In order to live, man consumes non-human lives, but he also feeds on the lives of other humans. It suddenly strikes me that the blades slicing the wounded meat, all this carnage of blood and steel, are there only to illumi-nate the awful meaning of that natural law to which we're inured from birth—man is an animal that eats.[185]

Although de Beauvoir expressed deep anguish over the plight of other-than-human animals, she appears to acquiesce in their domination as part of "man's" transition from nature to culture. Yet the masculinist model of transcending nature is precisely what contemporary ecofeminists critique. Rather than accepting the mass objectification of farmed animals as a cultural destiny, ecofeminists can identify and challenge the larger masculinist conceptual system within which it exists. In so doing, vegetarianism becomes an act of resistance against patriarchal forms of oppression.

Vegetarianism is often regarded as an ideology but, as authors Nick Fiddes and Melanie Joy point out, meat eating is equally ideological.[186] Joy goes so far as to coin the terms *carnism* and *carnist* to refer to "the ideology of meat production/consumption and its proponents."[187] As she argues, "At least in the industrialized world, meat production and consumption are choices . . . based upon . . . the speciesist assumption that humans are superior to other animals and that therefore, sacrificing nonhumans for the human palate is ethical and legitimate."[188] Similarly, Fiddes contends that meat functions to provide "the ultimate authentication of human superiority over the rest of nature."[189] This attitude of superiority is not simply an abstract philosophical perspective, however. As Fiddes points out, it is intimately connected to identity, particularly masculine identity. Meat dominance and male dominance are intimately intertwined as ideologies, practices, and norms.[190] In the vast majority of cultures, meat is accorded more prestige than plant-based foods, notwithstanding evidence that suggests it is harmful to human health and the larger environment. The low status accorded to plant foods finds a parallel in the similarly inferior social position assigned to women. Just as patriarchal society considers a woman to be incomplete without a man, vegan foods are considered mere supplements to the centrally important flesh foods.[191]

The higher prestige of flesh foods reflects their residual connection to acts of male dominance: hunting and animal sacrifice. As Fiddes points out, meat functions as a symbol of a masculine conquest over nature. He elaborates, "meat is almost ubiquitously put to use as a medium through which men express their 'natural' control, of women as well as of animals."[192] Conquest and control over women and other-than-human animals are expressed in related forms of consumption. Men consume women's bodies via sex shows, pornographic magazines, and prostitution; their sexual "appetites" are aroused by women's bodies in the same way in which their taste buds are aroused by animal flesh. Although women are not literally consumed by men, they commonly describe their experience of sexual objectification as one in which they are treated like a "piece of meat."[193] As Carol Adams points out, the oppression of women and of other-than-human animals follows a similar trajectory: "a cycle of objectification, fragmentation, and consumption." As she further argues, "Consumption is the fulfillment of oppression, the annihilation of will, of separate identity."[194]

The conceptual link between the perceptions of women and animals is also seen in the lives of ascetics who renounce meat eating as an integral part of a life of celibacy.[195] In many religious orders, women and other-than-human animals are viewed as inciters of the "animal" passions and as sources of defilement. Rather than exercising their prerogative to "consume" women and meat, "holy" men conquer their internal animal passions by abstaining from these temptations of the flesh. But whether a man "consumes" women and other animals to demonstrate his masculinity, or renounces both to attain spiritual purity, women and other animals function as symbols or objects in the quest to establish masculine identity.

While hunting and animal sacrifice both exhibit the long-standing connection between masculinity and meat eating, modern industrial agribusiness represents a new incarnation of masculine dominance and control, unprecedented in its extremity. The scale of objectification of other-than-human animals on factory farms is difficult to comprehend.[196] Reproduction—the creation of life—on large-scale corporate farms is the ultimate in assembly-line production, although the final goal is dismemberment, the destruction of the life created. In the dairy "industry," the life cycle typically begins with sperm obtained from select "stud" bulls, who are lured into mounting a dummy or a steer and climaxing in artificial vaginas. On some occasions, semen is obtained through the application of low-voltage pulses applied inside the bull's rectum or through manual manipulation. The semen is then flown to businesses around the country for implantation into cows. A female is impregnated either by allowing a bull unrestrained access while she is immobilized, or by inserting sperm into her cervix with a syringe.[197] When cows give birth, their offspring typically are wrenched away from them on their first day of life, an anguishing experience for both mother and infant.[198] "Dairy" cows are pumped full of hormones and antibiotics throughout their lives to maximize milk production. They are kept in a continual state of lactation until between five and seven years of age, at which point they are no longer able to sustain the high rate of milk production.[199] Cows are bred to generate abnormally large quantities of milk, a contributing factor in the frequent occurrence of mastitis.[200] Young male "dairy" cows are typically either raised to become veal, chained by the neck in two-by-five-feet stalls, where they cannot even turn around, or simply dumped, since they are of no use to the dairy industry. Young female "replacers" are also raised in tiny huts until they are ready to be used for dairy production.[201]

Bull calves are routinely de-horned, castrated, and branded without anesthesia. When they are ready for sale they are corralled and packed into trucks, where they spend days without food or water during transport to feedlots for fattening before slaughter. Feedlots can house up to 100,000 animals in a single facility. As Michael Pollan observes, "A feedlot is a city of cows. It's cattle pens, [where the animals stand] around in their manure all day long. When they go to sleep, that's what they lie down in. They're forced to exist with their feces all the time."[202]

The fate of pigs is equally grotesque. Taken away from their mothers at less than twenty days old (on average),[203] they are typically raised in dark or dim, overcrowded sheds, on concrete or wooden slatted floors, with little room to move around. The ends of their tails are cut off, their ears are "cropped," their teeth clipped, and the males are castrated, all without anesthesia. Instead of living up to their potential life span of twenty years, they are sent off to be slaughtered at five to six months of age. Although breeding sows live longer (three to four years) their lives are also filled with constant suffering. Eighty-five percent of sows on large commercial hog farms are now artificially inseminated.[204] After impregnation, "breeder" sows spend their entire pregnancy confined in "gestation crates," providing no room to walk or turn around. Shortly before giving birth, they are moved to almost equally confining "farrowing crates." Because of their abnormally large size, the unnatural conditions under which they live, and farm managers' fear that they will crush one of their young, they are forced to nurse their infants through the bars. Sows who are used for breeding are impregnated every five to six months.[205] Twenty to fifty percent of sows are regularly "culled" (i.e., killed) annually, most often for "reproductive failure."[206]

Chickens fare no better. "Broiler chickens" are confined to sheds with less than half a square foot of space, where they are forced to stand on cement floors littered with their own excrement until they are slaughtered at six weeks of age. Through a combination of genetic selection, antibiotics, and high levels of protein, chickens grow to an abnormally large size, often causing their bones to collapse due to the excess weight. Egg layers spend equally abysmal lives, crammed with four to six other chickens into stacked cages less than two feet square, unable to spread their wings or avoid the droppings that fall onto them from the cages above. Between 50,000 and 100,000 chickens are often confined in a single facility, where they never see the light of day. In a painful process, the tips of their beaks are seared off in order to prevent the injury to other chickens that would otherwise occur as a result of their stressful living conditions. Often their feet develop cracks and deformities, sometimes growing around the mesh flooring of their cages.[207] From eighteen months to two years old, when their egg production begins to decline, they are sent off to be slaughtered. Since egg layers are bred to be lean, the lean male chicks that are born are considered industrial waste, and are therefore killed just after birth. Most frequently, they are placed, fully conscious, into grinders in order to be made into fertilizer, while at some facilities they are thrown into trash bags where they die by suffocation.[208]

Animals who survive the living conditions on factory farms and the grueling transit to their slaughter face an agonizing death. No laws exist in the United States regarding the slaughter of farmed birds, who constitute 95 percent of all land animals slaughtered. The electrified water bath in which chickens are immersed paralyzes them, but does not render them unconscious. The baths are administered not out of concern for the bird, but rather to minimize thrashing that might damage the carcass. As many as three million birds may be boiled alive every year. Approbation of cruelty to other-than-human-animals is built into the U.S. legal system. As Jim Mason and Peter Singer observe, "There is no federal law regulating the welfare of farmed animals. Literally nothing." Most states that have large industries also exempt farmed animals from anti-cruelty laws.[209]

These forms of abuse can only exist in a system in which the feelings of other-than-human animals are considered nonexistent or irrelevant. The overriding goal of agribusiness owners is the profit they derive from the production and reproduction of the farmed animals' flesh. For some feminists, vegetarianism is a concrete means of disassociating from this pervasive rape culture.[210]

Ecofeminist philosophy provides an important lens through which to examine the practice of consuming flesh. By bringing the practice into critical scrutiny, and examining the nature of the relationships that surround it, ecofeminism can help to challenge the conceptual force that holds meat eating in place. Ecofeminist philosophy can thus open a space in which to plant the seeds of a new relationship to food and a new practice of care. In this dietary paradigm, meat eating is not renounced due to the compelling force of an abstract norm, nor is it renounced as an expression of asceticism. Instead, people are drawn to vegetarian food by its positive allure. The appeal of vegetarian foods flows at once from an urge to resist patriarchal forms of dominance and control, and from positive feelings of empathy and care for the other animals with whom we share the earth.

The exploitation of the natural world exists on a scale that is difficult to grasp. Every year in the United States billions of animals are killed for food, and thousands are killed or subjected to painful experiments in laboratories. In the face of these massive numbers people are psychically numbed. How is it possible to emotionally assimilate the reality of so much suffering and pain? How can people attain the realization that when they eat "meat," they are eating what once was a living being?

For many people, the path out of psychic numbness begins with a connection to an individual animal. Often people are unable to eat animals who resemble one with whom they have formed a bond. The impact of this emotional bonding is portrayed in an episode of the television series *The*

*Simpsons.* The young, sensitive girl Lisa befriends a lamb while on an outing to a petting zoo. That evening, when her mother serves "lamb" at dinner, Lisa announces to the family that she cannot "eat a lamb." Her father, Homer, protests that she is not eating *a* lamb, but rather *lamb.* However, Lisa, who through her empathic connection with an individual animal has broken through the mass construct, announces to her horrified parents that she will no longer eat *any* meat.[211]

Alice Walker describes a similar, real-life experience when she writes of the connection that she forged with a horse named Blue. She was haunted by the look of vacancy and loneliness that she saw in the eyes of the solitary horse. When another horse was brought to Blue to share his meadow, she saw a new look in Blue's eyes, a look of "independence, of self-possession, of in-alienable *horse*ness."[212] However, Blue's new friend was soon taken away. Walker learned that the mare had been brought to Blue only to mate, and when the act was accomplished, she was returned to her "owner." Walker sadly watched as Blue returned to his original despondency, only now she also noticed a new look of hatred in his eyes. Walker observes, "If I had been born into slavery, and my partner had been sold or killed, my eyes would have looked like that."[213] One evening after this occurrence, while Walker was talking to a friend about justice and freedom for all beings, she came to a re-alization:

> And I thought, yes, the animals are forced to become for us merely "images" of what they once so beautifully expressed. And we are used to drinking milk from containers showing "contented" cows, whose real lives we want to hear nothing about, eating eggs and drumsticks from "happy" hens, and munching hamburg-ers advertised by bulls of integrity who seem to command their fate.

As she sat down to dinner and began to eat a steak, she realized that she was "eating misery . . . and spit it out."[214]

The use of narrative as a mode of ethical instruction has received increas-ing attention in recent years.[215] Yet its relevance for facilitating ethical inter-actions with the natural world is only beginning to be appreciated. Animal stories have always appealed to young children; the enduring popularity of the 1995 movie *Babe* suggests that even adults enjoy them. *Babe* tells the story of a pig who, upon learning that he will one day become "meat," sets out to circumvent his destiny by becoming a sheepherder. Although the movie takes considerable license with reality, it conveys Babe's individual identity, much like the controversial wild animal stories discussed in chapter 3.[216] This kind of movie may be a more effective way to get people to question their di-etary choices than appeals to abstract constructs and rules.[217]

Children's storybooks also hold great potential for challenging patriarchal modes of thought, and for promoting care. The story of a bull named Ferdinand, who preferred to smell flowers rather than fight, is a case in point. Written in 1936 by Munro Leaf, *The Story of Ferdinand* was the subject of heated controversy. The book was published in the midst of the Spanish Civil War and critics believed that its opposition to violence was a veiled attempt to undermine the war. Gandhi hailed it as his favorite book, Hitler decreed that it be burned, and Spain banned it for many years. In the story, a group of men visit the field where Ferdinand lives in order to select the "biggest, fastest and roughest" bull for a bullfight in Madrid. As Ferdinand wanders off, knowing he will not be picked, he happens to sit on a bumble bee and gets stung. Reeling from pain, and "puffing and snorting," Ferdinand conveys the impression that he is the most ferocious bull of all and is therefore chosen. But when the day of the bullfight arrives and Ferdinand is placed in the ring, he notices the flowers in the "lovely ladies' hair" and sits down to quietly savor the experience. In the end, the frustrated matador is compelled to take Ferdinand home.[218]

The effectiveness of stories about real animals in evoking empathy and care is demonstrated by the story of a cow named Emily. Many animal stories are fixed in local lore, but the story of Emily the "dairy cow" gained national recognition. Emily arrived at the Arena slaughterhouse in Hopkinton, Massachusetts on November 14, 1995. The Boston Vegetarian Society newsletter wrote, "Seeing the horror which faced her, Emily jumped from a small holding pen, her 1,400 pound body clearing a five foot tall gate, and escaped the violent fate which befalls millions of 'worn out' dairy cows each year." Emily went on to "spend 40 days in the bitter cold and harsh snowstorms, foraging for food and cleverly evading the slaughterhouse crew bent on recapturing her." Touched by the story that received almost daily coverage in the local newspaper, numerous people tried to help Emily by placing hay throughout the woods. One editorial was headlined "Run, Emily, Run."[219]

Emily was fortunate to have inspired the compassion of the vegetarians Meg and Lewis Randa, who "offered to buy her so that she could live out her life in a sanctuary at the Peace Abbey, a project of The Life Experience School which they run in Sherborn." And since the school served special needs students, the owners of the slaughterhouse agreed to sell her for one dollar. Meg and Lewis exercised "patience and gentle persistence" in order to coax Emily into a trailer and introduce her to her new home. It was Christmas Eve. As the newsletter concludes, in a "cozy barn, with abundant food, and surrounded by only love and goodwill, it didn't take Emily long to realize that she was now safe."[220] Emily remained at the sanctuary until her death in the winter of 2004, attracting thousands of visitors, many of whom became vegetarian.[221] The following year, a life-size bronze replica of her was installed at her burial site, located in what is known as the Sacred Cow Animal Rights Memorial. Visitors continue to visit the statue to pay homage to her spirit of freedom and her resistance to her foreordained fate. Emily's story, which attracted national media coverage, is exceptional. But it may, perhaps, continue to promote concern for the fate of the majority of other animals whose stories will never be told.[222]

Stories like those of Babe and Emily the cow do not use abstract theories to advocate animal "rights" or obligations to the natural world. Nor do they rely on grand scientific or metaphysical narratives. Yet they can inspire humans to deepen their connection to other animals. Stories such as these help people to recognize that the lives of other animals follow story lines, representing a subjective identity. One way in which we can come to appreciate their subjectivity, therefore, is through telling their stories as best we can.

## CONCLUSION

Throughout this book, I have sought to distinguish ecofeminist philosophy from the holist orientations I have reviewed. My intent, however, has not been to drive a wedge between the two perspectives. On the contrary, I wish to encourage ongoing dialogue about what it means to care for and about the natural world. I also have sought to demonstrate the need for greater clarity about the terminology used in nature ethics.[223] While invocations to bestow "care," "love," and "respect" upon "wildlife" or "life forms" may appear admirable, they can conceal vastly divergent attitudes and practices.[224] According to Roosevelt, Leopold, and Rolston, these sentiments could be appropriately expressed by killing individual beings. The concern of all four figures studied is for the continued existence of "life forms" and "lineages," not individual beings. Although Fox does not explicitly endorse the killing of other than-human animals, his model of moral maturity similarly submerges them as individuals within a larger abstract construct, the transpersonal Self. For all four, individuals can be "sacrificed" on behalf of the larger whole.

Despite my criticisms, I do not seek to deny the contributions of these holists to the field of nature ethics. Roosevelt was an early harbinger of the message of limits, the notion that abundance should not be taken for granted. Leopold made a further contribution through his emphasis on the importance of a perceptual shift based on the ecological notion of interdependence, a theme often embraced by ecofeminists. Through their efforts, laws protecting thousands of acres of land from development were enacted. Rolston's discussion of narrative suggests the importance of lived experience and local stories, a concern also expressed by ecofeminists as a contrast to the notions of abstract obligations and rights. Fox's idea that humans, like other "species," are merely individual leaves on a metaphorical tree is also a beneficial antidote to the presumption of human superiority. And the idea of deep questioning, first advanced by Naess, perhaps provides the most help in evaluating these and other nature philosophies, as well as human conduct toward nature more generally.

Ecofeminists, however, can offer deeper questions, ensuring that the nature philosophies that are presented pertain not only to larger evolutionary processes, but also to individual beings. Ecofeminists might, for example, ask, Conservation of what? Preservation for whom? What are the origins of violent practices toward nature, and what role, if any, does masculine identity play in their expression? How can violent practices be prevented, rather than merely restrained? Where do domesticated animals figure in nature ethics? Why is the notion of species accorded so much importance in nature ethics?

While the nature philosophers that I have discussed all aligned themselves with movements to protect nature, their attitudes exemplify the ways in which "protection" can manifest as predation. For example, Roosevelt and Leopold attempted to preserve "species" of animals in order to perpetuate hunting, a violent manhood ritual. In so doing, they sought to link past and future generations of men and boys in a cross-generational legacy. The focus of Rolston and Fox on "species," evolutionary processes, and "ecosystems" echoes a similar "sacrifice" of individual lives in pursuit of transcendent experience.

The thread that I have traced in this book situates the protection of species in a long history of masculinist attempts to control the reproductive capacity of other animals.[225] Whether other species are preserved as the source of "game," symbols of the frontier, representatives of a lineage, "living drama," or an "intergenerational narrative," the focus of protection is on the fertility of nature, not the individual beings that nature generates.

Ecofeminists can not only deepen the questions posed in nature ethics, they can broaden the scope of concern. The holists in this study typify a common neglect of care within nature theories for the treatment of animals living in captivity. The suffering of the other-than-human animals who are subjected to experiments in laboratories or raised for food seemingly falls outside the purview of "nature." However, as the animal advocacy movement reminds us, nature is not only that which is perceived as the "wild"; nature is also inside laboratories, factory farms, fur ranches, and the many other places where other-than-human animals are subjected to manipulation and abuse. If we truly care about the natural world, then these beings should also be the focus of our concern.

Ecofeminists can add still another dimension to the scope of nature ethics. Nature consists not only of the external entities that surround us; it also resides within our own psycho-social natures and identities. Although definitive answers may always elude us, it is important to explore the relevance of gender identity as a major contributor to nature abuse. While it would be foolish to argue that destructive attitudes toward nature can be attributed entirely to the influence of masculine identity, I have argued that it is equally misguided to ignore its contribution.

A holist ecofeminist philosophy, as I conceive it, is not so much an ethic as a consciousness or ethos. It is a "way of life" or a mode of consciousness that invites us to be "responsible," not in the sense of conforming to obligations and rights, but in the literal sense of developing the ability for response. It is an invitation to dissolve the dualistic thinking that separates reason from emotion, the conscious from unconscious, the "domestic" from the "wild," and animal advocacy from nature ethics. It welcomes the larger scientific stories of evolutionary and ecological processes, but never loses sight of the individual beings who exist within these larger narratives. Ecofeminist philosophy never transcends or denies our capacity for empathy and care, our most important human connection with the natural world.

## NOTES

1. See, for example, the essays in Irene Diamond and Gloria Orenstein, eds., *Reweaving the World: The Emergence of Ecofeminism* (San Francisco: Sierra Club, 1990); Judith Plant, ed., *Healing the Wounds: The Promise of Ecofeminism* (Philadelphia: New Society Publishers, 1989); and Greta Gaard, ed., *Ecofeminism: Women, Animals, Nature* (Philadelphia: Temple University Press, 1993).

2. A large body of literature on ecofeminism exists. See Carol Adams, ed., *Ecofeminism and the Sacred* (New York: Continuum, 1993); Irwin Altman and Arza Churchman, *Women and the Environment* (New York: Plenum Press, 1994); Carol Bigwood, *Earth Muse: Feminism, Nature, and Art* (Philadelphia: Temple University Press, 1993); Léonie Caldecott and Stephanie Leland, eds., *Reclaim the Earth: Women Speak Out for Life on Earth* (London: Women's Press, 1983); Andrée Collard with Joyce Contrucci, *Rape of the Wild: Man's Violence against Animals and the Earth* (Bloomington: Indiana University Press, 1989); Erika Cudworth, *Developing Ecofeminist Theory: The Complexity of Difference* (New York: Palgrave Macmillan, 2005); Chris J. Cuomo, *Feminism and Ecological Communities: An Ethic of Flourishing* (New York: Routledge, 1998); Mary Daly, *Gyn/Ecology: The Metaethics of Radical Feminism* (Boston: Beacon Press, 1978); Diamond and Orenstein, *Reweaving the World*; Gaard, *Ecofeminism: Women, Animals, Nature*; Greta Gaard, *Ecological Politics: Ecofeminists and the Greens* (Philadelphia: Temple University Press, 1998); Susan Griffin, *Woman and Nature: The Roaring Inside Her* (New York: Harper and Row, 1978); Mary Mellor, *Breaking the Boundaries: Towards a Feminist, Green Socialism* (London: Virago, 1992); Mary Mellor, *Feminism and Ecology* (New York: New York University Press, 1997); Carolyn Merchant, *The Death of Nature: Women,*

Chapter 7

*Ecology, and the Scientific Revolution* (New York: Harper and Row, 1980); Maria Mies and Vandana Shiva, *Ecofeminism* (Atlantic Highlands, N.J.: Zed Books, 1993); Bonnie Mann, *Women's Liberation and the Sublime: Feminism, Postmodernism, Environment* (Oxford, Oxford University Pess, 2006); Vera Norwood, *Made from This Earth: American Women and Nature* (Chapel Hill: University of North Carolina Press, 1993); Plant, *Healing the Wounds*; Val Plumwood, *Environmental Culture: The Ecological Crisis of Reason* (New York: Routledge, 2002); Val Plumwood, *Feminism and the Mastery of Nature* (New York: Routledge, 1993); Catherine M. Roach, *Mother/Nature: Popular Culture and Environmental Ethics* (Bloomington: Indiana University Press, 2003); Rosemary Radford Ruether, *Gaia and God: An Ecofeminist Theology of Earth Healing* (San Francisco: Harper San Francisco, 1992); Rosemary Radford Ruether, *Integrating Ecofeminism, Globalization, and World Religions* (Lanham, Md.: Rowman & Littlefield, 2005); Rosemary Radford Ruether, ed., *Women Healing Earth: Third World Women on Ecology, Feminism, and Religion* (Maryknoll, N.Y.: Orbis Books, 1996); Ariel Salleh, *Ecofeminism as Politics: Nature, Marx, and the Postmodern* (Atlantic Highlands, N.J.: Zed Books, 1997); Catriona Sandilands, *The Good-Natured Feminist: Ecofeminism and the Quest for Democracy* (Minneapolis: University of Minnesota Press, 1999); Joni Seager, *Earth Follies: Coming to Feminist Terms with the Global Environmental Crisis* (New York: Routledge, 1993); Vandana Shiva, ed., *Close to Home: Women Reconnect Ecology, Health, and Development Worldwide* (Philadelphia: New Society Publishers, 1994); Vandana Shiva, *Earth Democracy: Justice, Sustainability, and Peace* (Cambridge, Mass.: South End Press, 2005); Vandana Shiva, *Staying Alive: Women, Ecology, and Development* (Atlantic Highlands, N.J.: Zed Books, 1988); Vandana Shiva and Ingunn Moser, eds., *Biopolitics: A Feminist and Ecological Reader on Biotechnology* (Atlantic Highlands, N.J.: Zed Books, 1995); Sally Sontheimer, ed., *Women and the Environment, A Reader: Crisis and Development in the Third World* (New York: Monthly Review Press, 1991); Noël Sturgeon, *Ecofeminist Natures: Race, Gender, Feminist Theory, and Political Action* (New York: Routledge, 1997); Karen J. Warren, ed., *Ecofeminism: Women, Culture, Nature* (Bloomington: Indiana University Press, 1997); Karen J. Warren, *Ecofeminist Philosophy: A Western Perspective on What It Is and Why It Matters* (Lanham, Md.: Rowman & Littlefield, 2000); Karen J. Warren, ed., *Ecological Feminism* (New York: Routledge, 1994); and Karen J. Warren, ed., *Ecological Feminist Philosophies* (Bloomington: Indiana University Press 1996).

3. Carol J. Adams, *Neither Man Nor Beast: Feminism and the Defense of Animals* (New York: Continuum, 1994), 79. As previously mentioned, some theorists use the word "ecofeminism" to refer to an essentialist philosophy that focuses exclusively on "women" and "nature," reserving terms such as "ecological feminism" for a more comprehensive philosophy concerned with the structure of multiple forms of abuse. While personally advocating the broader analysis, I use "ecofeminism" to refer to all theories that incorporate a focus on the domination of women and nature.

4. Images suggesting the foundational approach can readily be found in both book and article titles. See for example, Richard Cartwright Austin, "Beauty: A Foundation for Environmental Ethics," *Environmental Ethics* 7 (Fall 1985): 197–208; Eliot

Deutsch, "A Metaphysical Grounding for Nature Reverence: East–West," *Environmental Ethics* 8 (Winter 1986): 293–316; and Ernest Partridge, "Nature as a Moral Resource," *Environmental Ethics* 4 (Summer 1984): 101–130. Ecofeminists, by contrast, frequently employ images of healing or artistry. See for example, Diamond and Orenstein, *Reweaving the World*; Plant, *Healing the Wounds*; Heather Eaton, "Liaison or Liability: Weaving Spirituality into Ecofeminist Politics," *Atlantis* 21, no. 1 (1997): 109–122; and Ruether, *Gaia and God*. The contrast between these two approaches is intended to be suggestive and does not imply that overlap does not occur. Some ecofeminists, for example, object to images of nature that reinforce stereotypical nurturing traits. Chris Cuomo praises Donna Haraway's notion of the cyborg, a hybrid of machine and organism, for its "provocative model of transgressive, insubordinate nature- and culture-loving relationships and identities." In contrast to traditional notions of purity, "the power of the cyborg lies in the fact that she is an example of a border-dweller who *flourishes* on the borders." Cuomo, *Feminism and Ecological Communities*, 85–86. For more on the concept of the cyborg, see Donna J. Haraway, *Simians, Cyborgs, and Women: The Reinvention of Nature* (New York: Routledge, 1991).

5. Alison M. Jaggar, *Feminist Politics and Human Nature* (Totowa, N.J.: Rowman and Allanheld, 1983), 41.

6. Lynn White Jr., "The Historical Roots of Our Ecological Crises," *Science* 155, no. 3767 (1967): 1203–1207. Other works that trace historical influences on attitudes toward nature include H. Paul Santmire, *The Travail of Nature: The Ambiguous Ecological Promise of Christian Theology* (Philadelphia: Fortress Press, 1985); Donald Worster, *Nature's Economy: A History of Ecological Ideas* (New York: Cambridge University Press, 1990); Keith Thomas, *Man and the Natural World: A History of the Modern Sensibility* (New York: Pantheon, 1983); and Clarence Glacken, *Traces on the Rhodian Shore: Nature and Culture in Western Thought from Ancient Times to the End of the Eighteenth Century* (Berkeley: University of California Press, 1976).

7. For a notable exception to the neglect of the unconscious among ecofeminist and other environmental advocates, see Roach, *Mother/Nature*.

8. Warren, *Ecofeminist Philosophy*, 47.

9. Warren, *Ecofeminist Philosophy*, 47.

10. Karen Warren's and Val Plumwood's analyses of the "logic of domination" are perhaps the most commonly cited insights attributed to ecofeminists. See Warren, *Ecofeminist Philosophy*, 47–56; and Plumwood, *Feminism and the Mastery of Nature*, 41–68.

11. Plumwood, *Feminism and the Mastery of Nature*, 69.

12. Plumwood, *Feminism and the Mastery of Nature*, 141.

13. Plumwood, *Feminism and the Mastery of Nature*, 58.

14. Plumwood, *Feminism and the Mastery of Nature*, 195.

15. In fairness to Plumwood, her use of the word "instrumental" occasionally suggests the wider notion of a "psychological instrumentalism," as I have employed the term, and hence less conscious designs. For example, in her discussion of object relations theory, she argues that the development of the boy child entails an instrumental construction of identity. By and large, however, her analysis suggests more conscious motives. *Feminism and the Mastery of Nature*, 144.

16. The authors argue that "men who rape have something to teach us about the cultural roots of sexual aggression. They force us to acknowledge that rape is more than an idiosyncratic act committed by a few 'sick' men. . . . Understanding that otherwise normal men can and do rape is critical to the development of strategies for prevention." Diana Scully and Joseph Marolla, "'Riding the Bull at Gilley's': Convicted Rapists Describe the Rewards of Rape," in *Violence against Women: The Bloody Footprints*, ed. Pauline B. Bart and Eileen Geil Moran (Thousand Oaks, Calif.: Sage Publications, 1993), 36, 42–43. Originally printed in *Social Problems* 32, no. 3 (February 1985).

17. Scully and Marolla identify multiple motives for rape, although they argue that revenge and punishment are the most common. *Violence against Women*, 42.

18. Diana E. H. Russell, *The Politics of Rape: The Victim's Perspective* (New York: Stein and Day, 1975), 260. For the view that dominance and control are the central motives for rape, also see Susan Brownmiller, *Against Our Will* (New York: Simon and Schuster, 1975), 15; Peggy Reeves Sanday, "The Socio-cultural Context of Rape," *Journal of Social Issues* 37, no. 4 (Fall 1981): 5–27; and Anthony R. Beech, Tony Ward, and Dawn Fisher, "The Identification of Sexual and Violent Motivations in Men Who Assault Women: Implication for Treatment," *Journal of Interpersonal Violence* 21, no. 12 (December 2006): 1635–1653.

19. My views on the influence of the unconscious are not intended to deny the agency of the perpetrators of violence. As Susan Brownmiller's work demonstrates, men do not rape women because they are "out of control." Rather, they typically use rape as a conscious tool of intimidation. *Against Our Will*, 183. I would suggest that the two understandings of male violence are not mutually exclusive. Men may use violence as an active tool of intimidation *and* there may be larger, unconscious factors that contribute to this propensity.

20. Seyla Benhabib, "The Generalized and the Concrete Other: The Kohlberg-Gilligan Controversy and Moral Theory," in *Feminism as Critique*, ed. Seyla Benhabib and Drucilla Cornell (Minneapolis: University of Minnesota Press, 1987), 176, 94. On the importance of unconscious influences on moral conduct, see also Diana T. Meyers, "The Socialized Individual and Individual Autonomy: An Intersection between Philosophy and Psychology," in *Women and Moral Theory*, ed. Eva Feder Kittay and Diana T. Meyers (Totowa, N.J.: Rowman & Littlefield, 1987): 139–153; and Roach, *Mother/Nature*.

21. Diana Tietjens Meyers, *Subjection and Subjectivity: Psychoanalytic Feminism and Moral Philosophy* (New York: Routledge, 1994), 59.

22. Sarah Lucia Hoagland, *Lesbian Ethics: Toward New Value* (Palo Alto, Calif.: Institute of Lesbian Studies, 1988), 278.

23. Roach argues that "evil" and "badness" exist in the unconscious, along with goodness, as inherent aspects of the human condition. *Mother/Nature*, 138, 98–99. While agreeing with her emphasis on recognizing destructive drives, I do not concur that evil and badness are innate.

24. Merchant, *Death of Nature*.

25. Carolyn Merchant, "Mining the Earth's Womb," in *Machina Ex Dea: Feminist Perspectives on Technology*, ed. Joan Rothschild (New York: Pergamon Press, 1983),

100. For a divergent view that contends that "feelings for mothers are too complex for the mother-nature relation to function unequivocally as an environmental prod," see Roach, *Mother/Nature*, 71.

26. Merchant, *Death of Nature*, 103.

27. Merchant, *Death of Nature*, 41.

28. See, for example, Plumwood, *Feminism and the Mastery of Nature*; Wendy Brown, *Manhood and Politics: A Feminist Reading in Political Theory* (Totowa, N.J.: Rowman & Littlefield, 1998); and Genevieve Lloyd, *The Man of Reason: "Male" and "Female" in Western Philosophy* (Minneapolis: Minnesota University Press, 1984).

29. See Marija Gimbutas, *The Civilization of the Goddess: The World of Old Europe* (San Francisco: HarperCollins, 1991).

30. For the depiction of nature as a web, see Carol P. Christ and Kathryn Roundtree, "Humanity in the Web of Life," *Environmental Ethics* 28 (Summer 2006): 185–200. For discussion of the liabilities entailed in the image of nature as a mother, see Roach, *Mother/Nature*, 39–50. For ethical relations with nature as a partner, see Carolyn Merchant, *Earthcare: Women and the Environment* (New York: Routledge, 1995), 55–56. For the notion of respecting nature's "charm," see Chris Cuomo, *Feminism and Ecological Communities*, 71–72. For the argument that gendering the planet in a patriarchal society "inadvertently [reinforces] current hierarchical sociogender stereotypes," see Patrick D. Murphy, "Sex-Typing the Planet: Gaia Imagery and the Problem of Subverting Patriarchy," *Environmental Ethics* 10, no. 2 (Summer 1988): 166.

31. According to Lakoff and Johnson, the other major findings of cognitive science are that "abstract concepts are largely metaphorical" and that "mind is inherently bodied." George Lakoff and Mark Johnson, *Philosophy in the Flesh: The Embodied Mind and Its Challenge to Western Thought* (New York: Basic Books, 1999), 3.

32. Mark Johnson, *Moral Imagination: Implications of Cognitive Science for Ethics* (Chicago: University of Chicago Press, 1993), 62.

33. An article in the business section of the *San Francisco Examiner* encouraged businesses to avail themselves of metaphors in their marketing strategies. "For marketers, metaphors are essential for connecting with a busy, frequently stressed, consumer running on information overload." John Berger, "Master of Your Domain," *San Francisco Examiner*, April 11, 1990. The use of metaphors as a marketing ploy illustrates the diverse ways in which metaphors can be adapted, and points to the need for caution in their use.

34. The Gaia hypothesis, developed by scientists James Lovelock and Lynn Margulis, exemplifies the danger inherent in focusing on metaphors without addressing underlying psychological processes. Although the Gaia hypothesis was initially hailed by ecophilosophers for reviving the notion of earth as a living being, this enthusiasm was tempered when Lovelock subsequently concluded that the earth's self-regulating mechanisms made her perfectly capable of enduring humanity's onslaughts. Thus, an image of the earth as a living being was adapted to the underlying structures and attitudes of aggression, rather than challenging them. See James Lovelock, "Gaia: A Model for Planetary and Cellular Dynamics," in *Gaia, A Way of Knowing: Political*

*Implications of the New Biology*, ed. William Irwin Thompson (Hudson, N.Y.: Lindisfarne, 1987), 95. Lovelock, who has since expressed grave concern for the fate of the planet, given human energy consumption, advocates the development of nuclear energy to avert environmental catastrophe. Despite its stark contrast to his previous views, his most recent book perpetuates the personification of Gaia, now imaged as seeking "revenge." James Lovelock, *The Revenge of Gaia: Earth's Climate Crisis and the Fate of Humanity* (New York: Basic Books, 2006).

35. Warren, *Ecofeminist Philosophy*, 66–68.

36. Warren, *Ecofeminist Philosophy*, 108–109.

37. Warren, *Ecofeminist Philosophy*, 67.

38. Warren, *Ecofeminist Philosophy*, 109.

39. *The American Heritage Dictionary*, 4th ed., s.v. "gathering."

40. *The American Heritage Dictionary*, 4th ed., s.v. "gathering."

41. John Ayto, *Dictionary of Word Origins* (New York: Arcade Publishing, 1990). The Germanic *gath* also produced the German "*gatte*," meaning "husband, spouse, originally 'companion.'" 251.

42. Ayto, *Dictionary of Word Origins*, 289.

43. Research suggests that even among subsistence hunters, men often hunt for reasons other than necessity. According to Jared Diamond, men hunt even when other forms of subsistence are easier and more reliable. As he concludes, their primary motivation is the enjoyment, prestige, and other social rewards associated with hunting rather than simply food procurement. Jared Diamond, "What Are Men Good for?" *Natural History* (May 1993): 25–29.

44. See Shere Hite, *The Hite Report on Male Sexuality* (New York: Ballantine, 1981).

45. As Paul Shepard explains, "The human hunter in the field is not merely a predator, because of hundreds of centuries of experience in treating the woman-prey with love, which he turns back into the hunt proper. The ecstatic consummation of this love is the killing itself." *The Tender Carnivore and the Sacred Game* (Athens: University of Georgia Press, 1998), 173. For more on the connection between hunting and sexuality, see Karl Menninger, "Totemic Aspects of Contemporary Attitudes toward Animals" in *Psychoanalysis and Culture*, ed. George Browning Wilbur and Warner Muensterberger (New York: International University Press, 1951). More recently, see Brian Luke, "Violent Love, Heterosexuality and the Erotics of Men's Predation," *Feminist Studies* 24, no. 3 (1998): 627–655, and *Brutal: Manhood and the Exploitation of Animals* (Chicago: University of Illinois Press, 2007), 81–108; Collard with Contrucci, *Rape of the Wild*; Marti Kheel, "The Killing Game: An Ecofeminist Critique of Hunting," *Journal of the Philosophy of Sport*, 23 (May 1996): 38–40; Holmes Rolston III, *Environmental Ethics: Duties to and Values in the Natural World* (Philadelphia: Temple University Press, 1988), 81; and Charles Bergman, *Orion's Legacy: A Cultural History of Man as Hunter* (New York: Dutton, 1997).

46. While sport and play have commonalities, there are significant differences. Roger Caillois developed a framework listing six features common to play: (1) its outcome is uncertain, (2) it is an activity that is freely engaged in, (3) it is unproductive, (4) it is regulated, (5) it takes place in a separate area, and (6) it is make-believe.

Caillois, *Man, Play, and Games*, trans. Meyer Barash (New York: Free Press–Macmillan, 1961), 3–10. The distinction between sport and play is generally thought to reside in the greater complexity of sport. According to Carolyn Thomas, "Sport has elements of play but goes beyond the characteristics of play in its rule structure, organization, and criteria for the evaluation of success." Thomas ascribes a second distinguishing feature to sport: its agonistic quality. Carolyn E. Thomas, *Sport in a Philosophic Context* (Philadelphia: Lea and Febiger, 1983), 18. Play, by contrast, is viewed as an inherently "cooperative interaction that has no explicit goal, no end point, and no winners." Janet Lever, "Sex Differences in the Complexity of Children's Play and Games," *American Sociological Review* 43, no. 4 (1978): 473.

47. Jeffrey Moussaieff Masson and Susan McCarthy, *When Elephants Weep: The Emotional Lives of Animals* (New York: Delta, 1995), 132.

48. While earlier theorists, particularly in the eighteenth and nineteenth centuries, believed that play served some practical end, the Dutch researcher Johan Huizinga argued that play might be an end in itself. Huizinga proposed certain necessary conditions for an activity to be defined as play: it had to be voluntary and absorbing, contain an element of uncertainty and a sense of illusion or exaggeration, and it had to exist outside of the realm of ordinary life bounded by limits of time and place. Johan Huizinga, *Homo Ludens: A Study of the Play-Element in Culture* (Boston: Beacon Press, 1950).

49. Maria Lugones, "Playfulness, 'World-Traveling' and Loving Perception," *Hypatia* 2, no. 2 (Summer 1987): 3–19.

50. Sara Ebenreck, "Opening Pandora's Box: The Role of Imagination in Environmental Ethics," *Environmental Ethics* 18, no. 1 (Spring 1996): 3–18.

51. See John Seed, Joanna Macy, Pat Fleming, and Arne Naess, *Thinking like a Mountain: Toward a Council of All Beings* (Philadelphia: New Society Publishers, 1988).

52. Given the greater longevity and prevalence of the holistic approach, it is more accurate to refer to Western allopathic medicine as the "alternative." For a feminist critique of Western medicine, see Marti Kheel, "From Healing Herbs to Deadly Drugs: Western Medicine's War against the Natural World," in Plant, *Healing the Wounds*.

53. A chemical gas, nitrogen mustard, was a principal cancer therapy for many years, and continues to be administered. See John Curtis, "From the Field of Battle, an Early Strike at Cancer," *Yale Medicine* 39, no. 3 (Summer 2005): 16–17.

54. As Patrick Quillin points out, "chemotherapy is a spin-off product from the chemical warfare of World Wars I and II and is now given to 75% of all American cancer patients." Radiation is used to treat about 60 percent of all cancer patients. Patrick Quillin with Noreen Quillin, *Beating Cancer with Nutrition* (Carlsbad, Calif.: Nutrition Times Press, 2005), 72. Sadly, the "war on cancer," declared by President Richard Nixon in 1971, has produced more casualties than cures. For further discussion of the dangers posed by chemotherapy and the advantages of a holistic approach, also see Ralph W. Moss, *Questioning Chemotherapy* (Brooklyn, N.Y.: Equinox Press, 1995), and *Cancer Therapy: The Independent Consumer's Guide to Non-Toxic Treatment and Prevention* (Brooklyn, N.Y.: Equinox Press, 1992).

55. In previous centuries, philosophy did show a greater appreciation for the influence of what we now call unconscious drives. As Paul Crittenden points out, theories of psychological development were an integral part of philosophical theory until the latter part of the nineteenth century. Paul Crittenden, *Learning to Be Moral: Philosophical Thoughts about Moral Development* (Atlantic Highlands, N.J.: Humanities Press International, 1990).

56. John Stoltenberg, *Refusing to Be a Man: Essays on Sex and Justice* (New York: Penguin, 1990).

57. The current emphasis on male competitive sports has been shown to contribute to the aggressive aspect of masculine identity that I have identified. On the connection between masculinity and sport, see Michael A. Messner and Donald F. Sabo, eds., *Sport, Men and the Gender Order: Critical Feminist Perspectives* (Champaign, Ill.: Human Kinetic Books, 1990), and Mariah Burton Nelson, *The Stronger Women Get, the More Men Love Football: Sexism and the American Culture of Sports* (New York: Harcourt Brace, 1994).

58. Whitney Stewart, "The Dalai Lama on Love and Children," *L.A. Parenting Magazine* 8, no. 6 (June 1988): 71. On the importance of developing respect for insects, see Joanne Elizabeth Lauck, *The Voice of the Infinite in the Small: Revisioning the Insect–Human Connection* (Boston: Shambhala, 2002).

59. For an analysis of the connection between masculinity and the current global crisis, see the work of ecofeminist geographer Joni Seager. Seager is one of the few ecofeminists to argue specifically for the existence of a connection between masculine identity and the abuse of the natural world. Her critique of the masculinist underpinnings of exploitative attitudes and practices extends not only to military, corporate, and governmental institutions, but also to the major environmental organizations. Joni Seager, *Earth Follies: Coming to Feminist Terms with the Global Environmental Crisis* (New York: Routledge, 1994).

60. J. C. Smith, *The Psychoanalytic Roots of Patriarchy: The Neurotic Foundations of Social Order* (New York: New York University Press, 1990), 386.

61. Research has shown, for example, that children raised by lesbian parents are "equally healthy in terms of psychological well-being and social adjustment" as children of heterosexual couples. David K. Flaks, Ilda Ficher, Frank Masterpasqua, and Gregory Joseph, "Lesbians Choosing Motherhood: A Comparative Study of Lesbian and Heterosexual Parents and Their Children," *Developmental Psychology* 31, no. 1 (January 1995): 105–114; and A. Brewaeys, I. Ponjaert, E. V. Van Hall, and S. Golombok, "Donor Insemination: Child Development and Family Functioning in Lesbian Mother Families," *Human Reproduction* 12, no. 6 (1997): 1349–1359.

62. Miriam M. Johnson, *Strong Mothers, Weak Wives: The Search for Gender Equality* (Berkeley: University of California Press, 1988), 8.

63. In a similar vein, scholars and activists in the movement to stop violence against women underscore the reality and nature of that violence by using the word "femicide" rather than "homicide," exemplifying the importance of naming reality as a first step in social change. See Jill Radford and Diana E. H. Russell, eds., *Femicide: The Politics of Woman Killing* (New York: Twayne Publishers, 1992).

64. The debate over the ethic of care has spawned a voluminous body of literature, including a number of anthologies. See Mary M. Brabeck, ed., *Who Cares? Theory, Research, and Educational Implications of the Ethic of Care* (New York: Routledge, 1993); Mary Jeanne Larrabee, ed., *An Ethic of Care: Feminist and Interdisciplinary Perspectives* (New York: Routledge, 1993); Eve Browning Cole and Susan Coultrap-McQuin, eds., *Explorations in Feminist Ethics: Theory and Practice* (Bloomington: Indiana University Press, 1992); Marsha Hanen and Kai Nielsen, eds., "Science, Morality and Feminist Theory," supplementary volume, *Canadian Journal of Philosophy*, 13 (1987); Kittay and Meyers, *Women and Moral Theory*; and Virginia Held, ed., *Justice and Care: Essential Readings in Feminist Ethics* (Boulder, Colo.: Westview Press, 1995). See also Jean Grimshaw, *Philosophy and Feminist Thinking* (Minneapolis: Minnesota University Press, 1986); Joan Tronto, *Moral Boundaries: A Political Argument for an Ethic of Care* (New York: Routledge, 1993); and Susan J. Hekman, *Moral Voices, Moral Selves: Carol Gilligan and Feminist Moral Theory* (University Park: Pennsylvania State University Press, 1995).

65. Carol Gilligan, *In a Different Voice: Psychological Theory and Women's Development* (Cambridge, Mass.: Harvard University Press, 1993), 33.

66. In *In a Different Voice*, for example, Gilligan refers to "the possibility of a different truth" found in a women's ethic of care. She also maintains that "the vision of maturity can be seen to shift when adulthood is portrayed by women rather than men." *In a Different Voice*, 170, 67. As Susan J. Hekman points out, in this understanding, "Gilligan seems to be arguing that she is replacing one truth with another, attempting to correct the biased and incomplete masculinist theories of moral development by a truer, more objective theory." By and large, however, as Hekman argues, Gilligan is "introducing a new interpretation of the moral realm, which wholly reconstitutes it. She is opposing the 'truth' of the masculinist theories with other 'truths.'" *Moral Voices, Moral Selves*, 5.

67. In a similar vein, as Joan Tronto notes, "Gilligan . . . accepts much of Kohlberg's method and framework," including the notion of "stages and development [and] a commitment to the study of *cognitive* development." *Moral Boundaries*, 78.

68. Gilligan's model of development also diverges from Kohlberg's notion of three progressive stages of moral development, emphasizing the nonlinear path of moral decision-making that results as adolescent girls learn to ignore their inner voice. This point is emphasized in Lyn Mikel Brown and Carol Gilligan, *Meeting at the Crossroads* (New York: Ballantine, 1992), 6–7, which examines how girls often regress at adolescence.

69. Although Gilligan's ideas evolve, they do not follow a linear development. Different emphases can be found throughout her work.

70. Carol Gilligan, "Prologue: Adolescent Development Reconsidered," in *Mapping the Moral Domain: A Contribution of Women's Thinking to Psychological Theory and Education*, ed. Carol Gilligan, Janie Victoria Ward, and Jill McLean Taylor, with Betty Bardige (Cambridge, Mass.: Harvard University Press, 1989), xix.

71. Carol Gilligan and Jane Attanucci, "Two Moral Orientations," in Gilligan et al., *Mapping the Moral Domain*, 82.

72. See for example, Gilligan, *In a Different Voice*, 174. For a critical analysis of the use of the paradigm of "marriage" in relation to the justice and care orientations, see Marti Kheel, "The Heterosexist Subtext of the Justice/Care Debate" (paper, presented to the Society for Women in Philosophy Pacific Division Conference, Oceanside, Calif., May 31, 1997).

73. Gilligan, *In a Different Voice*, 174.

74. Gilligan and Attanucci, "Two Moral Orientations," 73–86; Carol Gilligan, "Moral Orientation and Moral Development," in Kittay and Meyers, *Women and Moral Theory*, 19–32.

75. Gilligan, "Moral Orientation and Moral Development," 30.

76. Gilligan, "Moral Orientation and Moral Development," 31.

77. Brown and Gilligan, *Meeting at the Crossroads*, 23. For further development of the metaphor of music for understanding ethical voice, also see Carol Gilligan, Annie Rogers, and Lyn Mikel Brown, "Epilogue: Soundings into Development," in *Making Connections: The Relational Worlds of Adolescent Girls at Emma Willard School*, ed. Carol Gilligan, Nona P. Lyons, and Trudy J. Hanmer (Cambridge, Mass.: Harvard University Press, 1990), 320–328.

78. See Catherine C. Greeno and Eleanor Maccoby, "How Different is the 'Different Voice?'" *Signs* 11, no. 2 (1986): 310–316; Zella Luria, "A Methodological Critique," *Signs* 11, no. 2 (1986): 316–321; Debra Nails, "Social-Scientific Sexism: Gilligan's *Mismeasure of Man*," *Social Research* 50, no. 3 (1983): 643–664; Lawrence J. Walker, "Sex Differences in the Development of Moral Reasoning: A Critical Review," in Larrabee, *An Ethic of Care*, 157–176; Sandra Harding, "The Curious Coincidence of Feminine and African Moralities: Challenges for Feminist Theory," in Kittay and Meyers, *Women and Moral Theory*, 296–315; Carol B. Stack, "Different Voices, Different Visions: Gender, Culture, and Moral Reasoning," in *Uncertain Terms: Negotiating Gender in American Culture*, ed. Faye Ginsburg and Anna Lowenhaupt Tsing (Boston: Beacon Press, 1990), 19–27.

79. Carol Gilligan, "Reply by Carol Gilligan," *Signs* 11, no. 2 (Winter 1986): 325–326.

80. Gilligan, "Reply by Carol Gilligan," 328.

81. See, for example, Ruth Smith, "Feminism and the Moral Subject," in *Women's Consciousness, Women's Conscience: A Reader in Feminist Ethics*, ed. Barbara Hilkert Andolsen, Christine E. Gudorf, and Mary D. Pellauer (Minneapolis: Winston Press, 1985), 235–250; Linda J. Nicholson, "Women, Morality, and History," in Larrabee, *An Ethic of Care*; and Tronto, *Moral Boundaries*.

82. Bill Puka, "The Liberation of Caring: A Different Voice for Gilligan's 'Different Voice,'" in Larrabee, *An Ethic of Care*, 215. For a response to Puka's criticism of Gilligan, see Elise Peeples, who argues that "there is no one 'discoverable' structure of moral development and that all forms of moral development are coping strategies, not just the coping that women adopt to deal with sexist oppression." Peeples, "Her Terrain Is Outside of His 'Domain,'" *Hypatia* 6, no. 2 (1991): 194. For Puka's reply to Peeples, see Bill Puka, "Comment Reply: The Science of Caring," *Hypatia* 6, no. 2 (1991): 200–210.

83. Puka, "The Liberation of Caring," 223.

84. Puka, "The Liberation of Caring," 219–220.

85. Joan C. Tronto, "Women and Caring: What Can Feminists Learn about Morality from Caring?," in *Gender/Body/Knowledge: Feminist Reconstructions of Being and Knowing*, ed. Alison M. Jaggar and Susan Bordo (New Brunswick, N.J.: Rutgers University Press, 1989), 184.

86. Tronto, *Moral Boundaries*, 96.

87. See Linda K. Kerber, "Some Cautionary Words for Historians," in Larrabee, *An Ethic of Care*, 102–107; John M. Broughton, "Women's Rationality and Men's Virtues: A Critique of Gender Dualism in Gilligan's Theory of Moral Development," in Larrabee, *An Ethic of Care*, 112–139; Tronto, *Moral Boundaries*; Barbara Houston, "Rescuing Womanly Virtue: Some Dangers of Moral Reclamation," in Kittay and Meyers, *Women and Moral Theory*, 237–262; Lawrence A. Blum, "Gilligan and Kohlberg: Implications for Moral Theory," in Larrabee, *An Ethic of Care*, 49–68.

88. Broughton, "Women's Rationality and Men's Virtues," 129; Alison Jaggar, "Sex Inequality and Bias in Sex Differences Research," in "Science, Morality and Feminist Theory," ed. Marsha Hanen and Kai Nielsen, supplementary volume, *Canadian Journal of Philosophy* 13 (1987): 38.

89. In her more recent work, Gilligan is particularly sensitive to the role of socialization. Thus, she and co-author Brown refer to the "pervasiveness of androcentric and patriarchal norms, values and societal structures," as well as to the need "to move beneath the prevailing conventions and to understand how those not heard as full human beings within such a system exist and resist, how they create and maintain their humanity both above ground and underground." Brown and Gilligan, *Meeting at the Crossroads*, 15, 30.

90. Gilligan, *In a Different Voice*, 67.

91. Gilligan, *In a Different Voice*, xix.

92. Gilligan, *In a Different Voice*, xvi.

93. Carol Gilligan and Grant Wiggins, "The Origins of Morality in Early Childhood," in Gilligan et al., *Mapping the Moral Domain*, 111–112.

94. Carol Gilligan, "Reply to Critics," in Larrabee, *An Ethic of Care*, 209.

95. Janie Victoria Ward, "Urban Adolescents' Conceptions of Violence," in Gilligan et al., *Mapping the Moral Domain*, 175.

96. Sara Ruddick, *Maternal Thinking: Toward a Politics of Peace* (Boston: Beacon Press, 1989); Hoagland, *Lesbian Ethics*; Annette C. Baier, *Moral Prejudices: Essays on Ethics* (Cambridge, Mass.: Harvard University Press, 1994); Claudia Card, ed., *Feminist Ethics* (Lawrence: University Press of Kansas, 1991); Robin Dillon, "Care and Respect," in Cole and Coultrap-McQuin, *Explorations in Feminist Ethics*, 69–81. This is not intended as a comprehensive enumeration of all the theories concerning the relations between an ethic of care and justice but rather the most common *feminist* ideas. For a detailed listing of additional conceptualizations of the relation between justice and care, see Lawrence Blum's eight-point categorization of "impartialist rejoinders to Gilligan." Blum, "Gilligan and Kohlberg," 53.

97. The essays in Claudia Card's anthology, *Feminist Ethics*, illustrate this "critical tradition" of feminists who seek to move the discussion of ethics beyond what is perceived as a glorification of women's role as caregiver. Card states that the articles

are united primarily by the *absence* of the typical themes of care, motherhood, and re-productive control. According to Card, the values promoted by her book are those of "feistiness" as opposed to "politeness." *Feminist Ethics*, 18.

98. Kathy Davis, "Toward a Feminist Rhetoric: The Gilligan Debate Revisited," *Women's Studies International Forum* 15, no. 2 (1992): 222–223.

99. Davis, "Toward a Feminist Rhetoric," 228.

100. Simone Weil, "Reflections on the Right Use of School Studies with a View to the Love of God," in *Waiting for God*, trans. Emma Craufurd (New York: G. P. Put-nam's Sons, 1951), 57–66.

101. Iris Murdoch, *The Sovereignty of Good* (Boston: Routledge and Kegan Paul, 1970), 40.

102. Marilyn Frye, *The Politics of Reality: Essays in Feminist Theory* (Trumans-burg, N.Y.: Crossing Press, 1983), 75.

103. Frye, *The Politics of Reality*, 67.

104. Hoagland, *Lesbian Ethics*, 300.

105. Hoagland, *Lesbian Ethics*, 264.

106. It is important to underscore that although Hoagland emphasizes the impor-tance of "choice," she is not referring to choice in the liberal sense of an abstract "right" to choose that disregards the reality of power imbalances. Her emphasis is first and foremost on the importance of *facilitating* choice for those who live under con-ditions of oppression. *Lesbian Ethics*, 13.

107. Hoagland, *Lesbian Ethics*, 14–15.

108. Hoagland, *Lesbian Ethics*, 285.

109. Hoagland, *Lesbian Ethics*, 20, 22.

110. Marilyn Frye, "A Response to Lesbian Ethics," in Card, *Feminist Ethics*, 58.

111. Holmes Rolston III, "The Human Standing in Nature: Fitness in the Moral Overseer," in *Values and Moral Standing*, ed. Wayne Sumner, Donald Callen, and Thomas Attig (Bowling Green, Ohio: Bowling Green State University, 1986), 95.

112. Warwick Fox, *Toward a Transpersonal Ecology: Developing New Founda-tions for Environmentalism* (Boston: Shambhala, 1990), 217.

113. Nel Noddings, *Caring: A Feminine Approach to Ethics and Moral Education* (Berkeley: University of California Press, 1984), 68.

114. According to Noddings, since "potential response in animals" in care-giving situations is "nearly static," they cannot "complete" the caring relation. Furthermore, "we do not have a sense of the animal-as-subject" with "projects to pursue." Even leaving aside the moot question of whether other-than-human animals are "subjects" with "projects," and the even more dubious claim that this determination has any moral significance, Noddings's argument is inconsistent with her overall critique of the overemphasis in Western culture on goal-directed consciousness, and the impor-tance of attaining a more receptive, goal-less kind of consciousness. In addition, de-spite her criticisms of abstract, "logical," or "utilitarian" ethical theories, Noddings readily dons the role of utilitarian theorist in her discussion of other animals, arguing against the notion of "pure sentiment," defending meat eating by imagining a bizarre scenario whereby, if other-than-human animals are not killed for the production of meat, they will overpopulate the earth. She thereby ties the morality of eating other

animals to logical, instrumental calculations, rather than to a direct caring response. In addition, although Noddings concedes a limited ethical obligation toward those animals with whom we have direct contact, there is nothing in her ethic that suggests any direct moral obligation to care for "wild" animals. *Caring: A Feminine Approach*, 87, 141–156.

115. For further discussion of "contextualized care," see Deane Curtin, "Toward an Ecological Ethic of Care," *Hypatia* 6, no. 1 (Spring 1991): 65–68; and Warren, *Ecofeminist Philosophy*, 97–123.

116. Margaret Urban Walker, *Moral Understandings: A Feminist Study of Ethics* (New York: Routledge, 1998), 128.

117. For further discussion of the importance of the act of attention with respect to other-than-human animals, see Josephine Donovan, "Attention to Suffering: Sympathy as a Basis for Ethical Treatment of Animals," in *Beyond Animal Rights: A Feminist Caring Ethic for the Treatment of Animals*, ed. Josephine Donovan and Carol J. Adams (New York: Continuum, 1996): 147–169.

118. Personal communication to author, March 12, 2000.

119. Georg Lukács, *History of Class Consciousness*, trans. Rodney Livingstone (Cambridge, Mass.: MIT Press, 1971), 169, quoted in Josephine Donovan, "Feminism and the Treatment of Animals: From Care to Dialogue," *Signs* 31, no. 2 (2006): 319.

120. Donovan, "Feminism and the Treatment of Animals," 320.

121. Donovan, "Feminism and the Treatment of Animals," 305.

122. Josephine Donovan, "Animal Rights and Feminist Theory," *Signs* 15, no. 2 (1990). Reprinted in Donovan and Adams, *Beyond Animal Rights*, 52.

123. Melanie Joy, "Humanistic Psychology and Animal Rights: Reconsidering the Boundaries of the Humanistic Ethic," *Journal of Humanistic Psychology* 45, no. 1 (Winter 2005): 122. See also James L. Kuhn, "Toward an Ecological Humanistic Psychology," *Journal of Humanistic Psychology* 41, no. 2 (2001): 9–24; Kenneth J. Shapiro, "Animal Rights versus Humanism: The Charge of Speciesism," *Journal of Humanistic Psychology* 30, no. 2 (1990): 9–37; M. Patricia Hindley, "'Minding Animals': The Role of Animals in Children's Mental Development," in *Attitudes to Animals: Views in Animal Welfare*, ed. Francine L. Dolins (Cambridge: Cambridge University Press, 1999), 186–199; and Theodore Roszak, Mary E. Gomes, and Allen D. Kanner, eds., *Ecopsychology: Restoring the Earth, Healing the Mind* (San Francisco: Sierra Club Books, 1995).

124. Joy, "Humanistic Psychology and Animal Rights," 122.

125. Donovan, "Feminism and the Treatment of Animals," 323–324.

126. Brian Luke, "Taming Ourselves or Going Feral? Toward a Nonpatriarchal Metaethic of Animal Liberation," in *Animals and Women: Feminist Theoretical Exploration*, ed. Carol J. Adams and Josephine Donovan (Durham, N.C.: Duke University Press, 1995), 303–311.

127. For decades, the meat and dairy industries have routinely created free materials for schools based on their version of the USDA dietary guidelines, including idealized images of "happy" animals on idyllic farms. Although the revamped 2005 government guidelines allow for a greater place for some vegetarian foods, animal products still retain their position of prominence. Government-sponsored subsidies to

schools in the form of "commodities" also typically feature animal products rather than vegetarian food. Schools that do not serve milk do not qualify for government reimbursement without special permission. On the advisory panel for the dietary guidelines published in 2000, six of the eleven panel members had ties to the meat, dairy, and egg industries. The end result of these government- and industry-sponsored programs is to convey the message that animal products are compulsory for human health. The USDA was originally developed to promote and assist farmers' interests, but is now mandated with the task of setting guidelines for consumers, clearly a conflict of interest. For a detailed discussion of industry and government's influence on food politics, see Marion Nestle, *Food Politics: How the Food Industry Influences Nutrition and Health* (Berkeley: University of California Press, 2002).

128. Aldo Leopold, "The Land Ethic," in *A Sand County Almanac and Sketches Here and There* (New York: Oxford University Press, 1968), 224–225.

129. Cuomo, *Feminism and Ecological Communities*, 73.

130. Warren, *Ecofeminist Philosophy*, 116.

131. For the argument that the notions of race and species are fictitious constructs, see Chaone Mallory, "Speci(es)al (as) Performance: Ecofeminism and the Regulatory Fictions of Race, Gender, and Species" (presented at the York University Nature Matters conference, Toronto, Canada, October 25–28, 2007). In a related debate, Andrew Brennan recognizes the lack of consensus concerning the definition of the term "species," but argues that it is nonetheless a useful tool, since recognition of biological differences among kinds of animals is necessary for determining what is necessary for them to flourish. Brennan concludes that dissimilar treatment of different species of animals is therefore not inherently discriminatory, and that the analogy sometimes made between racism and speciesism (as argued by Peter Singer, inter alia), does not hold. Andrew Brennan, "Humanism, Racism and Speciesism," *Worldviews* 7, no. 3 (2003): 282, 299. Nonetheless, I argue that although it may be useful to have a construct that facilitates assessing the distinct needs of kinds of animals, this does not necessitate that one of the most common criteria—the ability to reproduce—be the defining characteristic for making those distinctions, as is currently the case. According to the *New Encylopedia Britannica*, "to be members of the same species, individuals must be able to mate and produce viable offspring," 15th ed., vol. 11, s.v. "species," 76–77.

132. In the modern Western world, marriage has been conceived as a legal, contractual property relation between a husband and wife, allowing the husband access to his wife's sexual and domestic services. It is worthy of note that not until 1993 did marital rape become a crime in all fifty states, under at least one section of the sexual offense codes. Nonetheless, some legal exemptions from rape prosecution continue to be given to husbands. See Raquel Kennedy Bergen, *Wife Rape: Understanding the Response of Survivors and Service Providers* (Thousand Oaks, Calif.: Sage Publications, 1996).

133. Marti Kheel, "Animal Husbandry: Time for Divorce," *Feminists for Animal Rights Semiannual Publication* 12 (Autumn 2000–Winter 2001).

134. Rolston, *Environmental Ethics: Duties and Values*, 83.

135. Aldo Leopold, "The Wilderness and Its Place in Forest Recreational Policy," in *The River of the Mother of God and Other Essays by Aldo Leopold*, ed. Susan Flader and J. Baird Callicott (Madison: University of Wisconsin Press, 1991), 81.

136. Roderick Nash, *The Rights of Nature: A History of Environmental Ethics* (Madison: University of Wisconsin Press, 1989), 71.

137. Elizabeth Dodson Gray, *Green Paradise Lost* (Wellesley, Mass.: Roundtable Press, 1979), 148.

138. Mary Midgley, *Beast and Man: The Roots of Human Nature*, 2nd ed. (New York: Routledge, 1995).

139. The use of violence as a means of forging connections can perhaps best be understood by recollecting the psychosocial roots of masculine identity. Having established a second and alienated nature, it appears that the hyper-separated male then faces a lifelong urge to return to the original state of oneness left behind. The regression to this undifferentiated state, however, is precisely what must be avoided, since it constitutes an annihilation of the masculine self. This conflict between opposing drives may shed light on the hunter's urge to kill. The pursuit of the other-than-human animal expresses the hunter's yearning to repossess his lost female/animal nature. The death of the animal ensures that oneness with nature will not be attained. Violence becomes the only way in which the hunter can experience the sense of oneness while asserting his masculine status as an autonomous human being. By killing the animal, the hunter ritually enacts the death of his longing for a primordial female/animal world, a realm to which he cannot return. For a more general analysis of the psychological link between masculinity and violence, see Nancy C. M. Hartsock, *Money, Sex, and Power: Toward a Feminist Historical Materialism* (Boston: Northeastern University Press, 1985), 155–185.

140. Mary O'Brien, *The Politics of Reproduction* (Boston: Routledge and Kegan Paul, 1981), 59; Ruddick, *Maternal Thinking*, 209–211; Charlene Spretnak, introduction to *The Politics of Women's Spirituality: Essays on the Rise of Spiritual Power within the Feminist Movement*, ed. Charlene Spretnak (Garden City, N.Y.: Anchor Press, 1982), xvii–xviii.

141. I define veganism as an orientation that avoids the use of animal flesh and products derived from animals, such as eggs, milk, and leather. I use *vegetarian* to refer to a diet that omits animal flesh, but not necessarily other animal products. If only due to the relative scarcity of, and difficulty in obtaining flesh food, most of the world's populations have eaten a diet that is primarily plant-based. The term "vegetarian," however, is usually reserved for the conscious decision to avoid meat, based upon philosophical, religious, ethical, or nutritional beliefs. Although I personally advocate veganism in the following discussion, I often refer to vegetarianism, since that has been the focus of discussion among ecofeminists.

142. See for example, Lori Gruen, "Empathy and Vegetarian Commitments," in *Food for Thought: The Debate over Eating Meat*, ed. Steve Sapontzis (Amherst, N.Y.: Prometheus Books, 2004), 284–292; Deane Curtin, "Contextual Moral Vegetarianism," in Sapontzis, *Food for Thought*, 272–283; Josephine Donovan, "Animal Rights and Feminist Theory," *Signs* 15, no. 2 (1990): 350–375, reprinted in Donovan and

Adams, *Beyond Animal Rights*, 34–59; and Marti Kheel, "The Liberation of Nature: A Circular Affair," *Environmental Ethics* 7 (Summer 1985): 135–149, reprinted in Donovan and Adams, *Beyond Animal Rights*, 17–33.

143. For feminist critiques of the idea of rights with respect to other-than-human animals, see Donovan and Adams, *Beyond Animal Rights*. For a response to the feminist challenges, see Tom Regan, *Defending Animal Rights* (Urbana: University of Illinois Press, 2001), 53–64.

144. For example, Tom Regan argues that "reason compels us to recognize the equal inherent value of . . . animals and, with this, their equal right to be treated with respect." From "The Case for Animal Rights," in *In Defense of Animals*, ed. Peter Singer (New York: Basil Blackwell, 1985), 23–24.

145. Deane Curtin coined the term *contextual vegetarianism* in "Toward an Ecological Ethic of Care." For further discussion of contextual vegetarianism, see Curtin, "Contextual Moral Vegetarianism"; Cathryn Bailey, "We Are What We Eat: Feminist Vegetarianism and the Reproduction of Racial Identity," *Hypatia* 22, no. 2 (2007): 39–59; and Warren, *Ecofeminist Philosophy*, 125–145. For the development of a "context-sensitive semi-vegetarian position," see Val Plumwood, "Animals and Ecology: Toward a Better Integration," in Sapontzis, *Food for Thought*, 344–358. For an overview of vegetarianism and ecofeminism, see Greta Claire Gaard, "Vegetarian Ecofeminism: A Review Essay," *Frontiers: A Journal of Women Studies* 23, no. 3 (2002): 117–146.

146. Curtin, "Toward an Ecological Ethic of Care," 68–69.

147. Rolston, *Environmental Ethics: Duties and Values*, 79, 60.

148. Rolston, *Environmental Ethics: Duties and Values*, 79.

149. Warren, *Ecofeminist Philosophy*, 133.

150. Warren, *Ecofeminist Philosophy*, 125.

151. Warren, *Ecofeminist Philosophy*, 143.

152. Curtin, "Toward an Ecological Ethic of Care," 70.

153. Some ecofeminist animal advocates do argue for a universal ethical approach to vegetarianism. Thus, Josephine Donovan maintains that once we make an empathic connection with other animals, we can extrapolate a universal injunction to care for other-than-human animals. Donovan, "Feminism and the Treatment of Animals," 388–389. While agreeing with the desirability of extending one's capacity to care, I do not believe that empathy can be enjoined.

154. The information that I offer on behalf of veganism is based on my desire to remove the psychological blocks that impede caring conduct, and on my wish to attract people to veganism as a caring and life-giving practice. The information, thus, is designed to inspire rather than compel moral conduct. Arguments in favor of veganism are often refuted by the pronouncement that "I don't have a problem with killing animals," or "I don't equate animal and human life." While such pronouncements tend to (and no doubt, are designed to) end the dialogue, I encourage people to reflect upon why they lack empathy for other lives.

155. For example, according to Colin Spencer, during the persecution of the meat-abstaining Manicheans in the fourth century, avoidance of meat "became a sign of a heretic. . . . Timothy, Patriarch of Alexandria from AD 380 to 385, was so alarmed by

Manicheanism that he instituted food tests among his clergy and monks; those who refused to eat meat would then be interrogated." *The Heretic's Feast: A History of Vegetarianism* (Hanover, N.H.: University Press of New England, 1995), 142.

156. As Carol Adams points out, men who become vegetarian are particularly likely to be ridiculed as "effeminate, a 'sissy,' a 'fruit.'" *The Sexual Politics of Meat: A Feminist-Vegetarian Critical Theory* (New York: Continuum, 1990), 38.

157. Adrienne Rich, "Compulsory Heterosexuality and Lesbian Existence," in *Powers of Desire: The Politics of Sexuality*, ed. Ann Snitow, Christine Stansell, and Sharon Thompson (New York: Monthly Review Press, 1983), 177–205. Originally published in *Signs* 5, no. 4 (1979): 631–690. For further development of the notion of compulsory meat eating, see Marti Kheel, "Vegetarianism and Ecofeminism: Toppling Patriarchy with a Fork," in Sapontzis, *Food for Thought*. For a discussion of the social and cultural pressures experienced by vegetarians, see Carol J. Adams, *The Vegetarian's Survival Handbook: Living Among Meat Eaters* (New York: Three Rivers Press, 2001).

158. For a response to the charge that advocacy of vegetarianism is a form of cultural imperialism, see Chris J. Cuomo and Lori Gruen, "On Puppies and Pussies: Animals, Intimacy, and Moral Distance," in *Daring to Be Good: Essays in Feminist Ethico-Politics*, ed. Bat-Ami Bar On and Ann Ferguson (New York: Routledge, 1998), 140.

159. Thich Nat Hahn, "Cultivating Compassion, Responding to Violence" (lecture, Berkeley Community Theater, Berkeley, Calif., September 13, 2001). Audio and videotape copies are available from the Deer Park Monastery, attn. AV Team, 2499 Melru Lane, Escondido, CA, 92026 or via e-mail: dpavideo@earthlink.net, or fax: 760-291-1210. Clearly, advocacy of vegetarianism by a representative of a nonproselytizing cultural tradition, such as Buddhism, will be received differently from that of a person of privilege living in a dominant culture. Nonetheless, the view that all advocacy of vegetarianism as an ideal is inherently imperialist is an unjustified universal claim of its own.

160. It is interesting to note that while many theorists focus on the importance of understanding and respecting meat eating within the overall context of particular cultures, they often overlook less obvious cultural traditions, in particular those that link masculine identity and meat eating.

161. When, where, and how individuals express their ideals are important considerations for a contextual ethical approach. Since the vast majority of animal abuse occurs on factory farms that are owned and operated in the Western, developed world, it is most appropriate for vegetarian advocates living in the West to direct their central criticisms to this form of abuse.

162. Alice Walker, "Why Did the Balinese Chicken Cross the Road," in *Living by the Word: Selected Writings, 1973–1987* (San Diego, Calif.: Harvest Books, 1988), 172.

163. Ellen Bring, "Moving toward Coexistence: An Interview with Alice Walker," *Animals' Agenda* (April 1968): 9. For further discussion of the similarities between the enslavement of black people and the enslavement of other-than-human animals, see Marjorie Spiegel, *The Dreaded Comparison: Human and Animal Slavery* (New York: Mirror Books, 1988).

164. The significance of the prayers and rituals directed toward other-than-human animals among indigenous peoples is the subject of controversy. While many people view them as evidence of respect, other commentators have suggested that they were based on fears about retribution from the animals, or pragmatic concerns about ensuring a continued supply of animals for future hunts. See, for example, Shepard Krech III, *The Ecological Indian: Myth and History* (New York: W. W. Norton, 1999), 201–207; Tom Regan, "Environmental Ethics and the Ambiguity of the Native Americans' Relationship with Nature," in *All That Dwell Therein: Animal Rights and Environmental Ethics* (Berkeley: University of California Press, 1982), 227–235; and Calvin Martin, *Keepers of the Game: Indian-Animal Relationships and the Fur Trade* (Berkeley: University of California Press, 1978), 35–39. For challenges to the romantic contention that all indigenous cultures treated animals with reverence and respect, also see Clifford D. Presnall, "Wildlife Conservation as Affected by American Indian and Caucasian Concepts," *Journal of Mammalogy* 24, no. 4 (1943): 458–464.

165. "Indian" and "Native American," for example, are culturally constructed categories. Prior to European invasion, the indigenous population of North America did not see itself as a unified "race," but rather as separate peoples, often in hostile relation to one another. Recognition of this fact is growing among Anglo historians. See, for example, Richard White, *It's Your Misfortune and None of My Own: A New History of the American West* (Norman: University of Oklahoma Press, 1991). The question of whether Native Americans engaged in ecologically sound practices is often conflated with the issue of whether they held respect for individual animals. Krech, *Ecological Indian*, and Regan, "Environmental Ethics and the Ambiguity."

166. According to Martin W. Lewis, "Severe overhunting by so-called primal peoples has occurred in many different parts of the world. As it turns out, not only do hunter-gatherers (and hunter-farmers) sometimes slaughter their prey in a nonsustainable manner, but in several instances they have actually been encouraged to do so by their religious ideology." *Green Delusions: An Environmentalist Critique of Radical Environmentalism* (Durham, N.C.: Duke University Press, 1992), 63. Also see Martin, *Keepers of the Game*, 101–105, and Robert Brightman, "Conservation and Resource Depletion: The Case of the Boreal Forest Algonquians," in *The Question of the Commons: The Culture and Ecology of Communal Resources*, ed. Bonnie J. McCay and James M. Acheson (Tucson: University of Arizona Press, 1987), 121–141.

167. For further discussion of the ethical problems entailed in the use of truncated narratives, see Marti Kheel, "From Heroic to Holistic Ethics: The Ecofeminist Challenge," in Gaard, *Ecofeminism: Women, Animals, Nature*, 243–271.

168. Rolston, *Environmental Ethics: Duties and Values*, 82.

169. Stephan Lackner, *Peaceable Nature: An Optimistic View of Life on Earth* (San Francisco: Harper and Row, 1984), 12.

170. For research supporting the view that cats are obligate carnivores, see Debra L. Zoran, "The Carnivore Connection to Nutrition in Cats," *Journal of the American Veterinary Medical Association* 221, no. 11 (December 2002): 1559–1567.

171. Val Plumwood, "Integrating Ethical Frameworks for Animals, Humans, and Nature: A Critical Feminist Eco-Socialist Analysis," *Ethics and the Environment* 5, no. 2 (2000): 286. Reprinted in Sapontzis, *Food for Thought*.

172. Plumwood recognizes this visceral response in the natural aversion that humans have toward eating other humans. As she states, "Many animals do not eat their own kind for what appear to be ethical bonding and species life reasons." She fails to appreciate that this gut-level response to eating one's kind need not be restricted only to humankind; it is equally revolting to some humans to eat other animals. Plumwood, "Integrating Ethical Frameworks," 319.

173. For an effort to extend the notion of rights to the environment, see Christopher D. Stone, *Should Trees Have Standing? and Other Essays on Law, Morals and the Environment*, reprint edition (New York: Oxford University Press, 1996).

174. Ted Benton, *Natural Relations: Ecology, Animal Rights and Social Justice* (New York: Verso, 1993), 183.

175. Benton uses the terms "needs" and "interests" interchangeably. As he argues, meeting the needs of "living natural beings" must include "the satisfaction of all those conditions required for living of the mode of life characteristic of the species. These conditions, taken together, make up what I have sometimes referred to as 'basic interests' of individual animals, whether human or non-human." *Natural Relations*, 204.

176. Martha C. Nussbaum, *Frontiers of Justice: Disability, Nationality, Species Membership* (Cambridge, Mass.: Harvard University Press, 2006), 392.

177. Josephine Donovan, "Feminism and the Treatment of Animals," 315.

178. As John Robbins points out, "The livestock population of the United States today consumes enough grain and soybeans to feed over five times the entire human population of the country. . . . By cycling our grain through livestock, we end up with only 10% as many calories available to feed human mouths as would be available if we ate the grain directly. . . . For every sixteen pounds of grain and soybeans fed to beef cattle, we get back only one pound as meat on our plates." As Robbins further points out, "To supply one person with a meat food habit for a year requires three-and-a-quarter acres. To supply one lacto-ovo vegetarian with food for a year requires one-half acre. To supply one pure vegetarian requires only one-sixth of an acre. In other words, a given acreage can feed twenty times as many people eating a pure vegetarian diet-style as it could people eating the standard American dietary style." *Diet for a New America: How Your Food Choices Affect your Health, Happiness, and the Future of Life on Earth* (Walpole, N.H.: Stillpoint Publishing, 1987), 350–352.

179. Meat eating has been shown to be a major cause of disease due to the high levels of protein, bacteria, cholesterol, chemicals, hormones, and fat found in flesh foods. For more on the health hazards of meat eating see the monumental, cross-cultural epidemiological survey by T. Colin Campbell, published in *The China Study*. Campbell grew up on a dairy farm where he ate "plenty of meat and eggs," and went on to write a PhD dissertation on the ways animal protein could be used more efficiently. But after doing further research he concluded that a diet as low as possible in meat and animal products was a far healthier choice. T. Colin Campbell and Thomas M. Campbell II, *The China Study: Startling Implications for Diet, Weight Loss and Long-Term Health* (Dallas, Tex.: BenBella Books, 2006).

180. Henning Steinfield et al., *Livestock's Long Shadow: Environmental Issues and Options* (Rome: Food and Agriculture Organization of the United Nations, 2006), xx–xxiii.

181. Carol J. Adams, *Neither Man Nor Beast: Feminism and the Defense of Animals* (New York: Continuum, 1994), 27.

182. For further critique of the practice of framing moral dilemmas within a-contextual, truncated narratives, see Kheel, "From Heroic to Holistic Ethics," 243–271. On the importance of contextual narratives for ethical decision-making, see also Karen J. Warren, *Ecofeminist Philosophy*, 99, 102–105, and Jim Cheney, who argues that "to contextualize ethical deliberation is, in some sense, to provide a narrative, or story, from which the solution to the ethical dilemma emerges as the fitting conclusion." In "Eco-Feminism and Deep Ecology," *Environmental Ethics* 9, no. 2 (Summer 1987): 144.

183. While many of us will never visit a factory farm or slaughterhouse, we can nonetheless rely on depictions in films or upon vivid firsthand accounts.

184. Personal accounts, while powerful, cannot convey the full dimensions of sensory experience. De Beauvoir gropes at describing the stench of death, but words cannot adequately express her visceral response. While the relevance of odor to moral thought is rarely discussed, the producers of a documentary series on World War II contend that it is one of the most indelible aspects of war. Ken Burns and Lynn Novick, interview by Michael Krasny, *Forum*, KQED, March 1, 2007. A caller to the program recalled that his father always left when there was a barbecue, since the smell of burning flesh brought back painful memories of his wartime experience.

185. Simone de Beauvoir, *America Day by Day*, trans. Carol Cosman (Berkeley: University of California Press, 1999), 375–379. Used by permission of the University of California Press.

186. Nick Fiddes, *Meat: A Natural Symbol* (New York: Routledge, 1991), 5; Melanie Joy, "From Carnivore to Carnist: Liberating the Language of Meat," *Satya* 8, no. 2 (2001): 26.

187. Joy, "From Carnivore to Carnist," 26. See also Melanie Joy, "Psychic Numbing and Meat Consumption: The Psychology of Carnism" (PhD diss., Saybrook Graduate School, 2003).

188. Joy, "From Carnivore to Carnist," 26.

189. Fiddes, *Meat: A Natural Symbol*, 65.

190. Fiddes, *Meat: A Natural Symbol*, 144–155. Also see Adams, *Sexual Politics of Meat*, 26–27, 33–34.

191. The analogy between sexism and anti-vegetarian prejudice is made by Carol Adams in *Sexual Politics of Meat*, 33–34. The parallel is most pronounced in the respective threats posed by lesbians and vegetarians to male dominance and meat dominance. Just as heterosexuals often wonder how a lesbian can possibly find sexual fulfillment without a man, meat-eaters wonder how vegetarians can possibly obtain dietary fulfillment without meat. Vegetarians are asked, "What do you eat?" with the same mixture of incomprehension and bewilderment with which lesbians are asked, "What do you do?" In each case, the person is imagined to be deprived or incomplete, lacking a full dietary or sexual identity.

192. Fiddes, *Meat: A Natural Symbol*, 146.

193. The similarities in the objectification of women and other-than-human animals were brought to the fore in an infamous 1978 issue of *Hustler* magazine that fea-

tured a woman being fed into a meat grinder, an image echoed in a 2006 HBO promotional campaign. For further discussion of the link between pornography and meat, see Carol J. Adams, *The Pornography of Meat* (New York: Continuum, 2004).

194. Adams, *Sexual Politics of Meat*, 47.

195. Many of the early church fathers, including Clement of Alexandria, Tertullian, and John of Chrysostom, practiced celibacy and vegetarianism. As historian Colin Spencer underscores, however, their motivation was not respect for other-than-human animals, but rather their desire to establish "pre-eminence over their own flesh." *Heretic's Feast*, 128. For further discussion of vegetarianism in the early church, see *Heretic's Feast*, 108–125, and Rynn Berry, *Food for the Gods: Vegetarianism and the World's Religions* (New York: Pythagorean Publishers, 1998), 191–219.

196. For further details on the living conditions of animals on factory farms, as well as slaughterhouse practices, see Karen Davis, *Prisoned Chickens, Poisoned Eggs: An Inside Look at the Modern Poultry Industry* (Summertown, Tenn.: Book Publishing Company, 1996); Erik Marcus, *Meat Market: Animals, Ethics, and Money* (Boston: Brio Press, 2005). Although no longer current, a useful resource is still Jim Mason and Peter Singer's *Animal Factories*, rev. ed. (New York: Crown Publishers, 1990). For research on the emotions of farm animals, see Jeffrey Moussaieff Masson, *The Pig Who Sang to the Moon: The Emotional World of Farm Animals* (New York: Ballantine Books, 2003).

197. Sixty-six percent of all "dairy cows" are artificially inseminated. Stephen B. Blezinger, "Artificial Insemination: One of the Industry's Most Underutilized Tools" *Cattle Today* 19, no. 16 (May 6, 2006): 18.

198. One friend attributed her decision to become a vegan to her increased awareness while breast-feeding of how heart-wrenching it would be to have her daughter suddenly abducted. Personal communication to author, name withheld by request.

199. Peter Singer and Jim Mason, *The Way We Eat: Why Our Food Choices Matter* (Emmaus, Pa.: Rodale, 2006), 58.

200. As Keith Schillo points out, dairy scientists and dairy farmers manage udders, not cows. Email to author, September 15, 2006.

201. www.worldproutassembly.org/archives/2006/03/dairy_industry.html.

202. Michael Pollan, *Frontline*, "Modern Meat," program no. 2017, original airdate April 18, 2002. Written and directed by Doug Hamilton.

203. USDA, Swine 2000, Part I: Reference of Swine Health and Management in the United States (Fort Collins, Colo.: National Animal Health Monitoring Service, 2001), 16.

204. Allen Harper, "The NAHMS Survey on Sow and Gilt Management," *Livestock Update: Virginia Cooperative Extension*, Virginia Polytechnic Institute and State University, July 2002.

205. Marcus, *Meat Market*, 28–29.

206. W. E. Morgan Morrow, "Understanding Sow Wastage Rates," *Proceedings of the North Carolina Healthy Hogs Seminar* (Fayetteville, N.C.: North Carolina Swine Veterinary Group, 1997).

207. Davis, *Prisoned Chickens, Poisoned Eggs*, 57.

208. Walter Jaksch, "Euthanasia of Day-Old Male Chicks in the Poultry Industry," *International Journal for the Study of Animal Problems* 2, no. 4 (1981): 203–213, quoted in Marcus, *Meat Market*, 16. Although stuffing live birds into plastic bags is a common practice in poultry disposal, many viewers were aghast upon witnessing it firsthand during news coverage of the 2004 bird flu epidemic in Asia. More than 100 million chickens were killed, in terror of contagion, after twenty-two humans died from eating infected birds. Ed Cropley, "Bird Flu Epidemic Now under Control in Asia," Reuters News Service, March 15, 2004.

209. Singer and Mason, *The Way We Eat*, 45.

210. Animal activist Adam Weissman suggests that perhaps if meat eating were framed as a feminist issue, progressive activists might appreciate that serving meat/dairy was "creating an unsafe space for women and promoting rape culture." As he concludes, "Eating the bodies of raped animals is pretty compelling." Personal communication to author, May 3, 2005.

211. The Simpsons episode also illustrates how meat dominance and male dominance operate, as well as the notion of vegetarianism as a cross-cultural and counter-cultural tradition. After Lisa declares her vegetarianism, Homer enlists his son in a mocking jingle: "You can't win friends with vegetables!" He then insists on serving a roasted pig at a backyard barbecue (in hopes of impressing his neighbors with this symbol of status) and is enraged when Lisa sends the pig off on a roller coaster journey. Lisa, who is teased by her friends and despondent over the pervasiveness of flesh foods, ultimately finds solace from an Indian shopkeeper who, along with Paul and Linda McCartney (their real voices), comforts and teaches her the lesson of tolerance (the storekeeper is a vegan and thinks that it is wrong for her to eat dairy products).

212. Alice Walker, "Am I Blue?" in *Living by the Word: Selected Writings, 1973–1987* (San Diego, Calif.: Harvest Books, 1988), 6.

213. Walker, "Am I Blue?" 7.

214. Walker, "Am I Blue?" 8.

215. See, for example, Martha Nussbaum, *Love's Knowledge: Essays on Philosophy and Literature* (New York: Oxford University Press, 1990); Maria Pia Lara, *Moral Textures: Feminist Narratives in the Public Sphere* (Berkeley: University of California Press, 1998); T. Minh-Ha Trinh, *Woman, Native, Other: Writing Postcoloniality and Feminism* (Bloomington: Indiana University Press, 1989); and Walker, *Moral Understandings*.

216. As Val Plumwood notes, the message of the movie is ambiguous, for Babe survives by becoming an accomplice in the subjugation of other animals. As Plumwood concludes, although the movie does promote awareness about the subjectivity of other animals, it does not genuinely challenge the instrumental attitude toward factory-farmed animals, who exist only to become "meat." Thus, "the door opens to admit a few, but closes to keep the rest outside where they were." *Environmental Culture*, 164.

217. Elementary school dietitian Reed Mangels confirms that movies such as *Babe* and *Chicken Run* have influenced many young children to become vegetarian. Associated Press, "Vegetarian School Lunches Are Hard to Find," September 5, 2001.

218. Munro Leaf, drawings by Robert Lawson, *The Story of Ferdinand the Bull* (New York: Viking, 1936). Despite the book's underlying pacifist theme, the institution of bull-fighting is not challenged, as evidenced by the other bulls' eagerness to be selected to fight.

219. For further discussion of Emily the cow as a "teacher," see Mary Daly, *Amazon Grace: Recalling the Courage to Sin Big* (New York: Palgrave Macmillan, 2006), 119–121.

220. Evelyn Kimber, "Fleet, Sweet and Feisty: Emily the Celebrity Cow," *Newsletter of the Boston Vegetarian Society*, April 1996, 1.

221. Carol Beggy and Mark Shanan, "Sacred Cow Comes Home," *Boston Globe*, April 25, 2005. Also see www.peaceabbey.org/memorial/sacredcow.htm.

222. As Jason Hribal points out, "escapes from farms, slaughterhouses, laboratories, etc. are not unusual." Such resistance against human domination demonstrates that "our fellow creatures . . . [are] active beings each of whom has the ability to shape the world around them. Agency is not unique to the human animal. Cows, pigs, monkeys, and elephants can also resist their exploitation." Jason Hribal, "Emily the Cow and Tyke the Elephant: Resistance Is Never Futile," *Counterpunch*, May 17, 2007 online edition, www.counterpunch.org/hribal04172007.html.

223. For genuine dialogue to occur, it is important that the meaning of terms be understood. Just as the so-called generic "man" does not genuinely include women, so too, terms such as "species," "life forms," and "ecosystems" do not genuinely include individual beings.

224. For example, as Arne Naess points out, "unfortunately, the term 'life form' very often [is] interpreted to refer to species rather than specimens." Naess, "Response to Peder Anker," in *Philosophical Dialogues: Arne Naess and the Progress of Ecophilosophy*, ed. Nina Witoszek and Andrew Brennan (Lanham, Md.: Rowman & Littlefield, 1999), 447.

225. One of the standard definitions of species suggests the concern with procreation. As previously mentioned, the term "species" is commonly defined by an individual's ability to produce fertile offspring with her or his own kind.

# Bibliography

Abbagnano, Nicola. "Humanism." Translated by Nino Langiulli. In *The Encyclopedia of Philosophy*, vol. 4, edited by Paul Edward, 69–72. New York: Macmillan and Free Press, 1967.

Action News. "Bush Begins New Year by Bagging Quail." January 2, 2004.

Adams, Carol J., *The Sexual Politics of Meat: A Feminist-Vegetarian Critical Theory.* New York: Continuum, 1990.

———. ed. *Ecofeminism and the Sacred.* New York: Continuum, 1993.

———. *Neither Man Nor Beast: Feminism and the Defense of Animals.* New York: Continuum, 1994.

———. *The Vegetarian's Survival Handbook: Living Among Meat Eaters.* New York: Three Rivers Press, 2001.

———. *The Pornography of Meat.* New York: Continuum, 2004.

Adams, Carol J., and Josephine Donovan, eds. *Animals and Women: Feminist Theoretical Explorations.* Durham, N.C.: Duke University Press, 1995.

Aiken, William. "Ethical Issues in Agriculture." In *Earthbound: New Introductory Essays in Environmental Ethics*, edited by Tom Regan, 274–288. New York: Random House, 1984.

Allen, Reginald E., ed. *Greek Philosophy: Thales to Aristotle*, revised edition. New York: Macmillan Free Press, 1985.

Altherr, Thomas L. "'Chaplain to the Hunters': Henry David Thoreau's Ambivalence toward Hunting." *American Literature* 56, no. 3 (1984): 345–361.

Altman, Irwin, and Arza Churchman. *Women and the Environment.* New York: Plenum Press, 1994.

Anderson, J. K. *Hunting in the Ancient World.* Berkeley: University of California Press, 1985.

Andolsen, Barbara Hilkert, Christine E. Gudorf, and Mary D. Pellauer, eds. *Women's Consciousness, Women's Conscience: A Reader in Feminist Ethics.* Minneapolis: Winston Press, 1985.

Archer, John, ed. *Male Violence*. New York: Routledge, 1994.

———. "Male Violence in Perspective." In *Male Violence*, edited by John Archer, 1–20. New York: Routledge, 1994.

Ardrey, Robert. *African Genesis: A Personal Investigation into the Animal Origins and Nature of Man*. New York: Dell, 1961.

———. *The Territorial Imperative: A Personal Inquiry into the Animal Origins of Property and Nations*. New York: Atheneum, 1966.

———. *The Social Contract: A Personal Inquiry into the Evolutionary Sources of Order and Disorder*. New York: Atheneum, 1970.

———. *The Hunting Hypothesis: A Personal Conclusion concerning the Evolutionary Nature of Man*. New York: Atheneum, 1976.

Aristotle. *Aristotle's Politics*. Translated by Benjamin Jowett. New York: Oxford University Press, 1967.

Associated Press. "Vegetarian School Lunches Are Hard To Find." September 5, 2001.

Atkinson, Clarissa W., Constance H. Buchanan, and Margaret R. Miles, eds. *Immaculate and Powerful: The Female in Sacred Imagery and Social Reality*. Boston: Beacon Press, 1985.

Austin, Richard Cartwright. "Beauty: A Foundation for Environmental Ethics." *Environmental Ethics* 7 (Fall 1985): 197–208.

Ayto, John. *Arcade: Dictionary of Word Origins*. New York: Arcade Publishing, 1990.

Baden-Powell, Robert. *Scouting for Boys: A Handbook for Instruction in Good Citizenship*, reprint of original 1908 edition. New York: Oxford University Press, 2004.

Baer, Richard A., Jr. "Higher Education, the Church, and Environmental Values." *Natural Resources Journal* 17 (July 1977): 478–484.

Baier, Annette C. *Moral Prejudices: Essays on Ethics*. Cambridge, Mass.: Harvard University Press, 1994.

Bailes, Kendall E., ed. *Environmental History: Critical Issues in Comparative Perspective*. Lanham, Md.: University Press of America, 1985.

Bailey, Cathryn. "We Are What We Eat: Feminist Vegetarianism and the Reproduction of Racial Identity." *Hypatia* 22, no. 2 (2007): 39–59.

Bar On, Bat-Ami, and Ann Ferguson, eds. *Daring to Be Good: Essays in Feminist Ethico-Politics*. New York: Routledge, 1998.

Barringer, Judith. *The Hunt in Ancient Greece*. Baltimore: Johns Hopkins University Press, 2002.

Bart, Pauline. "Review of Chodorow's *The Reproduction of Mothering*." In *Mothering: Essays in Feminist Theory*, edited by Joyce Trebilcot, 147–152. Totowa, N.J.: Rowman & Littlefield, 1993.

Bart, Pauline, and Eileen Geil Moran, eds. *Violence against Women: The Bloody Footprints*. Thousand Oaks, Calif.: Sage Publications, 1993.

Barudy, Leo. *From Chivalry to Terrorism: War and the Changing Nature of Masculinity*. New York: Vintage, 2005.

Bataille, Georges. *Erotism: Death and Sensuality*. Translated by Mary Dalwood. San Francisco: City Lights Books, 1986.

Beard, George Miller. *A Practical Treatise on Nervous Exhaustion (Neurasthenia), Its Symptoms, Nature, Sequences, Treatment*. New York: William Wood and Company, 1879.

———. *American Nervousness: Its Causes and Consequences*. New York: G. P. Putnam's Sons, 1881.

Beauvoir, Simone de. *The Second Sex*. Translated by H. M. Parshley. New York: Vintage Books, 1974.

———. *America Day by Day*. Translated by Carol Cosman. Berkeley: University of California Press, 1999.

Bederman, Gail. *Manliness and Civilization: A Cultural History of Gender and Race in the United States, 1880-1917*. Chicago: University of Chicago Press, 1995.

Beech, Anthony, Tony Ward, and Dawn Fisher. "The Identification of Sexual and Violent Motivations in Men Who Assault Women: Implication for Treatment." *Journal of Interpersonal Violence* 21, no. 12 (December 2006): 1635–1653.

Beggy, Carol, and Mark Shanan. "Sacred Cow Comes Home." *Boston Globe*, April 25, 2005.

Benhabib, Seyla. "The Generalized and the Concrete Other: The Kohlberg-Gilligan Controversy and Moral Theory." In *Feminism as Critique*, edited by Seyla Benhabib and Drucilla Cornell, 77–95. Minneapolis: University of Minnesota Press, 1987.

Benhabib, Seyla, and Drucilla Cornell, eds. *Feminism as Critique*. Minneapolis: University of Minnesota Press, 1987.

Benjamin, Jessica. *The Bonds of Love: Psychoanalysis, Feminism, and the Problem of Domination*. New York: Pantheon Books, 1988.

Benton, Ted. *Natural Relations: Ecology, Animal Rights and Social Justice*. New York: Verso, 1993.

Benzoni, Francisco. "Rolston's Theological Ethic." *Environmental Ethics* 18 (Winter 1996): 339–351.

Bergen, Raquel Kennedy. *Wife Rape: Understanding the Response of Survivors and Service Providers*. Thousand Oaks, Calif.: Sage Publications, 1996.

Berger, John. "Master of Your Domain." *San Francisco Examiner*. April 11, 1990.

Bergman, Charles. *Orion's Legacy: A Cultural History of Man as Hunter*. New York: Dutton, 1997.

Berry, Rynn. *Food for the Gods: Vegetarianism and the World's Religions*. New York: Pythagorean Publishers, 1998.

Bettelheim, Bruno. *Symbolic Wounds: Puberty Rites and the Envious Male*. New York: Collier, 1962.

Biehl, Janet. *Rethinking Ecofeminist Politics*. Boston: South End Press, 1991.

Bigwood, Carol. *Earth Muse: Feminism, Nature, and Art*. Philadelphia: Temple University Press, 1993.

Binford, Lewis. "Human Ancestors: Changing Views of Their Behavior." *Journal of Anthropological Archaeology* 4, no. 4 (1985): 292–327.

Birch, Charles, and John B. Cobb Jr. *The Liberation of Life: From the Cell to Community*. Denton, Tex.: Environmental Ethics Books, 1990.

Blezinger, Stephen B. "Artificial Insemination: One of the Industry's Most Underutilized Tools." *Cattle Today* 19, no. 16 (May 6, 2006): 18.

Blum, Lawrence A. "Gilligan and Kohlberg: Implications for Moral Theory." In *An Ethic of Care: Feminist Interdisciplinary Perspectives*, edited by Mary Jeanne Larrabee, 49–68. New York: Routledge, 1993.

Bly, Robert. *Iron John: A Book About Men*. Reading, Mass.: Addison Wesley, 1990.

Bodian, Stephan. "Simple in Means, Rich in Ends: An Interview with Arne Naess." In *Deep Ecology for the 21ˢᵗ Century: Readings on the Philosophy and Practice of the New Environmentalism*, edited by George Sessions, 26–36. Boston: Shambhala, 1995.

Boehm, Felix. "The Femininity Complex in Men." *International Journal of Psycho-analysis* 11 (1930): 444–469.

Bookchin, Murray. "Social Ecology versus Deep Ecology: A Challenge for the Ecology Movement." In *Philosophical Dialogues: Arne Naess and the Progress of Ecophilosophy*, edited by Nina Witoszek and Andrew Brennan, 281–301. Lanham, Md.: Rowman & Littlefield, 1999.

Bordo, Susan. *The Flight to Objectivity: Essays on Cartesianism and Culture*. Albany: State University of New York Press, 1987.

Brabeck, Mary M., ed. *Who Cares? Theory, Research, and Educational Implications of the Ethic of Care*. New York: Routledge, 1993.

Brain, C. K. "New Finds at the Swartkrans Australopithecine Site." *Nature* 225 (March 21, 1970): 1112–1119.

——. *The Hunters or the Hunted? An Introduction to African Cave Taphonomy*. Chicago: University of Chicago Press, 1981.

Bramwell, Anna. *Ecology in the 20ᵗʰ Century: A History*. New Haven, Conn.: Yale University Press, 1989.

Brelich, Angelo. *Guerre, Agoni, e Culti Nella Grecia Arcaica*. Bonn: R. Habelt, 1961.

——. *Paides e Parthenoi*. Rome: Edizioni dell'Ateneo, 1969.

Brennan, Andrew. "Humanism, Racism and Speciesism." *Worldviews* 7, no. 3 (2003): 274–302.

Brewaeys, A., I. Ponjaert, E. V. Van Hall, and S. Golombok. "Donor Insemination: Child Development and Family Functioning in Lesbian Mother Families." *Human Reproduction* 12, no. 6 (1997): 1349–1359.

Brightman, Robert. "Conservation and Resource Depletion: The Case of the Boreal Forest Algonquians." In *The Question of the Commons: The Culture and Ecology of Communal Resources*, edited by Bonnie J. McCay and James M. Acheson, 121–141. Tucson: University of Arizona Press, 1987.

Bring, Ellen. "Moving toward Coexistence: An Interview with Alice Walker." *Animals' Agenda* (April 1968): 9.

Brod, Harry, and Michael Kaufman. *Theorizing Masculinities: Research on Men and Masculinities*. Thousand Oaks, Calif.: Sage Publications, 1994.

Brokaw, Howard P., ed. *Wildlife and America*. Washington, D.C.: Council on Environmental Equality, 1978.

Broughton, John M. "Women's Rationality and Men's Virtues: A Critique of Gender Dualism in Gilligan's Theory of Moral Development." In *An Ethic of Care: Feminist Interdisciplinary Perspectives*, edited by Mary Jeanne Larrabee, 112–139. New York: Routledge, 1993.

Brown, David E., and Neil B. Carmony, eds. *Aldo Leopold's Wilderness: Selected Early Writings by the Author of "A Sand County Almanac."* Harrisburg, Pa.: Stackpole Books, 1990.

Brown, Lyn Mikel, and Carol Gilligan. *Meeting at the Crossroads.* New York: Ballantine, 1992.

Brown, Wendy. *Manhood and Politics: A Feminist Reading in Political Theory.* Totowa, N.J.: Rowman & Littlefield, 1988.

Brownmiller, Susan. *Against Our Will: Men, Women and Rape.* New York: Simon and Schuster, 1975.

Buell, Lawrence. *The Environmental Imagination: Thoreau, Nature Writing, and the Formation of American Culture.* Cambridge, Mass.: Harvard University Press, 1995.

Bulliet, Richard W. *Hunters, Herders, and Hamburgers: The Past and Future of Human–Animal Relationships.* New York: Columbia University Press, 2005.

Burkert, Walter. *Homo Necans: The Anthropology of Ancient Greek Sacrificial Ritual and Myth.* Translated by Peter Bing. Berkeley: University of California Press, 1983.

Butler, Judith P. *Gender Trouble: Feminism and the Subversion of Identity.* New York: Routledge, 1990.

——. *Bodies That Matter: On the Discursive Limits of Sex.* New York: Routledge, 1993.

Caillois, Roger. *Man, Play, and Games.* Translated by Meyer Barash. New York: Free Press–Macmillan, 1961.

Calarco, Matthew, and Peter Atterton, eds. *Animal Philosophy: Essential Readings in Continental Thought.* New York: Continuum, 2004.

Caldecott, Léonie, and Stephanie Leland, eds. *Reclaim the Earth: Women Speak Out for Life on Earth.* London: Women's Press, 1983.

Callicott, J. Baird, ed. *A Companion to "A Sand County Almanac": Interpretive and Critical Essays.* Madison: University of Wisconsin Press, 1987.

——. "The Land Aesthetic." In *A Companion to "A Sand County Almanac": Interpretive and Critical Essays,* edited by J. Baird Callicott, 157–171. Madison: University of Wisconsin Press, 1987.

——. "Animal Liberation: A Triangular Affair." In *In Defense of the Land Ethic: Essays in Environmental Philosophy,* edited by J. Baird Callicott, 15–38. Albany: State University of New York Press, 1989.

——. "Animal Liberation and Environmental Ethics: Back Together Again." In *In Defense of the Land Ethic: Essays in Environmental Philosophy,* edited by J. Baird Callicott, 49–59. Albany: State University of New York Press, 1989.

——. "The Conceptual Foundations of the Land Ethic." In *In Defense of the Land Ethic: Essays in Environmental Philosophy,* edited by J. Baird Callicott, 75–99. Albany: State University of New York Press, 1989.

——. *In Defense of the Land Ethic: Essays in Environmental Philosophy.* Albany: State University of New York Press, 1989.

——. "Hume's *Is/Ought* Dichotomy." In *In Defense of the Land Ethic: Essays in Environmental Philosophy,* edited by J. Baird Callicott, 117–127. Albany: State University of New York Press, 1989.

——. "On the Intrinsic Value of Nonhuman Species." In *In Defense of the Land Ethic: Essays in Environmental Philosophy*, edited by J. Baird Callicott, 129–155. Albany: State University of New York Press, 1989.

——. "The Wilderness Idea Revisited: The Sustainable Development Alternative." In *The Great New Wilderness Debate: An Expansive Collection of Writings Defining Wilderness from John Muir to Gary Snyder*, edited by J. Baird Callicott and Michael P. Nelson, 387–394. Athens: University of Georgia Press, 1998.

——. "Holistic Environmental Ethics and the Problem of Ecofascism." In *Environmental Philosophy: From Animal Rights to Radical Ecology*, 4th ed., edited by Michael E. Zimmerman, J. Baird Callicott, George Sessions, Karen J. Warren, Irene J. Klaver and John Clark, 116–129. Upper Saddle River, N.J.: Prentice Hall, 2005.

——. "Turning the Whole Soul: The Educational Dialectic of *A Sand County Almanac*." *Worldviews* 9, no. 3 (2005): 365–384.

Callicott, J. Baird, and Michael P. Nelson, eds. *The Great New Wilderness Debate: An Expansive Collection of Writings Defining Wilderness from John Muir to Gary Snyder*. Athens: University of Georgia Press, 1998.

Campbell, T. Colin, and Thomas M. Campbell II. *The China Study: Startling Implications for Diet, Weight Loss and Long-Term Health*. Dallas, Tex.: BenBella Books, 2006.

Card, Claudia, ed. *Feminist Ethics*. Lawrence: University Press of Kansas, 1991.

Carlassare, Elizabeth. "Essentialism in Ecofeminist Discourse." In *Ecology*, edited by Carolyn Merchant, 220–234. Atlantic Highlands, N.J.: Humanities Press, 1994.

Carrigan, Tim, R. W. Connell, and John Lee. "Towards a New Sociology of Masculinity." *Theory and Society* 14, no. 5 (1985): 551–604.

Carson, Rachel. *Silent Spring*. Boston: Houghton Mifflin, 1962.

Carter, Jimmy. "A Childhood Outdoors." In *A Hunter's Heart: Honest Essays on Blood Sport*, edited by David Petersen, 35–46. New York: Henry Holt and Company, 1997.

Cartmill, Matt. *A View to a Death in the Morning: Hunting and Nature through History*. Cambridge, Mass.: Harvard University Press, 1993.

Cash, Mason. "Distancing Kantian Ethics and Politics from Kant's View on Women." *Minerva: An Internet Journal of Philosophy* 6 (November 2002): 103–150. www.mic.ul.ie/stephen/kantian.pdf

Cavalieri, Paola, and Peter Singer, eds. *The Great Ape Project: Equality Beyond Humanity*. London: Fourth Estate Limited, 1993.

Chapple, Christopher Key. *Nonviolence to Animals, Earth, and Self in Asian Traditions*. Albany: State University of New York Press, 1993.

Cheney, Jim. "Eco-Feminism and Deep Ecology." *Environmental Ethics* 9, no. 2 (Summer 1987): 115–145.

——. "The Neo-Stoicism of Radical Environmentalism." *Environmental Ethics* 11, no. 4 (1989): 293–326.

Chodorow, Nancy J. *The Reproduction of Mothering: Psychoanalysis and the Sociology of Gender*. Berkeley: University of California Press, 1978.

——. *Femininities, Masculinities, Sexualities: Freud and Beyond*. Lexington: University of Kentucky Press, 1994.

——. *The Power of Feelings: Personal Meaning in Psychoanalysis, Gender, and Culture*. New Haven, Conn.: Yale University Press, 1999.

——. "The Enemy Outside: Thoughts on the Psychodynamics of Extreme Violence with Special Attention to Men and Masculinity." In *Masculinity Studies and Feminist Theory: New Directions*, edited by Judith Kegan Gardiner, 235–260. New York: Columbia University Press, 2002.

Christ, Carol P., and Kathryn Roundtree. "Humanity in the Web of Life." *Environmental Ethics* 28 (Summer 2006): 185–200.

Chung, Carl. "The Species Problem and the Value of Teaching the Complexities of Species." *American Biology Teacher* 66, no. 6 (August 2004): 413–417.

Claridge, M. F., H. A. Dawah, and M. R. Wilson, "Practical Approaches to Species Concepts for Living Organisms." In *Species: The Units of Biodiversity*, 1–15. New York: Chapman and Hall, 1997.

——. eds. *Species: The Units of Biodiversity*. New York: Chapman and Hall, 1997.

Clark, Edward B. "Roosevelt on the Nature Fakirs." *Everybody's Nature Magazine* 16 (June 1907): 770–774.

Clifton, Merritt. "Killing the Female: The Psychology of the Hunt." *Animals' Agenda* 10, no. 7 (September 1990): 26–30, 57.

Cobb, John, Jr. "Deep Ecology and Process Thought." *Process Studies* 30, no. 1 (2001): 112–131.

Cole, Eve Browning, and Susan Coultrap-McQuin, eds. *Explorations in Feminist Ethics: Theory and Practice*. Bloomington: Indiana University Press, 1992.

Coleman, Sydney. *Humane Society Leaders in America*. Albany, N.Y.: American Humane Association, 1924.

Collard, Andrée, with Joyce Contrucci. *Rape of the Wild: Man's Violence Against Animals and the Earth*. Bloomington: Indiana University Press, 1989.

Collier, Richard. *Masculinities, Crime, and Criminology*. Thousand Oaks, Calif.: Sage Publications, 1998.

Condren, Mary. *The Serpent and the Goddess: Women, Religion, and Power in Celtic Ireland*. San Francisco: Harper and Row, 1989.

Connell, R. W. *Gender and Power: Society, the Person, and Sexual Politics*. Stanford, Calif.: Stanford University Press, 1987.

——. *Masculinities*. Berkeley: University of California Press, 1995.

——. "Hegemonic Masculinity: Rethinking the Concept." *Gender and Society* 19, no. 6 (2005): 829–858.

Cornwall, Andrea, and Nancy Lindisfarne, eds. *Dislocating Masculinity: Comparative Ethnographies*. New York: Routledge, 1994.

Crittenden, Paul. *Learning to Be Moral: Philosophical Thoughts about Moral Development*. Atlantic Highlands, N.J.: Humanities Press International, 1990.

Cropley, Ed. "Bird Flu Epidemic Now under Control in Asia." Reuters News Service, March 15, 2004.

Cudworth, Erika. *Developing Ecofeminist Theory: The Complexity of Difference.* New York: Palgrave Macmillan, 2005.

Cuomo, Chris. *Feminism and Ecological Communities: An Ethic of Flourishing.* New York: Routledge, 1998.

Cuomo, Christine J. "Ecofeminism, Deep Ecology, and Human Population." In *Ecological Feminism*, edited by Karen J. Warren, 88-105. New York: Routledge, 1994.

Cuomo, Chris, and Lori Gruen. "On Puppies and Pussies: Animals, Intimacy, and Moral Distance." In *Daring To Be Good: Essays in Feminist Ethico-Politics*, edited by Bat-Ami Bar On and Ann Ferguson. New York: Routledge, 1998.

Curtin, Deane. "Toward an Ecological Ethic of Care." *Hypatia* 6, no. 1 (Spring 1991).

———. "Contextual Moral Vegetarianism." In *Food for Thought: The Debate over Eating Meat*, edited by Steve Sapontzis, 272–283. Amherst, N.Y.: Prometheus Books, 2004.

Curtis, John. "From the Field of Battle, an Early Strike at Cancer." *Yale Medicine* 39, no. 3 (Summer 2005): 16–17.

Dahlberg, Frances, ed. *Woman the Gatherer.* New Haven, Conn.: Yale University Press, 1981.

Daly, Martin, and Margo Wilson. "Evolutionary Psychology of Male Violence." In *Male Violence*, edited by John Archer, 253–288. New York: Routledge, 1994.

Daly, Mary. *Gyn/Ecology: The Metaethics of Radical Feminism.* Boston: Beacon Press, 1978.

———. *Amazon Grace: Recalling the Courage to Sin Big.* New York: Palgrave Macmillan, 2006.

Dart, Raymond A. "The Predatory Transition from Ape to Man." *International Anthropological Linguistic Review* 1, no. 4 (1953): 201–219.

Dart, Raymond A., and Dennis Craig. *Adventures with the Missing Link.* Philadelphia, Pa.: Institute Press, 1967.

Darwin, Charles. *The Descent of Man and Selection in Relation to Sex*, reprint edition. New York: Barnes and Noble, 2004.

Davion, Victoria. "Is Ecofeminism Feminist?" In *Ecological Feminism*, edited by Karen Warren, 8–28. New York: Routledge, 1994.

Davis, Karen. *Prisoned Chickens, Poisoned Eggs: An Inside Look at the Modern Poultry Industry.* Summertown, Tenn.: Book Publishing Company, 1996.

Davis, Kathy. "Toward a Feminist Rhetoric: The Gilligan Debate Revisited." *Women's International Forum* 15, no. 2 (1992): 219–231.

D'Eaubonne, Françoise. *Le Feminisme ou la Mort.* Paris: Pierre Horay, 1974.

Defoe, William. *Robinson Crusoe.* Ann Arbor, Mich.: Ann Arbor Media, 2006.

Derr, Thomas Sieger. "Environmental Ethics and Christian Humanism." In *Environmental Ethics and Christian Humanism*, edited by Thomas Sieger Derr, James A. Nash, and Richard John Neuhaus, 17–104. Nashville, Tenn.: Abingdon Press, 1996.

Derr, Thomas Sieger, James A. Nash, and Richard John Neuhaus, eds. *Environmental Ethics and Christian Humanism.* Nashville, Tenn.: Abingdon Press, 1996.

Derrida, Jacques. "The Animal That Therefore I Am." In *Animal Philosophy: Essential Readings in Continental Thought*, edited by Matthew Calarco and Peter Atterton, 113–128. New York: Continuum, 2004.

DesJardins, Joseph, ed. *Environmental Ethics: Concepts, Policy and Theory.* New York: McGraw Hill, 1999.

Deutsch, Eliot. "A Metaphysical Grounding for Nature Reverence: East-West." *Environmental Ethics* 8 (Winter 1986): 293–331.

Devall, Bill. *Simple in Means, Rich in Ends: Practicing Deep Ecology.* Salt Lake City, Utah: Gibbs M. Smith, 1988.

———. "The Deep Ecology Movement." In *Ecology*, edited by Carolyn Merchant, 125–139. Atlantic Highlands, N.J.: Humanities Press, 1994.

Devall, Bill, and George Sessions. *Deep Ecology: Living as If Nature Mattered.* Salt Lake City, Utah: Gibbs M. Smith, 1985.

Diamond, Irene, and Gloria Orenstein, eds. *Reweaving the World: The Emergence of Ecofeminism.* San Francisco, Calif.: Sierra Club Books, 1990.

Diamond, Jared. "What Are Men Good For?" *Natural History* 102, no. 5 (May 1993): 24–29.

Diehm, Christian. "Arne Naess, Val Plumwood, and Deep Ecological Subjectivity: A Contribution to the 'Deep Ecology-Ecofeminism Debate.'" *Ethics and the Environment* 7, no. 1 (Spring 2002): 24–38.

Dillon, Robin. "Care and Respect." In *Explorations in Feminist Ethics: Theory and Practice*, edited by Eve Browning Cole and Susan Coultrap-McQuin, 69–81. Bloomington: Indiana University Press, 1992.

Dinnerstein, Dorothy. *The Mermaid and the Minotaur: Sexual Arrangements and Human Malaise.* New York: Harper and Row, 1976.

Dolins, Francine L., ed. *Attitudes to Animals: Views in Animal Welfare.* Cambridge: Cambridge University Press, 1999.

Donovan, Josephine. "Animal Rights and Feminist Theory." *Signs* 15, no. 2 (1990): 350–375.

———. "Attention to Suffering: Sympathy as a Basis for Ethical Treatment of Animals." In *Beyond Animal Rights: A Feminist Caring Ethic for the Treatment of Animals*, edited by Josephine Donovan and Carol J. Adams, 147–169. New York: Continuum, 1996.

Donovan, Josephine, and Carol J. Adams, eds. *Beyond Animal Rights: A Feminist Caring Ethic for the Treatment of Animals.* New York: Continuum, 1996.

Drengson, Alan R. "Social and Psychological Implications of Human Attitudes toward Animals." *Journal of Transpersonal Psychology* 12, no. 1 (1980): 63–74.

Drengson, Alan, and Yuichi Inoue, eds. *The Deep Ecology Movement: An Introductory Anthology.* Berkeley, Calif.: North Atlantic Books, 1995.

Drinka, George F. *The Birth of Neurosis: Myth, Malady, and the Victorians.* New York: Simon and Schuster, 1984.

Ducat, Stephen J. *The Wimp Factor: Gender Gaps, Holy Wars, and the Politics of Anxious Masculinity.* Boston: Beacon Press, 2004.

Dunayer, Joan. *Animal Equality: Language and Liberation.* Derwood, Md.: Recycle Publishing, 2001.

Dunlap, Thomas R. "Sport Hunting and Conservation, 1880–1920." *Environmental Review* 12 (Spring 1988): 51–60.

Eaton, Heather. "Liaison or Liability: Weaving Spirituality into Ecofeminist Politics." *Atlantis* 21, no. 1 (1997): 109–122.

Eaton, Randall, ed. *The Human/Animal Connection*. Incline Village, Nev.: Carnivore Journal and Sierra Nevada College Press, 1985.

———. "The Hunter as Alert Man: An Overview of the Origin of the Human/Animal Connection." In *The Human/Animal Connection*, edited by Randall Eaton. Incline Village, Nev.: Carnivore Journal and Sierra Nevada College Press, 1985.

Ebenreck, Sara. "Opening Pandora's Box: The Role of Imagination in Environmental Ethics." *Environmental Ethics* 18, no. 1 (Spring 1996): 3–18.

Edward, Paul, ed. *The Encyclopedia of Philosophy*. Vol. 4. New York: Macmillan and Free Press, 1967.

Ehrenreich, Barbara. *Blood Rites: Origins and History of the Passions of War*. New York: Henry Holt and Company, 1997.

Eisler, Josef Michael. "A Man's Unconscious Fantasy of Pregnancy in the Guise of Traumatic Hysteria." *International Journal of Psychoanalysis* 2 (1921): 255–286.

Elshtain, Jean Bethke. *Public Man, Private Woman: Women in Social and Political Thought*. Princeton, N.J.: Princeton University Press, 1981.

Emel, Jody. "Are You Man Enough, Big and Bad Enough? Wolf Eradication in the US." In *Animal Geographies: Place, Politics, and Identity in the Nature-Culture Borderlands*, edited by Jennifer Wolch and Jody Emel, 91–116. New York: Verso, 1998.

Fausto-Sterling, Anne. "The Five Sexes: Why Male and Female Are Not Enough." *Sciences* 2, no. 2 (March–April 1993): 20–24.

Fellman, Anita Clair, and Michael Fellman. *Making Sense of Self: Medical Advice Literature in Late Nineteenth Century America*. Philadelphia: University of Pennsylvania Press, 1981.

Ferré, Frederick. "Persons in Nature: Toward an Applicable and Unified Environmental Ethics." *Ethics and the Environment* 1, no. 1 (1996): 15–25.

Fiddes, Nick. *Meat: A Natural Symbol*. New York: Routledge, 1991.

Fischer, Louis. *The Life of Mahatma Gandhi*. New York: Harper and Row, 1950.

Fish and Wildlife Service, U.S. Department of Interior, and Bureau of the Census, U.S. Department of Commerce. *1991 National Survey of Fishing and Hunting and Wildlife Associated Recreation*. Washington, D.C.: U.S. Government Printing Office, 1993.

Fisher, Elizabeth. *Woman's Creation: Sexual Evolution and the Shaping of Society*. Garden City, N.Y.: Anchor Press, 1979.

Flader, Susan. *Thinking like a Mountain: Aldo Leopold and the Evolution of an Ecological Attitude toward Deer, Wolves and Forests*. Madison: University of Wisconsin Press, 1974.

Flader, Susan, and J. Baird Callicott, eds. *The River of the Mother of God and Other Essays by Aldo Leopold*. Madison: University of Wisconsin Press, 1991.

Flaks, David K., Ilda Ficher, Frank Masterpasqua, and Gregory Joseph. "Lesbians Choosing Motherhood: A Comparative Study of Lesbian and Heterosexual Parents and Their Children." *Developmental Psychology* 31, no. 1 (January 1995): 105–114.

Flax, Jane. "Reentering the Labyrinth: Revisiting Dorothy Dinnerstein's *The Mermaid and the Minotaur*." *Signs* 27, no. 4 (Summer 2002): 1037–1057.

Flügel, Ingeborg. "Some Psychological Aspects of a Fox-Hunting Rite." *International Journal of Psycho-Analysis* 12 (1931): 483–491.

Forester, Frank. *The Complete Manual for Young Sportsmen.* New York: Stringer and Townsend, 1856.

Forrest, Amy. "Hunting Heritage Starts at the Top." *Women in the Outdoors,* Spring 2004.

Fox, Warwick. "Deep Ecology: A New Philosophy of Our Time?" *Ecologist* 14, nos. 5–6 (1984): 194–200.

——. "Environment, Ethics, and Ecology Conference, Australian National University, August 26–28, 1983." *Ecophilosophy* 6 (May 1984): 11–12.

——. "On Guiding Stars to Deep Ecology: Warwick Fox Answers Naess's Response to Fox." *Ecologist* 14 (1984): 203–204.

——. "An Overview of My Response to Richard Sylvan's Critique of Deep Ecology." *Trumpeter* 2, no. 4 (Fall 1985): 17–20.

——. *Approaching Deep Ecology: A Response to Richard Sylvan's "Critique of Deep Ecology."* Hobart, Australia: University of Tasmania, 1986.

——. "The Deep Ecology-Ecofeminism Debate and Its Parallels." *Environmental Ethics* 11, no. 1 (Spring 1989): 5–25.

——. "On the Interpretation of Naess's Central Term 'Self-Realization.'" *Trumpeter* 2 (Spring 1990): 98–101.

——. "The Meanings of Deep Ecology." *Trumpeter* 7, no. 1 (Winter 1990): 48–50.

——. *Toward a Transpersonal Ecology: Developing New Foundations for Environmentalism.* Boston: Shambhala, 1990.

——. "Transpersonal Ecology and the Varieties of Identification." *Trumpeter* 8, no. 1 (Winter 1991): 3–5.

French, Marilyn. *Beyond Power: On Women, Men, and Morals.* New York: Summit Books, 1985.

French, William C. "Against Biospherical Egalitarianism." In *Philosophical Dialogues: Arne Naess and the Progress of Ecophilosophy,* edited by Nina Witoszek and Andrew Brennan, 127–145. Lanham, Md.: Rowman & Littlefield, 1999.

Freud, Sigmund. *Civilization and Its Discontents.* Translated and edited by James Strachey. New York: W. W. Norton, 1961.

——. *The Future of an Illusion.* Translated and edited by James Strachey. New York: W. W. Norton, 1961.

Fromm, Erich. *The Forgotten Language.* New York: Rinehart and Winston, 1951.

*Frontline.* "Modern Meat," program no. 2017. Interview with Michael Pollan. Written and directed by Doug Hamilton. Original airdate April 18, 2002.

Frye, Marilyn. *The Politics of Reality: Essays in Feminist Theory.* Trumansburg, N.Y.: Crossing Press, 1983.

——. "A Response to Lesbian Ethics: Why Ethics?" In *Feminist Ethics,* ed. Claudia Card, 52–59. Lawrence: University Press of Kansas, 1991.

Gaard, Greta, ed. *Ecofeminism: Women, Animals, Nature.* Philadelphia: Temple University Press, 1993.

——. *Ecological Politics: Ecofeminists and the Greens.* Philadelphia: Temple University Press, 1998.

——. Review of *Woman the Hunter*, by Marie Zeiss Stange. *Environmental Ethics* 22, no. 2 (Summer 2002): 203–206.

——. "Vegetarian Ecofeminism: A Review Essay." *Frontiers: A Journal of Women Studies* 23, no. 3 (2002): 117–146.

Garb, Yaakov J. "Perspective or Escape? Ecofeminist Musings on Contemporary Earth Imagery." In *Reweaving the World: The Emergence of Ecofeminism*, edited by Irene Diamond and Gloria Orenstein, 264–278. San Francisco, Calif.: Sierra Club Books, 1990.

Gardiner, Judith Kegan, ed. *Masculinity Studies and Feminist Theory: New Directions*. New York: Columbia University Press, 2002.

Gasset, José Ortega y. *Meditations on Hunting*. Translated by Howard B. Wescott. New York: Charles Scribner's Sons, 1972.

Gatens, Moira. *Imaginary Bodies: Ethics, Power and Corporeality*. New York: Routledge, 1996.

Gaylin, Willard. *The Male Ego*. New York: Penguin Books, 1992.

Gijswijt-Hofstra, Marijke, and Roy Porter, eds. *Cultures of Neurasthenia from Beard to the First World War*. Amsterdam: Rodopi, 2001.

Gilligan, Carol. "Reply by Carol Gilligan." *Signs* 11, no. 2 (Winter 1986): 325–326.

——. "Moral Orientation and Moral Development." In *Women and Moral Theory*, edited by Eva Feder Kittay and Diana T. Meyers, 19–33. New York: Rowman & Littlefield, 1987.

——. "Prologue: Adolescent Development Reconsidered." In *Mapping the Moral Domain*, edited by Carol Gilligan, Janie Victoria Ward, and Jill McLean Taylor, with Betty Bardige. Cambridge, Mass.: Harvard University Press, 1989.

——. *In a Different Voice: Psychological Theory and Women's Development*. Cambridge, Mass.: Harvard University Press, 1993.

——. "A Reply to Critics." In *An Ethic of Care: Feminist and Interdisciplinary Perspectives*, edited by Mary Jeanne Larrabee, 207–214. New York: Routledge, 1993.

Gilligan, Carol, and Jane Attanucci. "Two Moral Orientations." In *Mapping the Moral Domain*, edited by Carol Gilligan, Victoria Ward, and Jill McLean Taylor, 73–86. Cambridge, Mass.: Harvard University Press, 1988.

Gilligan, Carol, Nona P. Lyons, and Trudy J. Hanmer, eds. *Making Connections: The Relational Worlds of Adolescent Girls at Emma Willard School*. Cambridge, Mass.: Harvard University Press, 1990.

Gilligan, Carol, Annie Rogers, and Lyn Mikel Brown. "Epilogue: Soundings into Development." In *Making Connections: The Relational Worlds of Adolescent Girls at Emma Willard School*, edited by Carol Gilligan, Nona P. Lyons, and Trudy J. Hanmer, 314–329. Cambridge, Mass.: Harvard University Press, 1990.

Gilligan, Carol, Victoria Ward, and Jill McLean Taylor, with Betty Bardige, eds. *Mapping the Moral Domain*. Cambridge, Mass.: Harvard University Press, 1988.

Gilligan, Carol, and Grant Wiggins. "The Origins of Morality in Early Childhood Relationships." In *Mapping the Moral Domain*, edited by Carol Gilligan, Victoria Ward, and Jill McLean Taylor, 111–138. Cambridge, Mass.: Harvard University Press, 1988.

Gilmore, David D. *Manhood in the Making: Cultural Concepts of Masculinity*. New Haven, Conn.: Yale University Press, 1990.

———. *Misogyny: The Male Malady*. Philadelphia: University of Pennsylvania Press, 2001.

Gimbutas, Marija. *The Civilization of the Goddess: The World of Old Europe*. San Francisco, Calif.: HarperCollins, 1991.

Ginsburg, Faye, and Anna Lowenhaupt Tsing, eds. *Uncertain Terms: Negotiating Gender in American Culture*. Boston: Beacon Press, 1990.

Glacken, Clarence. *Traces on the Rhodian Shore: Nature and Culture in Western Thought from Ancient Times to the End of the Eighteenth Century*. Berkeley: University of California Press, 1976.

Glasser, Harold, and Alan Drengson, eds. *The Selected Works of Arne Naess*. New York: Springer, 2005.

Goffman, Erving. *Stigma: Notes on the Management of Spoiled Identity*. New York: Simon and Schuster: Prentice Hall, 1963.

Gottlieb, Roger S., ed. *This Sacred Earth: Religion, Nature, Environment*. New York: Routledge, 1996.

Graham, Frank, Jr. *Man's Dominion: The Story of Conservation in America*. New York: M. Evans, 1971.

Gramsci, Antonio. *Selections from the Prison Notebooks*. Edited and translated by Quintin Hoare and Geoffrey Nowell Smith. New York: International Publishers, 1971.

Gray, Elizabeth Dodson. *Green Paradise Lost*. Wellesley, Mass.: Roundtable Press, 1979.

Gray, Gary G. *Wildlife and People*. Chicago: University of Illinois, 1993.

Greek, Jean Swingle, and C. Ray Greek. *What Will We Do If We Don't Experiment on Animals? Medical Research for the Twenty-first Century*. Victoria, BC: Trafford Publishing, 2004.

Green, Martin. *The Adventurous Male: Chapters in the History of the White Male Mind*. University Park: Pennsylvania State University Press, 1993.

Greeno, Catherine C., and Eleanor Maccoby. "How Different Is the 'Different Voice?'" *Signs* 11, no. 2 (1986): 310–316.

Gregg, John R. "Taxonomy, Language, and Reality." *American Naturalist* 84, no. 819 (1950): 419–435.

Grier, Katherine C. "Childhood Socialization and Companion Animals: United States, 1820–1870." *Society and Animals* 7, no. 2 (1999): 95–120.

Griffin, Susan. *Woman and Nature: The Roaring inside Her*. New York: Harper and Row, 1978.

———. "Ecofeminism and Meaning." In *Ecofeminism: Women, Culture, Nature*, edited by Karen J. Warren, 213–226. Bloomington: Indiana University Press, 1997.

Grimshaw, Jean. *Philosophy and Feminist Thinking*. Minneapolis: University of Minnesota Press, 1986.

Grinnell, George Bird. "The Book of the Boone and Crockett Club." *Forest and Stream* 30 (March 1888).

Gruen, Lori. "Empathy and Vegetarian Commitments." In *Food for Thought: The Debate over Eating Meat*, edited by Steve Sapontzis, 284–292. Amherst, N.Y.: Prometheus Books, 2004.

Guha, Ramachandra. "Radical American Environmentalism and Wilderness Preservation: A Third World Critique." In *Philosophical Dialogues: Arne Naess and the*

*Progress of Ecophilosophy*, edited by Nina Witoszek and Andrew Brennan, 313–324. Lanham, Md.: Rowman & Littlefield, 1999.

——. "Radical American Environmentalism Revisited." In *Philosophical Dialogues: Arne Naess and the Progress of Ecophilosophy*, edited by Nina Witoszek and Andrew Brennan, 473–479. Lanham, Md.: Rowman & Littlefield, 1999.

Hall, Douglas. *The Steward: A Biblical Symbol Come of Age*. Grand Rapids, Mich.: Wm. B. Eerdmans Publishing, 1990.

Hamerton-Kelly, Robert G., ed. *Violent Origins: Walter Burkert, René Girard, and Jonathan Z. Smith on Ritual Killing and Cultural Formation*. Stanford, Calif.: Stanford University Press, 1987.

Hanen, Marsha, and Kai Nielsen, eds. "Science, Morality and Feminist Theory." *Canadian Journal of Philosophy*, 13 (1987), supplementary volume.

Haraway, Donna. *Primate Visions: Gender, Race and Nature in the World of Modern Science*. New York: Routledge, 1989.

——. "Teddy Bear Patriarchy: Taxidermy in the Garden of Eden, New York City, 1908–36." In *Primate Visions: Gender, Race and Nature in the World of Modern Science*, 26–58. New York: Routledge, 1989.

——. *Simians, Cyborgs, and Women: The Reinvention of Nature*. New York: Routledge, 1991.

Harding, Sandra. "The Curious Coincidence of Feminine and African Moralities: Challenges for Feminist Theory." In *Women and Moral Theory*, edited by Eva Feder Kittay and Diana Tietjiens Meyers, 296–315. Totowa, N.J.: Rowman & Littlefield, 1987.

Harding, Stephan. "What Is Deep Ecology?" *Resurgence* 185 (November–December 1997): 14–17.

Hargrove, Eugene. *Foundations of Environmental Ethics*. Englewood Cliffs, N.J.: Prentice Hall, 1989.

——. "From the Editor: After Twenty Years." *Environmental Ethics* 20, no. 4 (Winter 1998): 339–340.

Harper, Allen. "The NAHMS Survey on Sow and Gilt Management." *Livestock Update: Virginia Cooperative Extension*. Virginia Polytechnic Institute and State University, July 2002.

Harris, Adrienne, and Ynestra King, eds. *Rocking the Ship of the State: Toward a Feminist Peace Politics*. Boulder, Colo.: Westview Press, 1989.

Hart, Albert B., and Herbert Ferleger, eds. *Theodore Roosevelt Cyclopedia*. New York: Roosevelt Memorial Association, 1941.

Hart, Donna, and Robert W. Sussman. *Man the Hunted: Primates, Predators, and Human Evolution*. New York: Westview Press, 2005.

Hartsock, Nancy. *Money, Sex, and Power: Toward a Feminist Historical Materialism*. Boston: Northeastern University Press, 1985.

——. "Masculinity, Heroism and War." In *Rocking the Ship of the State: Toward a Feminist Peace Politics*, edited by Adrienne Harris and Ynestra King, 133–152. Boulder, Colo.: Westview Press, 1989.

Hawkins, Ronnie Zoe. "Ecofeminism and Nonhumans: Continuity, Difference, Dualism, and Domination." *Hypatia* 13, no. 1 (Winter 1998): 158–197.

Hays, Samuel P. *Conservation and the Gospel of Efficiency: The Progressive Conservation Movement, 1890-1920*. Cambridge, Mass.: Harvard University Press, 1959.

Heavey, Bill. "This Is Your Brain on Bucks." *Field and Stream*, November 2006.

Hekman, Susan J. *Moral Voices, Moral Selves: Carol Gilligan and Feminist Moral Theory*. University Park: Pennsylvania State University Press, 1995.

Held, Virginia, ed. *Justice and Care: Essential Readings in Feminist Ethics*. Boulder, Colo.: Westview Press, 1995.

Herbes-Sommers, Christine, producer and director, "The Difference Between Us." Episode 1 of the three-part PBS series *Race: The Power of An Allusion*. Created and produced by Larry Adelman. San Francisco: California Newsreel, 2003.

Herman, Daniel Justin. *Hunting and the American Imagination*. Washington, D.C.: Smithsonian Institution Press, 2001.

Hettinger, Ned. "Valuing Predation in Rolston's Environmental Ethics: Bambi Lovers versus Tree Huggers." *Environmental Ethics* 16, no. 1 (Spring 1994): 3–19.

Hindley, M. Patricia. "'Minding Animals': The Role of Animals in Children's Mental Development." In *Attitudes to Animals: Views in Animal Welfare*, edited by Francine L. Dolins, 186–199. Cambridge: Cambridge University Press, 1999.

Hite, Shere. *The Hite Report on Male Sexuality*. New York: Ballantine, 1981.

Hoagland, Sarah Lucia. *Lesbian Ethics: Toward New Value*. Palo Alto, Calif.: Institute of Lesbian Studies, 1989.

Hofacker, Al. "On the Trail of Wounded Deer: The Philosophy of Waiting." *Deer and Deer Hunting* 10, no. 6 (1986): 65–85, 104.

Hornaday, William T. *Our Vanishing Wild Life: Its Extermination and Preservation*. New York: Charles Scribner's Sons, 1913.

Horney, Karen. "The Denial of the Vagina: A Contribution to the Problem of the Genital Anxieties Specific to Women." In *Feminine Psychology*, edited by Harold Kelman, 147–161. New York: W. W. Norton, 1967.

———. "The Flight from Womanhood: The Masculinity-Complex in Women as Viewed by Men and by Women." In *Feminine Psychology*, edited by Harold Kelman, 54–70. New York: W. W. Norton, 1967.

Houston, Barbara. "Rescuing Womanly Virtue: Some Dangers of Moral Reclamation." In *Women and Moral Theory*, edited by Eva Feder Kittay and Diana Tietjiens Meyers, 237–262. Totowa, N.J.: Rowman & Littlefield, 1987.

Hribal, Jason. "Emily the Cow and Tyke the Elephant: Resistance Is Never Futile." *Counterpunch*, May 17, 2007.

Huizinga, Johan. *Homo Ludens: A Study of the Play-Element in Culture*. Boston: Beacon Press, 1950.

Hume, David. *A Treatise of Human Nature*. Oxford: Clarendon Press, 1960.

Isenberg, Andrew C. *The Destruction of the Bison: An Environmental History, 1750–1920*. Cambridge: Cambridge University Press, 2000.

Jaggar, Alison. *Feminist Politics and Human Nature*. Totowa, N.J.: Rowman and Allanheld, 1983.

Jaggar, Alison M., and Susan Bordo, eds. *Gender/Body/Knowledge: Feminist Reconstructions of Being and Knowing*. New Brunswick, N.J.: Rutgers University Press, 1989.

Jaksch, Walter. "Euthanasia of Day-Old Male Chicks in the Poultry Industry." *International Journal for the Study of Animal Problems* 2, no. 4 (1981): 203–213.

Jay, Nancy. "Gender and Dichotomy." *Feminist Studies* 7, no. 1 (Spring 1981): 38–56.

———. "Sacrifice as a Remedy for Having Been Born of Woman." In *Immaculate and Powerful: The Female in Sacred Imagery and Social Reality*, edited by Clarissa Atkinson, Constance H. Buchanan, and Margaret R. Miles, 283–309. Boston: Beacon Press, 1985.

———. *Throughout Your Generations Forever: Sacrifice, Religion, and Paternity.* Chicago: University of Chicago Press, 1992.

Jeanmaire, Henri. *Couroi et Courètes*, reprint edition. New York: Arno Press, 1975.

Johnson, Lawrence. "Humanity, Holism, and Environmental Ethics." *Environmental Ethics* 5 (Winter 1983): 345–354.

Johnson, Mark. *Moral Imagination: Implications of Cognitive Science for Ethics.* Chicago: University of Chicago Press, 1993.

Johnson, Miriam M. *Strong Mothers, Weak Wives: The Search for Gender Equality.* Berkeley: University of California Press, 1988.

Johnson, William Davidson. *T. R.: Champion of the Strenuous Life: A Photographic Biography of Theodore Roosevelt.* New York: Theodore Roosevelt Association, 1958.

Johnston, Jill. "Why Iron John Is No Gift to Women." *New York Times Book Review*, February 23, 1992.

Jones, Ernest. *Papers on Psychoanalysis.* London: Bailliere, Tindall and Cox, 1942.

———. "Psychology and Childbirth." In *Papers on Psychoanalysis.* London: Bailliere, Tindall and Cox, 1942.

Joy, Melanie. "From Carnivore to Carnist: Liberating the Language of Meat." *Satya* 8, no. 2 (2001): 26–27.

———. "Psychic Numbing and Meat Consumption: The Psychology of Carnism." PhD diss., Saybrook Graduate School, 2003.

———. "Humanistic Psychology and Animal Rights: Reconsidering the Boundaries of the Humanistic Ethic." *Journal of Humanistic Psychology* 45, no. 1 (Winter 2005): 106–130.

Kalechofsky, Roberta, ed. *Judaism and Animal Rights: Classical and Contemporary Responses.* Marblehead, Mass.: Micah Publications, 1992.

Kant, Immanuel. *Observations on the Feeling of the Beautiful and the Sublime.* Translated by J. T. Goldthwait. Berkeley: University of California Press, 1960.

———. *Groundwork of the Metaphysic of Morals.* Translated by H. J. Paton. New York: Harper and Row, 1964.

———. *Anthropology from a Pragmatic Point of View.* Translated by Victor Lyle Dowdell. Carbondale: Southern Illinois University Press, 1978.

Kapleau, Philip. *To Cherish All Life: A Buddhist Case for Becoming Vegetarian.* New York: Harper and Row, 1982.

Katz, Eric. "Against the Inevitability of Anthropocentrism." In *Beneath the Surface: Critical Essays in the Philosophy of Deep Ecology*, edited by Eric Katz, Andrew Light, and David Rothenberg, 17–42. Cambridge, Mass.: MIT Press, 2000.

Katz, Eric, Andrew Light, and David Rothenberg, eds. *Beneath the Surface: Critical Essays in the Philosophy of Deep Ecology.* Cambridge, Mass.: MIT Press, 2000.

Keen, Sam. *Fire in the Belly: On Being a Man.* New York: Vintage Books, 1991.

Keller, Catherine. *From a Broken Web: Separation, Sexism, and Self.* Boston: Beacon Press, 1986.

Keller, Evelyn Fox. *Reflections on Gender and Science.* New Haven, Conn.: Yale University Press, 1985.

Kelman, Harold, ed. *Feminine Psychology.* New York: W. W. Norton, 1967.

Kerber, Linda K. "Some Cautionary Words for Historians." In *An Ethic of Care: Feminist Interdisciplinary Perspectives*, edited by Mary Jeanne Larrabee, 102–107. New York: Routledge, 1993.

Kessler, S. J. D., Dean Ashenden, R. W. Connell, and G. W. Dowsett. *Ockers and Disco-Maniacs.* Sydney, Australia: Inner City Education Center, 1982.

Kheel, Marti. "The Liberation of Nature: A Circular Affair." *Environmental Ethics* 7, no. 2 (Summer 1985): 135–149.

———. "From Healing Herbs to Deadly Drugs: Western Medicine's War against the Natural World." In *Healing the Wounds: the Promise of Ecofeminism,* edited by Judith Plant, 96–111. Philadelphia: New Society Publishers, 1989.

———. "Ecofeminism and Deep Ecology: Reflections on Identity and Difference." In *Covenant for a New Creation: Ethics, Religion and Public Policy*, edited by Carol S. Robb and Carl J. Casebolt, 141–164. Maryknoll, N.Y.: Orbis Books, 1991.

———. "From Heroic to Holistic Ethics: The Ecofeminist Challenge." In *Ecofeminism: Women, Animals, Nature*, edited by Greta Gaard, 243–271. Philadelphia: Temple University Press, 1993.

———. "License to Kill: An Ecofeminist Critique of Hunters' Discourse." In *Animals and Women: Theoretical Explorations*, edited by Carol J. Adams and Josephine Donovan, 85–125. Durham, N.C.: Duke University Press, 1995.

———. "The Killing Game: An Ecofeminist Critique of Hunting." *Journal of the Philosophy of Sport* 23, no. 1 (May 1996): 30–44.

———. "The Heterosexist Subtext of the Justice/Care Debate." Paper presented at the Society for Women in Philosophy Pacific Division conference, Oceanside, Calif., May 31, 1997.

———. "Animal Husbandry: Time for Divorce." *Feminists for Animal Rights Semiannual Publication* 12 (Autumn 2000–Winter 2001).

———. "Vegetarianism and Ecofeminism: Toppling Patriarchy with a Fork." In *Food for Thought: The Debate over Eating Meat*, edited by Steve Sapontzis, 327–341. Amherst, N.Y.: Prometheus Books, 2004.

Kimber, Evelyn. "Fleet, Sweet and Feisty: Emily the Celebrity Cow." *Newsletter of the Boston Vegetarian Society*, April 1996.

Kimmel, Michael S. *Manhood in America: A Cultural History.* New York: Free Press, 1996.

Kimmel, Michael S., and Michael Kaufman. "Weekend Warriors: The New Men's Movement." In *Theorizing Masculinities: Research on Men and Masculinities*, edited by Harry Brod and Michael Kaufman, 259–288. Thousand Oaks, Calif.: Sage Publications, 1994.

King, Ynestra. "Toward an Ecological Feminism and a Feminist Ecology." In *Machina Ex Dea: Feminist Perspectives on Technology*, edited by Joan Rothschild, 118–127. New York: Pergamon Press, 1983.

Kipling, Rudyard. *The Jungle Book*. New York: Golden Press, 1963.

Kittay, Eva Feder. "Rereading Freud on 'Femininity' or Why Not Womb Envy?" *Women's Studies International Forum* 7, no. 5 (1984): 385–391.

——. "Mastering Envy: From Freud's Narcissistic Wounds to Bettelheim's Symbolic Wounds to a Vision of Healing." *Psychoanalytic Review* 82 (February 1994): 124–158.

——. *Love's Labor: Essays on Women, Equality, and Dependency*. New York: Routledge, 1998.

Kittay, Eva Feder, and Diana T. Meyers, eds. *Women and Moral Theory*. Totowa, N.J.: Rowman & Littlefield, 1987.

Klein, Ann Carolyn. *Meeting the Great Bliss Queen: Buddhists, Feminists, and the Art of the Self*. Boston: Beacon Press, 1995.

Klein, Melanie. "Love, Guilt and Reparation." In *Love, Guilt and Reparation and Other Works, 1921–1945*, 306–343. New York: Free Press, 1975.

——. "The Oedipus Complex in Light of Early Anxieties." In *Love, Guilt and Reparation and Other Works, 1921–45*, 370–414. New York: Free Press, 1975.

Klinger, Cornelia. "The Concepts of the Sublime and the Beautiful in Kant." In *Feminist Interpretations of Immanuel Kant*, edited by Robin Schott, 191–212. University Park: Pennsylvania State Press, 1997.

Kolodny, Annette. *The Lay of the Land: Metaphor as Experience and History in American Life and Letters*. Chapel Hill: University of North Carolina Press, 1984.

Krasny, Michael. Interview with Ken Burns and Lynn Novick. *Forum*, KQED, March 1, 2007

Krech, Shepard, III. *The Ecological Indian: Myth and History*. New York: W. W. Norton, 1999.

Kuhn, James L. "Toward an Ecological Humanistic Psychology." *Journal of Humanistic Psychology* 41, no. 2 (2001): 9–24.

Kundera, Milan. *The Unbearable Lightness of Being*. New York: Harper and Row, 1984.

Kyle, Donald G. *Spectacles of Death in Ancient Rome*. New York: Routledge, 1998.

Lackner, Stephan. *Peaceable Nature: An Optimistic View of Life on Earth*. San Francisco: Harper and Row, 1984.

Lakoff, George, and Mark Johnson. *Philosophy in the Flesh: The Embodied Mind and Its Challenge to Western Thought*. New York: Basic Books, 1999.

Langenau, E. E., Jr. "Factors Associated with Hunter Retrieval of Deer Hit by Arrows and Shotgun Slugs." *Leisure Sciences* 8, no. 4 (1986): 417–438.

*Lankavatara Sutra*. Translated by Daisetz Suzuki. London: Routledge, 1932.

Lara, Maria Pia. *Moral Textures: Feminist Narratives in the Public Sphere*. Berkeley: University of California Press, 1998.

Larrabee, Mary Jeanne, ed. *An Ethic of Care: Feminist and Interdisciplinary Perspectives*. New York: Routledge, 1993.

Lauck, Joanne Elizabeth. *The Voice of the Infinite in the Small: Revisioning the Insect–Human Connection*. Boston: Shambhala, 2002.

Laughlin, William S. "Hunting: An Integrating Biobehavior System and Its Evolutionary Importance." In *Man the Hunter*, edited by Richard B. Lee and Irven DeVore, 304–320. Hawthorne, N.Y.: Aldine de Gruyter, 1987.

Leaf, Munro. Drawings by Robert Lawson. *The Story of Ferdinand the Bull*. New York: Viking, 1936.

Lee, Richard B., and Irven DeVore, eds. *Man the Hunter*. Hawthorne, N.Y.: Aldine de Gruyter, 1987. Chicago: Aldine Publishing Company, 1986.

Leopold, Aldo. "To the Forest Officers of the Carson." In *River of the Mother of God*, edited by Susan L. Flader and J. Baird Callicott, 41–46. Originally published in *Carson Pine Cone* 15 (July 1913): n.p.

——. "On Killing the Limit," *Pine Cone* (July 1917).

——. "Forestry and Game Conservation." In *River of the Mother of God*, edited by Susan L. Flader and J. Baird Callicott, 53–59. Originally published in *Journal of Forestry* 16, no. 4 (April 1918): 404–411.

——. "Varmints." In *Thinking like a Mountain: Aldo Leopold and the Evolution of an Ecological Attitude toward Deer, Wolves and Forests*, edited by Susan L. Flader, xxvi. Madison: University of Wisconsin Press, 1974. Originally published in *Pine Cone*, no.12 (January 1919).

——. "Determining the Kill Factor for Black-Tail Deer in the Southwest." In David E. Brown and Neil B. Carmony, *Aldo Leopold's Wilderness*, 87–91. Originally published in *Journal of Forestry* 18, no. 2 (February 1920): 131–134.

——. "Wanted—National Forest Game Refuges." *Bulletin of the American Game Protective Association* 9, no. 1 (1920): 8–10.

——. "The Wilderness and Its Place in Forest Recreational Policy." In *River of the Mother of God,* edited by Susan L. Flader and J. Baird Callicott, 78–81. Originally published in *Journal of Forestry* 19, no. 7 (November 1921): 718–721.

——. "Pioneers and Gullies." In *River of the Mother of God*, edited by Susan L. Flader and J. Baird Callicott, 106–113. Originally published in *Sunset Magazine* 52, no. 5 (May 1924): 15–16, 91–95.

——. "Conserving the Covered Wagon." In *River of the Mother of God*, edited by Susan L. Flader and J. Baird Callicott, 128–132. Originally published in *Sunset Magazine* 54, no. 3 (March 1925): 21, 56.

——. "Wilderness as a Form of Land Use." In *River of the Mother of God*, edited by Susan L. Flader and J. Baird Callicott, 134–142. Originally published in *Journal of Land and Public Utility Economics* 1, no. 4 (October 1925): 398–404.

——. "A Plea for Wilderness Hunting Grounds." In *Aldo Leopold's Wilderness*, edited by David E. Brown and Neil B. Carmony. Harrisburg, Pa.: Stackpole Books, 1990. Originally published in *Outdoor Life* 56 (November 1925): 348–350.

——. "Game Management in the National Forests." In *Aldo Leopold's Wilderness*, edited by David E. Brown and Neil B. Carmony, 125–131. Originally published in *American Forests* 36, no. 7 (July 1930): 412–414.

——. "Game Methods: The American Way." In *River of the Mother of God*, edited by Susan L. Flader and J. Baird Callicott, 156–163. Originally published in *American Game* 20, no. 2 (March–April 1931): 20, 29–31.

——. "Game and Wild Life Conservation." In *River of the Mother of God*, edited by Susan L. Flader and J. Baird Callicott, 164–168. Originally published in *Condor* 34, no. 2 (March–April 1932): 103–106.

———. "An Outline Plan for Game Management in Wisconsin." In *A Study of Wisconsin: Its Resources, Its Physical, Social and Economic Background; First Annual Report*. Madison: Wisconsin Regional Planning Committee, December 1934.

———. "Threatened Species: A Proposal to the Wildlife Conference for an Inventory of the Needs of Near-Extinct Birds and Animals." In *Aldo Leopold's Wilderness*, edited by Brown and Carmony, 193–198. Orignally published in *American Forests* 42, no. 3 (1936): 116–199.

———. "The Farmer as a Conservationist." In *River of the Mother of God*, edited by Susan L. Flader and J. Baird Callicott, 255–265. Transcribed speech, originally published in Stencil Circular 210, Extension Service, College of Agriculture, University of Wisconsin, Madison (February 1939): 1–8.

———. "Wilderness as a Land Laboratory." In *River of the Mother of God*, edited by Susan L. Flader and J. Baird Callicott, 287–289. Originally published in *Living Wilderness* 6 (July 1941): 3.

———. "Review of Young and Goldman, The Wolves of North America." In *The River of the Mother of God and Other Essays by Aldo Leopold*, edited by Susan L. Flader and J. Baird Callicott, 320-322. Originally published in *Journal of Forestry* 43, no. 1 (January 1945): 928–929.

———. *A Sand County Almanac and Sketches Here and There*. New York: Oxford University Press, 1968.

———. "Some Fundamentals of Conservation in the Southwest." *Environmental Ethics* 1, no. 2 (Summer 1979): 131–141. Reprinted in *River of the Mother of God*, edited by Susan L. Flader and J. Baird Callicott, 86–97.

———. *Game Management*. Madison: University of Wisconsin Press, 1986.

———. "Ten New Developments in Game Management." In *Aldo Leopold's Wilderness*, edited by David E. Brown and Neil B. Carmony. Harrisburg, Pa.: Stackpole Books, 1990. Originally published in *American Game* 14, no. 3, 7–8, 20.

———. *Round River: From the Journals of Aldo Leopold*. Edited by Luna B. Leopold New York: Oxford University Press, 1993.

———. "The River of the Mother of God." In *River of the Mother of God*, edited by Susan L. Flader and J. Baird Callicott, 123–127.

———. "Wilderness" (transcribed speech). In *River of the Mother of God*, edited by Susan L. Flader and J. Baird Callicott, 226–229.

Lever, Janet. "Sex Differences in the Complexity of Children's Play and Games." *American Sociological Review* 43 (1978): 471–483.

Lewis, Joseph. *The Ten Commandments*. New York: Freethought Press Association, 1946.

Lewis, Martin W. *Green Delusions: An Environmentalist Critique of Radical Environmentalism*. Durham, N.C.: Duke University Press, 1992.

Linzey, Andrew. *Animal Theology*. Chicago: University of Illinois Press, 1995.

Livingstone, David. *Missionary Travels and Researches in South Africa*. London: Murray, 1857.

Lloyd, Genevieve. *The Man of Reason: "Male" and "Female" in Western Philosophy*. Minneapolis: University of Minnesota Press, 1984.

———. "Spinoza's Environmental Ethics." In *Philosophical Dialogues: Arne Naess and the Progress of Ecophilosophy*, edited by Nina Witoszek and Andrew Brennan, 73–90. Lanham, Md.: Rowman & Littlefield, 1999.

Lo, Y. S. "Non-Humean Holism, Un-Humean Holism." *Environmental Values* 10, no. 1 (2001): 113–123.

Long, William J. "The Modern School of Nature-Study and Its Critics." *North American Review* 176 (May 1903): 687–696.

Lovelock, James. "Gaia: A Model for Planetary and Cellular Dynamics." In *Gaia, A Way of Knowing: Political Implications of the New Biology*, edited by William Irwin Thompson, 83–97. Hudson, N.Y.: Lindisfarne, 1987.

———. *The Revenge of Gaia: Earth's Climate Crisis and the Fate of Humanity*. New York: Basic Books, 2006.

Lugones, Maria. "Playfulness, 'World-Traveling' and Loving Perception." *Hypatia* 2, no. 2 (1987): 3–19.

Lukács, Georg. *History of Class Consciousness*. Translated by Rodney Livingstone. Cambridge, Mass.: MIT Press, 1971.

Luke, Brian. "Taming Ourselves or Going Feral? Toward a Nonpatriarchal Metaethic of Animal Liberation." In *Animals and Women: Feminist Theoretical Explorations*, edited by Carol J. Adams and Josephine Donovan, 290–319. Durham, N.C.: Duke University Press, 1995.

———. "Violent Love, Heterosexuality and the Erotics of Men's Predation." *Feminist Studies* 24, no. 3 (1998): 627–655.

———. "Animal Sacrifice: A Model of Paternal Exploitation." *International Journal of Sociology and Social Policy* 24, no. 9 (2004): 18–44.

———. *Brutal: Manhood and the Exploitation of Animals*. Chicago: University of Illinois Press, 2007.

Luria, Zella. "A Methodological Critique." *Signs* 11, no. 2 (1986): 316–321.

Lutts, Ralph H. *The Nature Fakers*. Golden, Colo.: Fulcrum Publishing, 1990.

———. ed. *The Wild Animal Story*. Philadelphia: Temple University Press, 1998.

Lutz, Tom. *American Nervousness, 1903: An Anecdotal History*. Ithaca, N.Y.: Cornell University Press, 1992.

Maccoby, Eleanor E., and Carol Nagy Jacklin. *The Psychology of Sex Differences*. Stanford, Calif.: Stanford University Press, 1974.

MacKenzie, John. *The Empire of Nature: Hunting, Conservation, and British Imperialism*. Manchester, England: Manchester University Press, 1988.

Mallory, Chaone. "Acts of Objectification and the Repudiation of Dominance: Leopold, Ecofeminism, and the Ecological Narrative." *Ethics and the Environment* 6, no. 2 (2001): 59–89.

———. "Speci(es)al (as) Performance: Ecofeminism and the Regulatory Fiction of Race, Gender, and Species." Presented at the York University Nature Matters conference. Toronto, Canada, October 25–28, 2007.

Mangan, J. A., and James Walvin, eds. *Manliness and Morality: Middle-Class Masculinity in Britain and America, 1800–1940*. New York: St. Martin's Press, 1987.

Marcus, Erik. *Meat Market: Animals, Ethics, and Money*. Boston: Brio Press, 2005.

Marietta, Don. *For People and the Planet: Holism and Humanism in Environmental Ethics*. Philadelphia: Temple University Press, 1994.

Martin, Calvin. *Keepers of the Game: Indian-Animal Relationships and the Fur Trade*. Berkeley: University of California Press, 1978.

Maskit, Jonathan. "Deep Ecology and Desire: On Naess and the Problem of Consumption." In *Beneath the Surface: Critical Essays in the Philosophy of Deep Ecology*, edited by Eric Katz, Andrew Light, and David Rothenberg, 215–230. Cambridge, Mass.: MIT Press, 2000.

Maslow, Abraham. *Toward a Psychology of Being*. 2nd ed. Princeton, N.J.: Van Nostrand, 1968.

———. *The Farther Reaches of Human Nature*. New York: Viking, 1971.

Mason, Jim, and Peter Singer. *Animal Factories*. Rev. ed. New York: Crown Publishers, 1990.

Masson, Jeffrey Moussaieff. *The Pig Who Sang to the Moon: The Emotional World of Farm Animals*. New York: Ballantine Books, 2003.

Masson, Jeffrey Moussaieff, and Susan McCarthy. *When Elephants Weep: The Emotional Lives of Animals*. New York: Delacorte Press, 1995.

Matthiessen, Peter P. *Wildlife in America*. New York: Viking, 1987.

McCay, Bonnie J., and James M. Acheson, eds. *The Question of the Commons: The Culture and Ecology of Communal Resources*. Tucson: University of Arizona Press, 1987.

McDaniel, Jay B. *Of God and Pelicans: A Theology of Reverence for Life*. Louisville, Ky.: Westminster/John Knox, 1989.

Mead, Margaret. *Male and Female*. New York: William Morrow, 1949.

Meine, Curt. *Aldo Leopold: His Life and Work*. Madison: University of Wisconsin Press, 1988.

Mellon, Joseph. "Nature Ethics without Theory." PhD diss., University of Oregon, 1989.

Mellor, Mary. *Breaking the Boundaries: Towards a Feminist, Green Socialism*. London: Virago Press, 1992.

———. *Feminism and Ecology*. New York: New York University Press, 1997.

Menninger, Karl. "Totemic Aspects of Contemporary Attitudes toward Animals." In *Psychoanalysis and Culture*, edited by George Browning Wilbur and Warner Muensterberger, 42–74. New York: International University Press, 1951.

Merchant, Carolyn. *The Death of Nature: Women, Ecology, and the Scientific Revolution*. New York: Harper and Row, 1980.

———. "Mining the Earth's Womb." In *Machina Ex Dea: Feminist Perspectives on Technology*, edited by Joan Rothschild. New York: Pergamon Press, 1983.

———. "The Women of the Progressive Conservation Crusade: 1900–1915." In *Environmental History: Critical Issues in Comparative Perspective*, edited by Kendall E. Bailes, 153–170. Lanham, Md.: University Press of America, 1985.

———. *Radical Ecology: The Search for a Livable World*. New York: Routledge, 1992.

———. ed. *Ecology*. Atlantic Highlands, N.J.: Humanities Press, 1994.

———. *Earthcare: Women and the Environment*. New York: Routledge, 1995.

———. *Reinventing Eden: The Fate of Nature in Western Culture*. New York: Routledge, 2004.

Messerschmidt, James W. *Masculinities and Crime: Critique and Reconceptualization of Theory*. Lanham, Md.: Rowman & Littlefield, 1993.

Messner, Michael A. *Power at Play: Sports and the Problem of Masculinity*. Boston: Beacon Press, 1992.

Messner, Michael A., and Donald F. Sabo, eds. *Sport, Men and the Gender Order: Critical Feminist Perspectives*. Champaign, Ill.: Human Kinetic Books, 1990.

Meyers, Diana Tietjiens. "The Socialized Individual and Individual Autonomy: An Intersection between Philosophy and Psychology." In *Women and Moral Theory*, edited by Eva Feder Kittay and Diana Tietjiens Meyers, 139–153. Totowa, N.J.: Rowman & Littlefield, 1987.

——. *Subjection and Subjectivity: Psychoanalytic Feminism and Moral Philosophy*. New York: Routledge, 1994.

Midgley, Mary. *Beast and Man: The Roots of Human Nature*. 2nd ed. New York: Routledge, 1995.

Mies, Maria, and Vandana Shiva. *Ecofeminism*. Atlantic Highlands, N.J.: Zed Books, 1993.

Mighetto, Lisa. *Wild Animals and American Environmental Ethics*. Tucson: University of Arizona Press, 1991.

Mitchell, Silas Weir. *Camp Cure*. Philadelphia: J. B. Lippincott, 1877.

——. *Fat and Blood and How to Make Them*. Philadelphia: J. B. Lippincott, 1878.

Moen, Aaron N. "Crippling Losses." *Deer and Deer Hunting* 12, no. 6 (June 1989): 64–70.

Money, John, and Anke A. Ehrhardt. *Man and Woman, Boy and Girl: Differentiation and Dimorphism of Gender Identity from Conception to Maturity*. Baltimore: Johns Hopkins University Press, 1972.

More, Thomas. *The Latin Epigrams of Thomas More*. Edited and translated by Leicester Bradner and Charles Arthur Lynch. Chicago: University of Chicago Press, 1953.

Morrow, W. E. Morgan. "Understanding Sow Wastage Rates." *Proceedings of the North Carolina Healthy Hogs Seminar*. Fayetteville and Greenville, N.C.: North Carolina Swine Veterinary Group, 1997.

Moss, Ralph W. *Cancer Therapy: The Independent Consumer's Guide to Non-toxic Treatment and Prevention*. Brooklyn, N.Y.: Equinox Press, 1992.

——. *Questioning Chemotherapy*. Brooklyn, N.Y.: Equinox Press, 1995.

Muir, John. "The Wild Sheep of California." *Overland Monthly* 12 (1874): 359.

——. "Wild Wool." In *Wilderness Essays*. Salt Lake City, Utah: Peregrine Smith, 1980.

——. *Our National Parks*. Boston: Houghton Mifflin, 1901.

——. *The Yosemite*. San Francisco: Sierra Club, 1912.

Mumford, Lewis. "Man the Finder." *Technology and Culture* 6 (Summer 1965): 375–381.

Munson, Ronald, ed. *Man and Nature: Philosophical Issues in Biology*. New York: Harper and Row, 1971.

Murdoch, Iris. *The Sovereignty of Good*. Boston, Mass.: Routledge and Kegan Paul, 1970.

Murdock, G. P. "World Ethnographic Sample." *American Anthropologist* 59 (1957): 664–687.

——. *Ethnographic Atlas: A Summary*. Pittsburgh: University of Pittsburgh Press, 1967.

Murphy, Patrick D. "Sex-Typing the Planet: Gaia Imagery and the Problem of Subverting Patriarchy." *Environmental Ethics* 10, no. 2 (Summer 1988): 155–168.

298      *Bibliography*

Naess, Arne. "The Shallow and the Deep, Long-Range Ecology Movement: A Summary." *Inquiry* 16 (1973): 95–100.

——. *Gandhi and Group Conflict: An Exploration of Satyagraha.* Oslo: Universitetsforlager, 1974.

——. "Spinoza and Ecology." *Philosophia* 7, no. 1 (1977): 45–54.

——. "A Defense of the Deep Ecology Movement." *Environmental Ethics* 6, no. 3 (Fall 1984): 265–270.

——. "Identification as a Source of Deep Ecological Attitudes." In *Deep Ecology*, edited by Michael Tobias, 256–270. San Diego, Calif.: Avant Books, 1985.

——. *Ecology, Community, and Lifestyle: Outline of an Ecosophy.* Translated and revised by David Rothenberg. New York: Cambridge University Press, 1989.

——. "The Deep Ecology 'Eight Points' Revisited." In *Deep Ecology for the 21st Century: Readings on the Philosophy and Practice of the New Environmentalism*, edited by George Sessions, 213–221. Boston: Shambhala, 1995.

——. "Deepness of Questions and the Deep Ecology Movement." In *Deep Ecology for the 21st Century: Readings on the Philosophy and Practice of the New Environmentalism*, edited by George Sessions, 204–212. Boston: Shambhala, 1995.

——. "Self-Realization: An Ecological Approach to Being in the World." In *The Deep Ecology Movement: An Introductory Anthology*, edited by Alan Drengson and Yuichi Inoue, 13–30. Berkeley, Calif.: North Atlantic Books, 1995.

——. "An Answer to William C. French: Ranking, Yes, but the Inherent Value is the Same." In *Philosophical Dialogues: Arne Naess and the Progress of Ecophilosophy*, edited by Nina Witoszek and Andrew Brennan, 146–149. Lanham, Md.: Rowman & Littlefield, 1999.

——. "Comments on Guha's 'Radical American Environmentalism and Wilderness Preservation: A Third World Critique.'" In *Philosophical Dialogues: Arne Naess and the Progress of Ecophilosophy*, edited by Nina Witoszek and Andrew Brennan, 325–333. Lanham, Md.: Rowman & Littlefield, 1999.

——. "The Ecofeminism versus Deep Ecology Debate." In *Philosophical Dialogues: Arne Naess and the Progress of Ecophilosophy*, edited by Nina Witoszek and Andrew Brennan, 270–273. Lanham, Md.: Rowman & Littlefield, 1999.

——. "Environmental Ethics and Spinoza's Ethics: Comments on Genevieve Lloyd's Article." In *Philosophical Dialogues: Arne Naess and the Progress of Ecophilosophy*, edited by Nina Witoszek and Andrew Brennan, 91–99. Lanham, Md.: Rowman & Littlefield, 1999.

——. "Response to Peder Anker." In *Philosophical Dialogues: Arne Naess and the Progress of Ecophilosophy*, edited by Nina Witoszek and Andrew Brennan, 444–450. Lanham, Md.: Rowman & Littlefield, 1999.

——. *Life's Philosophy: Reason and Feeling in a Deeper World.* Athens: University of Georgia Press, 2002.

——. "The Encouraging Richness and Diversity of Ultimate Norms." In *The Selected Works of Arne Naess*, edited by Harold Glasser and Alan Drengson. New York: Springer, 2005.

Naess, Arne, and Ivar Mysterud. "Philosophy of Wolf Policies (I): General Principles and Preliminary Exploration of Selected Norms." In *Philosophical Dialogues:*

*Arne Naess and the Progress of Ecophilosophy*, edited by Nina Witoszek and Andrew Brennan, 339–359. Lanham, Md.: Rowman & Littlefield, 1999.

Nails, Debra. "Social-Scientific Sexism: Gilligan's *Mismeasure of Man.*" *Social Research* 50, no. 3 (1983): 643–664.

Nash, James A. "In Flagrant Dissent: An Environmentalist's Contentions." In *Environmental Ethics and Christian Humanism*, edited by Thomas Sieger Derr, James A. Nash, and Richard John Neuhaus, 105–124. Nashville, Tenn.: Abingdon Press, 1996.

Nash, Roderick. *Wilderness and the American Mind*, rev. ed. New Haven, Conn.: Yale University Press, 1978.

———. "Aldo Leopold's Intellectual Heritage." In *Companion to "A Sand County Almanac": Interpretive and Critical Essays*, edited by J. Baird Callicott, 63–90. Madison: University of Wisconsin Press, 1987.

———. *The Rights of Nature: A History of Environmental Ethics.* Madison: University of Wisconsin Press, 1989.

Nathan, George Jean. *The Theatre Book of the Year, 1950–1951: A Record and an Interpretation.* New York: Alfred A. Knopf, 1951.

National Shooting Federation, "What They Say About Hunting," http://www.nssf.org/lit/WTSAH2.pdf?AoI=hunting (accessed August 11, 2007).

Nelson, Mariah Burton. *The Stronger Women Get, the More Men Love Football: Sexism and the American Culture of Sports.* New York: Harcourt Brace, 1994.

Nelson, Michael. "Holists and Fascists and Paper Tigers . . . Oh My!" *Ethics and the Environment* 1, no. 2 (1996): 103–118.

Nelson, Richard. "A Letter from Richard Nelson, February 5, 1991." In *For Love of the World: Essays on Nature Writers*, edited by Sherman Paul, 163–218. Iowa City: University of Iowa Press, 1992.

Nerlich, Michael. "The Unknown History of Our Modernity." Center for Humanistic Studies Occasional Papers 3. Minneapolis: University of Minnesota, 1986.

Nestle, Marion. *Food Politics: How the Food Industry Influences Nutrition and Health.* Berkeley: University of California Press, 2002.

Neumann, Erich. *The Origins and History of Consciousness.* Translated by R. F. C. Hull. New York: Pantheon Books, 1949.

Nicholson, Linda J. "Women, Morality and History." In *An Ethic of Care: Feminist and Interdisciplinary Perspectives*, edited by Mary Jeanne Larrabee, 87–101. New York: Routledge, 1993.

Noddings, Nel. *Caring: A Feminine Approach to Ethics and Moral Education.* Berkeley: University of California Press, 1984.

Norwood, Vera. *Made from this Earth: American Women and Nature.* Chapel Hill: University of North Carolina Press, 1993.

Nussbaum, Martha C. *Love's Knowledge: Essays on Philosophy and Literature.* New York: Oxford University Press, 1990.

———. *Frontiers of Justice: Disability, Nationality, Species Membership.* Cambridge, Mass.: Harvard University Press, 2006.

Nye, Andrea. *Feminist Theory and the Philosophies of Man.* New York: Routledge, 1988.

O'Brien, Mary. *The Politics of Reproduction*. Boston: Routledge and Kegan Paul, 1981.

Ochs, Carol. *Behind the Sex of God: Toward a New Consciousness-Transcending Matriarchy and Patriarchy*. Boston: Beacon Press, 1977.

Oelschlaeger, Max, ed. *The Wilderness Condition: Essays on Environment and Civilization*. San Francisco: Sierra Club Books, 1992.

Orrieux, Claude, and Pauline Schmitt Pantel. *A History of Ancient Greece*. Translated by Janet Lloyd. Malden, Mass.: Blackwell Publishing, 2006.

Ortner, Sherry. "Is Female to Male As Nature Is to Culture?" In *Woman, Culture, and Society*, edited by Michelle Z. Rosaldo and Louise Lamphere, 67–87. Stanford, Calif.: Stanford University Press, 1974.

Partridge, Eric. *Origins: A Short Etymological Dictionary of Modern English*. New York: Macmillan, 1958.

Partridge, Ernest. "Nature as a Moral Resource." *Environmental Ethics* 4 (Summer 1984): 101–130.

Pateman, Carole. *The Disorder of Women: Democracy, Feminism and Political Theory*. Stanford, Calif.: Stanford University Press, 1989.

Paul, Sherman. *For Love of the World: Essays on Nature Writers*. Iowa City: University of Iowa Press, 1992

Peeples, Elise. "Her Terrain Is Outside of His 'Domain.'" *Hypatia* 6, no. 2 (1991): 192–199.

Perlman, David. "Clinton Bans Human Clone Funding." *San Francisco Chronicle*, March 5, 1997.

Perschel, Robert T., ed. *The Land Ethic Toolbox: Using Ethics, Emotion and Spiritual Values to Advance American Land Conservation*. Washington, D.C.: Wilderness Society, 2004.

Petersen, David, ed. *A Hunter's Heart: Honest Essays on Blood Sport*. New York: Henry Holt and Company, 1997.

Philippon, Daniel J. *Conserving Words: How American Nature Writers Shaped the Environmental Movement*. Athens: University of Georgia Press, 2005.

Phillips, D. C. *Holistic Thought in Social Science*. Palo Alto, Calif.: Stanford University Press, 1976.

Pinchot, Gifford. *The Use of the National Forest Reserves: Regulation and Instructions*. U.S. Department of Agriculture, Forest Service, 1905.

Plant, Judith, ed. *Healing the Wounds: The Promise of Ecofeminism*. Philadelphia: New Society Publishers, 1989.

Plato. *The Republic of Plato*. Translated with Introduction and Notes by Francis Macdonald Cornford. Oxford: Clarendon Press, 1941.

——. *Laws*, vol. 2. Translated by R. G. Bury. Cambridge, Mass.: Harvard University Press, 1952.

——. *The Phaedrus*. In *Greek Philosophy: Thales to Aristotle*, edited by Reginald E. Allen, rev. ed. New York: Macmillan Free Press, 1985.

——. *Laws: Plato*. Translated by Benjamin Jowett. Amherst, N.Y.: Prometheus Books, 2000.

Plumwood, Val. "Nature, Self and Gender: Feminism, Environmental Philosophy, and the Critique of Rationalism." *Hypatia* 6, no. 1 (1991): 3–27.

———. *Feminism and the Mastery of Nature.* New York: Routledge, 1993.

———. "Comment: Self-Realization or Man Apart? The Reed-Naess Debate." In *Philosophical Dialogues: Arne Naess and the Progress of Ecophilosophy*, edited by Nina Witoszek and Andrew Brennan, 206–210. Lanham, Md.: Rowman & Littlefield, 1999.

———. "Integrating Ethical Frameworks for Animals, Humans, and Nature: A Critical Feminist Eco-Socialist Analysis." *Ethics and the Environment* 5, no. 2 (2000): 285–322.

———. *Environmental Culture: The Ecological Crisis of Reason.* New York: Routledge, 2002.

———. "Animals and Ecology: Toward a Better Integration." In *Food for Thought: The Debate over Eating Meat*, edited by Steve Sapontzis, 344–358. Amherst, N.Y.: Prometheus Books, 2004.

Plutarch. *Moralia*, vol. 12. Translated by Harold Cherniss and W. C. Helmbold. Cambridge, Mass.: Harvard University Press, 1957.

Pollan, Michael. *The Omnivore's Dilemma: A Natural History of Four Meals.* New York: Penguin Press, 2006.

Popper, Karl R. *Objective Knowledge: An Evolutionary Approach.* New York: Oxford University Press, 1972.

Power, Mary James. *Poets at Prayer.* Freeport, N.Y.: Books for Libraries Press, 1977.

Presnall, Clifford D. "Wildlife Conservation as Affected by American Indian and Caucasian Concepts." *Journal of Mammalogy* 24, no. 4 (1943): 458–464.

Preston, Christopher J. "Intrinsic Value and Care: Making Connections through Ecological Narratives." *Environmental Values* 10 (2001): 243–263.

Proctor, Nicolas W. *Bathed in Blood: Hunting and Mastery in the Old South.* Charlottesville: University of Virginia Press, 2002.

Puka, Bill. "Comment Reply: The Science of Caring." *Hypatia* 6, no. 2 (1991): 200–210.

———. "The Liberation of Caring: A Different Voice for Gilligan's 'Different Voice.'" In *An Ethic of Care: Feminist Interdisciplinary Perspectives*, edited by Mary Jeanne Larrabee, 215–239. New York: Routledge, 1993.

Quillin, Patrick, and Noreen Quillin. *Beating Cancer with Nutrition.* Carlsbad, Calif.: Nutrition Times Press, 2005.

Radford, Jill, and Diana E. H. Russell, eds. *Femicide: The Politics of Woman Killing.* New York: Twayne Publishers, 1992.

Raymond, Janice. "Female Friendship: Contra Chodorow and Dinnerstein." *Hypatia* 1, no. 2 (Fall 1986): 37–48.

Reagan, Ronald. Campaign speech, meeting of Western Wood Products Association, San Francisco, Calif., March 12, 1966.

Regan, Tom. *All That Dwell Therein.* Berkeley: University of California Press, 1982.

———. *The Case for Animal Rights.* Berkeley: University of California Press, 1983.

———. ed. *Earthbound: New Introductory Essays in Environmental Ethics.* New York: Random House, 1984.

———. *The Thee Generation: Reflections on the Coming Revolution.* Philadelphia: Temple University Press, 1991.

———. *Defending Animal Rights.* Urbana: University of Illinois Press, 2001.

Reid, Mayne. *Wild Life, or Adventures on the Frontier*. New York: Robert M. De Witt, 1859.

———. *Afloat in the Forest*. New York: Thomas R. Knox, 1884.

———. *The Boy Hunters*. London: George Routledge and Sons, 1892.

Reiger, George. "Hunting and Trapping in the New World." In *Wildlife and America*, edited by Howard P. Brokaw, 42–52. Washington, D.C.: Council on Environmental Equality, 1978.

Reiger, John. *American Sportsmen and the Origin of Conservation*. Rev. ed. Norman: University of Oklahoma Press, 1986.

———. "Response to Thomas Dunlap." *Environmental Journal* 12 (Fall 1988): 94–96.

Reiter, Rayna R., ed. *Toward an Anthropology of Women*. New York: Monthly Review Press, 1975.

Rensberger, Boyce. "The Killer Ape Is Dead." *Alicia Patterson Foundation Reporter* 12, no. 8 (December 1973): 1–7.

Ribbens, Dennis. "The Making of *A Sand County Almanac*." *Wisconsin Academy Review* 28, no. 4 (1982). Reprinted in *Companion to "A Sand County Almanac": Interpretive and Critical Essays*, edited by J. Baird Callicott, 91–109. Madison: University of Wisconsin Press, 1987.

Rich, Adrienne. "Compulsory Heterosexuality and Lesbian Existence." In *Powers of Desire: The Politics of Sexuality*, edited by Ann Snitow, Christine Stansell, and Sharon Thompson, 177–205. New York: Monthly Review Press, 1983.

Riley, Glenda. "'Wimmin Is Everywhere': Conserving and Feminizing Western Landscapes, 1870 to 1940." *Western Historical Quarterly* 29 (Spring 1998): 5–23.

———. *Women and Nature: Saving the "Wild" West*. Lincoln: University of Nebraska Press, 1999.

Roach, Catherine M. *Mother/Nature: Popular Culture and Environmental Ethics*. Bloomington: Indiana University Press, 2003.

Robb, Carol S., and Carl J. Casebolt, eds. *Covenant for a New Creation: Ethics, Religion and Public Policy*. Maryknoll, N.Y.: Orbis Books, 1991.

Robbins, John. *Diet for a New America: How Your Food Choices Affect Your Health, Happiness, and the Future of Life on Earth*. Walpole, N.H.: Stillpoint Publishing, 1987.

Roberts, Charles G. D. *Kindred of the Wild: A Book of Animal Life*. Boston: L. C. Page, 1907.

Rohner, Ronald P. "Sex Differences in Aggression." *Ethos* 4 (1976): 57–72.

Rolston, Holmes III. "Is There an Ecological Ethic?" *Ethics: An International Journal of Social, Political, and Legal Philosophy* 85, no. 2 (January 1975): 93–109.

———. "Can and Ought We to Follow Nature?" *Environmental Ethics* 1, no. 1 (Spring 1979): 7–30.

———. "Duties to Endangered Species." *Bioscience* 35, no. 11 (December 1985): 718–726.

———. "The Human Standing in Nature: Fitness in the Moral Overseer." In *Values and Moral Standing*, edited by Wayne Sumner, Donald Callen, and Thomas Attig, 90–101. Bowling Green, Ohio: Bowling Green State University, 1986.

———. *Philosophy Gone Wild: Essays in Environmental Ethics*. Buffalo, N.Y.: Prometheus Books, 1986.

——. "Engineers, Butterflies, Worldviews." *Environmental Professional* 9 (1987): 295–301.

——. "On Behalf of Bioexuberance." *Garden Magazine* 11, no. 4 (July–August 1987): 2–4, 31–32.

——. *Science and Religion: A Critical Survey*. New York: Random House, 1987.

——. *Environmental Ethics: Duties to and Values in the Natural World*. Philadelphia: Temple University Press, 1988.

——. "In Defense of Ecosystems." *Garden* 12, no. 4 (July–August 1988): 2–5, 32.

——. "Treating Animals Naturally?" *Between the Species: A Journal of Ethics* 5, no. 3 (Summer 1989): 131–137.

——. "Genes, Genesis, and God in Natural and Human History." *Center for Theology and the Natural Sciences Bulletin* 11, no. 2 (Spring 1991): 9–23.

——. "Respect for Life: Christians, Creation, and Environmental Ethics." *Center for Theology and the Natural Sciences Bulletin* 11, no. 2 (Spring 1991): 1–8.

——. *Conserving Natural Value*. New York: Columbia University Press, 1994.

——. "Does Nature Need to Be Redeemed?" *Zygon* 29, no. 2 (June 1994): 205–229.

——. *Genes, Genesis and God: Values and Their Origins in Natural and Human History*. New York: Cambridge University Press, 1999.

Romano, Lois. "Kerry Hunting Trip Sets Sites on Swing Voters." *Washington Post*, October 21, 2004.

Roosevelt, Theodore. *The Wilderness Hunter: An Account of the Big Game of the United States and Its Chase with Horse, Hound and Rifle*. New York: G. P. Putnam's Sons, 1893.

——. *Ranch Life and the Hunting Trail*. New York: Century Co., 1899. Reprint ed. Lincoln: University of Nebraska Press, 1983.

——. *Hunting Trips of a Ranchman: Hunting Trips on the Praire and in the Mountains*. New York: G. P. Putnam's Sons, 1900.

——. *The Winning of the West*. New York: G. P. Putnam's Sons, 1907.

——. *Theodore Roosevelt: An Autobiography*. New York: Macmillan, 1914.

——. *Hunting the Grisly and Other Sketches*. Boston: Elibron Classics, 2000.

Rosaldo, Michelle, and Louise Lamphere, eds. *Woman, Culture, and Society*. Stanford, Calif.: Stanford University Press, 1974.

Rosenhek, Ruth. "Nature as Faith." *Chain Reaction* 94 (July 2005): 21.

Rosenthal, Michael. *The Character Factory: Baden-Powell and the Origins of the Boy Scout Movement*. New York: Pantheon Books, 1986.

Rossi, Alice. "On *The Reproduction of Mothering*: A Methodological Debate." *Signs* 6, no. 3 (Spring 1981): 482–514.

Roszak, Theodore, Mary E. Gomes, and Allen D. Kanner, eds. *Ecopsychology: Restoring the Earth, Healing the Mind*. San Francisco: Sierra Club Books, 1995.

Rothschild, Joan. ed. *Women, Technology and Innovation*. New York: Pergamon Press, 1982.

——. ed. *Machina Ex Dea: Feminist Perspectives on Technology*. New York: Pergamon Press, 1983.

Rotundo, Anthony. "Learning About Manhood: Gender Ideals and the Middle-Class Family in Nineteenth-Century America." In *Manliness and Morality: Middle-Class*

*Masculinity in Britain and America, 1800–1940*, edited by J. A. Mangan and James Walvin, 35–51. New York: St. Martin's Press, 1987.

Routley, Richard. "Is There a Need for a New, An Environmental Ethic?" In *Philosophy and Science: Morality and Culture: Technology and Man, Bulgarian Organizing Committee, Proceedings of the 15th World Congress of Philosophy*, no. 1, 205–210. Varna, Bulgaria: Sophia Press, 1973.

Ruddick, Sara. *Maternal Thinking: Toward a Politics of Peace*. Boston: Beacon Press, 1989.

Ruether, Rosemary Radford. *Gaia and God: An Ecofeminist Theology of Earth Healing*. San Francisco: Harper San Francisco, 1992.

——. ed. *Women Healing Earth: Third World Women on Ecology, Feminism, and Religion*. Maryknoll, N.Y.: Orbis Books, 1996.

——. *Integrating Ecofeminism, Globalization, and World Religions*. Lanham, Md.: Rowman & Littlefield, 2005.

Runte, Alfred. Review of *American Sportsmen and the Origins of Conservation*, by John Reiger. *Journal of Forest History* 20 (April 1976): 100–101.

Russell, Diana E. H. *The Politics of Rape: A Victim's Perspective*. New York: Stein and Day, 1975.

Sabo, Donald, and Ross Runfola, eds. *Jock: Sports and Male Identity*. Englewood Cliffs, N.J.: Prentice Hall, 1980.

Salleh, Ariel. "Deeper Than Deep Ecology: The Ecofeminist Connection." *Environmental Ethics* 6, no. 4 (1984): 335–341.

——. *"Staying Alive: Women, Ecology and Development*, by Vandana Shiva." *Hypatia* 6 (Spring 1991), 206–214.

——. "The Ecofeminism/Deep Ecology Debate: A Reply to Patriarchal Reason." *Environmental Ethics* 14, no. 3 (Fall 1992): 195–216.

——. *Ecofeminism as Politics: Nature, Marx, and the Postmodern*. New York: Zed Books, 1997.

——. "Class, Race, and Gender Discourse in the Ecofeminism/Deep Ecology Debate." In *Philosophical Dialogues: Arne Naess and the Progress of Ecophilosophy*, edited by Nina Witoszek and Andrew Brennan, 236–254, Lanham, Md.: Rowman & Littlefield, 1999.

Sánchez, José Luis García, and Miguel Angel Pacheco. *I Am a Wild Animal*. New York: Santillana Publishing, 1975.

Sanday, Peggy Reeves. "The Socio-cultural Context of Rape." *Journal of Social Issues* 37, no. 4 (Fall 1981): 5–27.

Sandilands, Catriona. *The Good-Natured Feminist: Ecofeminism and the Quest for Democracy*. Minneapolis: University of Minnesota Press, 1999.

Santmire, H. Paul. *The Travail of Nature: The Ambiguous Ecological Promise of Christian Theology*. Philadelphia: Fortress Press, 1985.

Sapontzis, Steve F., ed. *Food for Thought: The Debate over Eating Meat*. Amherst, N.Y.: Prometheus Books, 2004.

Scarce, Rik. *Eco-warriors: Understanding the Radical Environmental Movement*. Chicago: Noble Press, 1990.

Schott, Robin. *Cognition and Eros: A Critique of the Kantian Paradigm*. Boston: Beacon Press, 1988.

———. ed. *Feminist Interpretations of Immanuel Kant.* University Park: Pennsylvania State Press, 1997.

Schullery, Paul. *The Bear Hunter's Century: Profiles from the Golden Age of Bear Hunting.* Silver City, N.Mex.: High Lone-Some Books, 1988.

Schrepfer, Susan R. *Nature's Altars: Mountains, Gender, and American Environmentalism.* Lawrence: University Press of Kansas, 2005.

Schröder, Hannelore. "Kant's Patriarchal Order." Translated by Rita Gircour. In *Feminist Interpretations of Immanuel Kant*, edited by Robin Schott, 275–296. University Park: Pennsylvania State Press, 1997.

Scoville, Judith N. "Value Theory and Ecology in Environmental Ethics: A Comparison of Rolston and Niebuhr." *Environmental Ethics* 17 (1995): 115–133.

Scully, Diana, and Joseph Marolla. "'Riding the Bull at Gilley's': Convicted Rapists Describe the Rewards of Rape." In *Violence Against Women: The Bloody Footprints*, edited by Pauline B. Bart and Eileen Geil Moran, 15–30. Thousand Oaks, Calif.: Sage Publications, 1993.

Scully, Matthew. *Dominion: The Power of Man, the Suffering of Animals and the Call to Mercy.* New York: St. Martin's Griffin, 2002.

Seager, Joni. *Earth Follies: Coming to Feminist Terms with the Global Environmental Crisis.* New York: Routledge, 1993.

Sedgwick, Sally. "Can Kant's Ethics Survive the Feminist Critique?" In *Feminist Interpretations of Immanuel Kant*, edited by Robin Schott, 77–100. University Park: Pennsylvania State Press, 1997.

Seed, John. "Beyond Anthropocentrism." In *Thinking like a Mountain: Towards a Council of All Beings*, edited by John Seed, Joanna Macy, Pat Fleming, and Arne Naess, 35–40. Philadelphia: New Society Publishers, 1988.

Seed, John, Joanna Macy, Pat Fleming, and Arne Naess, eds. *Thinking like a Mountain: Towards a Council of All Beings.* Philadelphia: New Society Publishers, 1988.

Seidler, Victor. *Man Enough: Embodying Masculinities.* Thousand Oaks, Calif.: Sage Publications, 1997.

Sessions, George. "Spinoza and Jeffers on Man in Nature." *Inquiry* 20, no. 4 (1977): 481–525.

———. ed. *Deep Ecology for the 21st Century: Readings on the Philosophy and Practice of the New Environmentalism.* Boston: Shambhala, 1995.

Sewell, Anna. *Black Beauty.* New York: Sterling Publishing Company, 1954.

Shapiro, Kenneth. "Animal Rights versus Humanism: The Charge of Speciesism." *Journal of Humanistic Psychology* 30, no. 2 (1990): 9–37.

Shepard, Paul. *Man in the Landscape: A Historical View of the Esthetics of Nature.* New York: Alfred A. Knopf, 1967.

———. "Post-historic Primitivism." In *The Wilderness Condition: Essays on Environment and Civilization*, edited by Max Oelschlaeger, 40–89. San Francisco: Sierra Club Books, 1992.

———. *The Tender Carnivore and the Sacred Game.* Athens: University of Georgia Press, 1998.

Shipman, Pat. "Scavenging or Hunting in Early Hominids: Theoretical Framework and Tests." *American Anthropologist* 88, no. 1 (1986): 27–43.

Shiva, Vandana. *Staying Alive: Women, Ecology, and Development* (Atlantic Highlands, N.J.: Zed Books, 1988.

——. ed. *Close to Home: Women Reconnect Ecology, Health, and Development Worldwide*. Philadelphia: New Society Publishers, 1994.

——. *Earth Democracy: Justice, Sustainability, and Peace*. Cambridge, Mass.: South End Press, 2005.

Shiva, Vandana, and Ingunn Moser, eds. *Biopolitics: A Feminist and Ecological Reader on Biotechnology*. Atlantic Highlands, N.J.: Zed Books, 1995.

Short, William J. "Saints in the World of Nature: The Animal Story as Spiritual Parable in Medieval Hagiography, 900–1200." PhD diss., Pontificia Universitas Gregoriana, 1983.

Shrader-Frechette, Kristin. "Individualism, Holism, and Environmental Ethics." *Ethics and the Environment* 1, no. 1 (1996): 55–69.

Singer, Peter. *Animal Liberation: A New Ethics for Our Treatment of Animals*. New York: Avon Books, 1975.

——. *Practical Ethics*. New York: Cambridge University Press, 1979.

——. ed. *In Defense of Animals*. New York: Basil Blackwell, 1985.

Singer, Peter, and Jim Mason. *The Way We Eat: Why Our Food Choices Matter*. Emmaus, Pa.: Rodale, 2006.

Sjöö, Monica, and Barbara Mor. *The Great Cosmic Mother: Rediscovering the Religion of the Earth*. San Francisco: Harper and Row, 1987.

Slocum, Sally. "Woman the Gatherer: Male Bias in Anthropology." In *Toward an Anthropology of Women*, edited by Rayna R. Reiter, 36–50. New York: Monthly Review Press, 1975.

Slotkin, Richard. *Gunfighter Nation: The Myth of the Frontier in Twentieth-Century America*. Norman: University of Oklahoma Press, 1998.

Smith, Jonathan Z. "The Domestication of Sacrifice." In *Violent Origins: Walter Burkert, René Girard, and Jonathan Z. Smith on Ritual Killing and Cultural Formation*, edited by Robert G. Hamerton-Kelly, 191–205. Stanford, Calif.: Stanford University Press, 1987.

Smith, J. C. *The Psychoanalytic Roots of Patriarchy: The Neurotic Foundations of Social Order*. New York: New York University Press, 1990.

Smith, J. C., and Carla J. Ferstman. *The Castration of Oedipus: Feminism, Psychoanalysis, and the Will to Power*. New York: New York University Press, 1996.

Smith, Ruth. "Feminism and the Moral Subject." In *Women's Consciousness, Women's Conscience: A Reader in Feminist Ethics*, edited by Barbara Hilkert Andolsen, Christine E. Gudorf, and Mary D. Pellauer, 235–250. Minneapolis: Winston Press, 1985.

Smuts, Jan Christian. *Holism and Evolution: The Original Source of the Holistic Approach to Life*. Edited by Sanford Holst. Sherman Oaks, Calif.: Sierra Sunrise Books, 1999.

Snitow, Ann, Christine Stansell, and Sharon Thompson, eds. *Powers of Desire: The Politics of Sexuality*. New York: Monthly Review Press, 1983.

Sontheimer, Sally, ed. *Women and the Environment, A Reader: Crisis and Development in the Third World*. New York: Monthly Review Press, 1991.

Spencer, Colin. *The Heretic's Feast: A History of Vegetarianism*. Hanover, N.H.: University Press of New England, 1995.

Spiegel, Marjorie. *The Dreaded Comparison: Human and Animal Slavery*. New York: Mirror Books, 1988.

Spretnak, Charlene, ed. *The Politics of Women's Spirituality: Essays on the Rise of Spiritual Power within the Feminist Movement*. Garden City, N.Y.: Anchor Press, 1982.

——. *The Resurgence of the Real: Body, Nature and Place in a Hypermodern World*. New York: Routledge, 1999.

Spinoza, Benedict de. *Philosophy of Benedict de Spinoza*. Translated by R. H. M. Elwes. New York: Tudor Publishing, 1933.

Stack, Carol B. "Different Voices, Different Visions: Gender, Culture, and Moral Reasoning." In *Uncertain Terms: Negotiating Gender in American Culture*, edited by Faye Ginsburg and Anna Lowenhaupt Tsing, 19–27. Boston: Beacon Press, 1990.

Stange, Mary Zeiss. *Woman the Hunter*. Boston: Beacon Press, 1988.

Stanley, Autumn. "Daughters of Isis, Daughters of Demeter: When Women Sowed and Reaped." In *Women, Technology and Innovation*, edited by Joan Rothschild. New York: Pergamon Press, 1982.

Stegner, Page, ed. *Marking the Sparrow's Fall: The Making of the American West*. New York: Henry Holt and Company, 1998.

Stegner, Wallace. "Living on Our Principal." *Wilderness* 48 (Spring 1985), reprinted in *Marking the Sparrow's Fall: The Making of the American West*, edited by Page Stegner, 149–160. New York: Henry Holt and Company, 1998.

Steinem, Gloria. *Revolution from Within: A Book of Self-Esteem*. Boston: Little, Brown and Company, 1992.

——. Commencement speech. Wellesley College, Wellesley, Mass., May 28, 1993.

Steinfield, Henning, et al. *Livestock's Long Shadow: Environmental Issues and Options*. Rome: Food and Agriculture Organization of the United Nations, 2006.

Stevens, Jacqueline. "Pregnancy Envy and the Politics of Compensatory Masculinities." *Politics and Gender* 1, no. 2 (2005): 265–296.

Stewart, Whitney. "The Dalai Lama on Love and Children." *L.A. Parenting Magazine* 8, no. 6 (June 1988): 71.

Stoltenberg, John. *Refusing to Be a Man: Essays on Sex and Justice*. New York: Penguin, 1990.

Stone, Christopher D. *Should Trees Have Standing? and Other Essays on Law, Morals and the Environment*, reprint edition. New York: Oxford University Press, 1996.

Sturgeon, Noël. *Ecofeminist Natures: Race, Gender, Feminist Theory, and Political Action*. New York: Routledge, 1997.

Sumner, Wayne, Donald Callen, and Thomas Attig, eds. *Values and Moral Standing*. Bowling Green, Ohio: Bowling Green State University, 1986.

Sutter, Paul S. "'A Blank Spot on the Map': Aldo Leopold, Wilderness, and U.S. Forest Service Recreational Policy, 1909–1924." *Western Historical Quarterly* 29, no. 2 (Summer 1998): 187–214.

Swan, James A. *In Defense of Hunting*. New York: HarperCollins, 1995.

Sylvan, Richard, and David Bennett. *The Greening of Ethics*. Tucson: University of Arizona Press, 1994.

Taber, Richard D., and Neil F. Payne. *Wildlife, Conservation, and Human Welfare: A United States and Canadian Perspective.* Malabar, Fla.: Krieger Publishing Company, 2003.

Tarnas, Richard. *The Passion of the Western Mind: Understanding the Ideas That Have Shaped Our World View.* New York: Ballantine Books, 1991.

Taylor, Bron. "Earth First!: From Primal Spirituality to Ecological Resistance." In *This Sacred Earth: Religion, Nature, Environment,* edited by Roger S. Gottlieb, 545–557. New York: Routledge, 1996.

———. ed. *The Encyclopedia of Religion and Nature.* New York: Continuum, 2005.

Taylor, Bron, and Michael Zimmerman. "Deep Ecology." In *The Encyclopedia of Religion and Nature,* edited by Bron R. Taylor, 456–460. New York: Continuum, 2005.

Thich Nat Hahn. "Cultivating Compassion, Responding to Violence." Lecture, Berkeley Community Theater, Berkeley, Calif., September 13, 2001.

Thiébaux, Marcelle. *The Stag of Love: The Chase in Medieval Literature.* Ithaca, N.Y.: Cornell University Press, 1974.

Thomas, Carolyn E. *Sport in a Philosophic Context.* Philadelphia: Lea and Febiger, 1983.

Thomas, Keith. *Man and the Natural World: A History of the Modern Sensibility.* New York: Pantheon, 1983.

Thompson, William Irwin, ed. *Gaia, A Way of Knowing: Political Implications of the New Biology.* Hudson, N.Y.: Lindisfarne, 1987.

Tiger, Lionel, and Heather Fowler, eds. *Female Hierarchies.* Chicago: Beresford Book Service, 1978.

Tober, James A. *Who Owns the Wildlife: The Political Economy of Conservation in Nineteenth Century America.* Westport, Conn.: Greenwood Press, 1981.

Tobias, Michael, ed. *Deep Ecology.* San Diego, Calif.: Avant Books, 1985.

Tong, Rosemary Putman. *Feminist Thought.* Boulder, Colo.: Westview Press, 1998.

Trebilcot, Joyce, ed. *Mothering: Essays in Feminist Theory.* Totowa, N.J.: Rowman & Littlefield, 1993.

Trinh, T. Minh-Ha. *Woman, Native, Other: Writing Postcoloniality and Feminism.* Bloomington: Indiana University Press, 1989.

Tronto, Joan C. "Women and Caring: What Can Feminists Learn about Morality from Caring?" In *Gender/Body/Knowledge: Feminist Reconstructions of Being and Knowing,* edited by Alison M. Jaggar and Susan Bordo. New Brunswick, N.J.: Rutgers University Press, 1989.

———. *Moral Boundaries: A Political Argument for an Ethic of Care.* New York: Routledge, 1993.

Turner, James. *Reckoning with the Beast: Animals, Pain, and Humanity in the Victorian Mind.* Baltimore, Md.: Johns Hopkins University Press, 1980.

USDA. Swine 2000 Part I: Reference of Swine Health and Management in the United States. Fort Collins, Colo.: National Animal Health Monitoring Service, 2001.

Van Wyck, Peter C. *Primitives in the Wilderness: Deep Ecology and the Missing Human Subject.* Albany, N.Y.: SUNY Press, 1997.

Varner, Gary E. "The Schopenhauerian Challenge in Environmental Ethics." *Environmental Ethics* 7 (Fall 1985): 209–230.

————. *In Nature's Interests?: Interests, Animal Rights and Environmental Ethics.* Oxford: Oxford University Press, 1998.

Vidal-Naquet, Pierre. *The Black Hunter: Forms of Thought and Forms of Society in the Ancient Greek World.* Translated by Andrew Szegedy-Maszk. Baltimore, Md.: Johns Hopkins University Press, 1986.

Virtanen, Reino. *Claude Bernard and His Place in the History of Ideas.* Lincoln: University of Nebraska Press, 1960.

Vrba, E. S. "Some Evidence of Chronology and Palaeoecology of Sterkfontein, Swartkrans, and Kromdraai from the Fossil Bovidae." *Nature* 254 (March 6, 1975): 301–304.

Vyvyan, John. *In Pity and in Anger: A Study of the Use of Animals in Science.* Marblehead: Mass.: Micah Publications, 1969.

Waal, Frans de. *Good Natured: The Origins of Right and Wrong in Humans and Other Animals.* Cambridge, Mass.: Harvard University Press, 1996.

Waldau, Paul. *The Specter of Speciesism: Buddhist and Christian Views of Animals.* New York: Oxford University Press, 2002.

Walker, Alice. *Living by the Word: Selected Writings, 1973–1987.* San Diego, Calif.: Harvest Books, 1988.

Walker, Lawrence J. "Sex Differences in the Development of Moral Reasoning: A Critical Review." In *An Ethic of Care: Feminist Interdisciplinary Perspectives*, edited by Mary Jeanne Larrabee, 157–176. New York: Routledge, 1993.

Walker, Margaret Urban. *Moral Understandings: A Feminist Study of Ethics.* New York: Routledge, 1998.

Walsh, Diana. "The Peterson Trial: Defendant Moved to Tears." *San Francisco Chronicle*, section B-5, August 5, 2004.

Ward, Janie Victoria. "Urban Adolescents' Conceptions of Violence." In *Mapping the Moral Domain: A Contribution of Women's Thinking to Psychological Theory and Education*, edited by Carol Gilligan, Janie Victoria Ward, and Jill McLean Taylor, with Betty Bardige, 175–200. Cambridge, Mass.: Harvard University Press, 1989.

Warren, Karen J., *Ecological Feminism.* New York: Routledge, 1994.

————. ed. *Ecological Feminist Philosophies.* Bloomington: Indiana University Press, 1996.

————. ed. *Ecofeminism: Women, Culture, Nature.* Bloomington: Indiana University Press, 1997.

————. "Ecofeminist Philosophy and Deep Ecology." In *Philosophical Dialogues: Arne Naess and the Progress of Ecophilosophy*, edited by Nina Witoszek and Andrew Brennan, 255–269, Lanham, Md.: Rowman & Littlefield, 1999.

————. *Ecofeminist Philosophy: A Western Perspective on What It Is and Why It Matters.* Lanham, Md.: Rowman & Littlefield, 2000.

————. "The Philosophical Foundations of a New Land Ethic." In *The Land Ethic Toolbox: Using Ethics, Emotion and Spiritual Values to Advance American Land Conservation*, edited by Robert T. Perschel, 14–17. Washington, D.C.: Wilderness Society, 2004.

Washburn, Sherwood L., and C. S. Lancaster. "The Evolution of Hunting." In *Man the Hunter*, edited by Richard B. Lee and Irven DeVore, 293–303. Hawthorne, N.Y.: Aldine de Gruyter, 1987.

*The Watchdog Report on Animal Protection Charities.* Clinton, Wash.: Animal People, 2006.

Weil, Simone. "Reflections on the Right Use of School Studies with a View to the Love of God." In *Waiting for God*, translated by Emma Craufurd, 57–66. New York: G. P. Putnam's Sons, 1951.

Weir, Allison. *Sacrificial Logics: Feminist Theory and the Critique of Identity.* New York: Routledge, 1996.

White, Lynn, Jr. "The Historical Roots of Our Ecological Crisis." *Science* 155, no. 3767 (1967): 1203–1207.

White, Richard. *It's Your Misfortune and None of My Own: A New History of the American West.* Norman: University of Oklahoma Press, 1991.

Whitney, Elspeth. "Lynn White, Ecotheology, and History." *Environmental Ethics* 15, no. 2 (1993): 151–169.

Wilber, Ken. "Odyssey: A Personal Inquiry into Humanistic and Transpersonal Psychology." *Journal of Humanistic Psychology* 22, no. 1 (1982): 57–90.

———. *Eye to Eye: The Quest for the New Paradigm.* Garden City, N.Y.: Anchor Books, 1983.

Wilbur, George Browning, and Warner Muensterberger, eds. *Psychoanalysis and Culture.* New York: International University Press, 1951.

Wilkinson, Loren, ed. *Earthkeeping in the '90s: Stewardship of Creation.* Rev. ed. Grand Rapids, Mich.: Wm. B. Eerdmans Publishing, 1991.

Will, Barbara. "The Nervous Origins of the American Western." *American Literature* 70, no. 2 (1998): 293–316.

Wilson, Robert A., ed. *Species: New Interdisciplinary Essays.* Cambridge, Mass.: MIT Press, 1999.

Witoszek, Nina, and Andrew Brennan, eds. *Philosophical Dialogues: Arne Naess and the Progress of Ecophilosophy.* Lanham, Md.: Rowman & Littlefield, 1999.

Wolch, Jennifer, and Jody Emel, eds. *Animal Geographies: Place, Politics, and Identity in the Nature-Culture Borderlands.* New York: Verso, 1998.

Wood, Forrest, Jr. *The Delights and Dilemmas of Hunting: The Hunting versus Anti-Hunting Debate.* Lanham, Md.: University Press of America, 1997.

Worster, Donald. *Nature's Economy: The Roots of Ecology.* San Francisco: Sierra Club, 1977.

Xenophon. "Cynegeticus." In *Scripta Minora*, translated by E. C. Marchant. Cambridge, Mass.: Harvard University Press, 1968.

Young, Iris. *Throwing Like a Girl and Other Essays.* Bloomington: Indiana University Press, 1990.

Zihlman, Adrienne L. "Women in Evolution, Part II: Subsistence and Social Organization among Early Hominids." *Signs* 4, no. 1 (1978): 4–20.

Zihlman, Adrienne L., and Nancy Tanner. "Gathering and Hominid Adaptation." In *Female Hierarchies*, edited by Lionel Tiger and Heather Fowler, 163–194. Chicago: Beresford Book Service, 1978.

Zimmerman, Michael. "Feminism, Deep Ecology and Environmental Ethics." *Environmental Ethics* 9, no. 1 (1987): 21–44.

———. "Possible Political Problems of Earth-Based Religiosity." In *Beneath the Surface: Critical Essays in the Philosophy of Deep Ecology*, edited by Eric Katz, Andrew Light, and David Rothenberg, 169–194. Cambridge, Mass.: MIT Press, 2000.

Zimmerman, Michael E., J. Baird Callicott, Karen J. Warren, Irene J. Claver and John Clark, eds. *Environmental Philosophy: From Animal Rights to Radical Ecology*, 4th ed. Upper Saddle River, N.J.: Prentice Hall, 2005.

Zoran, Debra L. "The Carnivore Connection to Nutrition in Cats." *Journal of the American Veterinary Medical Association* 221, no. 11 (December 2002): 1559–1567.

Zucker, Arthur. "Ferré, Organicistic Connectedness—But Still Speciesistic." *Ethics and the Environment* 1, no. 2 (1996): 185–190.

# Index

Abraham (biblical figure), 35, 52
abstraction: in masculine identity,
    45–46; nature as, viii; in nature
    ethics, 164; and vegetarianism, 240
abuse: deep ecology and, 191;
    ecofeminist terminology for, 209–10;
    ethic of care and, 223–24;
    unconscious influences on, 210–11
Adams, Carol, 20, 208, 240, 243,
    267n156
admiration, of nature, 145, 158n61
adventure: Leopold on, 124; in
    masculinism, 4; Roosevelt on,
    88–90; sport hunting as, 53, 88–90;
    wilderness associated with, 124
advertising, metaphors in, 255n33
aesthetics: in Leopold's holism, 118–19,
    128; in preservation movement, 80;
    of sport hunting, 118, 128
affliction, in domestic animals, 152
African Americans, in sport hunting, 78,
    79
agency, 222, 225, 273n222
aggression: ethics as restraint of, 12,
    121–22; in holist philosophy, 16
    Leopold on, 12, 120–21; in
    masculinism, 3; Roosevelt on, 12;

sex difference in, 35, 58n2, 222; in
    sport hunting, 12, 71; and
    transcendence over nature, 35
agricultural food production: and
    development of empathy, 228–29;
    Rolston on, 148. *See also* domestic
    animals; factory farms
agricultural model: Leopold on, 112,
    119, 231; in refuges, 112; species
    preservation, applied to, 119, 231;
    wildlife management in, 110, 119
Agriculture, United States Department
    of (USDA), 1, 110, 231, 263n127
Ainu people, 101n34
alienation: in masculine identity, 50–51,
    53; in Self-realization, 183–84
allegories: charioteer, 53–54; coming-
    of-age, 114. *See also* narratives
allopathic ethics, 217
allopathic medicine, 216–17, 257n52
alternative medicine, 216–17, 257n52.
    *See also* holistic health
*American Sportsman* (journal), 79
*American Turf Register* (journal), 78
Anderson, J. K., 100n31
androcentrism: *vs.* anthropocentrism, 4,
    25, 188, 196n7; in deep ecology,

# About the Author

**Marti Kheel** is a prominent scholar and activist in the areas of ecofeminism, animal advocacy, and environmental ethics. Her articles have been widely published in journals and anthologies within the United States and abroad. Kheel developed the first feminist critique of the philosophical dualisms between environmental and animal liberation philosophies in a 1984 landmark essay, "The Liberation of Nature: A Circular Affair." Originally published in *Environmental Ethics*, the article has since been frequently cited and reprinted. Kheel holds a doctorate from the Graduate Theological Union in Berkeley, California, where she is currently a visiting scholar.